The Picturesque (a set of theories, ideas and conventions which grew up around the question of how we look at landscape) offers a valuable focus for new investigations into the literary, artistic, social and cultural history of the late eighteenth and nineteenth centuries. This volume of essays by scholars from various disciplines in Britain and America incorporates a range of historically and theoretically challenging approaches to the topic. It covers the writers most closely identified with the exposition of the Picturesque as a theory and also traces the influence and implications of its aesthetic in a variety of fields in the Romantic period, including literary and pictorial works, estate management and women's fashion. Several essays deal more specifically with radical critiques and appropriations of the Picturesque in the nineteenth century, while in others its influence is traced beyond traditionally accepted geographical or historical bounds.

THE POLITICS OF THE PICTURESQUE

THE POLITICS OF THE PICTURESQUE

Literature, landscape and aesthetics since 1770

EDITED BY

STEPHEN COPLEY AND PETER GARSIDE

School of English, University of Wales College of Cardiff

CAMBRIDGE
UNIVERSITY PRESS

Published by the Press Syndicate of the University of Cambridge
The Pitt Building, Trumpington Street, Cambridge CB2 1RP
40 West 20th Street, New York, NY 10011–4211, USA
10 Stamford Road, Oakleigh, Melbourne 3166, Australia

First published 1994

Printed in Great Britain at the University Press, Cambridge

Note: The essays in this volume are based on papers delivered at a conference on
'Romanticism and the Picturesque', held at the University of Wales Conference Centre,
Gregynog Hall, Mid Wales, in July 1991. The conference was sponsored by the University
of Wales Staff Colloquium Fund and the British Association for Romantic Studies.

A catalogue record for this book is available from the British Library

Library of Congress cataloguing in publication data

The politics of the Picturesque: Literature, landscape and aesthetics since 1770/edited by
Stephen Copley and Peter Garside.
p.   cm.
Essays based on papers delivered at a conference on 'Romanticism and the Picturesque',
University of Wales Conference Centre, July 1991.
Includes index.
ISBN 0 521 44113 7 (hardback)
1. Picturesque, The – Congresses.   2. Aesthetics, Modern – 18th century – Congresses.
3. Aesthetics, Modern – 19th century – Congresses.   I. Copley, Stephen, 1954–
II. Garside, Peter.
BH301.P53P65   1994
111'.85 – dc20   93-1970CIP
ISBN 0 521 44113 7 hardback

Contents

Illustrations

Tables

Notes on contributors

MALCOLM ANDREWS is a Senior Lecturer in English and American Literature at the University of Kent at Canterbury. He is the author of *The Search for the Picturesque* (1989), a study of landscape aesthetics and tourism in late eighteenth-century Britain, and is currently editor of *The Dickensian*.

ANN BERMINGHAM is Associate Professor of Art History at the University of California, Irvine. She is the author of *Landscape and Ideology: The English Rustic Tradition, 1740–1860* (1986), and is presently working on a study of drawing as a social practice in eighteenth- and nineteenth-century Britain.

MICHAEL CHARLESWORTH received his Ph.D. in the History and Theory of Art from the University of Kent at Canterbury. His research interests are interdisciplinary, and embrace both landscape studies and word and image studies. He teaches art history at the University of Texas at Austin.

STEPHEN COPLEY is a Lecturer in the School of English, University of Wales, Cardiff. His publications include *Literature and the Social Order in Eighteenth-Century England* (1983), *Beyond Romanticism: New Approaches to Texts and Contexts 1789–1832* (edited with John Whale, 1992), and articles on eighteenth-century polite culture.

STEPHEN DANIELS is a Senior Lecturer in Geography at the University of Nottingham. He is the author of *Fields of Vision: Landscape Imagery and National Identity in England and the United States* (1993) and a co-editor of *The Iconography of Landscape* (1988).

xiii

PETER GARSIDE is a Senior Lecturer in the School of English, University of Wales, Cardiff. He is an executive editor of the Edinburgh Edition of the Waverley Novels, for which he has edited *The Black Dwarf* (1993) and is preparing an edition of *Guy Mannering*; he is also one of the editors of *The Routledge Encyclopedia of Literature and Criticism* (1990).

ANNE JANOWITZ is Associate Professor of English at Rutgers University. She is the author of *England's Ruins: Poetic Purpose and the National Landscape* (1990), and is presently working on a study of Romantic communitarianism.

VIVIEN JONES is a Senior Lecturer in the School of English, University of Leeds. She has published books on Henry James and Jane Austen and articles on women and writing in the eighteenth century, and is the editor of *Women in the Eighteenth Century: Constructions of Femininity* (1990).

RAIMONDA MODIANO is Professor of English and Comparative Literature at the University of Washington. She is the author of *Coleridge and the Concept of Nature* (1985) and co-editor of volumes II–V of S. T. Coleridge, *Marginalia*, Bollingen Series LXXV (1980, 1984, 1992–).

DAVID PUNTER is Professor of English Studies at the University of Stirling. Among his books are *The Literature of Terror* (1980), *Romanticism and Ideology* (1981), *The Hidden Script* (1985) and *The Romantic Unconscious* (1988).

CHARLES WATKINS is a Lecturer in Geography at the University of Nottingham. He is the author of *Woodland Management and Conservation* (1990), co-author of *Justice Outside the City* (1991) and *Church and Religion in Rural England* (1991), and editor of *Ecological Effects of Afforestation* (1993).

JOHN WHALE is a Senior Lecturer in the School of English, University of Leeds. He is the author of a book on De Quincey and of articles on literature and politics in the Romantic period, and he is co-editor (with Stephen Copley) of *Beyond Romanticism: New Approaches to Texts and Contexts 1789–1832* (1992).

DAVID WORRALL is a Lecturer in English at St Mary's College, Strawberry Hill. He is the author of *Radical Culture* (1992) and co-editor of *Historicizing Blake* (1993).

Introduction

Stephen Copley and Peter Garside

'The Picturesque' is a notoriously difficult category to define. The term is clearly of considerable importance in British aesthetic debate of the 1790s and early 1800s. Offered by its original proponents as a third aesthetic category to set against Burke's 'Sublime' and 'Beautiful', it also plays an important part, directly or by default, in the definition of the 'Gothic' and the 'Romantic' in the period. By the time it enters theoretical debate in the 1780s, however, the word already has a prehistory which renders its deployment problematic. Subsequent debates between the proponents of the Picturesque aesthetic in the 1790s and early 1800s are marked by sharp disagreements over what it might entail, and over its possible applications in different areas; and these disagreements are compounded by disjunctures between Picturesque theory and the practices that are justified under its name – or, in other words, by conflicts between the status of the Picturesque as a theoretical category and its manifestations as a popular fashion. The widespread adoption of Picturesque terminology in conversational use in the late eighteenth century, in relation to a broad range of cultural practices, confirms the problematic nature of the aesthetic: even in this period, it can seem so ill-defined as to be virtually meaningless. This lack of precise definition is not an indication of its cultural or ideological insignificance, however. On the contrary, it can be argued that the cultural importance of the Picturesque stands in direct proportion to the theoretical imprecision of its vocabulary.

Unsurprisingly in this context, the Picturesque has never established itself as a rigorous category in aesthetic debate in the way that the Sublime or the Beautiful have done. Instead, work on the aesthetic has tended to concentrate on its historical manifestations. In the earlier twentieth century, commentators tended to examine the Picturesque largely through consideration of its links with the

Romantic movement. This is the approach adopted in Christopher Hussey's *The Picturesque: Studies in a Point of View* (1927), which has remained an important reference point in more recent accounts, even if Hussey's view of the historical progress of aesthetics from 'classic' to 'Romantic' achievement, through an 'interregnum' of pre- or proto-Romantic Picturesque experimentation, now seems inadequate.[1] Research on the topic in the 1950s and 1960s – notably by Walter J. Hipple – essentially followed the lineage and preserved the terms of debate set out by Hussey, even if the critical arguments that informed the later work were more sophisticated than his had been.[2]

Recently, the Picturesque has been exposed to revisionist rereading and reassessment of a kind that has also been apparent in work on the Gothic, the Sentimental, and other styles and modes of late eighteenth-century aesthetic discourse, which had earlier been securely placed and contained as more or less coherent facets of a notional 'pre-Romanticism'. This new work has not resulted in a confident new synthesis of the meanings of the Picturesque. Indeed, it may appear that the methodological problems of working across several disciplines and dealing with the variety of 'high cultural' and 'popular' contexts in which Picturesque terminology is used, and the questions raised in recent theoretical discussions of representation and cultural history, have confounded the attempts of commentators after Hussey to provide a comprehensive theorisation of the Picturesque aesthetic. It is perhaps more accurate to suggest that an awareness of the inadequacy of the grand narrative of aesthetic development that underpins Hussey's account, as a vehicle for writing larger cultural history, has led many commentators to the conclusion that totalising aesthetic theorisation is inappropriate in the face of the complex historical phenomenon represented by the Picturesque movement. In this context, studies have tended to approach the aesthetic by documenting and characterising its manifestations in particular sites or periods, in gardening, painting or literature, or in the tourist's search for aesthetically pleasing landscapes. The question that has underlain much recent work, whether voiced or not, has been whether it makes sense in any circumstances to speak of 'the Picturesque' as a single coherent category, or whether the multifarious versions of the Picturesque aesthetic produced by William Gilpin, Uvedale Price and Richard Payne Knight, by the tourist, the landscape gardener, the painter, the aesthetic theorist, the literary writer, in the late eighteenth and early nineteenth centuries, let alone by others in wider usages and later periods, are not so disparate and in some respects so incompatible as to resist homogenisation on any terms.

Certain broad characteristics of Picturesque theory and representation have been remarked by most modern commentators, however, although their readings of them have varied widely. The historical genealogy of the term offered initially by Hussey has been broadly accepted by later critics, even if it has been extended and qualified by several of them. Alan Liu, for instance, has suggested three overlapping phases in which the Picturesque aesthetic developed in the eighteenth century: a period from the 1710s to the 1760s in which broadly picturesque conceptions increasingly informed landscape painting and design; a period of the 'high Picturesque' in design and tourism from the 1770s; and an overlapping period of theorisation of the aesthetic in the 1790s, lasting perhaps until 1810.[3] As various critics have pointed out in this context, when the term 'picturesque' came into use early in the century as an anglicisation of the French 'pittoresque' or the Italian 'pittoresco' it was applied to all the subjects suitable for painting, rather than being restricted to landscape, and it only gradually acquired its later dominant focus and its characteristic emphases. The most striking of these for modern commentators is the apparent rejection by Picturesque theorists of self-conscious design and system and their recommendation instead of irregularity, variation, decay and wildness in 'natural' appearance as sources of aesthetic pleasure. This emphasis, and its manifestations in practice in a variety of fields, have come under the scrutiny of scholars in several different disciplines.

Recent work has taken two broad directions, which are by no means mutually exclusive, but which are worth distinguishing, at least provisionally. On the one hand, increasing interest in eighteenth-century cultural and social history since the late 1960s, combining with recent theoretical work devoted to reading aesthetics as ideology, has produced a number of substantial critiques of the ideological implications of the Picturesque movement, some of which have been written by contributors to this volume.[4] On the other hand, particularly in the last couple of years, attempts have been made to rehabilitate the Picturesque as a coherent category in aesthetic debate. Interestingly, these latter attempts have inverted earlier critical assumptions about the similarities between the

Picturesque and the Romantic: instead, the critics involved have celebrated the Picturesque as an aesthetic that is in many ways antithetical to Romanticism.

Two discussions in particular exemplify the attempts of recent commentators to revive the Picturesque as an aesthetic category. In *Inquiry into the Picturesque*[5] Sidney K. Robinson presents the aesthetic as an expression of contemporary liberalism whose sophistication has been undervalued. He concentrates mainly on the theoretical writings of Uvedale Price, arguing that in his case the Picturesque aesthetic arises from 'dissatisfaction with a compositional mode that seeks seamless control over all constituent elements' (p. xi). Price's identification of roughness and irregularity as the qualities of Picturesque appearance is only a partial statement made in response to the previously prevailing aesthetic. Underlying his claims, and unrecognised at the time by his opponents, is the 'much more challenging principle of mixture' (p. 5), which is ensured by 'abrupt variation' (p. 6). Picturesque design also deploys 'less power than is available to compose the parts in an arrangement that does not press for a conclusion' (p. xi). This, Robinson argues, implies 'a preexisting condition of plenitude' (p. xii). The relinquishment of fully visible compositional control does not imply the absence of such control: Price is ultimately concerned with the relation between parts of a composition, not with the parts for their own sake, and the devices of the Picturesque are strategies for maintaining the vividness of the whole design. In this context viewers' uncertainties about whether they are being 'misled, entertained, or challenged' (p. xii) by the Picturesque object are integral to their experience of it.

Robinson writes as an architectural historian: indeed his presentation and celebration of the Picturesque movement's eclecticism, refusal of fixity and authority, and exploitation of marginality, sometimes makes it sound disconcertingly like a programme for architectural Postmodernism. His overwhelming concentration on Price as a Picturesque theorist inevitably leads him to develop a monolithic version of the phenomenon, in which the claims of Gilpin's Picturesque, for instance, are scarcely mentioned; and his approach to the enormously varied sources and manifestations of Picturesque taste is notably more successful in some areas than in others. In his survey of the political implications of the Picturesque movement, for instance, the amorphousness of the category is not really clarified by discussion of Charles James Fox's 'picturesque' political behaviour – especially when Robinson admits that there is very little to connect Fox himself directly to use of the term, and when the vagaries of the politician's career and pronouncements look very much like those of many another pre- or post-Picturesque politician.

Robinson's selective endorsement of the Picturesque aesthetic is both complemented and countered in Kim Ian Michasiw's 'Nine Revisionist Theses on the Picturesque'.[6] Michasiw challenges the viability of the Picturesque itself as a unitary category. In particular, he attacks the assumption, most recently voiced by Frances Ferguson, that 'a writer like William Gilpin composes his guides to picturesque travel as a way of reconciling nature with art, making the walking tour itself the near relation and opposite number to the eighteenth-century landscape garden'.[7] Instead, Michasiw emphasises the distinctions between the projects of Picturesque tourism and land-scape management, and condemns the preference of earlier commen-tators for the landscape theorists Price and Knight over the supposedly naive tourist Gilpin. He identifies Gilpin's Picturesque writings as the repository of an aesthetic that is in some ways radically opposed to the claims of the later theorists, and that has been largely disregarded by commentators who have only been prepared to see Gilpin as a precursor of those theorists. He thus celebrates Gilpin's Picturesque for precisely the reasons that had earlier caused critics to denigrate his accounts of decorative scenery as trivial and frivolous in comparison with the Romantic engagement with nature. For Michasiw, Gilpin's 'Enlightenment game' (p. 94) with the artifices of perception and representation, his self-aware ironic playfulness, are the antithesis of Romantic mystificatory absolutism, even if the later Picturesque theorists themselves fall prey to that absolutism. The attraction of Gilpin's Picturesque in the context of current aesthetic debates is then clear: 'the implications of Gilpin's theories have some relevance to the necessary demystification of art and its ideolatry in the postmodern condition', and 'the fact that they were unsuited to their era should not license our continuing to condemn and dismiss them' (p. 96).

Despite his self-declared 'aesthetic' focus and dismissive references to earlier work on the politics of the Picturesque, Michasiw acknowledges that many of the most valuable recent discussions of the movement have developed from critiques of its political impli-cations. In the hands of some of its original expositors in the 1780s and 1790s, the Picturesque is an intensely and explicitly politicised aesthetic – Richard Payne Knight's famous footnote to *The Landscape*, setting his landscaping projects in the context of contemporary events in France, provides the clearest example of this level of engagement.[8] At the same time, and sometimes in the same texts, the Picturesque celebration of the spontaneously 'natural' appears to be based on the effacement of the political and the social. This latter aspect of the aesthetic has come in for particular scrutiny. Picturesque habits of viewing, representing or constructing aesthetically pleasing objects – whether they be landscapes, artefacts or human figures – have been seen to rest on the suppression of the interpretative and narrative signs which marked earlier representation. This characteristic has been identified by commentators as the basis on which the Picturesque translates the political and the social into the decorative, and so, as the route to the naturalisation of the Picturesque image.[9] The clearest instance of this translation is the Picturesque deployment of motifs for aesthetic effect which in other circumstances are the indicators of poverty or social deprivation, but critics have also identified the feature more generally, for instance in the oddly double-edged relation of the aesthetic to time and history. On the one hand, time and mutability are essential to, and indices of, Picturesque decorative effects; on the other, the Picturesque has been presented as resolutely ahistorical in its deflection of socially consequential interpretations of favoured aesthetic objects such as ruins.[10]

The Picturesque aesthetic emerges as strongly in literary narratives (in written tours and in fiction) as it does in visual art or practical landscaping. In turn this poses problems. If pictorial Picturesque representation suppresses narrative for decorative effect, this possibility is altogether more difficult to contrive in written narrative. Discussion of this aspect of the aesthetic has benefited considerably from comparative analysis of Picturesque and other scientific or exploratory writings of the period, and from more general historical and feminist work on the novel and on travel literature.[11] Recent criticism has also questioned the extent to which the Picturesque – initially and specifically a domestic landscape aesthetic – can be seen to shape British (or wider European) accounts of colonial landscapes and cultures. Even within the British Isles the discourse of the Picturesque intersects with and is shaped by the discourses of colonialism at various points. In the case of the Scottish Highlands, for instance, the combination of political repression, economic exploitation, and aesthetic sentimentalisation of the Scottish landscape in the early nineteenth century clearly renders the Picturesque 'invention' of the region a hegemonic cultural manifestation of the English colonising presence.[12] In a broader field, the shaping and constraining legacy of Picturesque assumptions can be discerned in European accounts of North America, India, Africa and Australia.

A number of commentators have pointed out that the development of the Picturesque aesthetic is closely dependent on contemporary economic and technological changes, although the latter may seem inimical to the values it appears to celebrate. This link involves both the enabling circumstances of the Picturesque and the representational constraints and conventions that mark it. In relation to the first, it is clear that the fashion for Picturesque domestic tourism stems in part from the development of a good road system, making previously inaccessible areas of Britain relatively accessible, although this development is driven by commercial (and in the case of some areas, such as the Scottish Highlands, military) imperatives apparently inimical to the claims of the aesthetic. Equally, interest in the Picturesque appearance of the countryside is intimately connected with changes in the agricultural and commercial economies, whether their effects are registered directly (in the booms and slumps in agricultural production during and after the Revolutionary and Napoleonic Wars, or in the Highland clearances), or indirectly, in the emergence of sections of society with the leisure and resources to cultivate an aesthetic of redundancy in those parts of the country least implicated in the economic changes from which their own prosperity derived.[13]

The popularisation of the aesthetic, which superficially seems to threaten its very nature, depends on technological advances in printing (such as the development of aquatint, which allowed Gilpin to reproduce his sketches commercially). More generally, it is intimately connected with the growth of consumerism in early industrial society.[14] In this light it is hardly surprising that the representational codes permitting, excluding or otherwise governing the treatment of commercial activity and industrial subjects in Picturesque visual art and description have been opened to considerable scrutiny. On the one hand, the suggestion that, at least in its early stages, the Picturesque is not as single-minded as it may appear in its exclusion of the industrial has led to interesting analysis of the precise bounds and grounds of its aesthetic exclusions. On the other, its boundaries have been marked in relation to other genres of painting such as the industrial Sublime.[15] More generally, the discourse of the Picturesque itself has been located ideologically in relation to contemporary political economy in a recently revised article by John Barrell, which draws on a number of the disparate strands in current debate.[16] Barrell points out that Picturesque 'taste' is often naturalised by contemporaries to the extent that 'Picturesque' appearance is often treated as 'natural' appearance, and 'the picturesque eye' is represented simply as 'the eye'. Taking as his example the Picturesque illustrations of social activities that make up William Pyne's *Microcosm* (1806), he suggests that the perspective offered by the Picturesque appears as the 'transcendent viewing-position which had through the eighteenth century been regarded as the perquisite of the gentleman' (p. 97): 'the picturesque eye', detached from all cramping restrictions or specialisation, surveys 'the natural' with 'pure unmediated vision', when 'the natural is located in picturesque forms devoid of ethical, political, or sentimental meanings' (p. 98). The Picturesque thus offers a rival version of transcendent vision to that offered in the political economist's survey of the multiple activities that constitute the economy and, by including the economically marginal (in the form of gypsies) as well as the productive, and leisure as well as labour, it turns out to offer 'an account of the variety of social activities no less expansive, though certainly less methodised, than that revealed to the economic philosopher' (p. 116).

The essays in this volume continue the exploratory projects of recent work and extend the arguments that have informed this work into new areas. They are written from various disciplinary standpoints and do not attempt to work from (or towards) a single definition of the Picturesque. Instead, they emphasise the variousness of the manifestations of the aesthetic in a wide range of areas in the eighteenth and early nineteenth centuries, and examine its continuance as a focus of aesthetic debate and political polemic beyond the point at which it is usually thought to have dissipated as a coherent (or potentially coherent) aesthetic category. The essays are weighted towards consideration of (but not exclusively concerned with) 'the politics of the Picturesque', defining 'politics' both in its narrow, and in its broader, ideological and textual senses.

The first four essays cover familiar – and less familiar – areas of cultural practice in which Picturesque taste manifested itself in the late eighteenth and early nineteenth centuries. Stephen Daniels and Charles Watkins dispel the vacuum in which the theoretical arguments about landscape of Price and Knight have often been discussed by modern commentators, and in doing so challenge the view that Picturesque landscaping in the period was a purely and impractically decorative concern. They dwell on the practical demands of estate management, which provided a countervailing or complementary set of imperatives to those of aesthetic landscaping, even for a Picturesque theorist such as Price, and suggest that the landscapes that he developed consequently cannot be read exclusively in terms of his aesthetic theories. Stephen Copley takes William Gilpin's account of a particular site in the Lake District as the focal point of a more general discussion of the projects of Picturesque tourism, and of eighteenth-century tourists' perceptions of the economic activities they encounter in the parts of the country they visit. Michael Charlesworth considers the implications of the aesthetic appropriation of that most popular of Picturesque sites – the ruined monastery – in the early nineteenth century. His arguments about the historical changes in perception that underlie representations of Rievaulx Abbey reinforce the suggestion that the Picturesque is an unstable and mutating aesthetic, even in the Romantic period. Ann Bermingham surveys an area in which the importance of the Picturesque aesthetic has not previously been much documented – the development of female fashion systems. In demonstrating the extent to which the vocabulary of the Picturesque informs female fashion, she also suggests how far the notion of fashion is central to the Picturesque aesthetic as it emerges in the area of mass taste.

The next group of essays have literary texts at their centre, although they 'place' these texts in distinctive ways in relation to the dual concerns of the volume as a whole. As Vivien Jones demonstrates in her essay, the gender politics of the Picturesque emerges particularly clearly when the Picturesque motifs that are deployed in fiction written by women in the period are examined in the context of gendered readings of the texts of Picturesque theory. Peter Garside's discussion of the relation between Scott's descriptions of the gypsy Meg Merrilies and contemporary illustrations of her sets both firmly in the tradition of Picturesque representation, drawing on eighteenth-century debates about the origin and social place of gypsies, as well as aesthetic assessments of their potential as

Picturesque figures. Further aspects of the relation between the Picturesque and the Romantic are negotiated in the next two essays. John Whale investigates the relevance of the Picturesque as an organising trope and as a point of departure in the exploratory writings about Africa of James Bruce and Mungo Park, and in the exploratory projects of Romantic poetry. Raimonda Modiano's treatment of the status of the destitute in the Picturesque draws on Freud and Melanie Klein in its consideration of the 'found object' and she extends her discussion into the area of German Romanticism and into later nineteenth-century British aesthetic debate. Finally in this group, David Punter's wide-ranging discussion also deploys a psychoanalytical vocabulary to suggest ways in which the terminology of the Picturesque can be deployed as an aesthetic category well beyond the historical period with which it is associated.

Three final essays extend historical discussion of the aesthetic forward to the later nineteenth century. Two tackle the specifically political controversies that surround discussion of the Picturesque from the 1790s on, marking both radical opposition to the aesthetic and the appropriation of its vocabulary for radical causes. David Worrall surveys the attacks on the Picturesque that are mounted by proponents of the Spencean programme for land in the early nineteenth century, and traces the ramifications of those attacks in radical political polemics and in middle-class literary texts of the time. Anne Janowitz analyses a later moment of nineteenth-century radical politics: the counter-hegemonistic deployment by Welsh artisan radicals in the Chartist movement of a vocabulary with its roots in the Picturesque, which links their native South Wales and the Australia to which their leaders were transported after the Newport Uprising. Finally, Malcolm Andrews marks the continuance of debate about many of the issues at stake in earlier discussions of the Picturesque, in his survey of a later nineteenth-century controversy over the social and political acceptability or unacceptability of the aesthetic, as it is manifested in photographic images of decay and decrepitude in the poorer areas of London.

NOTES

1 Christopher Hussey, *The Picturesque: Studies in a Point of View* (London and New York: G. P. Putnam's Sons, 1927).
2 See Walter J. Hipple, *The Beautiful, the Sublime and the Picturesque in*

Eighteenth-Century British Aesthetic Theory (Carbondale: Southern Illinois University Press, 1957).

3 See Alan Liu, *Wordsworth: The Sense of History* (Stanford University Press, 1989), pp. 533–4.

4 See Malcolm Andrews, *The Search for the Picturesque: Landscape Aesthetics and Tourism in Britain, 1760–1800* (Aldershot: Scolar Press, 1989); Ann Bermingham, *Landscape and Ideology: The English Rustic Tradition 1740–1860* (London: Thames and Hudson, 1986), especially chapters 2 and 3; John Dixon Hunt, *Gardens and the Picturesque: Studies in the History of Landscape Architecture* (Cambridge, Mass.: M.I.T. Press, 1992); Liu, *Wordsworth*, chapter 3. See also essays in Michael Clarke and Nicholas Penny (eds.), *The Arrogant Connoisseur: Richard Payne Knight, 1751–1824* (Manchester University Press, 1982); Denis Cosgrove and Stephen Daniels (eds.), *The Iconography of Landscape* (Cambridge University Press, 1988); and Simon Pugh (ed.), *Reading Landscape: Country–City–Capital* (Manchester University Press, 1990).

5 Sidney K. Robinson, *Inquiry into the Picturesque* (University of Chicago Press, 1991).

6 Kim Ian Michasiw, 'Nine Revisionist Theses on the Picturesque', *Representations*, 38 (1992), 76–100.

7 Frances Ferguson, *Solitude and the Sublime: Romanticism and the Aesthetics of Individuation* (London: Routledge, 1992), p. 138.

8 Richard Payne Knight, *The Landscape: A Didactic Poem in Three Books* (London, 1794), pp. 73–5.

9 See Andrews, *Search for the Picturesque*, part 1, and Liu, *Wordsworth*, pp. 65–84.

10 See Anne Janowitz, *England's Ruins: Poetic Purpose and the National Landscape* (Oxford: Basil Blackwell, 1990). See also Marjorie Levinson, 'Insight and Oversight: Reading "Tintern Abbey"', in *Wordsworth's Great Period Poems: Four Essays* (Cambridge University Press, 1986).

11 For the first see Barbara Maria Stafford, *Voyage into Substance: Art, Science, Nature, and the Illustrated Travel Account, 1760–1840* (Cambridge, Mass.: M.I.T. Press, 1984). For the second see Alistair M. Duckworth, *The Improvement of the Estate: A Study of Jane Austen's Novels* (Baltimore and London: Johns Hopkins Press, 1971); and Carole Fabricant, 'The Literature of Domestic Tourism and the Public Consumption of Private Property', in Felicity Nussbaum and Laura Brown (eds.), *The New Eighteenth Century: Theory, Politics, English Literature* (New York and London: Methuen, 1987).

12 See Peter Womack, *Improvement and Romance: Constructing the Myth of the Highlands* (Basingstoke: Macmillan, 1989).

13 See Liu, *Wordsworth*, chapter 3.

14 See Bermingham, *Landscape and Ideology*, chapter 2.

15 See Stephen Daniels, 'Loutherbourg's Chemical Theatre: *Coalbrookdale*

by Night', in John Barrell (ed.), *Painting and the Politics of Culture: New Essays on British Art 1700–1850* (Oxford University Press, 1992).

16 John Barrell, 'Visualising the Division of Labour: William Pyne's *Microcosm*', in *The Birth of Pandora* (Basingstoke: Macmillan, 1992), pp. 89–118.

CHAPTER I

Picturesque landscaping and estate management: Uvedale Price and Nathaniel Kent at Foxley

Stephen Daniels and Charles Watkins

INTRODUCTION

Georgian landscaping is conventionally studied as an example of high culture, in terms of the history of art, literature and aesthetics. We take a more down to earth view and look at landscaping as an example of estate management, in terms of such topics as farming, planting, leases and rents. We do not pretend that the study of estate management offers a sort of ground-truth for understanding landscaping. Terms like 'rent' and 'estate' are of course no more eternal, or less ideological, than terms like 'picturesque' and 'landscape'. We will not neglect high culture: indeed a central theme of the essay is how the aesthetics of painting helped frame estate management. Even a casual reading of the literature on 'improvement' in the eighteenth century reveals a complex overlapping not just of economic and aesthetic issues but also of moral and political ones. And the point of this essay is to reinsert landscaping and estate management into this complex.[1]

Uvedale Price (1747–1829) is best known today for his writings on Picturesque aesthetics. Of all landscape tastes the Picturesque has conventionally been seen as wilfully detached from the practice of rural production, even hostile to it. In his own lifetime Price was censured by self-consciously utilitarian writers for taking too ornamental a view of landscape improvement. But Price was a committed country landowner as well as a connoisseur, and the day-to-day demands of managing his estate at Foxley in Herefordshire engaged him no less than the finer points of Old Masters. When we read his *Essay on the Picturesque* in the light of his other writings, including his letters, and in terms of his estate records, we see his landscaping engage with his estate management. The very soil of his estate, his native clay, is a central theme of a discourse of

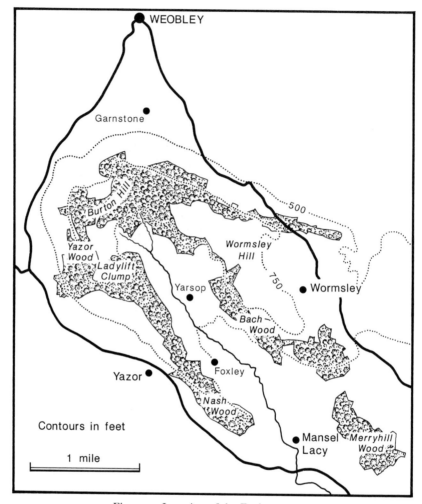

Fig. 1.1   Location of the Foxley estate.

improvement which emphasises the virtues of local knowledge and power.

Nathaniel Kent's (1737–1810) reputation as an agrarian reformer is now overshadowed by that of Arthur Young and William Marshall.[2] In his own lifetime he was more highly esteemed. Based in Norfolk, he established a major land agency business with prestigious contracts for estates throughout the country, including the royal estates at Richmond and Windsor. Kent specialised in rationalising

Fig. 1.2   General view of Foxley, 1855.

the layout of estates and drawing up leases. He set out his views in *Hints to Gentlemen of Landed Property* (1775) and *General View of the Agriculture of the County of Norfolk* (1794).[3] Influenced by Netherlandish practice, Kent emphasised the importance of small farms and cottages to the economic efficiency and moral welfare of estates. In 1774 Uvedale Price commissioned Kent to prepare a survey of the Foxley estate with a view to its complete reorganisation.[4]

The Foxley estate came into the Price family by marriage in 1679. Over the next century it grew through the purchase, inheritance and exchange of many small properties by successive members of the Price family. Foxley Court itself was situated in a small valley surrounded on all but its south-western side by a horseshoe-shaped belt of hills. The estate reached its greatest size in the early nineteenth century. By the time it was sold in the 1850s it comprised 4,330 acres, all virtually in one block (figures 1.1 and 1.2).

In this essay we examine the views of Price and Kent on the improvement of the Foxley estate. These views converged in the idea of 'connection'. Connection was a key word in the discourse of improvement. It denoted a condition of social and geographical interdependence, both a common interest and a coherent context for thought and action. A well connected landscape integrated a variety of physical, social and economic features in a model polity. As such it necessitated the inter-linking of landscaping and estate management.

CONNECTION

Connection was an axiom of Nathaniel Kent's doctrine of land management. In principle 'the landlord, tenant and labourer are intimately connected together', declared Kent but, in fact, he found labourers disconnected and at the mercy of avaricious farmers and advised landlords to intervene on their behalf to assume 'the superintendence and regulation of country-business more than they do', without being seen to relish the exercise of power and so lose the 'confidence of the country'.[5] In his *General View of the Agriculture of the County of Norfolk* (1794), Kent found that where landlords provided cottages, a patch of land and some livestock, labourers were 'so far from being prompt to riot that their attachment to their masters was exemplary'.[6] That same year, in what he described as 'the present crisis', Price wrote to the landscape gardener, Humphry Repton, on 'that great principle, connection' in both aesthetics and politics:

although the separation of the different ranks and their gradations, like those of visible objects, is known and ascertained, yet from the beneficial mixture, and frequent intercommunication of high and low, that separation is happily disguised, and does not sensibly operate on the general mind. But should any of these most important links be broken; should any sudden gap, any distinct undisguised line of separation be made, such as between noblemen and the roturier, the whole strength of that firm chain (and firm may it stand) would at once be broken.[7]

Upon learning of the French landing on the Pembrokeshire coast in 1797 and the financial panic it provoked, Price feared for the interconnection of rural society and issued a pamphlet, *Thoughts on the Defence of Property*, addressed to the county of Herefordshire, arguing that all property owners should be armed and trained. He had visited most of the farmers in the six parishes of his neighbourhood and found 'all were trembling, unarmed, without confidence or connection' at the prospect of being attacked by propertyless 'profligate and separate men'. Lately in the county there was proof of 'attention and benevolence towards the industrious labouring poor' but it was necessary to be more attentive to labourers 'for without their generous attachment, how firmly we may be united to each other, our union would be far from complete'; 'He who can scarcely buy bread will hardly buy arms unless driven to despair by long ill treatment.' Price upheld the cottager's 'attachment of his little spot' against the outlook of extravagant grandees: 'vast possessions give ambitious views, and ambitious views destroy local attachments'. It was important to maintain smallholders, 'a bold yeomanry, their country's pride'.[8]

Price considered that in their prosecution of the war, the Administration were guilty of great extravagance. In 1801, he trusted the British navy would be a match for Napoleon's, but 'our governors have been so lavish with our money, and so little disposed to economy, that I fear we must be exhausted even by victories'. Britain's navy, colonies and commerce might be lost but we might still 'possess freedom, security and happiness' if agriculture were secured.[9] Price's agrarianism was central to his plans for Local Associations. Farmers in his locality resisted volunteering for Price's own armed troop because of the fear of government sanction, of being subject to military law or being ordered far from their homes; he told Lord Abercorn:

A great part must at all events be stationary if only for the sake of agriculture, and why not turn those very men into a means of defence without altering their situations and habits? I greatly think, that even supposing such a military spirit did prevail, and would make every farmer wish to be a soldier, and to go where he is ordered, it would be an unfortunate spirit; for it would ruin industry and the habits of industry: what in my mind should be encouraged, is a spirit of confidence and union, and of security from the means of resistance in each quarter; not a spirit of general enterprise and military ardour.[10]

Price's local patriotism may be seen expressed in a painting produced towards the end of the Napoleonic Wars, G. R. Lewis's harvest scene set in the Upper Wye Valley, *Hereford, Dynedor and the Malvern Hills* (figure 1.3). John Barrell observes it is 'quite unlike any other image of the poor in its period' in giving labourers a 'manly dignity' and suggests it is a celebration of 'the bold peasantry from which were recruited the victors of Waterloo'.[11] We might suggest that while undoubtedly an image of the war effort, it shows the bold peasantry who stayed behind. Exhibited in London, it is an image with broad cultural implications (the familiar theme of harvest, the academy poses of the two outside figures), but it makes specifically local references, from the cider flagon to the recent rectilinear intakes inscribed on the hills. Herefordshire, as Barrell emphasises, was throughout the eighteenth century the 'home of the English georgic', that rhetoric of good husbandry which is found in poems like Dyer's

Fig. 1.3   G. R. Lewis. *Hereford, Dynedor and the Malvern Hills from the Haywood Lodge* (1816).

The Fleece and Philip's *Cyder* as well as agricultural reports on the region, and whose mixture of delicacy and practicability recommended it to sophisticated squires.[12] Price, as we will see, was a committed agriculturalist and took pleasure in georgical views of the Upper Wye Valley, not least from the summit of his own estate, the Ladylift, one of the most renowned viewpoints in the country. A guide-book of 1805 described 'The vast extent of country which is here spread out before the sight, the great diversity and variety of its features, now swelling into bold hills mantled with rich woods, and again declining into luxuriant vales teeming with fertility, and animated by a thousand springs, the numerous orchards, cornfields, hop-grounds, and meadows, intermingled with castles, seats, and villages, and bounded by a bold range of distant mountains'.[13]

In his advocacy of the Picturesque, Price was often accused, notably by William Marshall, of celebrating sterile landscapes – rocky, ruinous, weed-choked and so on[14] – and Lambin has argued that, in contrast to his father, Price turned his back on farming.[15] But there is abundant evidence of Price's commitment to agriculture and to farming his estate along progressive lines. He carried through Benjamin Stillingfleet's experiments on improved pasture; he added improving covenants (for example on draining) to new leases; his largest tenant and bailiff was a keen sheep-breeder and provided the foundation sheep for George III's Ryeland herd; Price's wife kept a flock of Ryelands crossed with Merino; his letters to Sir George Beaumont (then improving his own estate at Coleorton) are peppered with agricultural advice, for example on ploughing in cabbage and buckwheat as well as turnips and on the use of mineral tar as a dressing to protect trees from cattle and to protect sheep from flies.[16] Economy was central to Price's landscaping. For example, when making a series of pools in the bottom of the valley at Foxley to highlight the landscape and to blend it 'into one composition', he told Lord Abercorn 'they will pay me ample interest for the money I paid' by watering land and providing a harvest of fish.[17] It was, of course, possible for Price to preserve his agricultural values but to purge them from his writing on aesthetics and this is precisely what William Gilpin, who popularised Picturesque sterility, advocated.[18] There is no doubt that Price felt a conflict between the discourses of farming and of aesthetics in evaluating landscape, as did many agriculturalists, notably John Clark in his *General View of the Agriculture of Herefordshire*.[19] But in his *Essay on the Picturesque*, Price takes issue with Gilpin by celebrating landscapes that, if not luxuriantly fertile, are flourishing, populous, domesticated, and that need to be worked industriously to keep them so.[20] Above all, Price upheld detailed variety in landscape that had its basis in the look and management of the valley of the Upper Wye. This quality, he complained, was not understood by those who alternated between the 'tame cultivated country' of the English lowlands and the 'barrenness, desolation and deformity' of popular tourist country like the Peak District or North Wales.[21] Price wanted his notable friends to visit Foxley more often, to read him aright by reading his landscape on the ground.[22]

This is not to say that the test of Price's localism in landscape taste was purely topographical. His writings are replete with references to Old Masters like Claude and Rubens and to authorities on aesthetics like Burke and Sir Joshua Reynolds. Indeed, his purpose was to raise the moral seriousness of the Picturesque. He attempted to see local or vernacular associations in an artist like Claude (who was usually seen

Fig. 1.4   Cottage at Foxley and the Ladylift. Mid-nineteenth-century watercolour.

as elevated above such associations) and, perhaps more plausibly, looked to less polished Dutch-style painting (which the Price family collected) as a model for his ideas. If the 'higher schools of painting' presented 'magnificent' views which could only be contemplated by 'men of princely revenues', vernacular Dutch landscape art was appropriate to 'the power of men of moderate fortunes' who might see in it suggestions for improving their farm buildings and cottages, woods and lanes. Just as Nathaniel Kent modelled his views on land holding and management on Dutch precedent, so did Price.

For Price a painterly point of view was a benevolent one, for 'the lover of painting considers the dwelling, the inhabitants and the marks of their intercourse, as ornaments to the landscape'. Price upheld the cottage scenes of Gainsborough and recalled making excursions into the countryside with the painter (a friend of his father). Gainsborough was, he remembered, a man 'at times severe and sarcastic; but when we came to cottage or village scenes' his countenance assumed 'an expression of particular gentleness and complacency' (figure 1.4). Far from demolishing cottages, which was the fashion with Capability Brown-style landscaping, a love of painting would encourage landowners to build or improve them. Price recalled 'a beloved uncle' whose village bore 'strong marks' of his attentions. 'Such attentive kindnesses are amply repaid by affectionate regard and reverence'; and if they were general throughout the kingdom, they would do much more towards guarding us against democratical opinions 'then twenty thousand soldiers arm'd in proof'.[23]

Paralleling Price's advocacy of 'variety…and humanity' in landscape, and arguably mobilising it, is a sustained attack on Capability Brown and his imitators. Price saw this style as precisely eroding localism, reducing landscapes to a general plan, erasing humble detail such as hamlets, hedges and copses, isolating ambitious owners in vast empty parks and leaving 'the vacancy of solitary grandeur and power'.[24] Price was all the more virulent in his attacks on Brownism because at Foxley he himself had once fallen under the sway of the style, in particular in destroying an old elaborate formal garden near the house.[25] The Brown style was in every way one of disconnection and, in the political climate of the war years, was a dangerously destabilising fashion. And it had become a centralised, almost state style. Price had heard that, upon reading his *Essay on the Picturesque*, the king had declared himself 'a most zealous admirer of Mr Brown… I should like to see all Europe like a place of Mr Brown's'.[26] Like Goldsmith (whom he admired), Price found the Brown style a belligerent, military one, the clumps of trees 'drilled for parade like compact bodies of soldiers'. The 'humbler trees' which Brown felled were, no less than humble cottages, 'bonds of connection…which the judicious improver always touches with a cautious hand'. Brown's principle was a 'levelling' one, in a despotic rather than a democratic sense, 'a principle that, when made general and brought into action by any determined improver, either of grounds or governments, occasions such mischiefs as time slowly, if ever, repairs'.[27] For Price improvements in all spheres were piece-meal, pragmatic, local, gradual. Improvement was vested in men like himself, watchful squires. He would no more trust a professional landscaper with his estate than the regular militia with his county. Landscaping should be carried out by 'men of liberal education, who passed much of their time at their own country-seats'.[28] In letters to fashionable friends, he is as frequently making excuses not to leave Foxley as he is imploring them to visit. For example, he told Beaumont in 1803: 'one occupation follows another in such a manner, that it seems as if the place could not part with me. Planting is just over, now bark peeling comes on, and by the time it is over, London is so hot, dusty and so empty, that I shall e're stay here.'[29] To the end of his life, he laboured on his domain with a workman or two, hacking boughs, blowing up limestone, digging banks. Aged seventy-four, he was still, in his words, 'spaddling about in my native clay'.[30]

When Price had completed his belt of encircling wood and his pools, Foxley had achieved the compositional coherence he craved. He upheld his own estate as above any other in 'the appearance as well as reality of being one person's property'.[31] Price enjoyed, in his words, 'extensive distances' in views from the summit of Foxley,[32] but he was careful to distinguish these from the ambitious 'prospects' of Brown-style parks.[33] At Foxley, long views over the county were to be combined with, and controlled by, 'near views' focusing on such detail as trees, shrubs and earth banks.[34] Price's Picturesque was grounded or rooted in the land. This is not to say every visitor to Foxley endorsed Price's own view of his estate. After his visit in 1811, Wordsworth wrote to Beaumont of 'a strange fault that I am going to find [with Foxley], considering the acknowledged taste of the owner; viz., that small as it is compared with hundreds of places, the Domain is too extensive for the character of the country'. As much as Brown, Price 'monotonised' the landscape. And on Price's declared humanity in landscaping, Wordsworth observed that 'a man by little and little becomes so delicate and fastidious with respect to forms in scenery: where he has a power to exercise a control over them and if they do not exactly please him, in all mood, and every point of view, his power becomes his law'. Foxley 'lacked the relish of humanity' of a 'country left more to itself'.[35]

Price's models for the Picturesque were embanked and embowered 'hollow lanes and bye-roads' because they were not designed but the product of long-term, piecemeal changes and impressed into them were the gradual processes of nature mixed with the steady impact of men and livestock.[36] There were many sunken lanes at Foxley, notably that drawn by Gainsborough passing an embanked beech tree leading to the parish church (figure 1.5). But again, this is local topography construed in terms of painting. Gainsborough's drawing of Foxley recalled his earlier painting of a lane winding to a church through Cornard Wood in Suffolk (Tate Gallery) and both pictures recall the depiction of such lanes by Ruisdael. Price found the fabric of such lanes was easily destroyed by 'military style ... smoothing and

Fig. 1.5   Thomas Gainsborough, *Study of Beech Trees at Foxley* (1760).

levelling'. He had observed this 'not in a distant county' like his own 'but within thirty miles of London', the epicentre of ambition. Here two lanes, one with a single beech among whose roots sheep had made their tracks, had been streamlined by smoothing the banks and erecting new palings.[37] When Price was widening an embanked lane at Foxley, he was distressed that a labourer had made a perpendicular cut in the clay and himself got to work to make it look instantly 'as ancient as any year old bank did'.[38] Given the proverbially appalling state of local roads and his family's efforts to improve them, it is perhaps surprising that Price should uphold the look, at least, of old bye-roads. The reason may reside in Price trying to maintain a balance between the virtues of land and circulation, between Foxley as an integral place and its role in a network that extends to other places. A lane of the kind that Gainsborough depicted seems to be inscribed into the landscape and, rather than running over it, is as much an arena as a routeway.[39]

REMODELLING FOXLEY

In the 1770s two surveys of the Foxley estate were made within four years of each other. The first, which was made in 1770, consists of a set of maps of the estate, together with a terrier giving the acreages of the different tenancies and the size of fields.[40] The second survey was made by Nathaniel Kent in 1774. The last page of this survey is signed by Kent who states that 'This estate was surveyed, modelled and set out by me upon the agreements contained in this book in the year 1774.' The maps are much more accurately drawn than those in the 1770 survey, although the field boundaries are in some cases those which Kent intended should be made during the tenancy, rather than those actually present in 1774. Unfortunately maps were not drawn for some of the farms, nor for the land kept in hand (figure 1.6).

Why should two such dissimilar surveys have been drawn up for the same estate, for the same proprietor, within four years? The 1770 survey was made when Uvedale Price was twenty-three, a couple of years after he had come of age. It contains complete surveys of the remaining open fields, including land held by other proprietors, and would have formed a useful prelude for land exchanges with or purchases from these smaller owners. The 1774 survey, which was produced the year that Uvedale married, was drawn up to assist the complete reorganisation of the estate by Kent. The survey includes copies of the leases, general hints to the landlord and specific hints relating to particular fields and farms. Although Kent's *Hints to Gentlemen of Landed Property* was not published until the following year, Kent was clearly already well established as a land agent: while working on Foxley he was asked to value part of the Earl of Hardwicke's Gloucestershire estate; in 1775 he was collecting rents on Sir Charles Cocks's estates in Worcestershire and Gloucestershire.[41]

At the time of the 1770 survey, the estate consisted of at least 3,844 acres, while the area surveyed by Kent in 1774 was 3,537 acres; the areas are not comparable as the second survey did not include some of the outlying farms. As a result of his reorganisation, the rental on 'such parts of Mr Price's estate as have been modelled by N Kent and are mentioned in this book' rose by a fifth (21 per cent) from £2,031 to £2,461. He achieved this by amalgamating farms and fields, and consolidating holdings. In addition, leases of fifteen years were

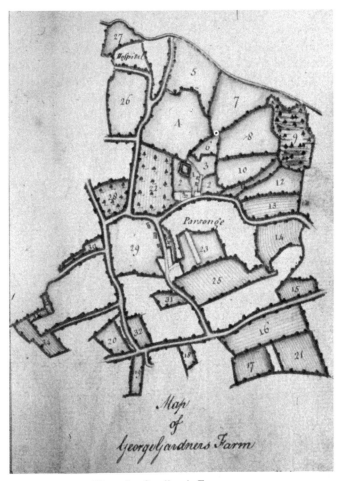

Fig. 1.6   Gardiner's Farm, 1774.

introduced and these included a series of covenants designed to
encourage good farming practice.

Kent was a strong advocate of small farms and small farmers. He
considered that as the small farmer 'has no great space to
superintend, it lies under his eye at all times, and seasons; he seizes all
minute advantages; cultivates every obscure corner'. In addition,
small farms encouraged independence and, moreover, industriousness which could be harnessed by the larger landlords as the
daughters of small farmers made 'the best dairy maids' while the sons

made 'the best gentlemen's bailiffs'.[42] Table 1.1 shows the distribution of holdings at Foxley by value in 1770 and 1774. For comparison equivalent figures based on Nathaniel Kent's model estate from his *Hints* are also given.[43] At first glance, Foxley falls well short of Kent's (1775) model. Kent suggests that 19 per cent of farms should be over £100 in value, while the figure for Foxley is 42 per cent in 1770 and 58 per cent in 1774. As a corollary, Kent places 56 per cent of farms in the £30–£60 range, while at Foxley the figure was 42 per cent in 1770 and this was reduced to 25 per cent in 1774.

Kent's model suggests that an estate of £2,000 should support thirty-two farm families, while both before and after reorganisation by Kent there were only twelve families with farms valued at £30 or more at Foxley. However, Kent points out that 'estates of this value usually support less than a third' of the number he suggests, so that Foxley would seem to be just above par in this respect. The comparison changes remarkably, however, if smallholders, who do not figure at all in Kent's model, are also considered. Thus in 1770 there were five tenants with holdings valued between £15 and £29, and this was increased to eight by the reorganisation of the estate. There were, moreover, twenty-nine tenants with holdings worth less than £15, but over 5 acres in area, although this number was reduced slightly by the reorganisation. Thirsk notes that the central Herefordshire plain was 'generally the home of smallholders' in the early eighteenth century and that the high number of smallholders compared to other parts of the country persisted well into the nineteenth century.[44] If smallholders are included in the calculations, then the Foxley estate supported more tenants than Kent's model estate.

As well as being an advocate of small farmers, Kent considered that 'cottagers are indisputably the most beneficial race of people we have'.[45] He states in his *Hints* that cottagers should have from half to one acre so that they could keep a cow. This is echoed in Kent's comment about a smallholding of 5 acres in six enclosures at Stoke Lacy: 'This is a very comfortable little place for an industrious man being just enough to enable him to keep one cow.'[46] It is difficult to ascertain what changes took place at the reorganisation of 1774 with respect to cottagers, as many holdings are not identifiable. It does appear, however, that the total number of cottagers with some land (but less than 5 acres) remained constant at about twenty-five, although there is some considerable turnover in tenants. Of the ten

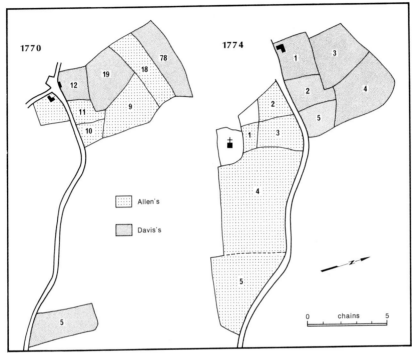

Fig. 1.7   Allen's and Davis's land.

cottagers who can be identified at both dates, the holding of one increased slightly; three remained exactly the same size, but six had reduced holdings.

Most cottagers had to pay increased rents as a result of re-organisation but, in some instances, Kent makes out specific cases as to why a cottager's rent should not be increased. In the case of a tenant who held a public house and ferry, for example, Kent notes that 'As the ferry is greatly fallen off since Bredwardine Bridge, it is dear enough at present rent which is to continue.'[47] The perhaps unwanted independence of at least one cottager is indicated by the case of Richard Evans who was paying £6 4s 6d for his holding of three enclosures and four open field strips. Kent considered that it was worth £7 10s, but noted that '[Evans] would not give it and Ridgeway [the bailiff] intimated that he was a man which it would be imprudent for Mr Price to have any dispute with'.[48]

Kent's 'remodelling' of 1774 consisted of as far as possible putting farms and smallholdings within a ring fence. This is easily appreciated if we consider the changes made for two holdings, Allen's and Davis's lands shown in figure 1.7. In 1770 their enclosures were intermixed; in 1774 they were consolidated on either side of the Hereford–Weobley road. In addition to consolidating holdings, Kent suggested that fields should be enlarged. This can be seen clearly with the two maps of Good's Farm (figure 1.8). In his survey Kent called for 'the hedges to be stubbed up so as to lay the fields as much like the map as may be found convenient'. The farm as remodelled consisted of 312 acres and was intended to have twenty-four enclosures; previously, excluding 22 acres in open fields, it consisted of 306 acres in forty-nine enclosures. Where fields were amalgamated, the old boundary banks had to be removed: 'No's 7, 9 and 10 have several banks in them should be levelled and mixed with lime for manure. As no 17 will not be a compleat inclosure all the banks which divided different persons land should likewise be levelled.'[49]

Wellson's Farm (figure 1.9) shows how scattered some farms remained even after reorganisation. Kent's detailed method can be illustrated by considering his hints to Price for this farm (table 1.2). The main recommendations are draining; removal of hedgerows to enlarge the fields according to his map (although in one case he recommends the stocking-up of a hedge between a hop yard and pasture); removal of alders and rushes which have spread onto fields; and removal of pollards.

Apart from the remodelling of the tenant farms, the reorganisation of 1774 brought about major changes in the 'in hand' estate. The area classed as in hand in 1770 was just over 860 acres but in 1774 this rose dramatically to 1,425 acres. Unfortunately there is no map of the in-hand land after reorganisation, but it appears that the opportunity was taken to transfer a considerable proportion of the tenanted land to Price. The bulk of this transfer came from the largest farms: and four of the five largest farms at Foxley in 1770 were reduced in size (table 1.3).

There is no certainty, however, that the land remained in hand for long. Table 1.4 shows Kent's summary of the land in hand in 1774. That land taken from farms is put in the pasture category is indicated by Kent's phrase 'Meadows, pastures, or designed to be so'.[50] Moreover, Kent compares the value of this land kept in hand to what it would be if it were tenanted, and shows that it is worth £45 more kept in hand (table 1.5). However, he concludes that although keeping the land in hand 'seems to be the best plan, it cannot be

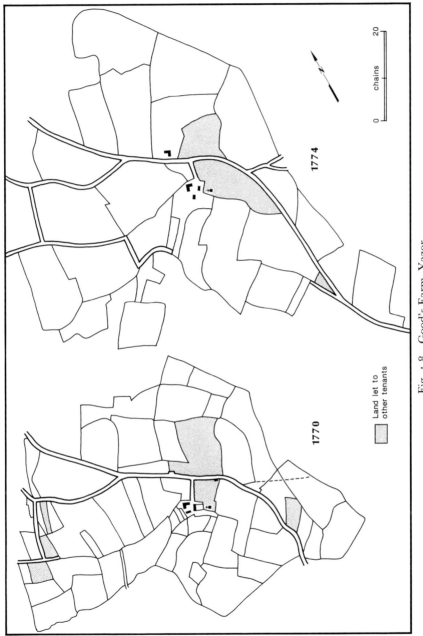

Fig. 1.8 Good's Farm, Yazor.

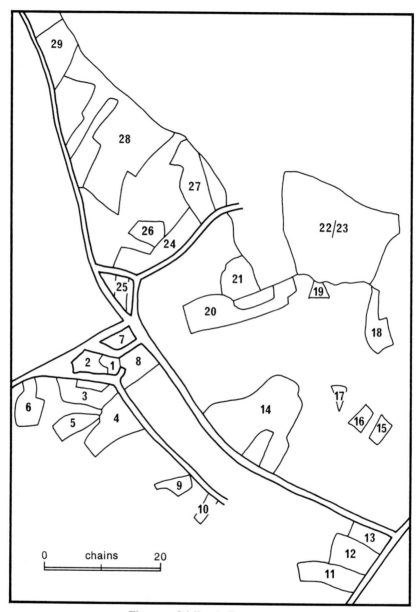

Fig. 1.9   Wellson's Farm, 1774.

expected to turn out so advantageously as the former because there will be some risk and expense in conducting it'.[51]

Kent's remodelling at Foxley increased the rental of the estate but allowed for the retention of that connection between landlord, tenant and labourer which both Price and Kent espoused. However, Price's control over the tenants was increased through the introduction of new leases, and further research is needed to establish the effect of the remodelling on the cottagers and labourers. The extent to which the farm consolidation and reorganisation proposed by Kent were instituted also needs to be examined in greater detail. The remodelling had perhaps its greatest direct effect upon the landscape of Foxley through the transfer of a considerable area of woodland from one of the tenants to Price himself.

THE FOXLEY WOODS

By the late eighteenth century the original core of ancient woodland at Foxley had been enlarged by the making of plantations by successive members of the Price family. There is only an incomplete record of this planting but the evidence does point to a number of conclusions about its nature. First, the plantings were not on a massive scale; a couple of fields were sown one year, while a few years later another planting would be made. Second, the successive members of the Price family all made important contributions to the development of the landscape. Third, the planting does not appear to have been made according to an explicit plan, although it is likely that the overall plan was determined to a large extent by the topography of the Yarsop valley. Finally, the fact that some of the new areas were specifically named as coppices indicates that the planting was justified by commercial as well as ornamental considerations.

By 1770, when Price was in his early twenties, the woodland landscape of Foxley had already undergone over a hundred years of planting, most of which tended to emphasise the sense of enclosure of the horseshoe-shaped valley of Yarsop. The 1770 survey provides for the first time a complete list of the woodland on the estate, and maps of its disposition. There are about 500 acres of woodland and this is mainly found along the inside slopes of the Yarsop valley. Over half (57 per cent) of the land in hand at this time was woodland. The area of woodland kept in hand increased from around 500 acres in 1770 to

about 700 acres in Kent's survey of 1774. Most of this increase can be
accounted for by the transfer of much of the woodland growing on
the hill slopes around the head of the Yarsop valley, which had been
tenanted by Prichard in 1770. Indeed, Prichard's farm was reduced
in size by 221 acres by the reorganisation (table 1.3). Thus the
remodelling of the estate by Kent appears to be a vital instrument in
enabling Price to take full control both of the woodland and of the
whole landscape at Foxley. There appear to be no surviving wood
books or timber accounts for this period, but there is a scatter of
evidence indicating that most of the woodland was managed
commercially.

More than half the woodland retained by Price was classed by
Kent as 'open woods and groves'. That the area was managed as
wood pasture in the 1770s is indicated by Kent's assessment that the
400 acres of grove pasture were worth £30 at 1s 6d an acre. In
addition to their grazing value, the 'necessary thinning' of the groves
would result in a further £50 income per year. The combined grazing
and timber value of the groves would therefore be about 4s per
annum. Unfortunately, apart from Kent's estimates, no records
survive to show income from timber while Price was in control of the
woods. Nationally, timber prices fell from 1760 to 1790 but began to
rise with demand for naval timber from 1790 to 1826.[52] Evidence that
Price was producing timber for this particular market is provided by
an advertisement of March 1795 in the *Hereford Journal* giving oak
timber 'fit for the navy' for sale at Yazor.[53] A further indication of
commercial management is provided by a covenant in a farm lease of
1799 which allowed Price 'to make saw pits or to coal wood' on any
part of the farm.[54]

The grove woodland was supplemented by about 300 acres of
coppice. There was a very strong market for coppice products in late
eighteenth-century Herefordshire. Kent in his Foxley survey notes
that 'Wood under regular course of felling is the most profitable
estate in the county of Hereford, being always a ready money article,
and the management of it is so well known that it is needless for me
to give any particular direction about it.'[55] This high price was partly
due to a local demand for hop poles, but Clark in his *General View*
notes that in addition, a 'vast quantity of wood is sent down the
Severn to Bristol and other markets for making hoops and hop
poles'.[56] This high demand is reflected in the value of the coppice at
Foxley. Kent suggests that about 12 acres should be felled each year,

and that the coppice should be worth 12s per acre, which is three times the value of the groves, and considerably more than the average value Kent gives to 'profitable land good and bad' (table 1.5). The market for coppice products held up, and if anything increased, through the last two decades of the eighteenth century: Clark gives its value at between 12s and 15s an acre per year in 1794 and Duncumb in 1805 gives a range of 11s to 22s an acre, though there is some evidence that there was a decline around 1810.[57]

Price's correspondence with Sir George Beaumont and Lord Aberdeen shows that with this decline in value of coppice, the coppices at Foxley became more important in *aesthetic* terms. He uses the analogy that in every block of marble there is a fine statue; it only requires to have the rubbish removed from around it:

So it is with this place; there are fine pictures without end, but concealed by rubbish to a degree you could hardly conceive...since the time you were here [four years previously], I have been busied in clearing away some of the mass of rubbish...the great blocks of marble are three distinct coppice woods; as such most unprofitable, but containing treasures of beauty; for a number of fine timber trees of various sorts have been left in them and likewise a number of old yews, thorns, nuts, hollies, maples...[58]

Price made the same analogy in a letter to Beaumont and noted that the coppice woods 'are brim full of beautiful groups and compositions both of a near and distant kind'. He described his method as follows:

I begin by taking away everything that may injure the trees and groups that are likely at last to be left, and I open up the compositions little by little but as I must have an eye to profit I leave a number of trees which do no other harm than that of hiding what is at last to be displayed.[59]

A letter of 1803 shows that the detailed mode of management he employed on his coppice woods when they were no longer profitable was not new. He writes that

Thinning and pruning with a proper mixture of caution and boldness is at least as necessary as planting, and should be exercised when wanting in every assemblage of trees, from the highest to the lowest growths, and from the oldest woods (but these with particular caution) to the youngest plantations.[60]

Apart from managing existing woodland, Price extended its acreage by the purchase of existing woodland, planting of new areas and through exchange. In 1773, for example, he purchased an area described as 'coppice wood ground' near to Ladylift at Yazor, from his neighbour Sir John Cotterell.[61] This purchase helped to thicken the existing border of woodland around Foxley. In addition, there is fragmentary evidence that he was planting new areas of woodland. A covenant on a lease of 1781 on a farm at Mansel Lacy, for example, permitted the landlord 'to plant with wood and take into his own hands as coppice ground any parts of the before mentioned premises making a reasonable deduction in the rent for the same'.[62] This particular covenant had not been put in any of the leases devised by Kent seven years earlier in 1774.

Price also extended his woodland by exchange. In 1812, there was a particularly interesting exchange between Thomas Andrew Knight and Price. Table 1.6 gives the valuation of timber on the 115 acres of land exchanged. It shows that Uvedale had gained a considerable number of trees by the exchange, particularly pollard oaks, but also oak and ash timber trees. In a letter to Sir George Beaumont in July 1812, Price describes this exchange as bringing to him 'new lands that are of real consequence to the beauty, connection and comfort of my place'.[63]

The value that Price put on the horseshoe of woodland around Foxley is shown by a letter from Peplowe, the owner of the Garnstone estate to the west of Foxley, to Knight, in which Peplowe states that in discussions Price had suggested that he 'was willing to give up to you [Knight] in exchange, whatever was not absolutely necessary, in his view of it, to complete the wooded boundary of his property'.[64] Indeed, for the purposes of the exchange, Knight's surveyor Harris was instructed to value fields 'in view of Foxley' at a shilling per acre more than the agricultural value.[65] In the final articles of agreement for the exchange (1813) no extra value was put on land because of its location, but they did state that:

in regard that some of those lands are in an uncultivated state and that the same have been for some time permitted to continue by the said Thomas Andrew Knight at the request and for the accommodation of the said Uvedale Price It hath been agreed that such Lands shall be valued as if the same were in a fair and proper state of cultivation according to the nature of the Land but that nothing shall be charged for locality of situation.[66]

This shows that before the exchange Price had arranged with Knight that some of the latter's land should remain in an uncultivated state.

The evidence of the timber valuations suggests that in all probability this was an area of old wood pasture as it had a high density of pollards and timber. Price had therefore been able to extend his influence over the landscape of a portion of a neighbouring estate until an exchange of land brought it fully under his control.

The remodelling of the estate in the 1770s was the springboard which allowed Price to achieve full control over the woodland landscape of Foxley. The management of this complicated mixture of ancient woodland, plantations and coppices became of immense importance to Price, as demonstrated through his published writing and private correspondence. The changing role of the coppices over his lifetime is of particular interest. William Mason's poem *The English Garden* emphasises the importance of coppice in creating texture, variety and intricacy as well as stimulating associations of humble comfort and economy. Both Price and Humphry Repton acknowledge Mason's poem as a formative influence and quote from it; in many ways coppicing provided a paradigm of the careful Picturesque style they both espoused.[67]

LANDSCAPE HUSBANDRY

While Price was often in his own lifetime dismissed as a dilettante, absurdly trying to convince down-to-earth Englishmen that their estates were potentially picture galleries, he was significantly the model for that most pragmatic of nineteenth-century improvers, John Claudius Loudon. Loudon found Foxley displayed 'the elegant and practical taste of the great reformer of landscape-gardening'. In his *Treatise on Farming, Improving and Managing Country Residences*, based on the axiom of connection, Loudon revived the old term 'husbandry', to encompass all kinds of estate design and management – arable and pastoral farming, planting and gardening; and he coined a new term 'Landscape Husbandry' to describe improvements, an 'awkward appellation', he admitted, but 'much better than Landscape Gardening'.[68] The term 'landscape husbandry' failed to gain any currency and this is unfortunate, both for the historiography of estate management in general and for the reputation of Uvedale Price in particular. For, better than any other term, 'landscape husbandry' describes what Price was doing at Foxley and probably what many other middling gentry were doing on their estates too.

Table 1.1. *Value of holdings at Foxley in 1770 and 1774*

Value (£)	1770 (£2,031)	1774 (£2,461)	Kent (1775 model for £2,000 estate)
160+	2	5	2
120–159	3	0	2
100–119	0	2	2
80–99	0	0	4
60–79	2	2	4
50–59	1	1	4
40–49	3	1	6
30–39	1	1	8
	12	12	32
20–29	1	2	—
15–19	4	6	—
< 15 (> 5 acres)	29	25	—
	46	45	32

Table 1.2. *Kent's hints to Price for Mr Wellson's premises (1774)*

4	composed of two pieces should have hedges removed and thrown together.
5	coppice of alders should be cut down and the blank parts planted with withey.
9 and 10	being overspread with alders and extremely wet coarse and rushy should be cleared and drained effectively.
12 and 13	should be thrown together.
14	consisting of a great number of pieces laid together wants a great deal of labour in draining and clearing of pollards, bushes and hedge rows and may be greatly improved by bringing the wash of the road over it.
15 and 16	draining.
18	effectually cleared of alders which are spread over a great part of it.
19 and 20	wants cleaning.
21	alders cut down and blank parts filled with withey.
22 and 23	will need a great deal of husbandry when the hedges are removed and the alders extirpated.
26	hedge taken away from middle.
27 and 8	miserably overspread with alder, bushes and lie wet. The former should be extirpated and likewise the pollards.
29	the hedge between the hop ground and pasture should be stocked up.

Table 1.3. *Area in acres of the five largest tenant farms at Foxley in 1770 and 1774*

Tenant	Area rented 1770	1774	Change 1770–1774
Ridgeway	436	328	−108
Prichard	428	207	−221
Gardiner	355	237	−118
Good	345	312	−33
Matthews	250	263	+13
	1814	1347	−467

Table 1.4. *Summary of land in hand, 1770 and 1774*

1770	Acres	Roods	Perches
House and garden	15	1	19
Pasture	340	2	12
Woodland*	504	1	35
Total in hand	860	1	26

* including some open land

1774			
Gardens, pleasure grounds etc.	16	3	31
Coppice ground under regular fall	294	0	4
Open woods and groves	403	3	11
Meadows, pastures, or designed to be so	710	2	28
Total in hand	1425	1	34

Table 1.5. *Kent's comparison of the value of the untenanted land at Foxley in 1774 let to a tenant and kept in hand*

Value of land in hand let to a tenant:	£ s d
Regular fall of wood @ 12 acres a year, £17 an acre on average	204 0 0
Necessary thinning of groves	50 0 0
400 acres of grove pasture at 1/6 acre	30 0 0
700 acres of profitable land good and bad together at 10 sh each	350 0 0
Total	634 0 0
Or, If Mr Price keeps it all in hand, it may turn out as follows:	
Grass and hay for 20 horses at £8 each	160 0 0
10 cows at £5 each	50 0 0
100 ewes and 400 weathers	125 0 0
70 Jack cattle at £2	140 0 0
The woods	204 0 0
Total	679 0 0

Table 1.6. *Exchange of land between Uvedale Price and Thomas Andrew Knight, 25 February 1812; valuation of timber*

Valuation of timber belonging to U. P. and going to T. A. K.:

5 Pollard Oaks; 15 Pollard Ash; 5 Maiden Oaks; 5 Maiden Ash; 23 Elm Timber Trees; Sundry Oak and Elm saplings etc.
Total Value £34 10s 0d

Valuation of timber belonging to T. A. K. and going to U. P.:

87 Pollard Oak Trees; 31 Maiden Oak ditto; 6 Maiden Ash ditto; 9 Pollard Ash ditto; 2 Asp Trees; Sundry oak and Ash saplings etc.
Value £114 0s 0d

Timber on 2 Acres of land along the head of the Shoaks:
2 Maiden Oaks; 4 Pollard ditto; 6 Ash Trees
Value £12 10s 0d

NOTES

1 An earlier version of this paper was published in the journal *Rural History*. See Stephen Daniels and Charles Watkins, 'Picturesque Land-scaping and Estate Management: Uvedale Price at Foxley, 1770–1829', *Rural History*, 2 (1991), 141–69. The general issue of this paper is also discussed in Stephen Daniels and Susanne Seymour 'Landscape Design and the Idea of "Improvement"', in R. Dodgshon and R. A. Butlin (eds.), *A New Historical Geography of England and Wales*, second edition

(London: Academic Press, 1990); Susanne Seymour 'Eighteenth Century Parkland "Improvement" on the Dukeries Estates of North Nottinghamshire', unpublished Ph.D. thesis (University of Nottingham, 1989); Stephen Daniels with Susanne Seymour and Charles Watkins, 'Landscaping and Estate Management in Later Georgian England', in J. D. Hunt (ed.), *Garden History: Issues, Approaches, Methods* (Washington D.C.: Dumbarton Oaks Research Library, 1992); and 'Parkland Design and Management', special issue of the *East Midland Geographer*, vol. 12 (1–2), 1989. For a detailed account of the Foxley estate see Denis A. Lambin, 'Foxley: the Prices' Estate in Herefordshire', *Journal of Garden History*, 7 (1987), 244–70. While there are important differences between Lambin and ourselves in interpreting Price and his estate, we wish to record our debt to both his article and his generous reading of an earlier draft of our essay here.

2 Pamela Horn, 'An Eighteenth-Century Land Agent: The Career of Nathaniel Kent (1737–1810)', *Agricultural History Review*, 30 (1982), 1–16.

3 Nathaniel Kent, *Hints to Gentlemen of Landed Property* (London, 1775); Nathaniel Kent, *General View of the Agriculture of the County of Norfolk* (London, 1794).

4 Nathaniel Kent, 'A Survey of Foxley and its Appendages in the County of Hereford, the Estate of Uvedale Price Esq'. This survey was discovered by Major D. J. C. Davenport in 1988. It is a small bound volume. The following statement is on the last page: 'This estate was surveyed, modelled and set out by me upon the agreements contained in this book in the year 1774 Signed Nath. Kent, Fulham 20.9.1774.' The authors would like to thank Major Davenport for letting them make use of this survey. This is referred to in the text as the '1774 survey'.

5 Kent, *Hints*, pp. 235, 239, 278.

6 Kent, *General View*, p. 46.

7 Uvedale Price 'A letter to H. Repton Esq.' in *An Essay on the Picturesque*, 3 vols. (London, 1810) vol. III, p. 178–9.

8 Uvedale Price, *Thoughts on the Defence of Property* (Hereford, 1797), pp. 11, 28, 20, 19.

9 Price to Lord Abercorn, 20 January 1801, British Museum (B.M.) Add. MSS.

10 Price to Lord Abercorn, 3 August 1798, B.M. Add. MSS.

11 John Barrell, *The Dark Side of Landscape: The Rural Poor in English Painting 1730–1840* (Cambridge University Press, 1980), pp. 116–17.

12 *Ibid.*, pp. 173–4.

13 E. W. Brayley and J. Britten, *The Beauties of England and Wales*, vol. VI (London, 1805), p. 581.

14 William Marshall, *A Review of the Landscape: Also of an Essay on the Picturesque* (London, 1795), pp. 185ff.

15 Lambin, 'Foxley', p. 262.

16 *Ibid.*, p. 259; Kent, *Hints*, pp. 35–6; Price letters to Beaumont, 24 April

1805, 17 August 1805, Coleorton MSS, Pierpont Morgan Library, New York.

17 Price to Lord Abercorn, 21 December 1800, B.M. Add. MSS.

18 William Gilpin, *Observations on the Mountains and Lakes of Cumberland and Westmorland*, 2 vols. (London, 1786), vol. II, p. 43.

19 Clark's text is discussed in John Barrell, *The Idea of Landscape and the Sense of Place 1730–1840: An Approach to the Poetry of John Clare* (Cambridge University Press, 1972), pp. 79–81.

20 Price, *Essay on the Picturesque*, vol. I, p. 351. Gilpin had pronounced the Upper Wye from Hereford to Ross 'tame'. Price's strictures on Gilpin were taken up by T. D. Fosbroke in his *Wye Tour, or Gilpin on the Wye with Picturesque additions from Wheatley, Price &c* (Ross, 1826).

21 Price, *Essay on the Picturesque*, vol. I, pp. 193–4.

22 Price to Beaumont, 29 April 1803, Coleorton MSS; Price to Lord Abercorn, 31 May 1796, B.M. Add. MSS. Abercorn read the proofs of Price's *Essay on the Picturesque* and was intent to erase provincial language, for example, 'tump' for which he substituted 'mound' even though Price considered it to be incorrect (Price to Abercorn, 2 February 1797; 11 March 1797).

23 Price, *Essay on the Picturesque*, vol. II, pp. 342, 367–8, 340.

24 *Ibid.*, vol. II, pp. 301–46.

25 *Ibid.*, vol. II, pp. 116–28.

26 Price to Beaumont, 2 February 1798, Coleorton MSS.

27 Price, *Essay on the Picturesque*, vol. I, p. 240.

28 *Ibid.*, vol. III, p. 120.

29 Price to Beaumont, 23 April 1803, Coleorton MSS.

30 Price to Lord Aberdeen, 22 November 1821, B.M. Add. MSS.

31 Price to Lord Abercorn, 12 June 1796, B.M. Add. MSS.

32 *Ibid.*

33 Price, *Essay on the Picturesque*, vol. III, p. 130.

34 On the importance of foregrounds to Price see Stephen Daniels, 'The Political Iconography of Woodland in Later Georgian England', in Denis Cosgrove and Stephen Daniels, *The Iconography of Landscape* (Cambridge University Press, 1988), pp. 59–60.

35 William Wordsworth to Sir George Beaumont, 28 August 1811, in Ernest de Selincourt (ed.), *The Letters of William and Dorothy Wordsworth: The Middle Years* (Oxford: Clarendon Press, 1937), p. 467.

36 Price, *Essay on the Picturesque*, vol. I, pp. 24ff.

37 *Ibid.*, vol. I, pp. 32–5.

38 Price to Beaumont, 24 July 1812, Coleorton MSS.

39 For a discussion of this idea in the local work of Humphry Repton see Daniels and Watkins, 'Picturesque Landscaping' pp. 163–5.

40 *A Book of Survey Containing the Manors of Yazor, Mancellacey, Bishopstone...with the Contents and Yearly Estimates of Uvedale Price Esq. of Foxley...in the Year of our Lord 1770*, Hereford County Record Office (H.C.R.O.) D 344. This is referred to in this essay as the '1770 survey'.

41 Horn, 'Eighteenth-Century Land Agent'.

42 Kent, *Hints*, p. 194.

43 Kent, *Hints*, p. 217.

44 Joan Thirsk (ed.), *The Agrarian History of England and Wales* (Cambridge University Press, 1985), vol. v, 1640–1750, part i, *Regional Farming Systems* (1984); Guy Robinson, 'Agricultural Depression, 1870–1900', *Transactions of the Woolhope Naturalists' Field Club*, 42 (1978), 259–78.

45 Kent, *Hints*, p. 208.

46 Kent, '1774 survey'.

47 *Ibid.*

48 *Ibid.*

49 *Ibid.*

50 *Ibid.*

51 *Ibid.*

52 Oliver Rackham, *Ancient Woodland: Its History, Vegetation and Uses in England* (London: Edward Arnold, 1980), p. 201.

53 *Hereford Journal*, 18 March 1795. David Whitehead kindly provided this information.

54 H.C.R.O. B 47/- D97.

55 Kent '1774 survey'.

56 John Clark, *General View of the Agriculture of the County of Hereford* (London, 1794).

57 Clark, *General View*; John Duncumb, *General View of the Agriculture of the County of Hereford* (London, 1805).

58 Uvedale Price to Lord Aberdeen, 6 February 1818, B.M. Add. MSS.

59 Uvedale Price to Beaumont, 11 November 1812, Coleorton MSS.

60 Uvedale Price to Beaumont, August 1803, Coleorton MSS.

61 H.C.R.O. B 47/- D303–307.

62 H.C.R.O. B 47/- H70–1 D97.

63 Uvedale Price to Beaumont, 14 August 1812, Coleorton MSS.

64 H.C.R.O. Knight papers T74 728.

65 H.C.R.O. Knight papers T74 728 5.

66 H.C.R.O. Knight papers T74 590.

67 See Daniels, 'Political Iconography'. For coppicing see Rackham, *Ancient Woodland* and Charles Watkins, *Woodland Management and Conservation* (Newton Abbot: David and Charles, 1990).

68 J. C. Loudon, *A Treatise on Farming, Improving and Managing Country Residences* (London, 1806), vol. III, p. 355.

CHAPTER 2

William Gilpin and the black-lead mine

Stephen Copley

In the course of his tour of the Lake District William Gilpin twice approaches, but does not actually visit, 'the celebrated black-lead mine'[1] above Seathwaite, at the head of Borrowdale. His representation and discussion of the distant appearance of the mine serves to differentiate his Picturesque narrative from other descriptive accounts of the region in the period, and to crystallise elements in the project of Picturesque tourism, particularly as it figures the relation between the aesthetic and the economic, and as it 'places' the tourist in relation to local society.

The new literature of Picturesque tourism that is produced in the last quarter of the eighteenth century represents one strand in the burgeoning array of contemporary forms of regional loco-descriptive literature. In the case of the Lake District, the numerous published and unpublished descriptive narratives of Picturesque tours of the area appear alongside the utilitarian descriptions offered in the *Northern Tour* of Arthur Young; the agricultural reports of Bailey, Culley and Pringle, eventually collected by William Marshall in his *Review and Abstract*; the county history of William Hutchinson; the *Survey* by the land surveyor James Clarke; and the commentaries of travellers such as Thomas Pennant, who are unsympathetic to the claims of the Picturesque.[2] Each of these accounts constructs its own distinctive discursive economy of the region, describing its natural features, history, social structures, agricultural and manufacturing economies, and trades; and assessing the role played by each in developing the manners of the inhabitants.

The Seathwaite black-lead, graphite, plumbago or wad mine figures widely, and perhaps disproportionately in relation to its economic importance, in accounts of the region in the period, and it offers a good focus for examination of the debates that run through these accounts. Forming part of the extensive, and in some cases ancient, quarrying, and lead-, copper-, iron- and coal-mining economy of the Lake District, the mine was first recorded in operation in 1555. It was then worked periodically, particularly in response to the massively increased demand for black lead in the eighteenth century, when the substance was transformed from a little-regarded local product, used for instance to mark sheep, into a valuable and much sought-after commercial commodity. The range of its applications in the late eighteenth century is indicated by James Clarke when he lists its 'several uses in medicine, dying, glazing of crucibles, keeping iron from rust, combs for fair-haired ladies etc', to which can be added casting bomb shells, round shot and cannon balls; and Clarke and others celebrate the mine as the source of the mineral in its purest known form in the world.[3] As Wordsworth records in the nineteenth century, black lead could 'scarcely be said any longer to exist'[4] in the area by the 1810s, and the mine itself was finally exhausted and closed in the 1830s. Its eighteenth-century boom years thus coincide with the flowering of that other regional boom industry of the period – Picturesque tourism.

The black-lead mine figures in contemporary accounts as much for the circumstances of its working as for its end product. In his county history William Hutchinson quotes Thomas Pennant's depiction of its operation: 'It is the property of a few gentlemen who, lest the markets should be glutted, open the mine only once in seven years, then cause it to be filled and otherwise secured from the depredations of the neighbouring miners.'[5] He also includes details of the mid-century Act of Parliament passed to protect it from these 'depredations' (25th Geo. II c.10), descriptions of it by earlier eighteenth-century visitors such as Bishop Nicolson in 1710 and Thomas Gray in 1769, and an account from the *Gentleman's Magazine* of 1751 of a trip to the 'Wad-Mines', in which the writer, 'G.S.', describes the scene of local people working through the spoil heaps for scraps of black lead as 'the most frightful that can be conceived'. 'G.S.' writes of the gleaners 'digging...in a great heap of clay and rubbish, where the mines had formerly been wrought', suggesting that although the spoils 'were now neglected by the proprietors, as affording nothing worth the search; yet these fellows could generally clear 6s or 8s a day, and sometimes more', and claiming that the mine supports an extensive black economy in Keswick, where 'the poorer inhabitants subsist chiefly by stealing or clandestinely buying of those that steal,

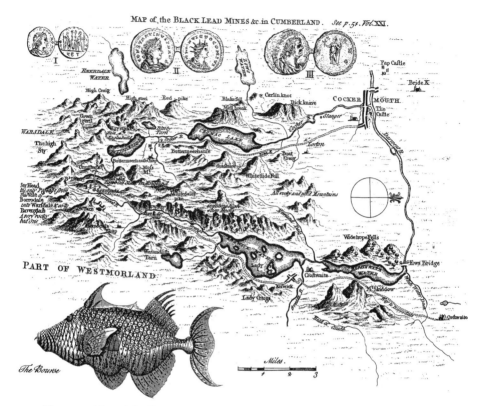

Fig. 2.1   *Map of the Black Lead Mines in Cumberland.* Illustration accompanying an
article in *The Gentleman's Magazine*, 1 June 1751.

the black lead, which they sell to Jews, or other hawkers'.[6] Other
eighteenth-century commentators note the mysterious appearances
of the mineral at various sites in other parts of Borrowdale and
Derwentwater, sometimes referring to ambitious local plans to
extract and exploit it. William Hutchinson, for instance, mentions its
presence on Vicar's Island in Derwentwater in the context of a
scheme by which 'the whole lake might be drained'[7] to recover it.
Usually, however, these appearances are taken simply as signs of the
extent of the contraband trade in the mineral, further and retrospective evidence for which is claimed by Wordsworth in the
nineteenth century, in the form of pieces of previously secreted ore,
which he suggests are regularly dug up in Borrowdale cottage
gardens.[8]

In surveys of the moral and political economy of the region, accounts of the mine feed into extended discussions of the place of the non-agricultural economies of manufacturing, quarrying, mining and trade in the rural economy as a whole. All are on the one hand celebrated as founts of wealth, and on the other decried as sources of luxury, corruption of manners, and crime. In this last regard, hostility to non-agricultural economic activity of all sorts is at its clearest among some of the agricultural improvers, whose programmes otherwise rest on claims for economic development as a route to local prosperity, but whose georgic ideology cannot embrace anything beyond purely agricultural bases for that prosperity, and who see all else as a source of corruption of manners. William Marshall's commentary on the region is pointed in its insistence on the benefits of agriculture and the dangerous intrusiveness of manufacturing. When the agricultural reporters comment that a few cotton mills are all the county of Cumberland has 'to boast of', he ripostes, 'Four or five cotton-mills to *boast* of! Their effects on the morals of Carlisle, at least, have been, for some time, *notoriously* ascertained.'[9]

Mining is at the centre of these debates. Its place in the rural economy as a whole is textualised by eighteenth-century commentators either as a disruptive intrusion into, or as an integral and organic part of, that economy. The categories are not entirely mutually exclusive, of course. In the context of the Lake District, quarrying and mining can clearly be presented as a traditional and integral part of the indigenous economy. In this context long-established immigrant communities, such as the German miners introduced to Keswick by the Company of the Mines Royal in the sixteenth century, are often naturalised and treated as local. At the same time, however, more recent settlements of Irish and other immigrant miners in various sites in the area are frequently condemned as disruptively intrusive. Clarke offers examples of each of these models. The black-lead mine is thus not represented as destructive of a previously harmonious rural economy, but as supportive of it, as are the adjacent 'valuable mines of blue slate in Borrowdale, which are of great service to the poor inhabitants, as the wages for working in them are very good'.[10] However, this descriptive model contrasts sharply with that which Clarke employs in relation to the common lead mines found in neighbouring Patterdale:

Patterdale, though now the poorest place that I am acquainted with, was once the seat of peace and plenty. Almost every man had a small freehold, whose annual produce, (though perhaps not equal to the daily expenditure of the rich and gay,) not only maintained him and his family in a comfortable manner, but even enabled many among them to amass small sums of money. The scene is now changed; vice and poverty sit pictured in almost every countenance, and the rustic fireside is no longer the abode of peace and contentment. This lamentable change took place about thirty years ago; at that time some lead mines were wrought in this Dale, and of course a number of miners were brought from different parts for that purpose. These fellows, who are in general the most abandoned, wicked, and profligate part of mankind, no sooner settled here, than they immediately began to propagate their vices among the innocent un-suspecting inhabitants … Thus we may see as it were in epitome, the baleful effects of vice upon society at large.[11]

This model of miners as a disruptive presence is widespread even in descriptions in which they are presented as an indigenous population. In the course of his *Northern Tour*, Arthur Young represents Yorkshire miners characteristically as the untamed, unruly elements in the rural economy, who can be controlled only by fixing and regulating their relation to enclosed and cultivated surface property. In a paean of praise to William Danby of Swinton for providing his miners with intake fields for their own cultivation, he thus writes that 'miners in general, I might almost say universally, are a most tumultuous, sturdy set of people, greatly impatient of controul'. In this context their landlord's management of them largely involves developing ways of exercising this 'controul'. Young summarises Danby's reasoning in these terms: 'If… I can give these fellows a better notion of local property and happiness, I shall gain a power over them, which I can easily turn to their good, and the benefit of their families, as well as to my own convenience'; and he reports that the outcome 'was of great service to the families, and it answered their landlord's purpose of rendering them more dependant, though at the same time more happy'.[12]

In his unpublished 'Tour of the Lakes', Wordsworth reflects many of the points of emphasis of these earlier commentaries, when he produces an account of the disruptive and corrupting effect of the Borrowdale black-lead mine on local manners. He reports that, in the previous century its presence has led to 'desperate' robberies, and premature deaths brought about by 'maladies caught in night watchings' at its mouth; and in the present, it has left a legacy of 'extravagant expectations & comparatively inordinate longings with a train of novel & reprehensible indulgences' such as the widespread taste for gaming in the dale. And the source of all this corruption is 'a material which the Reader is daily holding in his hand in the familiar shape of a Pencil'.[13]

What Alan Liu has referred to as William Gilpin's 'whimsical'[14] account of the black-lead mine stands at an interesting tangent to the other depictions of it mentioned so far. In its inclusions, exclusions and particularities of emphasis, it marks very clearly the project of the writer's Picturesque tourism. Obviously the mine is not the primary object of Gilpin's attention in the way it is for 'G.S.': instead, he sees it incidentally in the course of his search for the picturesque landscapes of the area. Viewing the mine from Borrowdale, he writes

Somewhat further, on this side, than Eagle's-crag lies on the other, rise those mountains, where the celebrated black-lead mine is wrought. I could not help feeling a friendly attachment to this place, which every lover of the pencil must feel, as deriving from this mineral one of the best instruments of his art; the freest and readiest expositor of his ideas. We saw the site of the mine at a distance, marked with a dingy yellow stain, from the ochery mixtures thrown from it's mouth, which shiver down the sides of the mountain.

He continues by explaining, 'During the periodical season of working it, for it is opened only once in seven years, many people pick up a comfortable subsistence from the scraps of black-lead, which escape amongst the coarser strata'; and he suggests that 'These are honest gains', unlike the designs of a 'late prolific genius in fraud', who

took a very indirect method of possessing a share of this rich mineral. A part of the mountain, contiguous to the mine, was his property. Here, at the expence of great labour, he sank a shaft, which he carried diagonally, till he entered the mine; where, with subterraneous wickedness, he continued his depredations for some time undiscovered. At length his fraud was brought to light; and he was tried at Carlisle. The peculiarity of his case had no precedent. He saved his life; but a law was obtained by the proprietors of the mine, to defend their property from such indirect attacks for the future

– the circumstances which had led to the passing of the Act of Parliament mentioned by Pennant and Clarke. Finally Gilpin admits that the lure of viewing a recommended landscape overcomes any desire on his part to investigate the mine further:

The sun was now declining, and it was too late to take a nearer view of the mine: nor indeed did it promise more on the spot, than it discovered at a distance. Besides, the beauties of Watenlath had been so strongly represented to us; that we were resolved to go in quest of those scenes, in preference to any other.[15]

The significance of this account of the mine can best be seen by setting Gilpin's description in the larger context of his and other journeys to and from the Lake District, and travels within it. The accumulation of sights seen and places visited – or pointedly not visited – on these journeys, helps define the characteristics of Picturesque tour literature, and sets the terms of the debates that run through it.

Eighteenth-century Picturesque tours do not generally or necessarily exclude accounts of agricultural, manufacturing or industrial activity in the regions through which the tourist passes, or visits to the sites where it occurs. However, they accommodate those sites in particular and peculiar ways, as they negotiate a place for the Picturesque as a specialised category of perception in contestation first with competing aesthetics of landscape, and second with the claims of political economy and morality. Various sites of economic activity are thus regularly described in tour texts, even if they are not regarded as Picturesque in themselves; equally, various forms of such activity are acknowledged as Picturesque – or potentially Picturesque – in particular perspectives; while the 'natural' landscapes sought by the tourists are themselves inevitably inscribed with evidence of the workings of the local economy.[16]

This is true even in the case of Gilpin, where the project of Picturesque description seems at times to be to efface the signs of economic activity entirely from the landscape. In this attempt, the visible signs of agriculture are in many cases more difficult to accommodate within the vocabulary of the Picturesque than are the signs of industrial activity or trade. On the Wye tour, for instance, Gilpin condemns signs of cultivation as intrusions into the natural landscape, but accepts the limited traces of industry that he encounters, insofar as they are translated into decorative forms. He thus lists 'abbeys, castles, villages, spires, forges, mills, and bridges' as attractive features of the tour, without marked distinctions between them, and at Lidbroke-wharf, sees coals being loaded and writes that 'The contrast of all this business, the engines used lading and unlading, together with the solemnity of the scene, produce all

together a picturesque assemblage'.[17] In the context of this description, the economic activities surveyed are assessed according to
a distinctive system of hierarchies and priorities. The smoke of
charcoal furnaces on the banks of the river is thus pleasing because it
harmonises the elements of the pictorial composition seen by the
tourist, not because it betokens industry. Similarly, 'the stone
quarries...on the right; and on the left, the furnaces of Bishop's
Wood' are acceptable because they 'vary the scene', though, with no
account of their economic significance, they are said to be 'of no great
importance in themselves'.[18]

In this connection, Ann Bermingham's suggestion that the often
assumed opposition of Picturesque nature and unpicturesque industry should be seen as a historical development in the period rather
than as a founding assumption of the Picturesque aesthetic[19] is borne
out widely in the literature of the Lakes. Thomas West, for example,
does not need to negotiate any changes of perceptive framework
when he suggests that the visitor to Ulverston 'Make an excursion to
the west, three miles, and visit the greatest iron mines in *England*'. His
account of the innocuousness of the mine is couched in functional as
well as aesthetic terms: he insists that 'This mineral is not hurtful to
any animal or vegetable. The verdure is remarkably fine about the
workings, and no one ever suffered by drinking the water in the
mines, though discoloured and much impregnated with the ore',
before going on in the next sentence, without needing to negotiate a
transition, to write 'Proceed by *Dalton* to the magnificent ruins of
Furness Abbey'.[20]

Following Bermingham's claim, it is clear that the problems that
characterise Picturesque representation of all forms of economic
activity stem in large part from the abandonment in Picturesque
writings of the aesthetic argument of *dulce et utile*. This feature of the
new aesthetic is repeatedly emphasised by Gilpin, for instance when
he writes of 'the picturesque eye' that 'it is not it's business to
consider matters of utility. It has nothing to do with the affairs of the
plough, and the spade; but merely examines the face of nature as a
beautiful object'.[21] This insistence involves the abandonment of a key
trope in which economic provision and aesthetic pleasure are united
within the terms of a discourse of morality in much earlier eighteenth-
century loco-descriptive writing, and indeed in which they continue
to be united, as Barbara Maria Stafford points out,[22] in the
'scientifically' descriptive landscape writing that appears in parallel

with Picturesque texts in the later part of the century. The abandonment of the argument of utility inevitably renders links between the economic, the socially ameliorative and the aesthetic problematic on several fronts. In particular, it leaves the claims of aesthetics at odds with the claims of morality whenever the benefits of cultivation, improvement and economic progress, and the moral values of industry, come into conflict with the aesthetic pleasures of the spectacle of wildness or decay.

Severing the connection between beauty and utility leaves tour writers with considerable problems of self-justification over their own position as tourists, and with particular problems over the place of labour, luxury and leisure in their narratives. Gilpin's tours, in common with the other Picturesque tours of the period, invite readings which see them as symbolic journeys through landscapes inscribed with over-determined moral values. As such, they construct their own symbolic geography of the country. The tourists' journeys from city to country, sophistication to simplicity, civilisation to nature, are articulated largely in relation to the trope of luxury. The Picturesque tour is presented as an escape both from the privileges and from the impositions of the luxury economy. The tourist visibly – if temporarily – renounces city luxury and domestic security for rural simplicity, and beyond that, for exposure to, and confrontation with, an imagined Other, the natural, outside the realms of the social and the economic. However, the tour journey is potentially compromised at every stage, involving as it does a search for aesthetic pleasure beyond the bounds of the moral, and so, at an extreme, offering a route to illicit gratification.

Tour writers are thus consistently wrong-footed when it comes to justifying their own position as tourists. Embarrassingly for them, the tourist, as observer of the rural scene, is repeatedly associated, explicitly or by default, with the negative terms in the binaries which structure the tour narratives. The problems involved stem in particular from the justifications they propose for their own leisure in relation to the labour they survey – or pointedly do not survey – in the course of their journeys. Tourists travel at leisure and for pleasure, and are unconstrained by the economic disciplines which govern the conduct of the population in the country through which they pass. The privilege of their position is their leisure, which offers a freedom symbolised by the freedom of digressive travel itself. As William Hutchinson puts it, 'On parties of pleasure time should never be limited... The speculative traveller is never confined to roads, times, or seasons; but as the circumstances exciting his curiosity lay either to the right or left, he pursues the objects of his attention, without regard to hours or rules...'[23]

For Hutchinson's 'speculative traveller', there is considerable pleasure to be derived from watching the economic activity in the 'living landscape', where 'the busy cottagers' are 'all abroad in the several occupations of the field'. Indeed this form of observation provides him with a means of associating himself vicariously with the industrious population he observes, and launching an attack on indolence and luxury. He thus lambastes the 'Half mankind [who] know nothing of the beauties of nature, and waste in indolence and sleep the glorious scene which advancing morning presents'.[24] Other tourists deploy, and fall victim to, some of the same terminology. When Thomas Newte, gentleman, tours the Lakes, he sets out from the seat of scholarly and gentlemanly leisure – Oxford – and travels via Birmingham, where he laments that 'this being unfortunately the time of their fair, we could not see any of the manufacturers at work'. The circumstance provokes him to the claim that there is a 'natural and indeed necessary connection between industry and economy, as there is between both and the prosperity of a nation', except that, under the influence of luxury, 'indolence and pleasure, the parents of idleness and corruption, have begun to sap the foundations of a state which was raised on industry, temperance, and frugality'.[25] The striking absence at the centre of this claim, however, is any consideration of his own position as the leisured observer of the scene.

As a clergyman with a developed sense of his social and moral duties and obligations, Gilpin faces the problem of the moral justification of Picturesque tourism in pressing form from the start of the tour of the Lakes. Travelling for aesthetic pleasure is a trivial pastime in comparison to useful travel in search of knowledge or on business: in moral terms the Picturesque traveller occupies a less justifiable position than the philosophic or scientific traveller. Equally, the kind of painting he practices cannot be afforded the substantial moral justification that can be extended to serious genres such as history painting. This is clear when Gilpin's attempts to present the Picturesque aesthetic as transgressive of the hierarchies of earlier eighteenth-century painting are repudiated by Reynolds, who insists on identifying the Picturesque with the low.[26] Throughout, then, Gilpin's justifications for touring and for the unambitious art to be produced by the tourist remain in many ways apologetic – or, in Alan Liu's phrase, quoted earlier, 'whimsical'. In the preface to the Lakes tour he presents the activities of touring and sketching as mere amusements. As a clergyman, however, he must defend himself against the charge of according them an importance they should not have in relation to his spiritual concerns, and repeatedly seeks means of justifying them in more morally elevated terms. He thus concedes that 'The only danger is, lest the *amusement* – the fascinating amusement – should press on improperly, and interfere too much with the employment';[27] and employment, leisure and pleasure figure largely and problematically alongside luxury in the debates that underlie his narrative.

The tour itself reaches its conclusion with an apocalyptic vision of the suburbs of London, as the Purgatory through which Gilpin and his party must pass before their return through 'the quiet lanes of Surrey' to the domestic security of Cheam: 'London comes on apace; and all those disgusting ideas, with which it's great avenues abound – brick-kilns, steaming with offensive smoke – sewers and ditches sweating with filth – heaps of collected soil, and stinks of every denomination – clouds of dust, rising and vanishing, from agitated wheels, pursuing each other in rapid motion...'[28] London, as the city, and as the seat of luxury, corruption and contamination, serves as the antitype to the rural ideals discovered and celebrated in the Lake District, and makes explicit the terms within which the earlier descriptions of that region have been articulated.

Additionally, the ideal landscapes of the Lake District are seen in the context of journeys from the South-East to the North-West of England and back, in the course of which Gilpin and his party travel through other regions of the country, in which other sites and objects of interest are sought out and celebrated. The terms in which these are presented differ at different stages of the journey. These differences mark one striking aspect of the symbolic organisation of the *Tour* – the separation of the country into geographically discrete domains of industry and pleasure. However, the value-judgements about each region produced in Gilpin's descriptions contaminate each other in the narrative as a whole, and all contribute to the problematic framework within which the eventual account of the Lake District is cast. The economically productive agricultural landscapes of the Home Counties and Midlands are thus dismissed as unpicturesque, and contribute to establishing the troubling division between aesthetic perception and productive utility which runs through the account of the Lakes themselves. Passing through the Midlands on the return journey Gilpin notes that 'In these plains, as rich, as they are unpicturesque, we had nothing to observe, but the immense herds of cattle, and flocks of sheep, which graze them.'[29]

Similarly, each time the party visits – or chooses not to visit – sites of industrial manufacturing, problems are introduced which frame the account of the economic activities of the Lakes, including the account of the black-lead mine. In the Midlands Gilpin writes that 'we wished for time to have visited the potteries of Mr Wedgwood; where the elegant arts of old Etruria are revived. It would have been pleasing to see all these works in their progress to perfection; but it was of less moment; as the forms of all his Tuscan Vases are familiar to us'.[30] The product is available, so the site and circumstances of its production need not be inspected. When the party does encounter large-scale industrial production, however, Gilpin reacts in terms which are diametrically opposed to those in which Adam Smith celebrates such production in *The Wealth of Nations*. He writes

Near Birmingham we went to see Boulton's hard-ware manufactory. It is a town under a single roof; containing about seven hundred work people. But notwithstanding it is a scene of industry, utility, and ingenuity, it is difficult to keep the eye in humour among so many frivolous arts; and check it's looking with contempt on an hundred men employed in making a snuff box.[31]

The contempt engendered by the spectacle of frivolous arts supplying the luxury economy outweighs the laudable fact that the activity described involves labour. The comment places nicely Gilpin's later celebration of his own frivolous pursuit of amateur painting as one that supplies nothing and produces its best results when it involves 'little labour'.[32]

At the other extreme to London, in the Lake District, are found the state of nature and the pastoral economy which ideally merges into it. Gilpin's celebration of the second is not complete – at Watenlath, for instance, he has to admit that 'the life of a shepherd, in this country, is not an Arcadian life'.[33] At Rosthwait, however, he finds an ideal, and insists that 'Here the sons, and daughters of simplicity enjoy health, peace, and contentment, in the midst of what city-luxury would call the extreme of human necessity.' Their pastoral existence keeps them free of commercial exchange and merges their activities and their appearance into their natural surroundings: 'Their herds afford them milk; and their flocks, cloaths; the shepherd himself being often the manufacturer also. No dye is necessary to tinge their wool: it is naturally russet-brown; and sheep and shepherds are cloathed alike; both in the simple livery of nature.'[34]

Idealisation of the pastoral economy as the next best thing to nature itself is widespread in the regional literature of the period. In the process definitions of the pastoral must be very accommodating. This is clear when Thomas West attempts to subsume the economic activities of local life to the pastoral ideal. In the *Guide*, he writes that after coming over Newland pass, where 'all is barrenness, solitude, and silence', 'Some traces of industry obtruding themselves at the foot of the glen, disturb the solemn solitude with which the eye and mind have been entertained, and point out your return to society; for you now approach the village of *Buttermere*.' Here, as West puts it, 'The life of the inhabitants is purely pastoral. A few hands are employed in the slate quarries; the women spin woollen yarn and drink tea'[35] – a construction of the pastoral economy which offers the inhabitants the leisure and moral simplicity of traditional pastoral life, a provision of employment allowing the men the economic benefits of industriousness, and the backup of an extended trade network bringing the women into the luxury economy by way of their consumption of tea.

This formulation draws attention to a central complexity in the tourists' accounts of the region. For Gilpin, the simplicity of life enjoyed by Lake District villagers is protected by their isolation from the contaminations of luxury, and specifically by their distance from the roads which would bring trade and allow the development of a taste for luxury goods: 'At a distance from the refinements of the age, they are at a distance also from it's vices... It is some happiness indeed to these people, that they have no great roads among them.' They have, however, roads great enough to bring tourists, and in this context tourism is dangerous for the local inhabitants, partly in introducing them to material luxury, but more urgently in offering them contact with a potentially infectious display of conspicuous leisure. Gilpin thus accuses some travellers of giving the local population 'a taste for pleasures, and gratifications, of which they had no ideas – inspiring them with discontent at home – and tainting their rough, industrious manners with idleness, and a thirst after dishonest means'.[36] Similarly, James Clarke outlines the corrupting effect of leisured tourists on the manners of the region when he comments on their new linguistic construction of its geography. He complains that

> Since so many of the curious have visited these lakes, *our native rusticks* have pretended to imitate them. Within these few years, not half a dozen persons in Keswick knew what the word *Lake* meant; it was either called *Daran* (that is, *Derwent*) or *Keswick* water, and had only two or three fishing boats upon it: now every cottager attempts to be polite, and to speak better language; and the name of *Daran* is not known, but the *Lake* only.

His satiric narrative illustrating this point plays on the local dialect meaning of 'laking' as 'playing': a local mother whose daughter has come home from a Sunday afternoon on 'the lake' asks 'What lake wast? Tennis, or Anthony Blindman [i.e. Blind Man's Buff]?' and tells her it is time to stop 'laking' and get back to her usual labours instead.[37]

Gilpin attempts to avoid the accusation of endangering local manners in his own case by representing his own aesthetic interests as transcending materially corrupting ones and by offering his vicarious participation in the rigours of country life as a means of moral self-justification: his project is to examine the region's 'grandeur, and beauty – or to explore it's varied, and curious regions with the eye of philosophy' and he advises responsible fellow tourists to 'be content with such fare as the country produces; or, at least reconcile themselves to it by manly exercise, and fatigue'.[38] He remains a compromised figure, however. Although he attempts to sustain a distinction between city luxury and his own leisure, he cannot escape the fact that his leisure is a token of his own economic privilege; and as such, is associated, however indirectly, with the luxury economy he claims to have left behind. It is thus in itself potentially corrupting of the values of industry which, with one breath, he seeks to celebrate in the rural population he surveys.

At the same time, however, it is leisure rather than visible industry that is central to the Picturesque image of the country that he seeks to create. The nearest he comes to accepting the visible signs of the continuance of local economic life is when he encounters groups of apparently leisured young people travelling to new employment at the time of 'a statute fair', and writes that 'we were not a little entertained with the simplicity, and variety of the several groups and figures we met, both on horseback, and on foot'. His ensuing discussion of their appearance elides a predictable rejection of luxury with a much more troubled rejection of labour. He writes first that 'These are the picturesque inhabitants of a landscape. The dressed-out figures, and gaudy carriages, along the great roads of the capital, afford them not. The pencil rejects with indignation the splendor of art.' Then, however, he jumps without transition to claim that 'In grand scenes, even the peasant cannot be admitted if he be employed in the low occupations of his profession: the spade, the scythe, and the rake are all excluded.'

Signs of economic activity must therefore be effaced in the rural scene, despite the claims of morality, apparently to enable the observer's unmediated confrontation with 'the natural':

Moral, and picturesque ideas do not always coincide. In a moral light, cultivation, in all its parts, is pleasing; the hedge, and the furrow; the waving corn field, and the ripened sheaf. But all these the picturesque eye, in quest of scenes of grandeur, and beauty, looks at with disgust. It ranges after nature, untamed by art, and bursting wildly into all it's irregular forms.

However, the announcement of what is permissible suggests that the secondary reason is to dignify and justify the oberver's own leisure: 'In a moral view, the industrious mechanic is a more pleasing object, than the loitering peasant. But in a picturesque light, it is otherwise. The arts of industry are rejected; and even idleness, if I may so speak, adds dignity to a character.'[39]

The models of attractive idleness that are offered in response to this problem leave the tourist uncomfortably positioned. The figures that are deemed appropriate as *'picturesque appendages'* in the landscape are not just those whose activity can be taken as being leisured – such as the fisherman – but those such as the gypsies, beggars and banditti familiar from Salvator Rosa, who 'impress us with some idea of greatness, wildness, or ferocity' verging on the Sublime, through their visible refusal of work discipline. On other counts, Gilpin obviously regards these latter figures as socially and morally reprehensible. At Penrith, for instance, he sees the Beacon as 'a monument' to earlier 'tumultuous times' before the Union with Scotland, and indulges in 'pleasing reflections on a comparison of present times with past', when the security of the region was disturbed by 'the ravages of banditti, with whom the country was always at that time infested'.[40] The tourist remains disconcertingly associated with the figures he sentimentalises in his aesthetic view, however, even when those figures are disconcerting or dangerously intrusive elements in the landscape he idealises. The reader is reminded of the telling moment on the Wye tour, when, at Tintern Abbey, Gilpin's account of the Picturesque appeal of the ruined abbey must struggle to negotiate the culpable 'indolence' both of its former inhabitants, the monks, and of its present tenants, the beggars, if he is to distinguish those forms of indolence from the laudable contemplative leisure of its present observer, the Picturesque tourist.[41]

What then of the black-lead mine, that centre of industry, commerce, prosperity, corruption and crime at the heart of the domain of the Picturesque? The mine cannot quite be bypassed in the way that the Cornish tin mines are on the Western Tour, when Gilpin nicely demonstrates the limits of normal Picturesque concern with the conditions of economic production, and comments: 'We had not, however, the curiosity to enter any of these mines. Our business was only on the surface.'[42] In this case that option is not open. The mine obtrudes into the account in a peculiarly literal way, leaving its own graphic trace on the otherwise Picturesque landscape. However, description of the unpicturesque appearance of the mine – the yellowish ochery stain it leaves on the mountainside – is preceded and overridden by an expression of affection for it, and a momentary acknowledgement of the conditions of production which enable Picturesque observation and representation in the first place. Only one aspect of the black-lead economy is mentioned. The detritus of the mine provides the material from which the economically marginal product – the amateur artist's pencil – is wrought, so that he can spend his leisure reproducing the scene of its origin – or rather, producing a Picturesque version of it which will efface the signs of that origin. Gilpin takes reassurance that the mine is a source of comfortable subsistence for the local population, but the distraction of another aesthetic experience prevents a minuter examination of what gaining that subsistence might involve. He ignores the accounts of its generally corrupting effects on local society offered by some other commentators. Instead he provides a narrative of its recent legal history, in which the boundaries of property, which he demands be effaced when they are visible on the surface and disturb the appearance of 'the natural' are unambiguously celebrated as they extend underground. The problematic blurring of categories seen to be involved in the operation of the mine in some other accounts – between commodity and spoil, legitimate exploitation and theft, moral and immoral economies – is largely ignored in this account, as it continues by condemning, but to some extent also heroising, a single illicit figure – the 'late prolific genius in fraud' tried but released under the inadequately protective property laws earlier in the century. Significantly, his 'subterraneous wickedness' is marked by, and carried on only at the expense of, 'great' but criminally invisible 'labour' – a category of activity notably missing in the depiction of the behaviour of the honest surface gleaners at the site of the mine, in the artist's celebration of his own pursuits of tourism and landscape painting, and in the landscape images of the area that he creates. The account of the mine offers a partial and momentary glimpse of the economic structures that underlie and underpin the tourist's vision of ideal natural landscape, and a partial recognition that those structures involve and affect both the local population and the observer of the scene. In this light, the description stands as a telling index of the textual negotiations through which the Picturesque ideal is constructed and sustained in eighteenth-century tour literature.[43]

NOTES

1 William Gilpin, *Observations Relative Chiefly to Picturesque Beauty, Made in the Year 1772, on Several Parts of England; Particularly the Mountains, and Lakes of Cumberland, and Westmoreland*, 2 vols. (London, 1786), vol. I, p. 205.

2 See Arthur Young, *A Six Months' Tour through the North of England*, second edition, corrected and emended, 4 vols. (London, 1771); William Marshall, *The Review and Abstract of the County Reports to the Board of Agriculture; from the Several Agricultural Departments of England*, 4 vols. (London, Edinburgh and York, 1818), vol. I, *Northern Department*; William Hutchinson, *The History of the County of Cumberland*, 2 vols. (Carlisle, 1794–7); James Clarke, *A Survey of the Lakes of Cumberland, Westmorland and Lancashire* (London, 1787); Thomas Pennant, *A Tour in Scotland and Voyage to the Hebrides MDCCLXXII* (London, 1774).

3 See Clarke, *Survey*, p. 82. Hutchinson quotes Thomas Gray's comment in 1769 that black lead 'will undergo no preparation by fire, not being

fasible', and his estimate that 'when it is pure, soft, black, and close grained, it is worth sometimes 30s a pound' (*History*, vol. II, p. 212); and the opinion of 'Dr Campbell in his *Political Survey of Great Britain*' that 'as it is used without any preparation, it is more valuable than the ore of any metal found in this island' (*ibid.*, p. 216). Further indications of the value of black lead are common in the period. In his unpublished 'Journal of a Tour through the North of England & Parts of Scotland; In Company with George Harvey & Thomas Clutterbuck Esqrs. during the Summer of 1795' (Central Library, Cardiff, MS 3.277) Robert Clutterbuck mentions the existence of mines near Castleton in Derbyshire for 'plumbago, or black-lead, at which the Miners work naked, that they may not embezzle any quantity of it, being of so precious a quality'. On the medical uses of the substance, Hutchinson quotes 'Mr Robinson in his *Natural History of Westmoreland and Cumberland*', who claims that it is a 'remedy for the colic, [and] easeth the pain of gravel, stone and strangury' (*History*, vol. II, p. 212). Esther Moir surveys eighteenth-century tourists' visits to 'mills, mines and furnaces' in *The Discovery of Britain: The English Tourists 1540–1840* (London: Routledge and Kegan Paul, 1964), chapter 8.

4 'An Unpublished Tour', in William Wordsworth, *Prose*, ed. W. J. B. Owen and J. Worthington Smyser (Oxford: Clarendon Press, 1974), Appendix II, p. 348.

5 Hutchinson, *History*, vol. II, p. 215.

6 *Ibid.*, vol. II, pp. 216–18. For the passages quoted from 'G. S.' see *The Gentleman's Magazine*, vol. 21 (London, 1751), 51–3. For the accompanying map see Fig. 1.

7 William Hutchinson, *An Excursion to the Lakes in Westmoreland and Cumberland, August 1773* (London, 1774), p. 151.

8 Wordsworth, *Prose*, p. 348.

9 Marshall, *Review and Abstract*, vol. I, p. 170.

10 Clarke, *Survey*, p. 83.

11 *Ibid.*, p. 33.

12 Young, *Tour*, vol. II, Letter X, p. 261. Robert W. Malcolmson discusses the reputation of miners earlier in the eighteenth century in '"A Set of Ungovernable People": The Kingswood Colliers in the Eighteenth Century', in John Brewer and John Styles (eds.), *An Ungovernable People: The English and their Laws in the Seventeenth and Eighteenth Centuries* (London: Hutchinson, 1980), pp. 85–127.

13 Wordsworth, *Prose*, p. 347.

14 See Alan Liu, *Wordsworth: The Sense of History* (Stanford University Press, 1989), p. 93.

15 Gilpin, *Lakes*, vol. I, pp. 205–6. On another occasion, in Gatesgarthdale, Gilpin comments that 'This valley is not more than six miles from the black-lead mines; and would have led us to them, if we had pursued it's course' (*Lakes*, vol. I, p. 237), but his party does not take this way.

16 For discussion of this point see John Barrell, 'The Public Prospect and the Private View: The Politics of Taste in Eighteenth-Century Britain', in Simon Pugh (ed.), *Reading Landscape: Country–City–Capital* (Manchester University Press, 1990), pp. 19–40; Ann Bermingham, *Landscape and Ideology: The English Rustic Tradition, 1740–1860* (London: Thames and Hudson, 1986), chapter 2; Liu, *Wordsworth: The Sense of History*, chapter 3.

17 William Gilpin, *Observations on the River Wye, and Several Parts of South Wales, etc. Relative Chiefly to Picturesque Beauty; Made in the Summer of the Year 1770* (London, 1782), pp. 14, 22.

18 *Ibid.*, p. 20.

19 See Bermingham, *Landscape and Ideology*, chapter 2.

20 Thomas West, *A Guide to the Lakes in Cumberland, Westmorland, and Lancashire*, third edition, revised and enlarged (London and Kendal, 1784), pp. 36–7.

21 William Gilpin, *Remarks on Forest Scenery, and Other Woodland Views, Relative Chiefly to Picturesque Beauty* (London, 1791), p. 298.

22 See Barbara Maria Stafford, *Voyage into Substance: Art, Science, Nature, and the Illustrated Travel Account, 1760–1840* (Boston, Mass.: M.I.T. Press, 1984), Introduction.

23 Hutchinson, *Excursion*, p. 21.

24 *Ibid.*, pp. 21, 26.

25 Thomas Newte, *A Tour in England and Scotland in 1785* (London, 1788), pp. 11, 19.

26 See the exchange of letters between Joshua Reynolds and William Gilpin, reprinted in William Gilpin, *Three Essays: On Picturesque Beauty; On Picturesque Travel; and On Sketching Landscape: To Which is Added a Poem, On Landscape Painting*, second edition (London, 1794), pp. 34–7.

27 Gilpin, *Lakes*, vol. I, pp. xxii–xxiii.

28 *Ibid.*, vol. II, p. 267.

29 *Ibid.*, vol. II, p. 252.

30 *Ibid.*, vol. I, p. 69.

31 *Ibid.*, vol. I, p. 51. Compare Adam Smith, *An Inquiry into the Nature and Causes of the Wealth of Nations*, ed. R. H. Campbell, A. S. Skinner, and W. B. Todd (Oxford: Clarendon Press, 1976), pp. 13–26, 131.

32 Gilpin, *Lakes*, vol. II, p. 13.

33 *Ibid.*, vol. I, p. 223.

34 *Ibid.*, vol. I, p. 197.

35 West, *Guide*, pp. 131–2.

36 Gilpin, *Lakes*, vol. II, pp. 66–7.

37 Clarke, *Survey*, p. 69.

38 Gilpin, *Lakes*, vol. II, p. 67.

39 *Ibid.*, vol. II, pp. 43–4.

40 *Ibid.*, vol. II, p. 86.

41 Gilpin, *Wye*, pp. 31–7.

42 William Gilpin, *Observations on the Western Parts of England, Relative Chiefly to Picturesque Beauty; To Which are Added a Few Remarks on the Picturesque Beauties of the Isle of Wight* (London, 1798), p. 196.

43 For further discussion of the projects of Gilpin's tourism, see the essays in this volume by John Whale (pp. 175–80) and Ann Bermingham (pp. 82–90).

CHAPTER 3

The ruined abbey: Picturesque and Gothic values

Michael Charlesworth

The politics of the Picturesque come into prominence when the Picturesque way of seeing engages with another similarly vigorous aesthetic discourse or theory. In this essay I have chosen to study the changing and evolving discourse that focuses on the most controversial of eighteenth-century ruins, the ruined abbey. I have concentrated on the responses to a single abbey, in the belief that such a narrow yet extended focus will allow changes in the discourse to emerge clearly.

The starting-point for my essay is a book – an archetypally slim volume – entitled *A Series of Views of the Abbeys and Castles in Yorkshire, Drawn & Engraved by W. Westall A.R.A. and F. Mackenzie with Historical and Descriptive Accounts by Thomas Dunham Whitaker*, published in London in 1820. The book is very tall and broad, and very slim. Contrary to the expectations set up by the title, the only building it discusses is Rievaulx Abbey in Yorkshire. The book amounts to the vestige of a publishing venture that failed. It cannot legitimately be described as dealing with 'the Abbeys and Castles of Yorkshire'. Nor are there any companion volumes, so it's not one of a 'Series' in that sense.[1] If the modern critic is tempted to explore possible reasons why this publishing enterprise foundered, it seems that s/he does not need to look very far.

The only image that shows the whole abbey is the frontispiece to the book (figure 3.1). This image, by its size and placing, has a paramount importance in the volume. The view it presents was taken by the artist Westall from the standpoint of an eighteenth-century landscape garden known as Rievaulx Terrace, made in 1758 by the local landowner, Thomas Duncombe III, of Duncombe Park near Helmsley.[2]

On page 15 of the book Whitaker regrets that the Abbey

Fig. 3.1 William Westall, *Rievaulx Abbey from Duncomb Terrace*. Engraving.

is not better connected with Helmsley or Duncombe Park than by a terrace on the brow of a hill...looking down upon the ruins, as into the funnel of a chimney, and detecting all the windings of the little glens to the first poverty of their sources; the eye is next fatigued by a tiresome expanse of unfeatured and barren slopes, terminated by the desert of Blackmore, which is not entitled, by elevation or outline, to the name of mountain.

Instead of this view from above, he wishes that a drive from Duncombe Park could 'approach the ruins at the lowest, that is, the really picturesque point of access...such were the charms which the monks of Rievaulx contemplated at the origin, and enjoyed during the continuance of their house'.

Then Whitaker ventures a statement that is quite extraordinary in the light of the frontispiece of the book: '[These are the] charms which a landscape painter of the present day would have selected.' The effect of these words is to stigmatise William Westall, in the text of his own book, as not a landscape painter or at least as an old-fashioned one. It would therefore appear that we could explain the failure of the publishing venture in terms of human eccentricities of personality, whereby the clash of individual psychologies interfered with the money-making process; and we could leave the inquiry at this convenient point.

Instead, the rest of this paper is concerned to explore the conflicting discourses that are speaking themselves through Westall's *image* and Whitaker's *words*, in the hope that by paying attention to them we can elucidate the cultural dynamics at issue when Gothic architecture became the object of the Picturesque way of seeing.

In particular, I want to concentrate on the relationship between the ruined abbey and the landscape garden that preoccupies, in different ways, both writer and artist. Initially I want to compare Whitaker's text with Arthur Young's description of Rievaulx from half a century earlier. Unlike Whitaker, Young liked the terrace and its views. He visited it in 1768 and published his description in the second edition of *A Six Months' Tour in the North of England* in 1771. He had this to say: 'at your feet winds an irriguous valley, almost lost in scattered trees:... upon the edge of the valley, an humble cottage is seen in a situation elegant in itself, and truly picturesque in the whole view.'[3] Two phrases, Whitaker's 'really picturesque' and Young's 'truly picturesque', are used to endorse contradictory viewpoints. Between them lies over half a century of discourse. How do we resolve their contradiction? Do we discredit one writer as incompetent and praise the other as knowing what he is talking about? Do we theorise that the idea of the Picturesque evolved, *from* one position *to* another position? Or do we account the aesthetics of the Picturesque as unable to bring about a resolution and concede that some other factor is involved?

It is worth considering further what Young has to say. Whitaker saw 'a tiresome expanse of unfeatured and barren slopes, terminated by the desert of Blackmore'; Young saw 'The distant hills which are seen above, are waste grounds, with fern, whins, etc. which seem to bound the little paradise in view, and add to the enjoyment of beholding it, that which results from contrast and unexpected pleasure.'[4] He returns to the same figure when the abbey comes into view as he continues his progress along the terrace, which is over half a mile long: 'You look...down immediately upon a large ruined abbey, in the midst... of a small but beautiful valley; scattered trees appearing among the ruins in a stile too elegant to admit description: it is a casual glance at a little paradise, which seems as it were in another region.' Young's cheerfulness and relish are quite surprising. Nowhere does he write on Rievaulx Abbey in terms of melancholy, even though modern commentators have asserted that ruined abbeys were signifiers of melancholy in this period, and indeed Young does rhapsodise over the melancholy qualities of Fountains Abbey, which he inspects on his visit to Studley Royal later in the volume.[5]

One explanation for the fact that Young did not find Rievaulx melancholy is that he was reacting subconsciously to the *distancing* that the abbey is put through by the landscape garden. As the terrace is the main viewing station, the abbey is looked down on, it is distanced or put in perspective. An optical control or ideology is introduced by the way the objects are laid out in three-dimensional space. If Whitaker could become involved in a nostalgic vision of monks while endorsing the view from the bottom, it surely does not over-stretch our understanding of the power of viewing mechanisms to suppose that Young would be sensitive to such subconscious suggestion in, as it were, the opposite direction (against nostalgia). In contrast, at Studley, Young was able to get to the ruins and clamber all over them, the close-quarters view allowing melancholy to permeate.

The same determination of seeing happens in the garden at Duncombe Park. The owners of Rievaulx Terrace lived at this house, situated some two miles down the valley of the Rye, approximately three-quarters of a mile from the town of Helmsley. The terrace at Rievaulx formed a remote extension to the famous earlier terraced garden around the house. At Duncombe the northern Yew Walk gave a view across the park towards Helmsley Castle that distanced it, looked down on it and put it in perspective. The history it embodied was therefore also distanced.[6] The castle had been ruinated in the Civil War, and the passage of time from that era to the mid-eighteenth century amounted to an interval of history marked by constitutional changes designed to avoid a repeat of civil conflict. The passing of time that is implied in the contemplation of the ruined castle is explicitly dramatised further along the garden terraces at Duncombe by Jan Nost's statue of Time consulting a sun-dial. There is also a contrast between old Gothic architecture and the modern classical architecture of the garden buildings. In other words, the terrace, by the way it is laid out in space, by the nature of the architecture built on it, by the emblem that it contains and by being newer than the overlooked ruined Gothic buildings, sets up a *rhetoric*

Fig. 3.2   J. C. Bentley after J. M. W. Turner, *Rievaulx Abbey, Yorkshire*. From *The Gallery of Modern British Artists* (1835).

of viewing that discriminates between alternative ways of seeing ruins in favour of one particular way.

With the exception of the statue, the same elements are repeated at Rievaulx. Both terraces provide a distancing view from above. Yet Thomas Gray and William Mason had identified the view from the bottom as the truly Picturesque view in the 1770s, taking this as a general rule, without specific relation to Rievaulx or even to abbeys in particular,[7] and they had done so as part of a purely aesthetic debate, without the investment of nostalgic cultural value in the abbey that Whitaker exemplifies by his comments about the monks.[8] Mason even characterised abbeys as emblematic of 'ruthless superstition'.[9]

Between 1770 and 1820, the Picturesque tourists had been busy. From 1798 to 1806, for example, Rievaulx Abbey had been painted from the lower and closer viewpoint by Thomas Girtin, John Sell Cotman and Paul Sandby Munn. The same viewpoint was adopted in the 1820s and 1830s by Copley Fielding and J. M. W. Turner, whose later view (figure 3.2) has been adapted as a postcard for sale in the Tourist Information Office in Helmsley. However, Turner at least distances himself from the abbey by yielding the foreground to people going about their daily business and acknowledges the Olympian situation of the Ionic Temple on the terrace above.[10]

A preliminary conclusion would therefore be that the search for the Picturesque promoted a sentimental or nostalgic way of viewing abbeys, a path that was pioneered by Picturesque artists seeking out a closer and lower involvement with them as subject-matter.

Yet Whitaker's cultural investment of value is dependent upon other factors. To elucidate them, we need to return to Young's text, and ask of it, how can you view a ruin and see it as 'a little paradise'?

The motif Young was employing was that of the oasis in desolation, a popular topos in all kinds of eighteenth-century literature. When the Roman Catholic poet Alexander Pope employs it in 'Eloisa to Abelard' in 1717, we can recognise a consistency because the building he describes is both whole and new. Eloisa describes Abelard founding her lonely nunnery in the desert in these terms:

> From the false world in early youth they fled,
> By thee to mountains, wilds and deserts led.
> You raised these hallowed walls; the desert smil'd
> And Paradise was open'd in the Wild. (lines 131–4)[11]

No such wholeness or newness exists at Rievaulx.

William Shenstone can help to resolve the problem. Early in 1743 he projected a poem on 'Rural Elegance', which would, as he put it, 'end up with a vista terminated by an old abbey, which introduces an episode concerning the effects of Romish power, interdicts, etc. in imitation of Lucretius's 'Plague of Athens', taken from Thucydides, Virgil's Murrain, and Ovid's Pestilence, etc.'[12] The poem was not written, but a poem entitled 'The Ruin'd Abbey, Or the effects of Superstition' appeared later. Shenstone begins this poem with an allusion to the recent hostilities of the 1745 Jacobite rebellion: 'At length fair Peace, with olive crown'd, regains / Her lawful throne, and to the sacred haunts / Of wood or fount the frighted muse returns'. As the poet roams around, he encounters an abbey:

> And see betwixt the grove's extended arms
> An Abby's rude remains attract thy view,
> Gilt by the mid-day sun: with lingering step
> Produce thine axe... with timorous hand
> Remove th'obstructive bough.

To improve the view of the abbey, the poet has to cut down a pine tree that he had planted earlier. An interesting point is that we are in a garden, and even before moralising starts, the first step is an act of gardening or landscape improvement.

There follows a long section about Roman Catholicism and English history. Thomas à Becket, we learn, 'Bid murd'rous Priests the sov'reign frown contemn / And with unhallow'd crosier bruis'd the Crown'. Monks are given varied epithets: 'Some murderous monk,' 'monks: gluttony, extortion, fraud, av'rice, envy, pride, revenge and shame', 'monks libidinous'. Liberation happened under Henry VIII:

> Then from its towering height with horrid sound
> Rush'd the proud Abby. Then the vaulted roofs
> Torn from their walls, disclosed the wanton scene
> Of Monkish chastity! Each angry Friar
> Crawl'd from his bedded strumpet, muttering low
> An ineffectual curse.[13]

The passages endorse and highlight the significance of Shenstone's framing device. What made his assault urgent in the mid-century were the activities of Jacobites, who sought to place a Roman Catholic king in power and therefore at the head of the Church of England. Shenstone wrote to Winny Fletcher during the Jacobite rebellion in late 1745, referring to the fact that her brother had joined the Hanoverian army: 'you will, upon Confession, pardon me, as you expect Pardon from your Confessor shou'd ye Benedictines & Friars get a footing in this Island – which I find, your Brother is endeavouring to prevent'.[14]

In a way entirely characteristic of Hanoverian Whig discourse, the threat of the return of a Roman Catholic monarch is viewed as the threat of a return to servitude under the monastic system. It was that system which was constantly held up, along with the practice of burning people to death, by Hanoverian Protestant Whigs, as the chief iniquity of Roman Catholicism and therefore its chief threat. Shenstone wrote a further prospect-poem in 1746, entitled 'Elegy XXI':

> Here if my vista point the mould'ring pile,
> Where Hood and Cowl devotion's aspects wore,
> I trace the tott'ring reliques with a smile,
> To think the mental bondage is no more![15]

The Jacobite threat amounts to the mental and economic threat of a restitution of the monastic system. This is how a ruin can be 'a little paradise', a cause for delight and rejoicing. We notice that in each poem the ruin is only ever seen from a distance. It is too dangerous to wander through.

In 1758 Shenstone built his ruined priory in a valley comfortably overlooked by his house, repeating on a smaller scale the arrangement at Rievaulx. We must interpret the priory in the light of Shenstone's poetry: 'these were thy haunts, thy opulent abodes / O Superstition!' The priory is an emblem of the overthrow of superstition, rather than a melancholy feature.

Our second conclusion must therefore be that Whitaker's nostalgic attitude would not have been possible without the decline in the Jacobite threat. Whitaker was both a magistrate in Burnley and a Church of England vicar, and as such incarnated the cosy relationship between state and Church of England that successive seventeenth- and eighteenth-century legislation had been enacted to create and protect. It was precisely this relationship that Jacobitism threatened to upset. Whitaker's indulgence in a nostalgic attitude to abbeys is an indication that the Jacobite threat to church–state relations was well past. The last active Jacobite plot was in 1759, the year after Rievaulx Terrace was completed. Prince Charles Edward died in 1788, and the last Stuart, his brother Cardinal York, in 1807. York was by then a pensioner of George III and left the Stuart Papers to that Hanoverian monarch.[16] And Whitaker's praise for the charms enjoyed by Rievaulx's monks appeared thirteen years later, nine years before the passing of the Catholic Emancipation Act of 1829.[17]

As both low and elevated views of abbeys were available to visitors throughout the second half of the eighteenth century, it is worth dwelling on the claim that their responses would be at least heavily influenced (to put it no more strongly) by specific cultural factors. These factors (including party political loyalty) were partially encoded in differing viewing strategies. The rhetorical strategy underlying what I am calling the earlier Hanoverian discourse of abbeys is *metonymy*, the reduction of a whole to a mere part of itself. This makes possible a reading of Rievaulx Abbey as representative of the Dissolution of the Monasteries (and Helmsley Castle as representative of the Civil War). The important metonymic objects are fragmented in themselves as well as being pieces of larger wholes (civil strife, superstition) and are perceived as metonymies as a function of the viewing-station: high vantage-platforms giving clear and distant views are necessary to maintain the buildings as metonymies, and celebrate their ruination. At Rievaulx this way of seeing was constructed with and by the terrace, which brings into existence its view of the abbey. In contrast, if they were seen from below, the completely shattered state of the ruins would become obscured, or they could appear to surround and embrace the artist. Whitaker encourages artists to become nostalgically absorbed in just this way, by arguing for what might be termed a perspectival synecdochic assimilation, whereby we can reconstruct the pleasures of the monks by, quite literally, adopting their point of view. In the Hanoverian view the fragments have to be kept fragmented and apart (therefore controlled) by the dominant overseeing eye, for the danger of diminished vigilance is that of becoming absorbed in a violent and superstitional history that we want instead to celebrate having put behind us.[18]

A further idea of what is at stake in the 'dominant overseeing eye' can be gained from a consideration of the pedigree, as it were, of the strategy that William Westall used in his frontispiece of the abbey ruins. The pictorial technique he employed in his image of Rievaulx was developed as a result of his participation as draughtsman in the colonialist adventurism of the Matthew Flinders expedition to chart the coast of Australia in 1800–3.[19] Many of his Australian drawings are partial panoramas, showing views from high places with prominent landmarks labelled. In 1809 the Admiralty commissioned from him a series of large oil paintings illustrating parts of the Australian coast. All show wide views from high viewpoints and depict the distant landscape (based on his original drawings) with remarkable accuracy. The foregrounds are occupied by natural terraces or brows exhibiting specimens of plants and native figures. The pictures have 'a middle distance enshrouded in deep shadow and an elevated foreground platform'.[20] The view of Rievaulx is remarkably consistent with this pictorial practice. The figures in the foreground are just who we would expect to meet at that exact place. They have had a chance to explore the terrace and gather some boughs from the flowering shrubs that Arthur Young described as growing at the edges of the wood. In Westall's Australian views there is an overlap with mapping,[21] and at Rievaulx we can trace the glens 'to the first poverty of their sources': precisely what one can do with maps and cannot do in the view from the bottom.

Westall's training and early experience, perpetuated in the view of Rievaulx, therefore brings up the entire equation between vision and power. The exercise of power and domination of subjugated peoples demands knowledge, which is essential for control. The main instrument for gathering knowledge of topography is sight, aided by tools such as compass and theodolite, and maps and pictures are the main records of the knowledge gained. Hanoverian colonialist strategies came to rely on artists for military intelligence, and such strategies were first practised upon the populations of the British Isles during the 1745 Jacobite rebellion and its aftermath, when the brothers Thomas and Paul Sandby were the artists involved.[22] In their activities mapping and watercolour views dovetailed together in the process of subjugating peoples (the Highland Scots) and conducting military campaigns. Their art was thereafter institutionalised in Hanoverian service by Paul Sandby's employment on the Ordnance Survey of Scotland and his position as drawing instructor at the Military Academy at Woolwich.[23] Hanoverian power grew across half the world once the Jacobite threat had been removed, and its servant William Westall exemplified its institutionalised pictorial strategies.[24] Arthur Young similarly served Hanoverian Whig aspirations in his agricultural writings and later as president of the Board of Agriculture.[25] Both endorsers of the view from above at Rievaulx were therefore closely involved with political and cultural strategies generated by Whig ambitions.

It would be inappropriate to suggest that every view drawn or painted from a high place inscribes colonialist aspirations to subjugation and therefore is fatally compromised by connotations of political repression. Yet such considerations are relevant in the present case because of the potent conjunction of two factors. The idea of the monastery had been constructed by the eighteenth-century Whigs as a threatening and alien Other to Hanoverian supremacy. Furthermore, William Westall applied to the depiction of the abbey an art that he had learned, in part at least, as a servant of Hanoverian imperialism.

We have not yet fully explored what is involved in Westall's sympathy for the mid-eighteenth-century Hanoverian viewpoint however. To do so we have to keep in mind the materiality of Rievaulx Terrace as a garden. Like all gardens, its chief ingredients are weather, time and light. These factors might seem to elude academic analysis by their ephemeral and changing nature. Yet it is precisely attention to them that unlocks another dimension in the terrace's relationship with the abbey.

One of the classical temples on the terrace contains a dining-room (figure 3.3), and had a fully equipped kitchen beneath it. When John Sell Cotman visited Rievaulx in 1803 in the company of the Cholmondeleys and Lady Melbourne, the company dined at Rievaulx Terrace.[26] And this itself is strange, in that Duncombe Park is only some two miles away, and no one would have suffered terminal discomfort while they drove back to the house to eat. Or was there some other reason why they would have wanted to while away some hours in that particular place? I believe there was, and that the clue lies in the angle of the sunbeams in this photograph. Apart from the other obvious reasons for its construction, the terrace was made as a place to view the sunset from. The subject matter of the wall-paintings in the temple also hints that it was used by night. One shows Endymion visited by Selene at night, and the main painting in the ceiling depicts Aurora, the dawn.

As the sun sets, it casts shadows over the ruined abbey first, so that the ruins drown in a pool of darkness while the terrace still enjoys direct sunlight. This is precisely the moment depicted in Westall's view.[27] The dining temple would furnish the means for occupying the time between a daylight view of the abbey and a sunset view in the most delightful way possible. In the spectacle of the darkened abbey we have an intimation of Gothic terror and the Gothic novel. If the mid-day response to the ruins in the mid-eighteenth century is a rejoicing about a victory over superstition conceived in *national* terms, contemplation of the ruins by night would surely evoke what, in that earlier moment, had been suppressed – but which could only be allowed to resurface in a diametrically opposed form. Thus the ruins become superstitional in a *personal* or individual way – ultimately, that is, by providing ghosts or visions.

William Mason described such an experience of abbey ruins in his poem, 'Ode V. To a Friend':

> To thee, whose young and polished brow
> The wrinkling hand of Sorrow spares;
> Whose cheeks, bestrewed with roses, know
> No channel for the tide of tears;
> To thee yon Abbey dank, and lone,
> Where Ivy chains each mouldering stone

Fig. 3.3   Interior of the Ionic Temple, Rievaulx Terrace, late afternoon.

That nods o'er many a Martyr's tomb,
May cast a formidable gloom.
Yet some there are, who, free from fear,
Could wander thro' the cloysters drear,
Could rove each desolated aisle,
Tho' midnight thunders shook the pile;

And dauntless view, or seem to view,
(As faintly flash the lightnings blue)
Thin shivering ghosts from yawning charnels throng,
And glance with silent sweep the shaggy vaults along.[28]

These responses to ruins depend not only on age and experience but on being able to contemplate the ruins at the appropriate time of night. Visitors to Rievaulx would have had the opportunity to do so, and to feel the sublime emotions aroused by that activity.

This insight gives us access to the Gothic novel, where Terror keeps its 'noctuary',[29] and whose characters have their greatest trouble with the supernatural precisely during the hours of darkness. It also allows us some purchase on the two main types of late-eighteenth-century Gothic architecture: the actually ancient ruins and the modern pastiches or conversions of such ruins into dwellings like Milton Abbas or Newstead Abbey. To pursue this section of the inquiry, I intend to take Ann Radcliffe's *The Romance of the Forest* (1791) as my example.

When the heroine Adeline's party take refuge in 'the vast forest of Fontainville' they discover the immense ruins of a former abbey. La Motte first approaches them in a way Shenstone might have admired: 'As he contemplated its ruins, fancy bore him back to past ages. "And these walls" said he "where once Superstition lurked, and austerity anticipated an earthly purgatory, now tremble over the mortal remains of the beings who reared them!"'[30] However, this confident dismissal of monkish superstition, which Shenstone has shown us is grounded in ultra-Protestantism and Whig hatred and fear of the Jacobite threat, quickly starts to veer towards its antithesis:

As he walked over the broken pavement, the sound of his steps ran in echoes through the place, and seemed like the mysterious accents of the dead, reproving the sacrilegious mortal who thus dared to disturb their precincts. Adeline inquired of La Motte, if he believed in spirits. The question was ill-timed, for the present scene impressed its terrors upon La Motte, and, in spite of endeavour, he felt a superstitious dread stealing upon him. He was now, perhaps, standing over the ashes of the dead. If spirits were ever permitted to revisit the earth, this seemed the hour and the place most suitable for their appearance!

La Motte feels the threat to the person posed by individual spirits. It is as well for the travellers that they manage to locate a different type of architecture:

They passed a suite of apartments and expressed their surprise at the incongruous appearance of this part of the edifice with the mouldering walls they had left behind.

They entered a long vaulted room. La Motte surveyed it with a scrutinizing eye. The room appeared to have been built in modern times upon a gothic plan. Adeline approached a large window that formed a kind of recess raised by one step over the level of the floor: she observed to La Motte that the whole floor was inlaid with mosaic work; which drew from him a remark, that the style of this apartment was not strictly gothic...[31]

The characters have become students of architectural history, and there is clearly some urgency behind this study. In this room they start to live a kind of parody of life at Strawberry Hill or Newstead Abbey or Fonthill.

In one set of rooms – the modern ones fitted up within the ancient shell – they can live tolerably without too many irrational fears. It is the other set – those of the ancient abbey itself – that can drag them back from the comforts of their modern anti-superstitious deism to the screaming spirits of terror. Thus when Adeline explores a room in another part of the abbey at night, 'holding up the lamp to examine it more fully, she was convinced by its structure that it was part of the ancient foundation', and we know that she is in trouble. She soon finds herself 'overcome by superstitious dread'.[32]

The abbey ruins are the focus of Protestant Whig hatred of Roman Catholicism – and they focus Hanoverian Whig guilt about the violent damage they have done to the body politic by their usurpation of the 'true' kings, and consequent damage to the divine and natural order of relations between a king and his people and country. Paul Monod has argued that the High Church and Jacobite theory of kingship, which viewed the nation as an extension of the king's body (the 'body politic'), for all its mysticism, also amounted to a coherent intellectual theory that had no counterpart in Hanoverian Whig ideology.[33] The Hanoverians simply had recourse to ultra-Protestant anti-Catholicism as the essential justification for their presence in power. The Whigs had twice intervened violently, once to usurp the throne against Roman Catholic monarchs in 1688, and again in 1714/15 to exclude a possible Stuart resurgence after Queen Anne's death.[34] In addition they were constantly vigilant and at work demolishing the seven other Jacobite plots between 1688 and 1759. My suggestion, based on the evidence of the ruined abbey, is that vestigial Whig doubt and guilt about their desecration of the sacred relationship between king and nation contributed to the Gothic novel.

It is not fanciful, surely, to see a reduced image of royal dynastic strife in the aristocratic fratricide of the plot of *The Romance of the Forest*. Many years before the present time of the book the Marquis had murdered his brother, Adeline's father, in the ruins of that object of Whig hatred, the abbey:

It is probable, that on the night of [the Marquis's] abrupt departure from the Abbey, the solitary silence and gloom of the hour, in a place which had been the scene of his former crime, called up the remembrance of his brother with a force too powerful for fancy, and awakened horrors which compelled him to quit the polluted spot. If it was so, it is certain however that the spectres of conscience vanished with the darkness.[35]

At the bottom of many plots of Gothic novels lies a usurpation, provoking spectres of conscience. This mechanism is seen most dramatically, perhaps, in Horace Walpole's *The Castle of Otranto*, where usurpation motivates the entire plot and the return of a scion of the 'true' possessors precipitates the appearance of the spectre of Alfonso the Good.

Our third conclusion must therefore be this. The Gothic novelists were not only tapping into two centuries of anti-papist and anti-monastic poetry that had flourished ever since the Reformation. They were also developing and elaborating habits of mind and thought that had first arisen in the landscape garden.

Other sacro-political discourses would encourage differing responses to abbey ruins. One reason that Arthur Young could clamber over Fountains Abbey and feel melancholy over past greatness is that the ruins had been protected from further slighting by the Roman Catholic Messenger family, 'through respect to the ancient religion of the place'. The Messengers refused to sell the ruins to the Aislabies of Studley Royal until 1768.[36] There might even have been Roman Catholic Jacobites who would have endorsed the monastic system and viewed ruined abbeys as a cause for lamentation.

The domination of aesthetic responses by sacro-political discourse accounts for some of the apparent inconsistencies in William Mason's writings (to take only one example). In particular, it helps to account for the persistence of 'yawning charnels' of 'ruthless superstition' in a sensibility that was simultaneously evolving an endorsement of the close-up view from the bottom as a main Picturesque mode of perception. The Picturesque artists exploited views from the bottom, but in doing so they challenged pictorial orthodoxy in so far as that orthodoxy was embodied in government institutions.

Beyond the celebration of Hanoverian power in the view from high places, beyond an indulgence in Whig guilt (the night view of the Gothic novel), and beyond a Jacobite refusal of both of these, the Picturesque mode of seeing provided a fourth alternative for the viewing of abbeys. One of its attractions was to be unencumbered by a close identification with party politics. After the Jacobite threat had waned, Picturesque artists demanded their lower and closer viewpoints, implicitly contradicting the equation between power and vision as necessarily involving the view from the top that Hanoverian military and political strategy had strengthened and institutionalised. Picturesque artists thus helped rehabilitate abbeys, so highly charged with political passions earlier in the century, as objects of historical interest rather than as the breeding-grounds for spectres of conscience.

NOTES

1 John Gough Nichols, in his 'Biographical Memoir' of Whitaker (1768–1821) prefaced to the latter's *An History of the Original Parish of Whalley and Honor of Clitheroe* (fourth edition, London, 1872), reprints the original Prospectus for the work, which projects serial publication monthly from November 1819, each 'number' to contain three plates. It is difficult to ascertain whether this plan was followed. Nichols asserts that only two 'numbers' appeared, but there are twelve plates in the copy of the book in the British Library. The prospectus states that the book will 'correspond' to *The Caves of Yorkshire*, a work of Westall's from 1818 in which Whitaker was not involved (pp. xxxii–xxxiii). William Westall (1781–1850) was the younger half-brother of the artist Richard Westall whose work is discussed by Peter Garside, 'Picturesque Figure and Landscape: Meg Merrilies and the Gypsies', in this volume.

2 The only date for the terrace comes from the local historian T. Gill and is reported by Christopher Hussey, *English Gardens and Landscapes 1700–1750* (London: Country Life, 1967), pp. 140–6. If 1758 represents completion of the work, commencement of such a large engineering project may have been as much as five years earlier in an age when garden-making proceeded very slowly.

3 Arthur Young, *A Six Months' Tour through the North of England*, second edition, 4 vols. (London, 1771), vol. II, p. 83. Young's descriptions of houses first appeared in this edition.

4 *Ibid.*

5 *Ibid.*, pp. 301–3.

6 For a fuller account of this history, see Michael Charlesworth, 'The Idea

of the Sacred in Neo-classical British Gardens of the Eighteenth and Twentieth Centuries', unpublished Ph.D. thesis, University of Kent at Canterbury, 1990, pp. 108–67.

7 See Malcolm Andrews, *The Search for the Picturesque: Landscape Aesthetics and Tourism in Britain, 1760–1800* (Aldershot: Scolar Press, 1989), p. 61.

8 Whitaker's Prospectus to the work only discusses monasteries, and does not mention castles, despite the title. He aspires to 'rescue from oblivion these precious and slowly perishing remnants of ancient wealth, elegance and devotion' (Nichols, 'Biographical Memoir', p. xxxiii). As vicar of Whalley and Burnley, and perpetual curate of Holme, near Cliviger (a position to which he nominated himself), Whitaker might have been particularly interested in spiritual matters.

9 William Mason, *The English Garden* (1772), Book I, line 362.

10 All these views except Turner's are in the Victoria and Albert Museum. Turner's is in the Tate Gallery.

11 More discussion of this topos is given in Charlesworth, 'The Idea of the Sacred', pp. 125–8.

12 Letter to Richard Graves, February 1743, in Marjorie Williams (ed.), *The Letters of William Shenstone* (Oxford: Basil Blackwell, 1939), pp. 62–3.

13 The poem is in William Shenstone, *The Works in Verse and Prose* (fourth edition, 2 vols., 1773); extracts quoted from lines 60–4, and 344–9.

14 Williams (ed.), *Letters of Shenstone*, p. 99.

15 'Elegy XXI. Taking a view of the country... Written at the time of a rumoured tax upon luxury, 1746', lines 17–20.

16 The recent resurgence in Jacobite studies includes Eveline Cruikshanks, *Political Untouchables: The Tories and the '45* (London: Duckworth, 1979); Cruikshanks (ed.), *Ideology and Conspiracy: Aspects of Jacobitism 1689–1759* (Edinburgh: John Donald, 1982); and Paul Monod, *Jacobitism and the English People* (Cambridge University Press, 1989).

17 While Whitaker wrote a history of the '45 rebellion in Latin, in imitation of Tacitus, entitled *De Motu per Britanniam Civico Annis 1745 et 1746* (1809), he found his main domestic enemy in working-class radicalism. He made a speech at Blackburn in 1817 at a meeting 'called to support the arm of Government and to check the nefarious designs of the lower ranks' (Nichols, 'Biographical Memoir', p. xlii). In Burnley in 1819 he read the Riot Act, an event evoked by Nichols with predictable heroic pomposity: Whitaker exhibited 'haughty independence of manner', a 'fine voice' and 'dignified bearing' (p. xliii). After suffering an 'attack of paralysis' in 1820, he was presented with a public testimonial for his 'patriotic services' (p. xlv).

18 It is useful to note that the builder of the Rievaulx Terrace, Thomas Duncombe III, was an orthodox Hanoverian Whig, serving as Deputy Lord-Lieutenant of the North Riding of Yorkshire in the 1740s. For the terms 'metonymic reduction' and 'synecdochic assimilation' used in this paragraph, see Stephen Bann's sustained interdisciplinary rhetorical

analysis in *The Clothing of Clio: A Study of the Representation of History in Nineteenth-Century Britain and France* (Cambridge University Press, 1984).

19 Westall was chosen as draughtsman on the advice of Benjamin West, President of the Royal Academy, while a student of the Academy aged nineteen, after West's first recommendation, William Daniell, had resigned the appointment to marry Westall's sister. The expedition was shipwrecked off the east coast of Australia after completing its work, but Westall managed to salvage all his drawings. He made his way home through China and India.

20 Bernard Smith, in T. M. Perry and Donald H. Simpson (eds.), *Drawings by William Westall: Landscape Artist on H.M.S. Investigator during the Circumnavigation of Australia by Captain Matthew Flinders R..N. in 1801–1803* (London: The Commonwealth Society, 1962), p. 27. This lighting was, of course, a technique of Claude Lorrain and therefore probably learned during Westall's period in the Royal Academy Schools.

21 For example, in Perry and Simpson (eds.), *Drawings by William Westall*, no. 76, 'Mount Westall: View North across Strong-tide Passage and Townshend Island' still shows a grid of construction lines visible in the upper part of the sheet, a distant view of an archipelago. Six horizontal lines and 23 vertical produce a grid of 138 squares, into which the complicated coastlines can be plotted with some accuracy. Other drawings by Westall record compass bearings, which may have provided him with the origin of the 23 vertical lines. The horizontals took the sea's horizon as their initiation. The vantage-point was named Mount Westall by Matthew Flinders as a compliment to this drawing by Westall.

22 See Michael Charlesworth, 'Elevation and Succession: The Representation of Jacobite and Hanoverian Politics in the Landscape Gardens of Wentworth Castle and Wentworth Woodhouse', *New Arcadian Journal*, 31/32 (Summer/Autumn 1991), 7–65.

23 Thomas Sandby also occupied institutional positions: Professor of Architecture at the Royal Academy and Deputy Ranger of Windsor Forest. Compare Martin Hardie, *Water-Colour Painting in Britain: I. The Eighteenth Century* (London: B. T. Batsford, no date), p. 98, and Jessica Christian, 'Paul Sandby and the Military Survey of Scotland', in *Mapping the Landscape: Essays on Art and Cartography*, ed. Nicholas Alfrey and Stephen Daniels (Nottingham: University Art Gallery and Castle Museum, 1990), pp. 18–22.

24 Westall was first taught painting by his brother, Richard, before entering the Academy schools. One assumes that this prepared him for academic landscape painting of the Claude variety. Many of his topographical techniques must have therefore been picked up from surveyors on the Flinders expedition.

25 See Patrick Eyres, 'A Patriotic Landscape: Wentworth Woodhouse: Landscape of Patriotic Opposition and of Patriotic Husbandry', *New Arcadian Journal*, 31/32 (1991), 77–128 especially 106–16.

26 Andrew J. Moore, *John Sell Cotman 1782–1842* (Cotman Bicentenary Exhibition – Norfolk Museums Service), p. 24.
27 Westall's Australian drawings often contain inscriptions of the time of day the sketch was made – e.g. 'taken Jan 26 at five p.m.' – and his awareness of changing time and light was very precise and exact.
28 Stanza III, as printed in Mason's *Poems* (1764), p. 41.
29 C. R. Maturin, *Melmoth the Wanderer: A Tale* (1820) (Harmondsworth: Penguin Books, 1977), p. 266: 'minutes are hours in the *noctuary* of terror, – terror has no *diary*' (i.e. a noctuary is a journal of nightly events).
30 Ann Radcliffe, *The Romance of the Forest*, ed. Chloe Chard (Oxford University Press, 1986), pp. 15–16.
31 *Ibid.*, p. 20. Previous quotation, p. 18.
32 *Ibid.*, pp. 114–15.
33 Monod, *Jacobitism and the English People*, especially p. 43.
34 See Charlesworth, 'Elevation and Succession', pp. 22–5, for expectations of Stuart intervention in 1713–14 from opposite sides of the ideological spectrum.
35 Radcliffe, *Romance of the Forest*, p. 346.
36 Thomas Pennant, *A Tour from Alston-Moor to Harrowgate and Brimham Crags* (London, 1804), p. 75.

CHAPTER 4

The Picturesque and ready-to-wear femininity

Ann Bermingham

In the 1920s Bullock's, a department store in Los Angeles, divided their women customers into six types: the romantic; the statuesque; the artistic; the modern; the conventional; and the picturesque.[1] This remarkable endurance of the Picturesque as a style and its curious migration from the aesthetic discourse of eighteenth-century landscape design to the commercial discourse of twentieth-century fashion retailing is not as odd and inexplicable as it might, at first glance, appear. For, as I hope to show, both the picturesque as a style category and the picturesque woman as a fashion type are not the creations of our modern, or even postmodern, consumer culture but were already anticipated in the eighteenth century's aestheticisation of nature and commercialisation of fashion. Unlike Edmund Burke's categories of the Beautiful and the Sublime, the Picturesque was an aesthetic uniquely constituted to serve the nascent mass-marketing needs of a developing commercial culture; one in which appearances were construed as essence and commodities were sold under the signs of art and nature. Like the Beautiful, the Picturesque was coded as feminine, but, unlike the Beautiful, it indexed a femininity that embodied and responded to variety and change. For this reason it was perfectly suited to the ever-changing woman of fashion and her world. In exploring the relationship between the Picturesque and commercial fashion's construction of femininity, it will be necessary to review a series of cultural events: the popularisation of the Picturesque as a way of seeing; the impact of the French Revolution on British fashion; the aestheticisation and commercialisation of British fashion; the creation of the fashion magazine as both a commercial and feminine discursive space; and the exclusion of women from public life and from institutions of high culture. By way of suggesting their importance, I hope to illuminate their role in the construction of fashion and femininity under commercial capitalism. What I am pro-

posing is that commercial capital's attempts to aestheticise our lives
through the mass marketing of commodities as style choices have contributed significantly to our understanding of ourselves as gendered,
psychological subjects. As exemplified by Bullock's taxonomy of
female customers, my underlying thesis is a simple one: in a commercial culture, consumption is stimulated and managed through
images of subjectivity. In this process, style is both aestheticised
and naturalised, that is to say, it is marketed as both ornament and
essence. With this in mind I wish to explore the Picturesque aesthetic
at the end of the eighteenth century as the paradigm of this
commercialised conception of style and, consequently, the importance of the Picturesque in producing images of femininity suited to
the period's 'fashion revolution' and to the new role of women as
consumers.[2]

PICTURESQUE FEMININITY

While the Beautiful and the Sublime were aesthetics of space, the
Picturesque was an aesthetic of the detail. The best way to illustrate
this is through a negative example.

From Cambridge the road to Ely led us immediately among fens. Trees,
groves, extensive distances, and all the variety of landscape, are now totally
gone. All is blank. The eye meets nothing but dreary causeways... Stretches
of flat, swampy ground; and long ditches running in strait lines... In the
room of such beautiful objects as often adorn landscape, the only ornaments
of this dreary surface are windmills... Their use is to pump off the water into
the channel of the river.[3]

Undistinguished and unmarked, the fens of Cambridge defied all of
the Rev. William Gilpin's powers of Picturesque analysis. Unpicturesque in the extreme, they lacked all ornamental detail. 'All is
blank.' Like a white sheet of drawing paper, to be filled with rocks,
trees, groves, mountains and extensive distances, landscape was a
surface to be decorated. Details gave the landscape depth and
volume and provided it with character and visual interest. Details are
thus crucial to the Picturesque landscape; in fact, one could say that
for Gilpin they *are* the landscape.

   Gilpin's contribution to landscape aesthetics was precisely to teach
viewers how to appreciate landscape as a series of fragments rather
than a unified whole. In his *Three Essays* (1791) he explained:

Our amusement... arises from the employment of the mind in examining the
beautiful scenes we have found. Sometimes we examine them under the idea

of a *whole*: we admire the composition, the colouring, and the light, in one *comprehensive view*.... But as we have less frequent opportunities of being thus gratified, we are more commonly employed in analyzing the parts of scenes; which may be exquisitely beautiful, tho unable to produce a whole. We examine what would amend the composition; how little is wanting to reduce it to the rules of our art; how trifling a circumstance sometimes forms the limit between beauty, and deformity. Or we compare the objects before us with other objects of the same kind: – or perhaps we compare them with the imitations of art. From all these operations of the mind results great amusement.[4]

As this reveals, the whole aesthetic apparatus of Picturesque viewing was attuned to aestheticising the part – the minutia of trifling circumstances – rather than the whole. What others might view as mere landscape details, of trees, rock and *staffage* – Gainsborough's 'a little business for the eye' – became for Gilpin the essential 'ornaments' from which the landscape was composed. Picturesque composition and variety depended on these ornamental elements which, as early as his tour of the Wye (1782), he characteristically began ordering into categories and increasingly minute sub-categories under such headings as: grounds; woods; rocks; animals; figures; and buildings.[5] His popular guide-books, in turn, directed the viewer's gaze to these fragmentary and decorative aspects of the scene. For instance, in describing New Weir on the Wye he writes:

The river is wider, than usual, in this part; and takes a sweep round a towering promontory of rock; which forms the side-screen on the left; and this is the grand feature of the view. It is not a broad, fractured face of rock; but rather a woody hill, from which large projections, in two or three places, burst out, rudely hung with twisting branches, and shaggy furniture; which, like the mane round the lion's head, gives a more savage air to these wild exhibitions of nature. Near the top a pointed fragment of solitary rock, rising above the rest, has rather a fantastic appearance: but it is not without its effect in marking the scene.[6]

The viewer is thus encouraged to perform a close analysis of the features of the 'promontory of rock' which is the 'grand feature of the view'. Put another way we might say that the Picturesque tourist is directed to look at the details within the detail. As if in anticipation of critics who might find him too preoccupied with incidentals Gilpin warned his readers that 'the province of the picturesque eye is to *survey nature*; not to *anatomize matter* ... It examines *parts*, but never descends to *particles*.'[7] Nevertheless, in books like the Wye tour and

Remarks on Forest Scenery he set out elaborate instructions as to the proper Picturesque grouping of trees, rocks, mountains, livestock and figures.[8] In his one stab at a theoretical treatise on the Picturesque, his *Three Essays*, Gilpin attempted to pay some homage to Reynolds's theory of great style, arguing that the goal of the Picturesque artist or viewer was to transcend the particulars in order to embrace the total effect, yet as his remarks on the aesthetic pleasure to be derived from 'parts of scenes' reveal, the Picturesque eye found its greatest delight in these bits of nature's 'furniture'.[9] For his part, Reynolds was clear that Gilpin's Picturesque, with its visually intuitive marshalling of odds and ends into the semblance of a landscape, was the antithesis of the 'great style'. Picturesque variety and ornamentation had no place in the work of Raphael and Michelangelo. In a letter to Gilpin he likened the Picturesque to the aesthetic of the 'inferior schools' of painting (the Flemish and Venetian) that depended on such incidentals as colour, light, texture and a variety of gorgeous detail for their aesthetic effect.[10]

As Reynolds understood, the Picturesque prized the visually ornamental not the intellectually abstract. Consequently, the purpose of the Picturesque was, as Gilpin so often noted, to 'please', 'delight', and 'amuse' the Picturesque eye and not to challenge the intellect.[11] The Picturesque ordering or reordering of landscape parts was entirely for the sake of the arrangement itself, so that it might strike the eye and please it with its disposition of effects. This sensual approach to landscape composition meant that in addition to focusing on the ornamental details and fragments of natural scenery, Gilpin was also concerned with the colour and light that played over them. For as he observed:

Different lights make so great a change even in the *composition* of landscape – at least in the *apparent* composition of it, that they create a scene perfectly new ... Hills and vallies are deranged: awkward abruptness and hollows are introduced: and the effect of woods, and castles, and all the ornamental detail of a country, is lost. On the other hand, these ingredients of landscape may in reality be awkwardly introduced; but through the magical influence of light, they may be altered, softened, and rendered pleasing.[12]

Whereas in Reynolds's theories the insubstantialities of colour and light were seen as trivial components secondary to the composition, for Gilpin they are treated as constituents of compositional form. Moreover, their mutability animated the landscape and gave it its mercurial character, thus contributing to its endless variety of

Picturesque effects. In summation then it can be observed that those elements of landscape painting which academic theory deemed secondary and unimportant because they were merely decorative or ornamental, became in Gilpin's writings of primary importance to the Picturesque aesthetic. Whereas academic theory taught unity of effect, Picturesque theory delighted in details, change, variety, contrasts and surprising juxtapositionings. The Picturesque eye comprehended landscape as pure spectacle, a lively surface animated by a *mélange* of ornamental details and decorative effects. Like the light and atmosphere Gilpin so admired, the Picturesque eye played lightly over this surface. Picturesque viewing was 'superficial' in that it was content to examine the appearances of things without necessarily seeking their cause or meaning. It delighted in textures, colours, and shapes as formal elements to be appreciated for their contrasting variety and unexpected harmonies. In Gilpin's guide-books, landscape becomes the object of a gaze trained precisely to relish its inexhaustibly amusing and ephemeral trivialities.

In Gilpin's guide-books the beholder is imagined as a discriminating connoisseur trained to consume the ever-changing spectacle of nature. The popularity of Gilpin's guides undoubtedly had to do not only with the way they aesthetically packaged the landscape, but also with the way in which they codified the Picturesque into a discourse that was as easily consumed as the scenery it described. For as much as it was a way of seeing, the Picturesque was what we might call a 'lingo', and the rapidity with which its terms could be learned, and the extravagant way in which they could be flaunted as a sign of aesthetic sensibility were often made the butt of satire. As proof that fluency in the Picturesque demanded little more than a flair for the obvious, the objects of this humour are often women: ignorant girls like Catherine Morland in Jane Austen's *Northanger Abbey*; or pretentious ones like Miss Beccabunga Veronique in James Plumptre's 'comic opera' *The Lakers*; or feminised men like William Combe's the Rev. Dr Syntax. The barbs were most often directed at Gilpin's jargon and his often hyperbolic descriptions of natural scenery. Here, for instance, is Miss Beccabunga's description of Derwentwater:

How frigidly frozen! What illusions of vision! The effect is inexpressibly interesting. The amphitheatrical perspective of the long landscape; the peeping points of the many coloured crags of the head-long mountains, looking out most interestingly from the picturesque luxuriance of the bowery foliage, margining their ruggedness, and feathering the fells; the delightful differences of the heterogeneous masses; the horrific mountains, such scenes of ruin and privation... I must take a sketch.[13]

True to the Picturesque love of detail, and in particular 'natural furniture', Miss Beccabunga, by the end of the opera, is engaged to a botanist whom she has examined through her Gray's glasses and found to be 'gorgeously glowing'. Imagining their future bliss as both Picturesque and 'perfectly botanic' she exclaims, 'We will be *connate* like the twin flowers on the same *peduncle*, and I trust our love will be *supervivent* and perennial.'[14]

As Plumptre's satiric account of Miss Beccabunga's visit to the Lakes reveals, the popularity of the Picturesque cannot be seen apart from its feminisation nor from the commercialisation of tourism in Britain at the end of the eighteenth century. The war with France virtually sealed off the Continent, and tours of England, Scotland and Wales replaced the Continental 'Grand Tours' of an earlier generation. Local touring, as Gilpin often reminded his readers, was not only more affordable but it was also morally improving, for Picturesque tourists communed with the most beautiful creations of divine intelligence and not with the corrupt and corrupting works of men.[15] For as Elizabeth Bennet observed in true Gilpin style, 'What are men to rocks and mountains!'[16] Unlike the Grand Tour, Picturesque touring was suited to the pockets and moral sensibilities of the middle classes. In short, Britain became for the middle classes what the Continent had been for the wealthy, that is a spectacle to be consumed. Moreover, the Picturesque aesthetic, with its emphasis on vision and on landscape as an ornamented surface affording endless occasions for diversion, provided an incentive for tourism and an education in how to do it properly. With Gilpin in hand, one could be sure not only that one was seeing the proper spot from the proper vantage point but also that one was having the proper aesthetic response in the presence of such natural wonders. As a Picturesque tourist, one shared in a sensibility or, as the Picturesque was so often called, a 'cult'. For in aestheticising the view the Picturesque ultimately validated the good taste of the viewer.

The popularisation of the Picturesque aesthetic was also its commercialisation. It was perhaps the first aesthetic to demand that its initiates literally buy into it. In addition to Gilpin's guides, the tourist in search of the Picturesque might also invest in a wide variety of what Plumptre called 'travelling knick-knacks'; that is, optical gadgets, art supplies, maps and hiking equipment.[17] Moreover, one could not seek and find the Picturesque without the aid of a suitable travelling costume. In the case of Plumptre, who was himself accomplished in the art of Picturesque touring, this meant breeches with a special pocket for a knife, fork and pedometer. In addition he carried two nightcaps, a Gray's glass, a Claude glass, a drawing book and lead pencil, two volumes of Cowper's poems, a compass, a pedometer, a telescope, a magnifying glass and a barometer. Suitably outfitted, the common traveller was transformed into a 'Picturesque tourist'.[18] As Plumptre's list of travelling knick-knacks shows, the fad for Picturesque touring resulted in commercial tie-ins to the fashion industry as well as to dealers in a variety of sundries: stationers who supplied amateur artists with paper, paints and drawing manuals; optical equipment makers; publishers of maps and guide-books. In addition, when the Picturesque had finally been located, there were rooms and meals at the local inn to be purchased, guides to be hired, and fees to be paid for securing access to the most Picturesque viewing spots. The economic boost this provided to local economies, such as the towns of the Lake District, was of course a mixed blessing, for increased tourism brought with it its own problems in the form of congestion and petty crime.[19]

In aestheticising the natural and often commonplace scenery of Britain, the Picturesque awakened a large segment of the population to the realisation that aesthetic judgement was not the gift of the privileged few but could be learned by anyone and applied to just about anything. The Picturesque's most important and abiding effect was that it encouraged the middle classes to aestheticise their lives. For in teaching people how to look at nature as if it were a picture the Picturesque accustomed its practitioners to exercising a connoisseur's gaze, one that could be trained not only on landscapes and paintings but on a whole variety of familiar scenes and objects: cityscapes; architecture; gardens; animals; furniture; pottery; fabrics; interior decoration; and dress. Just as Gilpin had conceived of the landscape as a surface to be decorated, so the consumer of Picturesque scenery could easily transpose Picturesque ideas onto the actual domestic sphere. The specific elements of Picturesque taste, in particular its attention to variety, ornamentation, and detail, were perfectly suited to the kinds of domestic objects easily afforded by the middle-class consumer and supplied in increasing volume by a whole host of domestic manufacturers.

As a result, the Picturesque became more than an aesthetic, it became a life style. That is to say, it became not simply a mode of viewing and judging art but a conscious choice to extend aestheticism to encompass one's way of life. The Picturesque was capable of embracing not only landscapes, paintings and manufactured objects, but people and personalities as well. The most striking and significant examples of this come from Uvedale Price's *Essay on the Picturesque* (1794). In describing the unconventional nature of Picturesque beauty, Uvedale Price observed:

There are several expressions in the language of a neighbouring people, of lively imagination, and distinguished gallantry and attention to the other sex, which seem to imply an uncertain idea of some character, which was not precisely beauty, but which, from whatever causes, produced striking and pleasing effects: such are *une physionomie de fantaisie*, and the well-known expression of *un certain je ne sais quoi*; it is also common to say of a woman – que sans être belle elle est *piquante* – a word, by the by, that in many points answers very exactly to picturesque.[20]

In another place, he describes Marmontel's heroine Roxalana as an example of the Picturesque. In creating her face, Price claims, Marmontel

certainly did not intend to give the *petit nez retroussé* as a *beautiful* feature; but to show how much such a striking *irregularity* might accord and co-operate with the same sort of irregularity in the character of the mind. The playful, unequal, coquetish Roxalana, full of sudden turns and caprices, is opposed to the beautiful, tender, and constant Elvira; and the effects of irritation, to those of softness and languor: the tendency of the qualities of beauty alone towards monotony, are no less happily insinuated.[21]

The obvious question raised by Price's analogy is by what means did the Picturesque aesthetic come to colonise not only the objects of everyday life but subjectivity as well? The answer I think has very much to do with the way the Picturesque was constituted as an aesthetic of both art and nature. When applied to paintings, the Picturesque spoke the language of nature and pictorial effects were judged on the basis of their imitation of Picturesque nature. When applied to landscape it spoke the language of art and natural scenery was weighed according to how well it conformed to the rules of Picturesque painting.[22] By naturalising art and aestheticising nature, the Picturesque continually transgressed the boundary between the two, collapsing them into versions of each other. Price's equation of the Picturesque landscape with a certain type of woman whose temperament is mercurial and whose beauty is individual is characteristic of this co-mingling. What is striking about Price's analogy is not only how it aestheticises subjectivity but how, in doing so, it makes physical appearances an index of character and temperament. From the conscious choice of life style we move to the unconscious drives of psychological temperament.

That such readings are performed on feminine bodies is significant. Price's analogy between the Picturesque and a type of femininity follows in large part from Gilpin. For it was Gilpin who established the Picturesque as a subset of Burke's feminised category of the Beautiful. According to Gilpin 'picturesque beauty' was that kind of beauty that 'looks good in a picture'.[23] In his *Enquiry*, Burke had associated the Beautiful with the social, affecting and sexual feelings provoked by the 'feminine' qualities of smoothness, smallness, weakness and delicacy. He contrasted the paternalistic impulses provoked by the Beautiful to the feeling for self-preservation stimulated by the awesome, virile terror of the Sublime. As a species of the Beautiful, Gilpin and Price's Picturesque assumed the feminine colouration of the original Burkean category. Nevertheless, while it was a kind of beauty, the Picturesque was not *the* Beautiful. It differed from the Beautiful in that its characteristics were not conventionally pleasing. In place of regularity, smoothness and delicacy, the Picturesque offered irregularity, variety and roughness. It was, as Price pointed out, an aesthetic of the 'piquant'. The Picturesque object was freed from traditional rules of beauty and decorum and demanded on the part of the beholder a certain sophisticated appreciation for that which was novel and unconventional. Moreover, unlike the Beautiful, which appealed to all the senses, the Picturesque appealed, as both Gilpin and Price explained, exclusively to the sense of vision.[24] Moreover, instead of soothing the eye and awakening protective feelings of affection in the viewer, as did the Beautiful, the Picturesque stimulated, excited and irritated the eye and provoked feelings of curiosity, interest and amusement. Consequently, the Picturesque should be understood as a supplement to the Beautiful, one that was all the more dangerous by virtue of the fact that it made the Beautiful look boring, or as Gilpin so often described it when he encountered it in a landscape – 'simply disgusting'.

As an aesthetic of ornamental detail intended to appeal to the eye and not the intellect or the deeper emotions, the Picturesque was all surface and thus all femininity. For what could be more quintessentially feminine than a lack of depth? The Picturesque emphasis on details, ornamentation, and variety complemented a familiar cultural discourse which characterised femininity as all petty surface and masculinity as all profound depth, and which imagined women to be changeable and sentimental and men to be stable and rational. Yet what is remarkable about the Picturesque is its demand that surfaces be taken seriously, that they be treated, not in depth, but *as* depth. Thus the Picturesque not only conformed to essential notions of gender difference but it also complemented an emerging commercial discourse which sought to identify appearances with essence. Hence it is not surprising to find Picturesque ideas emerging in women's fashion magazines of the last decade of the eighteenth century. In these publications, the Picturesque delight in variety, detail and spectacle is the prerequisite for an appreciation of fashion, and the 'piquant' character of Picturesque beauty complements a new kind of femininity under construction.

(EN)GENDERING FASHION

In his classic study of fashion, *The Psychology of Clothes* (1930), J. C. Flugel attributed changes in male clothing in the eighteenth century to changes in class relations brought about by the French Revolution. While women's dress was simplified, it still remained ornamental whereas men's dress became austere and uniform. 'Man', he wrote, 'abandoned his claim to be considered beautiful. He henceforth aimed at being only useful.'[25] The 'Great Masculine Renunciation', as Flugel called this development, served to integrate and unite men of all classes by inhibiting older forms of aristocratic display of masculine sartorial sumptuousness. At the same time that it softened signs of class divisions, however, it also, as Kaja Silverman has remarked, hardened the signs of gender difference.[26] 'Sexual difference', she notes, '[became] the primary marker of power, privilege and authority, closing the specular gap between men of different classes, and placing men and women on opposite sides of the great visual divide.' While styles in women's dress continued to change, male dress remained largely unchanged. The effect of this she claims was to 'define male sexuality as stable and constant, and so align it with the symbolic order. In other words... to conflate the penis with the phallus.'[27] Or as Flugel observed, 'The whole relatively "fixed" system of [man's] clothing is in adherence to the social code (though at the same time, through its phallic attributes, it symbolizes the most fundamental features of his sexual nature).'[28] The 'Great Masculine Renunciation' thus expressed both the socially inclusive and sexually exclusive nature of bourgeois democracy.

In contrast to the male dress, feminine fashion reconstructed the female body on at least a yearly basis. Bosoms, hips and waists waxed and waned, as they were padded, pressed, plumped, pushed and prodded into an ever-changing shape.[29] Thus fashion established femininity as a radically unstable category, a kaleidoscope of shifting images.[30] Furthermore, if sober masculine dress is aligned with phallic power and with the new democratic social order, then feminine fashion is not only a sign of impotence but is also a threat to that order. Thus for revolutionary radicals, such as the Jacobins in France, fashion was seen as a reactionary social force, one that threatened to reinstate distinctions of class and rank and thus one that continually needed to be policed for its sumptuous excesses.[31] By contrast in England, conservatives complained that fashion was too democratic; fashionable dress was so pervasive that it was erasing all social distinctions. Fashion thus inscribed on the bodies of women the old notions of female excess and inconstancy which, in turn, justified the exclusion of women from the political process. Naturalised as feminine fickleness and narcissism, fashion helped call forth a large body of literature at the end of the century demanding a reform in female manners.

As it is engendered in the last decade of the eighteenth century, commercial fashion had much in common with the popular Picturesque aesthetic. In order to trace these parallels it is necessary to return to Flugel. As a result of the 'Great Masculine Renunciation', Flugel claimed that the masculine desire for exhibitionism was now expressed in demonstrations of knowledge and expertise, in scopophilia and in the projection of exhibitionistic desire onto women. These three modes of displacing exhibitionism – expertise, scopophilia and objectification – are embedded in the Picturesque aesthetic. Since Picturesque theory valued the unconventional it was not – unlike Burke's categories – a universal emotion of taste. Instead it demanded a certain amount of cultivation; cultivation readily available and easily enough obtained, yet cultivation all the same. The 'Picturesque eye' had to be trained by first looking at pictures and learning to discriminate between their individual styles of beauty. Only after absorbing the rules of

Picturesque beauty from Claude, Gaspar and Salvator could the student of Picturesque beauty apply his special visual knowledge and terminology to natural objects. As a vulgarised form of connoisseurship, Picturesque viewing carried a certain *cachet* at a time when connoisseurs like Sir George Beaumont and Richard Payne Knight were gaining considerable reputations and influence over the practice and exhibition of art. The ability to distinguish a good picture or a good landscape was a sign of refinement; the exercise of aesthetic judgement was thus valued for the status and authority it conferred. The woman of fashion and the Picturesque object must be seen in conjunction with a particular construction of masculinity as the bearer of the gaze – as, for example, the true connoisseur of Picturesque beauty or the Picturesque tourist. In this sense, the Picturesque eye, like the eye of the connoisseur, may be described not only as an aestheticising eye but as a fetishising one as well.

This is not to say that Picturesque touring and viewing was reserved exclusively for men. Women were of course Picturesque tourists. Yet as the satires on the Picturesque reveal, while drawn by some magnetic, almost irrational, force to the Picturesque, women appear to be either incapable of understanding it or are blinded by it to 'reality'. In the case of Miss Beccabunga Veronique, Picturesque clichés become a babble of misunderstood and inappropriately applied terms; as a result she fails repeatedly to see the 'real' landscape of the Lakes, imagining 'horrors' where there are none and 'sudden variation and intricacy' in the most undistinguished view. In her case Picturesque viewing becomes a hallucinatory experience. Justifying her 'little sketch', which bears no resemblance to the landscape before her, she announces: 'If it is not like what *is*, it is what it *ought* to be. I have only made it picturesque.'[32] Blinded by the Picturesque, she wilfully misrecognises the landscape. Her wildly over-stimulated imagination is continually opposed to the true Picturesque eye of Sir Charles Portinscale, a native of the Lake District, which is sober and scientific. By contrast, Miss Beccabunga is incapable of seeing Picturesque nature in a detached aesthetic way because as a creature of enthusiasm, imagination and instability she *is* Picturesque nature. She cannot be both a connoisseur and the object of connoisseurship.

Her Picturesque objecthood leads us again to Flugel's observations. For in addition to demanding a certain expertise and detachment, Picturesque viewing, with its emphasis on the pleasure to be derived from looking implies, in Flugel's terms, a certain scopophilia where the 'desire to be seen is transformed into a desire to see'.[33] While certainly motivated by a desire to see, Miss Beccabunga's seeing is self-reflexive. That is to say, she desires to be seen seeing. Her sighs and sketches are calculated to charm her male companions. More typically scopophilic is Sir Charles's discriminating and scientific gaze. Following Freud, Flugel believed 'this desire to see may itself remain unsublimated and find its appropriate satisfaction in the contemplation of the other sex, or it may find expression in the more general desire to see and know'.[34] 'It is perhaps', he notes, 'no mere chance that a period of unexampled scientific progress should have followed the abandonment of ornamental clothing by men.'[35] Scopophilia is closely connected to Flugel's third category of masculine exhibitionism, the male identification of women as spectacle or as objects of the scopophilic gaze. The exclusively visual nature of the Picturesque, and its tendency to aestheticise things that were old, dilapidated and worn out or which were feminised in other ways by being characterised as lacking gravity and stability suggest to me an intimate psycho-sexual connection between the scopophilic gaze and the Picturesque eye. Thus the 'Great Masculine Re-nunciation' in the 1790s of extravagant and showy modes of male dress, signalled a repression of masculine exhibitionism, and a sublimation and channelling of this desire into other more acceptably 'masculine' forms. As a connoisseur of Picturesque beauty, a man could confirm his masculinity by displaying his specialised knowledge of painting, aesthetics, landscape and nature, and satisfy his connoisseur's love of looking by aestheticising and specularising women and impotent feminised Others – the poor, the old, the dilapidated – through a process of detached Picturesque viewing. In this way the Picturesque eye established a scopic dominion over what it viewed, and in doing so differentiated itself from the object of vision.

In writing to her sister Cassandra, Jane Austen noted: 'Miss Langley is like any other short girl with a broad nose & wide mouth, fashionable dress, & exposed bosom', and, again to Cassandra, she reported that Charlotte Craven 'looks very well, and her hair is done up with an elegance to do credit to any education'.[36] Clearly exposed bosoms and elegant hair functioned for Austen as metonymic signs of character.[37] Conversely what made Austen, and many of her contemporaries, uncomfortable was fashion's potential to obscure and falsify character. It was an anxiety which was shared by British commercial society at large, but which was played out largely on the text of the woman of fashion. The criticisms of fashion came in two forms. The first was that fashion was vanity, that it effeminised men and turned women into frivolous and rapacious consumers. This criticism turned on the idea that fashion could not only obscure character but could also cover an essential lack of individual authenticity. It played on the old conception of woman as lack, as having no true subjectivity, no real essence, as being a creature of dissemblance and masquerade. Men who followed fashion thus threatened their masculine prerogative, their phallic essence and power. The second criticism of fashion followed from this. It claimed that fashion was the enemy of individuality, that it erased distinctions of class and character. When required 'to salute the Ladies', Defoe complained, 'I kis'd the chamber jade into the bargain for she was as well dress'd as the rest.'[38] When not confusing rank and class, fashion could also threaten individuality through standardisation. When the *Lady's Monthly Museum* introduced a fashion page into the magazine in November 1798, a male reader responded, 'Now, Sir, I desire to know whether you do not conceive it a most preposterous and absurd thing that any fashion should be universally followed, that is without respect to age or form, to size or complexion?'[39] The writer went on to note that dress should be used to display the 'peculiar beauty' of the individual, and suggested that when introducing a new fashion the magazine should show how it 'suits a certain kind of figure, – and then to point out wherein it would be ludicrous if worn by a form of a different description'.[40] By doing so, the writer claimed the *Lady's Monthly Museum* would 'save my wife...from continuing to be a laughing-stock of those who generally set the fashion'.[41] This concerned husband's advice underscores the general suspicion in Britain that fashion was the great leveller, for not only did it permit chamber jades to look like ladies, but it erased individual uniqueness and substituted in its place a standardised and often unsuitable vestimentary persona.

Women, of course, were especially prone to fashion's maleficent influences for they were by nature imitative and impressionable, easily led into situations that were detrimental to their happiness and to their reputations. Thus they needed to be guided in dress as well as in most other things. In this context it is important to note that while Austen could spend pages of a letter to Cassandra describing the lace trim for a cap, she was loath to display her fashion expertise by entering into minute descriptions of dress in her novels. There fashion – or at least an over-concern with fashion – is a sign of superficiality and vulgar materialism.[42] Authenticity is signalled by a lack of preoccupation with one's appearance (one thinks of Elizabeth Bennet's muddy skirts) if not an outright indifference to fashion. In this sense Austen is typical of many women writers of the period – the 'bluestockings' being only the most obvious examples – who, in resisting the prevailing notions of women as nothing more than narcissistic fashion dolls, resisted fashion itself – at least in their public writings.[43] In Austen's fiction, fashion figures as an ever-present temptation:

Dress is at all times a frivolous distinction, and excessive solicitude about it often destroys its own aim. Catherine knew all this very well; her great aunt had read her a lecture on the subject only the Christmas before; and yet she lay awake ten minutes on Wednesday night debating between her spotted and her tamboured muslin, and nothing but the shortness of the time prevented her buying a new one for the evening.[44]

While tempted by fashion, heroines like Catherine Morland are always mortified to succumb to its vanity. For good girls like Catherine, fashion is a guilty pleasure. Austen's heroines are described as neat about their dress, but not over-concerned with its fashionability. Their deafness (or resistance) to fashion's siren call signals that they are individuals with sense *and* sensibility, women with minds as well as bodies.

Yet as Catherine's sleeplessness makes plain, dress was an important consideration for women and, as the domestic fashion industry became successfully industrialised, an ever-present temptation. Numerous changes in marketing were instituted to facilitate feminine consumption. As Neil McKendrick has noted, the old-fashioned pedlar was replaced by the 'Scotch draper' who provided provincial house-wives with the latest London fashions and by the 'Manchester man' who sold fashionable articles at wholesale prices directly to provincial shopkeepers.[45] Yet the most glamorous changes came about in the cities and in the way in which stores displayed their wares. As *Ackerman's Repository of the Arts* makes plain there was a growing sensitivity to the aesthetics of merchandise display and an increasing diversification of commodities carried by the larger shops. In the March 1809 issue we find this description of the interior of Harding, Howell and Company's Grand Fashionable Magazine at

Number 98 Pall-Mall: 'immediately at the entrance is the first department, which is exclusively appropriated to the sale of furs and fans. The second contains articles of haberdashery of every description, silks, muslins, lace, gloves, etc. In the third shop, on the right, you meet with a rich assortment of jewelry, ornamental articles in *ormolu*, French clocks, etc., and on the left, with all the different kinds of perfumery necessary for the toilette. The fourth is set apart for millinery and dresses; so that there is no article of female attire or decoration, but that may be here procured in the first style of elegance and fashion.'[46] Harding and Howell had been founded in 1789 and in 1809 employed forty people on the premises. In addition, they engaged a large number of artisans from all parts of the country to supply them with their stock of clothing and novelties.

While gratified by elegant shops like Harding and Howell, feminine desire was also stimulated by the fashion illustration. In 1771 *The Lady's Magazine* ran their first fashion illustrations; these illustrations became *de rigueur* for other women's periodicals, setting the stage ultimately for the publication of the first fashion magazines. The virtual explosion of women's fashion magazines in the 1790s and the early decades of the nineteenth century, with titles like *The Gallery of Fashion* (1794–1802), *The Temple of Taste* (1795), and *The Elegant Repository* (1791–2), is an important sign of the successful commercialisation of feminine fashion. Part of the impetus behind this creation and exploitation of feminine desire came from the cloth industry. Improvements in the dyeing and manufacture of cloth meant that a greater variety of fabrics was available at more affordable prices. Since the seventeenth century Britain had gradually taken over the finishing as well as the weaving of cloth, which strengthened the overall economy. As E. P. Thompson, John Foster, Chandra Mukerji and Grace Lovat Fraser among others have noted, the industrialisation of the British cotton industry destroyed not only native hand-weaving but also the indigenous cotton industries of India which had supplied England in the seventeenth century with fine cotton painted and printed with delicate floral patterns. In addition, industrialisation transformed Yorkshire and Lancashire into major textile centres.[47] English calicos and chintzes not only competed successfully at home and abroad against Indian cloth but also against French silk. The export trade in British cotton increased dramatically in the later half of the eighteenth century. Thus when foreign trade was depressed by the wars with France, the domestic market and the domestic consumption of textiles needed to be stimulated. The fashion for thin cotton and muslin dresses during the war years was a boon to British cotton manufactures. Consumer interest in British cloth was stimulated by publications like *Ackerman's Repository of the Arts* which in addition to running fashion plates also attached swatches of material produced by native manufacturers that would be appropriate to use in order to make the costumes shown in the illustrations.

In addition, the revolution in France resulted in the influx of a wave of well-to-do émigrés and of artisans employed in the French fashion industry. Their presence in Britain is acknowledged by fashion magazines like the *Mirror de la Mode* which was printed in English, French and Italian. French modistes, dress designers, fabric cutters and seamstresses were integrated into the domestic fashion industry. Since Paris had always been jealously regarded as the capital of fashion, these artisans' skills were especially prized. It is possible that many of the fashion magazine editors of the 1790s, like the famous Nicholaus Heideloff, were refugees from the upheavals on the Continent. Their presence in England gave English cloth and the domestic fashion industry a prominence that they had formerly lacked.

While writers like Austen might lament the effects of fashion on the female mind and character, it was clear that dress was one of the means, perhaps the major one, that women had at their disposal to improve their social status by marrying up. The scopic regime of the marriage market, where in the public spaces of cities and spa towns unmarried women were paraded before the male gaze at balls and assemblies, operas and concerts, placed a premium on appearance. In thinking about fashion it is helpful to remember that in the eighteenth and nineteenth centuries, the marriage market was a *real* market – that is an economic space for the exchange of goods and services, regulated by specific rules of decorum, brokered by institutions and protected by laws governing property. As a space of exchange it was characterised by bargaining, negotiation and contractual agreements. It was a space in which speculators made and lost fortunes. As a market it intersected with and supported other markets such as those that supplied women with the commodities – dresses, hats, gloves and shoes – that they needed in order to establish their social credi(t)bility.[48]

Within the marriage market, the marketing of women as com-

modities and the marketing of commodities for women was wholly
naturalised. It was a market that followed a seasonal and cyclical
pattern. A woman was inserted into this pattern through specific
codings of dress and deportment that signalled her availability – the
fact that she had 'come of age' and was 'out' – as well as through the
very temporal and seasonal character of the annual visits to London
and to spa towns like Bath. Walter Benjamin has remarked that 'if
the soul of the commodity which Marx occasionally mentions in jest
existed, it would be the most empathetic ever encountered in the
realm of souls, for it would have to see in everyone the buyer in whose
hand and house it wants to nestle'.[49] Women's empathetic relation to
the commodities of fashion must be seen within the context of their
own commodification. Within the discursive space of the marriage
market women continually had to discriminate between the tasteful
and vulgar consumption of goods, cultural events and novelties. For
how a woman consumed, that is to say how she identified with other
commodities, would determine how, in turn, she was consumed.
Thus, in addition to empathising with the potential buyer in whose
hand and home she might want to nestle, she had to first empathise
with those things that would secure for her that haven. Thus her
position as a commodity and a consumer of commodities was
institutionally assured.

Consumption then was intimately tied to the feminine sphere, and
to the commodification of women in the marriage market. For as
'Peter Scribble' notes in a letter to the editor of the *Mirror de la Mode*,
'The influence of dress on the various and extensive relations of
society is very great, it is a powerful auxiliary to those who *have been*,
and to those who *would be* brides; and when we consider that these
two classes comprehend nearly the whole sex, we shall hardly deny
the interest which mankind ought to feel on the subject.'[50] However,
even after marriage the important role of fashion and clothing in
women's lives was assured through the laws governing a married
woman's separate property. In her discussion of 'pin money', a
payment made by husbands to their wives, Susan Staves has noted
that while it afforded the married woman some form of economic
independence, there were laws drawn up to govern the way in which
it was to be expended.[51] Pin money could not be saved or spent as
capital, and if it was found that a woman was saving up her pin
money her husband was justified in stopping all payments. By law,
pin money *had* to be spent only on clothes, personal articles and trivial

amusements.[52] The kind of consumption this restriction on saving and spending encouraged was, of course, often condemned as frivolous and schemes to police it were not uncommon. One such plan, made no less obnoxious by the fact that it is an imaginary one, can be found in William Gilpin's *Dialogues on Various Subjects*. Remarking on the fact that mothers are often 'the great seducers of their daughters', Gilpin's Mr Willis proposes that 'a censor might be appointed, by authority, at the corner of every street, to question each lady passenger, on what errand she was bent; and, if she would not give a good account of herself, to stop her progress'. His interlocutor, Sir Charles, replies,

I should be highly amused to see you execute an office of that kind. When each fair itinerant made her request, – Pray, sir, let me go to the opera – I beg, sir, you will not prevent my going to a play – or to a rout – or perhaps a shopping – with what gravity you would turn to the coachman, and, without vouchsafing the poor lady an answer, order him to turn his horses round, and carry his lady immediately home. – I like your scheme mightily. If you could bring it to bear, it would keep many a gadding female out of mischief – it would save the shopkeeper much trouble – it would make the streets more comfortable, and commodious for those who had real business; – and above all it would keep mothers from misleading their daughters.[53]

The passage makes clear that women's access to the culture and the public sphere was largely through consumption, and that removing gadding females from sites like the opera and the shops was seen as desirable by reformers of feminine manners. Gilpin's dialogue underscores the growing social trend in the later eighteenth century to exclude women from the public sphere of culture and commerce and to limit their activities to the home in the name of maternal duty.

FASHION'S REVOLUTIONS

In his *Passagen-Werk*, Benjamin described fashion as 'the modern measure of time', a process of repetition and novelty that in evoking the cycles of nature and history denies the finality of death.[54] For Benjamin fashion was an emblem of hell, for it instituted a cycle of novelty without progress. Fashion expressed modern commodity society's sadistic craving for sameness disguised as innovation. Fashion's mendacious claims to revolutionary progress, Benjamin believed, disguised the fact that under capitalism real revolutionary change – a change in social and economic relations – cannot occur.[55]

Rather than see fashion's claims to revolution as simply fraudulent, I would suggest that fashion provided a comforting model of history, one that demanded, in an almost subliminal way, that 'revolution' be understood as both rupture – the myth of progress – and as continuity – the myth of historical repetition. In speaking to a need to believe simultaneously in progress and in continuity, fashion's revolutions provided modern industrial society with an image of the past as both a point of difference against which modern progress could be measured and as a point of continuity legitimating that progress as the logical extension of a historical tradition.[56]

Fashion was not only a way to mark the time of day – with morning, afternoon and evening dress – and to note the passing of the seasons but also, and increasingly, it was a system through which the past was reinvented as a style. Fashion illustrations of the later eighteenth century conform to this dual model of time. Illustrations in Heideloff's *Gallery of Fashion*, for instance, show fashion figures in everyday situations. Like those found in medieval books of hours, these pictures tell time by constructing 'typical' daily events and seasonal pastimes. Unlike the books of hours, however, the daily and annual circularity of events as depicted in *The Gallery of Fashion* is highlighted by a change of dress. While times of day and seasons are indicated by the change from 'morning dresses' to 'evening dresses' and by fabrics, accessories and cuts appropriate to the seasonal climate, years are differentiated one from the other by changes in over-all styles. Increasingly these styles were re-workings of fashions from the past. The rage for seventeenth-century Van Dyck dress, for instance, which swept aristocratic circles the 1770s, was the first of many revivals that were to mark fashion's revolutions in the later part of the century. It was followed by the taste for the Rubens, the Roman and the Grecian modes.[57] In the world constructed by the fashion illustration, days and years are differentiated one from the other not by individual acts or historical events but by stylistic novelty. In this sense the individual's ability to act, to direct her own life or create her own history, is presented exclusively in terms of her ability to consume and manipulate new fashion styles.

The variety of styles presented in fashion magazines signals the increasing commercialisation of fashion and an appeal to consumerism and to a diversity of tastes by trading on the novel and the exotic. In March 1804, 'Florio Honeysuckle' reports in *The Elegancies of Fashion* that present-day fashion includes: 'Grecian or Turkish

Costume', 'Dresses à l'enfant' or (for the more Amazonian in spirit) 'à la Sauvage' and 'Calypso drapery'.[58] The eclecticism represented by this list was embodied by the woman of fashion who was encouraged to mix modes and to top off, for instance, a Grecian gown with a 'Chinese' hair style or a seventeenth-century style 'Spanish hat'. As reported by magazines like *The Elegancies of Fashion* fashion's revolutions were abrupt and never-ending. In April 1804, a month after noting that 'Egyptian and Algerian turbans' are all the rage, Honeysuckle hints that 'The Spanish hat, hitherto scarcely exhibited, except at the opera, will be introduced at the ensuing great assemblies.'[59] The next month his intuition is validated for he reports with triumph, 'Turbans now are worn only by Turks, they are completely out.'[60] However, by July he admits that turbans have been 'revivified' but adds they are 'of a lighter, more delicate, and more seasonable construction'.[61] The vicissitudes of fashion were never-ending, for as Honeysuckle reminds his readers who might be tempted to believe that they had attained the height of fashion for the season and thus rest secure in their achievement (and perhaps even to cancel their subscriptions for the summer): 'Nothing can be more erroneous than the idea, that on the 4th of June costume is fixed for the summer... for though fashion changes her seat, she resigns not her sceptre for a moment, and admits of no interregnum. Those therefore, if any there be, who removing from the capital think they may disband their artificers, and safely consign personal ornament to the hands of domestic seamstresses, will commit a miserable error.'[62] The endless cycle of fashion was a cycle of sudden breaks and equally sudden repetitions. Repetitions, moreover, that were always a little bit different from what had come before, but which were just similar enough to feel familiar. Knowing when one could anticipate these changes was the desire of every fashionable woman – a desire created and fulfilled by the fashion magazine.

A variety of styles was felt to express and complement the 'genius' of women. Far from avoiding the old saw that women were by nature frivolous and inconstant, the fashion magazines embraced it, and celebrated it as part of the feminine civilising influence. A letter to the editor of the *Mirror de la Mode* notes,

Variety is allowed to be the essence of beauty in the works of genius as well as nature; and where is such variety to be found as in woman? Far from cloying us with sameness, she is never for two successive minutes the same; and every occurrence in life produces a change in her inclination, and these are as faithfully followed by every feature of her face, as the hand of the dial moves to the wheels. Let man trudge on in the same beaten track, in supposed consequence of his own superiority. The inexhaustible genius of Woman will invent methods of her own to display her accomplishments, in such an endless variety of ways, that the most Austere Cynic must acknowledge the justness of the remark,

'O woman, woman, you were born to temper
man, we had been brutes without you.'[63]

As this passage makes clear, women's desire for change is legitimated as a form of social and material progress. Civilisation is equated with feminine things like fashion and accomplishments, and implicitly with the feminine propensity to consume.

Rather than standardising feminine taste and dress, the writers on fashion insisted that the variety of styles prevalent in any one time provided every woman with a mode of dress appropriate to her figure and her mood. For as the anonymous author of *The Mirror of the Graces* explained, fashion enabled her to put on 'a variety of interesting characters. In one, a youthful figure, we see the lineaments of a wood-nymph... Another fair one appears with the chastened dignity of a vestal... Between the two lie the whole range of female character in form.'[64] Thus in affirming women's genius for variety, fashion also constructed and mapped a range of femininities from a dignified sobriety to an elfin-like sprightliness. Intimately connected to this valorisation of feminine variety was the idea of freedom. The fashion revolution at the end of the century was most often described as a 'liberation' for women. 'By following the style of dress, and the arrangement of drapery in these fine remains of antiquity,' *Ackerman's Repository of the Arts* declared, 'the present taste has happily emancipated the ladies from all the ridiculous lumber of the late fashions; from systems and powder, whalebone and cork, flounces and furbelows, and pockets and pincushions...'[65] It was conceived as a liberation from stays and corsets, and as a liberation of feminine self-expression. For as *The Mirror of the Graces* noted, '...an English woman has the extensive privilege of arraying herself in whatever garb may best suit her figure or her fancy. The fashions of every nation and every era are open to her choice. One day she may appear as the Egyptian Cleopatra, then a Grecian Helen, next morning the Roman Cornelia; or if these styles be too august for her taste, there are Sylphs, Goddesses, Nymphs of every region, in earth or air, ready to lend her their wardrobe.'[66] As this suggests, this liberation of the female body and of feminine self-expression was understood in terms of the freedom to appropriate and consume the costume of every land and every age.

In this sense fashion's empire should be seen not only within the context of late eighteenth-century consumption but also of nascent British and French imperialism. For the fashionable woman expressed more than just herself in her appropriation of exotic dress. Her freedom to consume the dress of other countries confirmed Britain's growing international economic and political power, and its proprietary interests in the Middle and Far East. Her dress signalled an increasing awareness of other races and other cultures, and mapped their difference onto her fashionable form. Femininity thus becomes the exotic Other in need of colonisation while the exotic Other becomes feminised and in need of political and economic domination. The mapping of the exotic Other onto the fashionable bodies of women implicitly invited an imperial gaze. A letter dated 1804 to the editor of *The Elegancies of Fashion* recommends with tongue in cheek that given the extreme *décolleté* of women's dresses, ladies take to painting their breasts as celestial and terrestrial globes. In addition to educating gentlemen in geography, the terrestrial globe would appeal especially to military men for 'how delightful an amusement it will be [for them] to point out to the enamored fair one, *upon her own globe*, the different fields of action where they underwent the toils of war'.[67] As this suggests, fashion magazines saw the exotic and the erotic as mutually reinforcing. The body they constructed was mutable, erotically diffuse and thus wholly sexualised: its very lack of libidinal focus was seen as inviting phallic domination.[68] In exotic fashions the cultural Other was subsumed by the more familiar and easily managed feminine Other, and the patriarchal model used to deny women their place in modern commercial society on the basis of sexual difference was extended to the colonial subjects of the British Empire on the basis of racial difference.

Similarly the revival of historical styles of dress signalled an ambivalence about the past and therefore a need to rewrite it through/as fashion. As Benjamin has noted, fashion is a denial of closure: through it the past is continually recycled and endlessly consumed anew. In feminine fashion, history is transformed from a text of specific political events into an image, artefact and style, that is to say into an aesthetic that is trans-historical and universal. British fashion magazines were intent upon depoliticising the classical past

after the period when in France antiquity had been ideologically re-
invested with radical political meaning. The rupture of revolutionary
politics from absolutism in France signalled by the republican
simplicity in masculine and feminine styles of dress, was packaged in
England as a revival of Grecian and Roman modes of costume
emptied of any radical political content. Instead, the revivals of
classical styles of dress were seen in terms of national rivalries:
'France has given her dresses to other nations, but it was reserved for
the Graces of Great Britain to take the lead in Fashion, and show
that, if they do not surpass, they certainly equal the elegance of the
most celebrated Grecian dress.'[69] In March of 1809 *Ackerman's
Repository of the Arts* reported that the Greek style of dress which
liberated so much of the female body was a typically lascivious
French misreading of ancient art: 'the exposure of a fine arm in some
of the draped statues, led them to suppose that the Grecian *belles*
always exposed their arms and shoulders, which was by no means the
case. A Grecian lady *sometimes* suffered her right arm to escape from
its cincture...but this was done occasionally, and in private only, as
when playing on the lyre.'[70] The British woman's refined elegance
and modesty, her superior fashion sense, in short her true femininity
thus becomes the subject of these discussions of classical dress. 'It is
surprising', the essayist for *Ackerman's Repository of the Arts* continued,
'during the frenzy of revolutionizing, that the French, with the
Brutuses and Catos constantly before them, made no efforts to effect
a similar revolution in the male costume.'[71] Revolution now becomes
simply a revolution in feminine fashion. The Grecian and Roman
modes were celebrated in the fashion magazines as the liberation of
the female body and imagination but not as a liberation of the female
body politic. The fashion revolution applauded the British woman's
freedom to consume instead of her freedom to participate in the
political process; in place of her political rights it gave her the
opportunity to 'express' herself.[72]

   In the context of the contemporaneous revolutionary writings of
Mary Wollstonecraft, Mary Ann Radcliffe and numerous anonymous pamphleteers like the author of *An Appeal to the Men of Great
Britain on behalf of Women* (1794) (which urged an extension of
political and legal rights to women), fashion's 'revolution' seems
trivial and tawdry. For in constructing progress as a change in style,
that is as a change in the image repertoire of femininities always/
already culturally constructed, fashion's revolution displaced the

political revolution. In doing so, fashion produced a revolution without change. The fashionable woman became the 'eternal feminine', ever-changing and ever the same. The 'liberation' of the female body at the end of the century from the architectural constraints and excrescences of stays and hoops, and the introduction of a softer more 'body conscious' mode of dressing that draped the female form with the sheerest fabrics and that revealed bare necks, arms and bosoms, emphasised the natural female body as both a sight and a site of sexual difference. Moreover, this 'natural' costume's variety of ever-changing historic and exotic decorative touches mimicked change while containing it within a particular discourse of history as continuity. In addition, it suggested that the exotic is naturally feminine and the feminine is naturally exotic. While celebrating the revolutions in fashion as the progress of civilisation, the fashion magazines also implicitly linked these changes to older ideas of feminine mutability, ideas which reinforced sexual difference and which invited scopophilia and paternalistic domination. Thus the revolution in feminine fashion supplanted the 'revolution in feminine manners' called for by reformers like Wollstonecraft. Their attempts to construct a new woman who would be a free political subject were subsumed by another less threatening and more economically advantageous social subject, the woman as consumer.

While in no way wishing to minimise commercial fashion's collusion with the culture's systematic oppression of women, I would like to suggest how it might also have offered women possibilities for creative and economic activity denied them elsewhere. It is important to note that the emergence of the commercial fashion industry coincides with women's increasing exclusion from institutions of high culture and from the industrialised work place. Fashion provided one of the few aesthetic and professional spaces in which women were allowed to work.[73] While perhaps not capable of producing political change, or of resisting the commodification of the subject under capital, wearing clothes and making clothes may in fact be seen as acts of psychological and economic empowerment.[74] Following from the work of Hans Magnus Enzensberger and Fredric Jameson, one could say that commercial fashion could not have succeeded with women in the way that it did if it had not appealed to real needs and desires, no matter how distorted they may have become when seen reflected back in the mirror of fashion.[75] It is important for instance to observe that at the end of the eighteenth and beginning of the nineteenth centuries the female body was increasingly made the site of cultural struggle. While a woman's property in her own body was never secure it became even less so as liberal political philosophies defining citizens as 'owners' of private property took hold, conferring citizenship on men and not women. The female body was pathologised as medical doctors attempted to professionalise their calling by excluding women practitioners who had specialised in women's health; it was incarcerated in the home and turned over to the production of children, and it became a subject that was off limits to any woman who attempted to become a professional artist. One way in which a woman could take some control over her body was through fashion. The culture's devaluing of fashion as trivial, feminine nonsense was of course a devaluing of this control. Since so many avenues for professional and aesthetic self-expression and economic self-sufficiency were closed to women in the late eighteenth and the nineteenth century, it is important for historians to examine the social functions and meanings of those few occupations and spheres of influence the culture ceded to them. While I cannot embark on such a project here I want nevertheless to recognise its importance. The move from the ideology of fashion to an examination of fashion's place in women's lives has been inhibited by older Marxian critiques of mass culture and avant-garde critiques of 'kitsch'. Yet the potency of such criticism seems increasingly diluted by the fact that as cultural historians we are hard pressed to find examples in the modern period of uncommodified relations or cultural practices. Indeed, commercial fashion and the specular aesthetics of the popular Picturesque may well have been 'feminised' by the late eighteenth century because they so obviously embodied this growing commodification of culture and social relations under capital. Nevertheless, repressed by patriarchy as feminine and Other, commercialised culture has had the disconcerting habit of returning again and again as culture itself.

THE PICTURESQUE AS NATURE AND FASHION TYPE

Fashion's emphasis on the female body as a surface of changing appearances, effects and signs cut against the idea of the body as an expression of inner character or psychological essence. Roy Porter has observed that in the eighteenth century fashion found itself in opposition to the renewed interest in physiognomy. In Britain new translations of pseudo-Aristotle's *Physiognomy*, and the wide-spread dissemination of LeBrun's *Character of the Passions*, Camper's *Dissertation on...the Physiognomy of Men of Diverse Climates*, and Lavater's *Fragments of Physiognomy*, were followed by Dr Gall's publications on phrenology in the early decades of the nineteenth century.[76] The renewed interest in physiognomy should be read as part of the period's preoccupation with the natural sign – that is the sign which bears a transparent relationship to the thing it represents.[77] In the age of sensibility, it was essential that the body be able to be read as a reflection of the soul, that the features of face describe the moral character of the individual and that these natural signs of interior states of being not be obscured by the artifice of make-up or clothing.

Fashion books and magazines took note of the temper of the times and attempted to defend fashion against the accusations that it was nothing more than deception. For their part defenders of fashion insisted on its transparency. In remarking on the fact that dress did not necessarily obscure character, one fashion commentator noted, 'In all cases the mind shines through the body.'[78] In response to the prevailing criticism that rouging falsified the blush, thus simulating feminine modesty where in fact there was none, *The Mirror of the Graces* sought to reassure with the observation that, 'rouging leaves three parts of the face and the whole of the neck and arms to their natural hues. Hence the language of the heart, expressed by the general complexion, is not yet entirely obstructed.'[79] It is within this concern for transparency and the natural sign that one should contextualise the extremely light and revealing dresses of the period – so thin and fine that they could be passed through a wedding ring.[80] Clearly, more than the mind shone through them. Worn over pink tights or sheer slips, these semi-transparent chemises were the cause of the so-called 'muslin disease'. Women would often become seriously ill after immersing themselves fully dressed in a tub and then standing before a fire so that when the gown dried it would cling to their body.[81] Yet despite the defence of fashion's transparency and the naturalising styles of the period, the fashionable woman was suspect, for she was seen as an artificial construction, a persona rather than a person. It was not until the early nineteenth century that there was an attempt to resolve the tension between nature and artifice by mapping physiognomy onto fashion so as to arrive at 'natural' categories of 'fashion types'.

In 1815 Mary Anne Schimmelpenninck published a book on the theory and classification of Beauty and Deformity, in which she developed the idea of the 'fashion type' from the physiognomic theories of Lavater and the aesthetic writings of Burke and the Picturesque theorists.[82] Schimmelpenninck's book is important for our analysis of the Picturesque and fashion, for it attempted to map physical, emotional and fashion types by using the categories of the Sublime, the Beautiful and the Picturesque. Like Price and Gilpin she enlarged the category of the Beautiful to include the Picturesque, for as she explained an 'error consists not in supposing that there is a fixed standard of beauty, but only, in supposing that standard to be one, instead of several'.[83] Her book set out a 'systematically arranged classification of agreeable and disagreeable perceptions' that would 'afford fixed and definite rules for giving characteristic and appropriate expression...[not only] in PAINTING, SCULPTURE, ARCHITECTURE, LANDSCAPE GARDENING, POETRY and other branches of the fine arts and of elegant literature; but which likewise would be of no less constant service, in all those minor departments of good taste, which constitute the agreeable every-day scenery of life,...which the informed intellect and cultivated tastes, as well as the good sense of our British ladies, ought to institute upon the permanent and inexpensive principles of good taste, instead of leaving them to the caprices of desultory fashions...'[84] Her purpose in reconciling fashion to nature was to form and reform the taste of the female consumer by providing her with universal types that she could use as unchanging typological standards in order to judge the vicissitudes of fashion.

In excusing herself from presuming to undertake such a difficult and learned subject, Schimmelpenninck explained that she had studied Lavater as a child, and amused herself by drawing Lavater-like profiles of family and friends and then 'travestying these profiles with every variety of costume'.[85] 'It could not fail,' she wrote, 'to strike the most inattentive eye, that whilst some of them [the costumes] only travestied the individual, so as to completely disguise him; and others produced a burlesque incongruity of appearance; some of them, on the other hand, imparted a new and bold relief to the expression; and...bid the original character start up to light, in all its native magnitude.'[86] Schimmelpenninck's purpose was not to travesty character but to make fashion a transparent sign of it. Unlike Lavater who was concerned with the relationship between humans and animals and with the correspondence between their appearances and their emotional natures, that is to say with the relationship between *natural* phenomena, Schimmelpenninck was concerned with the relationship between character and costume, in other words the relationship between nature and artifice. For as she asked: 'What common point of accordance can exist between dress and countenance, which can possibly afford a basis for any congruity or incongruity between two things of so dissimilar a nature.'[87] The points of accord that she discovered were the three universal types of the 'genus' beauty – the sublime, the sentimental, the sprightly – and the three universal types of the 'genus' deformity which devolved from them – the inflated, the porcine and the flippant. Unlike Lavater's zoomorphic categories of animal types, Schimmelpenninck's aesthetic categories could be applied to both natural and man-made objects. Schimmelpenninck was thus able to track these universal types as they were found expressed in the five senses, moral character, manner, countenance, dress, architecture, sculpture, music, language, writing style, fictitious characters, animals, trees, flowers and shrubs.

While deriving from Burke, her genus of the sublime was divided into two types, the active sublime, characterised by 'force and vigour', 'overwhelming impetuosity' and 'heroic beauty', and the passive sublime, characterised by 'firmness and permanence', 'calm, inextricable power' and 'saintly beauty'.[88] Her category of the sentimental was drawn completely from Burke's and the Picturesque theorists' ideas of the Beautiful for it was 'beautiful', 'flexible', 'weak', 'yielding', 'submissive', 'restful', 'affectionate', 'elegant' and 'graceful', and with 'its parts imperceptibly combined'.[89] In creating her category of the sprightly, Schimmelpenninck explained, in the manner of Price, that because 'the mind of man cannot be always immersed in the enervating softness of the Sentimental, a new class of beauty is elicited, called by the French...piquant; and by us...the pretty, the smart, or Sprightly'.[90] In contrast to the sentimental, therefore, the sprightly was 'pretty', 'versatile', 'various', 'elastic', 'spirited', 'vivacious', 'cheerful', 'lively', 'witty', 'playful', 'brilliant and amusing', with 'its parts numerous and contrasted'.[91] In landscape scenery the sentimental was best represented by Virgil's Grove in the Leasowes, whereas the sprightly was embodied by Italian scenery. While the appearance of the sentimental inspired love, the sprightly inspired amusement. In extending these categories to the human figure, Schimmelpenninck turned them into fashion types. The sentimental type was soft, languorous and uniformly coloured, the sprightly was bright, active and multi-coloured. The hair of the sentimental type was silken and waving while the hair of the sprightly was polished and strongly ringleted; the sentimental eye was soft, liquid, long and not too open, whereas the sprightly eye was sparkling, glancing and full. The dress of the sentimental type was light and limp, falling in graceful folds, its ornaments were few and not glittering. It was best represented by Grecian costume. The dress of the sprightly was made of very light and stiff material, it was short so as not to impede motion, and it abounded in small areas of distinct colours and glittering ornaments. It was best represented by the Highlander's costume or the Harlequin's dress.

The sprightly and its deformation as the flippant recall the character of the Picturesque and of the fashionable woman in both their positive and negative aspects. The sprightly type is 'naturally' piquant and exhibits the characteristics most often prized by Gilpin and Price in a landscape as being various and irregular, as well as by the fashion magazine as belonging to the woman of fashion, who is pretty rather than beautiful, and displays in her dress a taste for smartness, variety and wit. The degeneration of the sprightly into the flippant makes explicit its intrinsic connection to fashion, for then the clever and amusing woman of fashion becomes a vain, hardened creature, a grotesque caricature of her former self. The flippant was characterised by 'caprice', 'affectation', 'tawdry finery', 'vanity', 'restlessness', 'frivolousness', 'pettiness', 'heartless dissipation' and 'coquetry'.[92] The flippant types could be found 'in the pump room at Bath, and in the gardens of the Thuilleries in Paris'; all of them 'aped finery' and their taste in it ran toward the over-loaded and ostentatious.[93] While not limited to women, the flippant was effeminate in that it characterised the 'liveliness of persons of hard hearts, narrow minds, active bodies, capricious tempers, and petty passions'.[94] In short, it was the moral type of the vain, the superficial and the narcissistic, and the only emotion it could inspire was 'contempt'.

Given their love of variety and constant movement, the categories most susceptible to fashion's influence were the sprightly and the flippant. The sublime (in both its forms) and the sentimental seem less easily moved, being either too lofty, too grave or too languid. The fact that the sublime and the sentimental remain apart from fashion suggests that there was room in Schimmelpenninck's system for women to ignore fashion's revolutions. That is to say, both the sublime and sentimental emerge as fashion types without necessarily being fashionable. Unlike *The Mirror of the Graces*, which had assumed there were only two kinds of women, the fashionable woman and her unfashionable sister, and thus encouraged women with pretensions to fashion to experiment on a daily basis with many different styles and personas, Schimmelpenninck urged women to find their fashion type and stick to it in order to avoid the mistakes that can come from following fashion's fluctuations indiscriminately. In advising women to anchor their style of self-presentation in the permanence of their character type, Schimmelpenninck, in effect, attempted to rescue femininity from the charge of instability and fashion from the charge of feminine dissimulation and masquerade. By reconciling fashion to the 'science' of physiognomy she made it both technical and transparent. Her weaving of aesthetics with nature under the signs of physiognomy and the various fashion types was a way to read psychological depth onto artificial surfaces. In a similar way, modern fashion typing calls for a 'scientific' differential distribution of multiple separations and discriminations among individuals.[95] Modern fashion typing is the sorting of women into groups according to body shape, colouring, tastes, professions and, most importantly, personality. It pays homage to the notion of 'individual style' while enforcing standardisation. It acknowledges a variety of consumer fashion types which it addresses through manipulations, not of the basic style, but of its ornamental details. An example would be the mini-skirt of the 1960s which came in a variety of fabrics, colours, textures and detailing: lace for romantics; denim for politicos; leather and fringe for hippies.

Before its commercialisation in the eighteenth century, dress had signalled differences in class, occupation and social status, and sumptuary laws were periodically enforced in order to maintain these distinctions. After the commercialisation of fashion, dress came to signal individual character and sumptuary laws disappeared. This is perhaps fashion's greatest revolution. As a witness to the birth of modern consumer society, the eighteenth century in Britain brought to a close an era of primitive accumulation. In the new urban and urbane commercial culture, where one engaged in the public sphere through economic and intellectual exchange, sociability was valued as much as wealth. Wealth by itself was of no use if it could not also function in the symbolic realm of bourgeois individualism. Fashion is the place where the body and the symbolic intersect, it is the place where society's values become mapped onto the body and become naturalised as the body. Moreover, like the Picturesque, fashion aestheticises nature and naturalises aesthetics. It too is an aesthetic of everyday life. In addition then to sharing the same discourse and mode of visuality emanating from the period's commercialisation of nature and aesthetics, fashion and the Picturesque also shared a tendency to blur the boundaries between nature and aesthetics, between the natural and the symbolic, between essence and appearance. With its recognition of the specular nature of modern culture, its dependence on appearance and on the desire for variety and change, the Picturesque aesthetic provided a paradigm for the commercialisation of aesthetics and the aestheticisation of everyday life. Flugel's theory of the 'Great Masculine Renunciation' speaks to this. For finally what is renounced in the late eighteenth century is the possibility of aestheticising and thus commercialising the male body. In the eighteenth and nineteenth centuries men are men and not 'fashion types', their bodies are not intended to be read aesthetically, nor are they intended to be classed and sorted for the cultural archive. Instead, the archive exists as a point of difference between the seeing and the seen, the knowing and the known.

In dignifying fashion with a veneer of science, Schimmelpenninck did nothing more than what Burke, Gilpin and Price had done with their aesthetic categories. By insisting on the material reality of sublimity, beauty and picturesqueness, they had attempted to place taste on an equally empirical footing. Their materialism was countered, of course, by Kant, Alison and Knight's theories of idealism and associationism. Nevertheless, the tendency to classify objects as beautiful, sublime or picturesque on the basis of their physical characteristics continued throughout the nineteenth century, and, as Schimmelpenninck's treatise suggests, it intersected easily with other such systems of visual and psychological classification. Her particular technology of fashion coincided not only with the revival of popular interest in physiognomy at the end of the eighteenth and the beginning of the nineteenth centuries, but also with a whole constellation of other pseudo-sciences related to it, such as phrenology and craniometry and, more ominously, with the origins of physical anthropology and racial theory. Her work suggests that within fashion's micropolitics of sexual difference, consumerism, exoticism and 'revolution' we may also trace a curious link between the empirical aesthetic theories of the eighteenth century, with their implicit gendering of aesthetics, and the nineteenth century's empirical theories of racial and biological determinism. The de-naturalisation of the body through fashion or, for that matter, through tattooing or mutilation has since the eighteenth century, and until recently, been understood in the West as a violation of the body by culture. Such bodies are inferior, dominated sights of social inscription. Thus the history of commercial fashion in the eighteenth century is also the history of the construction of the 'natural body', of the body that cannot be contained by aesthetics, commerce or culture. It provides us with a starting point to consider the male body that has hidden from the cultural gaze, thus remaining mysterious and potent. It is this body, of course, that we have only just begun to see and to know.

NOTES

1 Paul H. Nystrom, *Economics of Fashion* (New York: Ronald Press Company, 1928), pp. 479–81. Quoted in Elizabeth Wilson, *Adorned in Dreams: Fashion and Modernity* (Berkeley and Los Angeles: University of California Press, 1985), p. 124.

2 Neil McKendrick, John Brewer and J. H. Plumb, *The Birth of a Consumer Society: The Commercialization of Eighteenth-Century England*, (London: Europa, 1982). In particular, see McKendrick's informative chapter on 'The Commercialization of Fashion', pp. 34–99.

3 William Gilpin, *Observations on Several Parts of the Counties of Cambridge, Norfolk, Suffolk and Essex. Also Several Parts of North Wales Relative Chiefly to Picturesque Beauty...* (London, 1809), pp. 15–16.

4 William Gilpin, *Three Essays: On Picturesque Beauty; On Picturesque Travel; and On Sketching Landscape* (London, 1792), pp. 49–50.

5 See his *Observations on the River Wye... Relative Chiefly to Picturesque Beauty; Made in the Summer of the Year 1770* (London, 1782), pp. 10–14, as well as his organisation of the two volumes of *Remarks on Forest Scenery* (London, 1791).

6 Gilpin, *Observations on the River Wye*, p. 24.

7 Gilpin, *Three Essays*, p. 26.

8 Gilpin, *Forest Scenery*. See books 1 and 2 of volume 1.

9 Gilpin, *Three Essays*, p. 26. Gilpin's concessions to Reynolds can be found in his broadly sketched wash drawings rather than in his actual descriptions of landscape which, by contrast, are quite Picturesque in their attention to detail. In the first decade of the nineteenth century, as the Picturesque aesthetic came to dominate the perception of landscape, Gilpin's drawing style was attacked as the inept bungling of an

insensitive generaliser by younger drawing masters. On this subject see
my 'System, Order, and Abstraction: the Aesthetics of Landscape
Drawing Around 1800', in *The Power of Landscape*, ed. W. J. T. Mitchell,
(University of Chicago Press, forthcoming).

10 Quoted in William Gilpin, *Three Essays*, pp. 34–5.

11 It should be noted that Gilpin's attempt to define the Picturesque, and
this is true in a lesser degree of Uvedale Price too, emerges not so much
from a coherent theory, despite his efforts in the *Three Essays*, but rather
from the examination of a variety of natural landscape scenes. His rather
loose grip on abstract thinking led him to dismiss as unimportant the
theoretical controversy surrounding the origin of the Picturesque. While
Price claimed that picturesqueness was a quality innate to certain scenes
and objects, Richard Payne Knight believed that the experience of
picturesqueness arose in the mind as the result of certain mental and
emotional associations. With a mental wave of the hand Gilpin dismissed
such wrangling, observing that, 'inquiries into *principles* rarely end in
satisfaction...enough has been said to shew the difficult of *assigning
causes*: let us then take another course, and amuse ourselves with *searching
after effects*' (*Three Essays*, pp. 30, 41). His remark is significant for it
demonstrates not only how important 'effects' were to the Picturesque,
but also how much his own understanding of the Picturesque derived not
from a theoretical overview but from a visual examination of particulars.

12 Gilpin, *Observations on the River Wye*, p. 44.

13 James Plumptre, *The Lakers: A Comic Opera in Three Acts* (London, 1798),
p. 19.

14 *Ibid.*, p. 59.

15 See Gilpin's 'Dialogue on the Advantages of a Town Life and a Country
Life Compared', in *Dialogues on Various Subjects* (London, 1807), pp.
146–82.

16 Jane Austen, *Pride and Prejudice*, ed. R. W. Chapman (Oxford University
Press, 1982), p. 154.

17 The term is Plumptre's and was first pointed out to me by Peter Bicknell
many years ago. On Plumptre see Bicknell, *The Picturesque Scenery of the
Lake District 1752–1855: A Bibliographical Study* (Winchester and Detroit:
St Paul's Bibliographies, 1990); and Malcolm Andrews, *The Search for the
Picturesque: Landscape Aesthetics and Tourism in Britain, 1760–1800* (Alder-
shot: Scolar Press, 1989), p. 67.

18 These are items selected by Plumptre for his own 'pedestrian journeys'.
See Bicknell, *Picturesque Scenery*, p. 39.

19 On these subjects as well as on Picturesque touring in general see Esther
Moir, *The Discovery of Britain* (London: Routledge and Kegan Paul,
1964).

20 Uvedale Price, *On the Picturesque, with an Essay on the Origin of Taste*, ed. Sir
Thomas Dick Lauder, Bart (Edinburgh, 1842), p. 92.

21 *Ibid.*

22 On this subject see my *Landscape and Ideology: The English Rustic Tradition, 1740–1860* (Berkeley and Los Angeles: University of California Press, 1986), pp. 57–73.

23 Gilpin, *An Essay on Prints* (London, 1768), p. 2; and Uvedale Price, *A Dialogue on the Distinct Characteristics of the Picturesque and the Beautiful* (London, 1801), pp. 15–16.

24 Price, *On the Picturesque*, p. 79. Because it privileged both vision and an unconventional sense of beauty the Picturesque became a subject of controversy when, as Jonathan Crary has described it, the model of vision shifted from a disembodied objective mode of seeing to an embodied subjective mode of perception. This shift is anticipated in the paper war between Uvedale Price, who embraced the Burkean notion of vision which was largely objective, and Richard Payne Knight, who shared Archibald Alison's notions of subjective associationism. Given the importance of this debate for nineteenth-century aesthetics generally, it is surprising that Crary does not mention it. Instead he locates the origin of the new mode of vision in later nineteenth-century, Continental theories of vision and optics. See Crary, *Techniques of the Observer: On Vision and Modernity in the Nineteenth Century* (Cambridge, Mass. and London: M.I.T. Press, 1990).

25 J. C. Flugel, *The Psychology of Clothes* (London: Hogarth Press, 1930), p. 111.

26 Kaja Silverman, 'Fragments of a Fashionable Discourse', in *Studies in Entertainment: Critical Approaches to Mass Culture*, ed. Tania Modleski (Bloomington and Indianapolis: Indiana University Press, 1986), pp. 139–52.

27 *Ibid.*, p. 147.

28 Flugel, *Psychology of Clothes*, p. 113.

29 The aesthetics of eighteenth- and nineteenth-century corsetry turned on an image of the female body as essentially boneless, made to be trussed and squeezed into shape by various kinds of 'foundations'. It was only after the discovery of x-rays (1895), when the fact of ribs and their deformation by corsets could be proven beyond a doubt, that the movement to reform female dress for health reasons succeeded in gaining public attention. On the corset see David Kunzle's *Fashion and Fetishism* (Totowa, New Jersey: Rowman and Littlefield, 1982).

30 See Silverman, 'Fragments', pp. 148–9. In his essay 'Femininity' (1933), Freud acknowledged that the process of becoming feminine was a complicated one and that 'true' femininity was perhaps never fully achieved. Femininity's instability is imaged in fashion's ever-changing construction of the female body. See Sigmund Freud, 'Femininity', *New Introductory Lectures on Psychoanalysis* (Harmondsworth: Penguin, 1973).

31 A little discussed project of Jacques Louis David's is his design for a civilian uniform for the French. In May 1794 the Convention gave David the task of 'presenting it with his views and proposals on how to

improve the present national costume, adapting it to the republican way of life and to the character of the revolution'. Several watercolour designs for this uniform can be found today in the Musée Carnavelet.

32 Plumptre, *The Lakers*, p. 20.

33 Flugel, *Psychology of Clothes*, p. 118.

34 *Ibid.*

35 *Ibid.* Freud connected scopophilia to the sexual drive and saw it as perverted only when it was restricted exclusively to the genitals, when it was connected with overriding disgust and when it supplanted the normal sexual aim (see Sigmund Freud, *Three Essays on the Theory of Sexuality* (1905), New York: Basic Books, 1975, pp. 22–3). Insofar as in Freudian analysis this fetishism or voyeurism stems from an Oedipal curiosity and anxiety about the presence or the absence of the penis, this gaze is gendered as male. When it takes the place of sex, scopophilia is connected to the compulsion to exhibit the penis which, Freud noted, was 'a means of constantly insisting upon the integrity of the subject's own (male) genitals and it reiterates his infantile satisfaction at the absence of a penis in those of women' (*Three Essays*, from a note added in 1920, p. 23). Moreover, scopophilia, Freud believed, can sublimate sex in the direction of art by shifting attention away from the genitals onto the body as a whole (*Three Essays*, p. 22). Scopophilia thus lent itself to an aestheticisation of the object of vision. When focused on the genitals and connected with an excessive disgust and fear of castration, scopophilia could lead to the fetishisation and/or voyeuristic objectification of the object of vision (Freud, 'Instincts and their Vicissitudes' (1915), in *Collected Papers of Sigmund Freud*, 5 vols. (London: Hogarth Press, 1925–50), vol. IV, p. 60).

36 W. and R. A. Austen-Leigh (eds.), *Jane Austen: Her Life and Letters, A Family Record* (New York, 1913), pp. 129 and 308.

37 See James Thompson, 'Jane Austen's Clothing: Things, Property, and Materialism in Her Novels', *Eighteenth-Century Life*, 7 (1981), 218.

38 Daniel Defoe, *Everybody's Business is Nobody's Business* (1725), quoted by Neil McKendrick in 'The Commercialization of Fashion', in McKendrick, Brewer and Plumb, *Birth of Consumer Society*, p. 59.

39 *Lady's Monthly Museum* (December 1798), p. 475.

40 *Ibid.*, p. 477.

41 *Ibid.*

42 See Thompson, 'Jane Austen's Clothing', p. 219.

43 There is evidence that many literary women, unlike Austen, resisted fashion even in their private lives. There is a great deal of discussion in the periodical literature of the late eighteenth century about the disagreeable singularity of dress and general slovenliness of 'literary ladies'. For instance, the anonymous author of *The Mirror of the Graces; or the English Lady's Costume* (London, 1811) warns her readers that 'there is a race of women, who priding themselves on their superior rank, or

wealth, or talents affect to despise what they deem the Adventitious aids of dress. Their appearances, in consequence, are frequently as ridiculous as disgusting. When this folly is seen in female authors, or, what is much the same thing, ladies professing a particularly literary taste, we can at once trace its motive. A conceited neglegence of outward attractions, and a determination to raise themselves in the opinions of men, by displaying a contempt for what they deem the vain occupations of meaner sorts' (pp. 64–5).

44 Jane Austen, *Northanger Abbey*, ed. R. W. Chapman (Oxford University Press, 1980), pp. 73–4.

45 For more information on 'The Commercialization of Fashion', see McKendrick in McKendrick, Brewer and Plumb, *Birth of Consumer Society*, pp. 34–98.

46 *Ackerman's Repository of the Arts*, vol. III (March 1809), p. 187.

47 E. P. Thompson, *The Making of the English Working Class* (new edition, Harmondsworth: Penguin, 1968); John Foster, *Class Struggle and the Industrial Revolution* (London: Weidenfeld and Nicolson, 1974); Chandra Mukerji, *From Graven Images: Patterns of Modern Materialism* (New York: Columbia University Press, 1983); and Grace Lovat Fraser, *Textiles by Britain* (London: George Allen and Unwin: 1948).

48 With the exception of Alan MacFarlane's *Marriage and Love in England 1300–1840* (Oxford: Basil Blackwell, 1986), little has been done in the way of a cultural analysis of the eighteenth-century marriage market. Most work on marriage patterns and markets has been done by demographers interested in nineteenth-century patterns of age, income, fertility and geographical distribution. For example see R. I. Woods and P. R. Andrew Hinde, 'Nuptiality and Age at Marriage in Nineteenth-Century England', *Journal of Family History*, 10 (1985), 126; P. R. Andrew Hinde and E. M. Garrett, 'Work Patterns, Marriage and Fertility in Late Nineteenth-Century England', in Richard M. Smith (ed.), *Regional and Spatial Demographic Patterns in the Past*, forthcoming.

49 Walter Benjamin, *Charles Baudelaire: A Lyric Poet in the Era of High Capitalism*, trans. Harry Zorn (London: New Left Books, 1973), p. 55.

50 *Mirror de la Mode* (April 1803), p. 29.

51 Susan Staves, *Married Women's Separate Property in England, 1660–1833* (Cambridge University Press, 1990), pp. 131–61.

52 The fear was that pin money would make a married woman independent, thus laws governing its expenditure and women's property tended to turn on definitions of what could be said to constitute feminine 'paraphernalia'. Usually this was defined as a wife's clothes and personal ornaments. See Staves, *Married Women's Property*, pp. 147–57.

53 Gilpin, *Dialogues on Various Subjects*, p. 152.

54 See Susan Buck-Morss, *The Dialectics of Seeing: Walter Benjamin and the Arcades Project* (Cambridge, Mass.: M.I.T. Press, 1989), p. 97.

55 *Ibid.*, pp. 95–6.

56 On this topic see Edward W. Said, *Beginnings: Intention and Method* (New York: Basic Books, 1975).

57 On revivals of clothing styles see Arleen Ribero, 'Dress Worn at Masquerades in England, 1730 to 1790, and Its Relation to Fancy Dress in Portraiture', Ph.D. thesis submitted to the University of London and Courtauld Institute of Art, 1975; C. W. and P. Cunnington, *Handbook of English Costume in the Eighteenth Century* (Philadelphia: Dufour Editions, 1957); and Edward Maeder, *An Elegant Art: Fashion and Fancy in the Eighteenth Century*, Exhibition Catalogue, Los Angeles County Museum of Art, New York, 1983.

58 Florio Honeysuckle, *The Elegancies of Fashion and General Remembrancer of Taste and Manners or Imperial Record of Painting, Music, Elegant Literature, the Theatre Costume and Arts Conductive to the Ornament or Amusement of Polished Life* (March 1804), pp. 2–4.

59 *Ibid.* (April 1804), p. 23.

60 *Ibid.* (May 1804), p. 37.

61 *Ibid.* (July 1804), p. 70.

62 *Ibid.* (July 1804), p. 69.

63 *Mirror de la Mode* (April 1803), pp. 45–6.

64 *The Mirror of the Graces*, pp. 26–7.

65 *Ackerman's* vol. III (March 1809), p. 171.

66 *The Mirror of the Graces*, pp. 59–60.

67 *The Elegancies of Fashion* (March 1804), p. 13.

68 On the diffuseness of the sexual libido in women see Flugel *Psychology of Clothes* (p. 106) and also Silverman 'Fragments' (pp. 147–8).

69 Nicholas Heideloff, *The Gallery of Fashion*, 2 (1795), n.p.

70 *Ackerman's* vol. III (March 1809), p. 171.

71 *Ibid.*, p. 171.

72 This is a paraphrase from Walter Benjamin's 'The Work of Art in the Age of Mechanical Reproduction', in *Illuminations*, ed. Hannah Arendt (New York: Shocken, 1969), p. 241.

73 See McKendrick's 'Commercialization of Fashion', in McKendrick, Brewer and Plumb, *Birth of Consumer Society*. See also David Alexander, *Retailing in England during the Industrial Revolution* (London: Athlone Press, 1970), and Bridget Hill, *Women, Work, and Sexual Politics in Eighteenth-Century England* (Oxford: Basil Blackwell, 1989).

74 While I believe fashion can be a means of expression and self-empowerment, I do not see these individual and collective acts of expression and empowerment outside the frame of commercialisation and commodification. This is not to say that they merely maintain the status quo, they may in fact change it; nevertheless, they do not overturn it. Just as they are acts that signal a cultural and economic situation that precludes certain kinds of political future (a proletarian revolution) they are acts that also preclude the possibility of certain forms of political oppression (fascism and totalitarianism). In this sense, I take issue with

Benjamin's, Horkheimer's and Adorno's critiques of consumer culture. On the topic of cultural resistance and fashion see Stuart Hall and Tony Jefferson (eds.), *Resistance through Rituals: Youth Subcultures in Post-War Britain* (London: Hutchinson, 1979); Dick Hebdige, *Subculture: The Meaning of Style* (London: Routledge, 1979).

75 Hans Magnus Enzensberger, *The Consciousness Industry: On Literature, Politics, and the Media* (New York: Seabury, 1974); Fredric Jameson, 'Reification and Utopia in Mass Culture', *Social Text*, 1 (1979), 130–48.

76 Roy Porter, 'Making Faces: Physiognomy and Fashion in Eighteenth-Century England', *Etudes Anglaises*, No. 4 (October–December, 1985), 385–96. See too Jurgis Baltrusaitis, on animal physiognomy in *Aberrations: Essai sur la légende des formes* (Paris: Flammarion, 1983), pp. 10–52.

77 On the construction of the natural sign in this period and its political implications, see my 'System, Order, and Abstraction', in *The Power of Landscape*, ed. W. J. T. Mitchell (University of Chicago Press, forthcoming).

78 *The Mirror of the Graces*, p. 50.

79 *Ibid.*, p. 52.

80 Flugel, *Psychology of Clothes*, p. 158.

81 Bill Cunningham, *Facades* (Harmondsworth: Penguin Books, 1978), p. 27.

82 Mary Anne Schimmelpenninck, *Theory on the Classification of Beauty and Deformity* (London, 1815). This book was followed forty-four years later by another published posthumously, *The Principles of Beauty as Manifested in Nature, Art, and Human Character, with a Classification of Deformities. An Essay on the Temperaments with Illustrations, and Thoughts on Grecian and Gothic Architecture*, ed. Christiana C. Hankin (London, 1859).

83 Schimmelpenninck, *Theory*, p. 6.

84 *Ibid.*, p. iv.

85 *Ibid.*, p. vi.

86 *Ibid.*

87 *Ibid.*

88 *Ibid.*, pp. 23–30.

89 *Ibid.*, pp. 30–3.

90 *Ibid.*, p. 33.

91 *Ibid.*, pp. 33–5.

92 *Ibid.*, charts 1 and 2, np.

93 *Ibid.*, chart 1, np.

94 *Ibid.*, chart 2, np.

95 On this subject as it relates to early twentieth-century retailing, in particular the standardisation of sizes and styles, see Nystrom, *Economics of Fashion*, pp. 452–81.

CHAPTER 5

'The coquetry of nature': politics and the Picturesque in women's fiction

Vivien Jones

The political significance of women's fiction in the decades following the French Revolution has now been firmly established. Current feminist work in the area is concerned to define the complex relationships between fictional form and cultural change: to explore, in other words, the overdetermined politics of plot.[1] Through an analysis of the sexual/textual politics of writings on the Picturesque, this essay will, I hope, contribute to that larger project. Using Mary Wollstonecraft's critique of the (Burkean) 'libertine imagination'[2] as a starting-point, I shall be examining ways in which three novels by women negotiate the voyeuristic gaze: the gaze through which, in other contexts, the Picturesque aesthetic exerts its uncertain control over landscape and property. The novels I have chosen represent a particular variant on the familiar identification of property – and particularly the country house – with women. Within the Picturesque therefore, my main concern is with the domesticated Picturesque of landscape gardening rather than the peripatetic quests of Gilpin and his imitators, and thus with the points at which the 'Picturesque' intersects with the 'Gothic', understood both as a narrative mode and as a discourse combining issues of aesthetics, erotics and history.[3]

My fictional paradigm is the romance topos of the socially marginal heroine, discovered in an isolated rural house, subjected metonymically to 'improvement' and eventually revealed as true heir, either actually or metaphorically, to the estate. In the revolutionary and post-revolutionary period, this class-resonant motif becomes particularly charged: like the well-documented controversy between Uvedale Price, Humphry Repton and Richard Payne Knight on landscape gardening, stories of discovery, improvement and inheritance are figurative participants in contemporary political crises.[4] Charlotte Smith's *The Old Manor House* and Sydney Morgan's *The*

Wild Irish Girl are about the historical definition and future inheritance of the nation – as, of course, is Jane Austen's rewriting of the same plot paradigm in *Mansfield Park*.

A set of flexibly analogous signifiers – woman/estate/nature/ nation – underlies the polemical import of both Picturesque theory and the novels. Of these, 'woman' has received scant attention, at least in discussions of the Picturesque. The writings of Price and Payne Knight are concerned to naturalise and fix the country house in the face of political instability, and various recent commentaries have analysed the class and party allegiances implicit in their project. By comparison, the gendered politics of desire in these texts are frequently noted, but never fully explored. In theories of the Picturesque, anxieties about private property and national identity are articulated in terms of voyeurism and sexual possession.[5] My three novels reproduce a version of the Picturesque's structure of desire/knowledge, but to increasingly subversive effect as their heroines move outside that objectifying frame.

But before turning to the fiction, I want to draw on recent political readings of the Picturesque in order to develop an idea of it as a manifestation of a crisis of libertinism, and to explore the culturally transitional texts of the second generation of Picturesque writers in terms of their shifting definitions of masculinity.

For Gilpin's Picturesque traveller, nature is the primary object:

The love of novelty is the foundation of this pleasure. Every distant horizon promises something new; and with this pleasing expectation we follow nature through all her walks. We pursue her from hill to dale; and hunt after those various beauties, with which she every where abounds.[6]

It is the 'formal separations of property – the houses, and towns' which 'disgust'.[7] In the work of Uvedale Price and Richard Payne Knight on landscape gardens, however, Gilpin's erotic chase is brought within the sphere of private ownership. Rather than being pursued, nature is reproduced for private consumption, and Picturesque features are used to minimise precisely those 'formal separations of property' which underwrite their production.[8] This becomes most explicit in Knight's poem *The Landscape* where property, specifically the country house, is justified through a naturalising act of substitution. In the following passage, the object of desire finally revealed by the landscape's seductive charms is not, as

in Gilpin, female nature's 'various beauties', but 'the stately
mansion':

> But still in careless easy curves proceed,
> Through the rough thicket or the flow'ry mead;
> Till bursting from some deep-imbower'd shade,
> Some narrow valley, or some op'ning glade,
> Well mix'd and blended in the scene, you shew
> The stately mansion rising to the view.[9]

There is an obvious tension here between the pleasure of surprise
('bursting') and a rhetoric of control and containment ('shew';
'stately'; 'Well mix'd and blended'). Desire itself, Gilpin's 'love of
novelty', is under threat in a managed landscape.

To that extent, the passage provides a neat illustration of Kim Ian
Michasiw's important concern with distinctions within Picturesque
discourse: specifically, between Gilpin 'the disempowered traveler'
and the proprietorial 'drive to mastery' in the work of the second-
generation improvers Price and Payne Knight. Difference of economic status, Michasiw argues, manifests itself in 'the *seductiveness* of
the landscape': 'The landowner inevitably perceives his land as
subject to him, as an extension of himself – the fiction of ownership
banishes the otherness of the land and subsumes the figures on that
land under legal categories: tenant, hireling, trespasser, poacher'.[10]
One legal category absent from this list is 'wife' – and necessarily so,
since to maintain itself as a state of 'novelty', 'curiosity', 'irritation',[11] the domesticated Picturesque must disrupt domesticity:
for desire and pleasure to survive, 'the otherness of the land'
(including its buildings) must be perpetuated, if only in fantasy.
Sidney K. Robinson's recent characterisation of the Picturesque in
terms of an 'underutilization of... power' is perhaps more useful here
than the idea of a straightforward 'drive to mastery'.[12] For at the
level of erotic discourse, it is less possible, because less stimulating, for
the Picturesque improving landowner to perceive the land as, in
Michasiw's phrase, 'an extension of himself': a tantalising distance
must be maintained between viewer and object, desire and attainment, a distance symptomatic of the Picturesque's flight from the
'tyranny of beauty'.[13] Within the dominant Burkean system of
gendered aesthetic categories, the figure of the wife is, of course,
associated with the Beautiful, with the sphere of custom, comfort,
familiarity – and submission: the equivalent, perhaps, of the 'stately

mansion' which *fails* to 'burst' on the viewer. The type of femininity imagined as the object of Picturesque desire must be less respectable, less legally categorisable – but also, potentially, less biddable.

This other femininity is particularly evident in a passage later in *The Landscape*, in which Knight rejects neo-classical follies as unsuitable in an English garden:

> Such buildings English nature must reject,
> And claim for art th'appearance of neglect:
> No decoration should we introduce,
> That has not first been nat'ralized by use;
> And at the present, or some distant time,
> Become familiar to the soil and clime:
> For as the cunning nymph, with giddy care,
> And wanton wiles, conceals her study'd air;
> And each acquired grace of fashion tries
> To hide in nature's negligent disguise;
> While with unseen design and cover'd art
> She charms the sense, and plays around the heart:
> So ev'ry pleasing object more will please,
> As less th'observer its intention sees;
> But thinks it form'd for use, and plac'd by chance
> Within the limits of his transient glance.[14]

The nationalistic argument in favour of native Gothic ruins rather than incongruous classical follies was already familiar within landscape theory. In this particular passage, however, Knight is more equivocal than has sometimes been suggested.[15] The argument shifts from the demand that these unnecessary landscape features are only allowable if 'nat'ralized by use' to the suggestion that they need only *appear* 'form'd for use' – indeed, that the pleasure they give depends on such deception. 'English nature' is what is at stake in this passage, defined through an idiosyncratic version of the familiar middle way: the deceptive combination of use with pleasure becomes a way of transforming ('claiming' is Knight's term), rather than straightforwardly rejecting, the threat posed at a time of national crisis by irresponsible luxury and exotic taste. The type of femininity evoked to embody this ambiguous mixture of indigenous usefulness and foreign beauty is the 'cunning nymph', who 'charms the sense' through 'wanton wiles' and 'cover'd art'. According to standard ideologies of femininity, this fantasy figure is an impossible mixture of innocence and knowledge, naturalness and artifice.[16] Nevertheless, within the larger nationalist argument of the poem, she has the status of an ideal, and I want to define the implications of this sexual fantasy by reading it against the poem's wider political context.

The identification of second-generation Picturesque theorists with Foxite liberalism is now firmly established; both Liu and Robinson have recently demonstrated the way in which the 'true Whiggish liberty' figured in the work of both Knight and Price could be read by a conservative contemporary audience as 'the Jacobinism of taste'.[17] This partisan label should not, however, be allowed to obscure the more conservative allegiances within the broad church of Whig reformism – or within Picturesque theory.

The Landscape is certainly a poem haunted and fascinated by the French Revolution. Essentially sympathetic, it deals with the Terror by breaking down at the end into a long footnote in which Knight speculates with prescient pessimism on the likely outcome of events. The poem argues optimistically that 'from these horrors, future times may see / Just order spring, and genuine liberty'; the footnote foresees a military dictatorship, brought about largely by the Pitt government's war policy, which will 'endanger the very existence of civilized society'.[18] By way of defence and warning against such a threat, the poem celebrates traditional English landscape as 'the seat of native liberty'. The studied negligence of the Picturesque is set against the ruthless authority of improvers; the 'various shapes' of the 'rich, high-clustering oak' against the 'haughty bows' of the foreign cedar, 'image apt of man's despotic power'.[19] It is a mistake, I think, to identify this image of despotism exclusively with the *ancien régime*.[20] The poem's Whig ideal of 'native liberty' works more flexibly, and consequently has a less confident identity, than that. It is primarily the accommodating alternative to 'man's despotic power' in any form: the *ancien régime*; the 'military democratic despotism'[21] of the Revolutionary government; the collusive rigidity of Tory war policy; – or the bourgeois commodification of Picturesque taste itself. And the exclusive, elusive mode of femininity used in the passage above to represent that accommodating ideal betrays a more anxious element in Knight's apparently confident celebration of 'native liberty': '[W]ith unseen design ... / She charms the sense', threatening loss of control.

For Price, liberty is similarly 'unconstrained' – and undefined:

A good landscape is that in which all the parts are free and unconstrained . . . . I do not see how a good government can be more exactly defined; and as this definition suits every style of landscape, from the plainest and simplest to the most splendid and complicated, and excludes nothing but tameness and confusion, so it equally suits all free governments, and only excludes anarchy and despotism. It must be always remembered however, that despotism is the most complete leveller; and he who clears and levels every thing round his own lofty mansion, seems to me to have very Turkish principles of improvement.[22]

Later, in the *Letter to Repton*, which draws on Knight's poem, Price objects to Repton's mechanical identification of standard landscape gardening with the constitution:

That the English constitution is the happy medium between the liberty of savages and the restraint of despotic government, I do not merely acknowledge, – I feel it with pride and exultation; but that pride and exultation would sink into shame and despondency, should the parallel between it and modern gardening ever become just; should the freedom, energy, and variety of our minds give place to tameness and monotony; should our opinions be prescribed to us, and they like our places be moulded into one form.[23]

It is not simply the 'cold monotony' of Capability Brown's artificial 'belts and clumps' (which Repton had defended) that is under attack here: more generally, Price rejects any kind of levelling consensus, or 'prescribed' opinions. His own Picturesque aesthetic translates into an anti-interventionist political model which is more dynamic in its attention to change, but also, as Ann Bermingham has pointed out, more élitist.[24] Dependent on 'accident and neglect [as] two principal causes of those beauties', and rejecting the predictable taste of 'false ideas of refinement' in favour of 'natural judgment',[25] it is a model no less concerned than Repton's formulation with a middle way, but which stresses individualism and accommodation – 'freedom, energy, and variety' – rather than static compromise. In terms of gardening practice, it presupposes an estate old enough to show the effects of accident and neglect in the first place: 'the rash hand of false taste completely demolishes what time only, and a thousand lucky accidents, can mature'.[26] This is a standard of taste – and a political position – dependent not on money, but on the cumulative effects of time, a defence of exclusivity against commodification.

At the level of aesthetic theory, Price's concern with process, accommodation and flexibility represents a rejection of Burke's static

aesthetic categories; but read politically, this stress on the accumulation of effects through time has much in common with the
Burke of the *Reflections on the Revolution in France*, with its rejection of
the abstract mechanisms, the 'sophisters, oeconomists, and calcu-
lators', of Revolutionary government.[27] It is certainly true, as Alan
Liu argues, that Repton's attack on Price's Picturesque, and
particularly his suggestion that 'experiments of untried theoretical
improvement be made in some other country', shows 'the clear
influence of Burke's *Reflections*'.[28] It is nevertheless equally true that
Price's counter-attack on the 'tameness and monotony' threatened
by Repton works from the same Burkean hatred of system. This is
Burke, in a striking echo of Price on 'false taste':

> it is with infinite caution that any man ought to venture upon pulling down
> an edifice which has answered in any tolerable degree for ages the common
> purposes of society.[29]

And this is Burke on government and liberty flourishing through, in
Price's terms, 'accident and neglect' rather than the 'rash hand' of
impertinent intervention:

> the great principles of government... the ideas of liberty... were understood
> long before we were born, altogether as well as they will be after the grave
> has heaped its mould upon our presumption, and the silent tomb shall have
> imposed its law on our pert loquacity.[30]

This appeal to an organic ideal of liberty and government as the
mature products of historical process ('At once to preserve and to
reform'[31]) is again closely echoed by Price. Immediately following his
remarks, quoted above, on Repton's definition of the constitution,
Price offers a corrective analogy between politics and painting:

> A much apter and more instructive parallel might have been drawn
> between our constitution and the art you have so much wronged. That art,
> like the old feudal government, meagre, hard, and gothic in its beginning,
> was mellowed and softened by long experience and successive trial and not
> less improved in spirit and energy. Such was the progress of our constitution,
> such is its character....[32]

A focus on particular controversies emphasises the antagonism
between Burkean and Picturesque politics: Knight was attacked in
the *Anti-Jacobin*, for example, and both Price and Knight opposed

Burke on the question of war with France. But immediate differences do not erase a deeper ideological alliance, based in class allegiance and 'Country' values, and manifest in a shared sexual politics.

In her *Vindication of the Rights of Men*, Mary Wollstonecraft identifies Burke's 'libertine imagination'[33] as both symptom and cause of his wider political position. Reading Burke's politics through his aesthetic theory, she locates a degraded femininity – 'spurious, sensual beauty' – as the object of desire motivating not simply Burke's sexual chivalric ideal, but also the 'gothic notions of beauty'[34] which determine his defence of traditional institutions:

> Is hereditary weakness necessary to render religion lovely? and will her form have lost the smooth delicacy that inspires love, when stripped of its Gothic drapery? Must every grand model be placed on the pedestal of property? and is there no beauteous proportion in virtue, when not clothed in a sensual garb?
>
> Of these questions there would be no end, though they lead to the same conclusion; – that your politics and morals, when simplified, would undermine religion and virtue to set up a spurious, sensual beauty, that has long debauched your imagination, under the specious form of natural feelings.[35]

Wollstonecraft's crucial recognition is that sexual ideologies are central to other modes of power. Burke's betrayal of Whig values is attributed to a 'debauched', aristocratic masculinity, whose falsifying aesthetic sacrifices liberty on 'the pedestal of property'. 'Gothic', used as a recurrent term of abuse, both evokes and condemns a particular way of reading history: it describes the political taste which prefers Picturesque British traditions to rational principles in an aestheticised legitimation of existing political structures; at the same time, it rejects such taste as itself barbaric, obfuscating and, significantly, outmoded.[36] The convenient libertine identification of women with 'beautiful weakness', which avoids the 'tinctured' affection which rational respect would involve, is seen by Wollstonecraft as continuous with the landowner's 'disgust' at 'the distresses of poverty', which he avoids by building 'sweeping pleasure-grounds, obelisks, temples, and elegant cottages, as *objects* for the eye'. And in a startling rereading of the feminised landscape, Burke's whole political structure becomes just 'another Chinese erection', an object of ridicule to Wollstonecraft's female view and that of 'the plain country people...who bluntly call such an airy edifice, a folly'.[37]

Wollstonecraft's critical method, her use of sexual politics to define other political allegiances, as well as the historically specific terms of her critique, can be readily applied to the modified Burkean discourses of Picturesque writings. In Picturesque texts, as we have seen, landscape is used for a more orthodox Whig celebration of liberty, but in erotic terms which make Wollstonecraft's focus on the 'libertine imagination' equally pertinent.

According to Price, the Picturesque connoisseur is motivated by 'irritation' and a 'curiosity' which the 'intricacy' of landscape *excites and nourishes*', a form of pleasure which Price glosses by sexual analogy: 'Many persons... may feel the effects of partial concealment in more interesting objects, and may have experienced how differently the passions are moved by an open licentious display of beauties, and by the unguarded disorder which sometimes escapes the care of modesty, and which coquetry so successfully imitates...'[38] Again, as in Knight, the difference between the 'unguarded' modest woman and the knowing coquette who successfully imitates her is minimised. Sexual sophistication masquerades as artlessness, and the knowing libertine gaze effectively dismisses the bourgeois values it claims to respect by turning them through deceptive imitation to sheer aesthetic effect. In a later passage, the anti-bourgeois, anti-commercial significance of this economy of desire for new sensations becomes more explicit. Price rejects Brown's 'clumps' both for their reproducible uniformity – they are 'as like each other as so many puddings turned out of one common mould' – and because they resist or, worse, do not even invite, penetration. 'Natural groups', in contrast, are full of tantalising 'openings and hollows': 'all deep coves, hollows, and fissures (such as are usually found in this style of scenery) invite the eye to penetrate into their recesses, yet keep its curiosity *alive, and unsatisfied...*' [my emphasis].[39]

Carole Fabricant has argued that the sexual and political ideology articulated in eighteenth-century writings on landscape is essentially one of control: like the relationship between painter and model it is 'rooted in the distinction between capturer and captured, definer and defined', so that within the privacy of the garden, even nature's 'hidden retreats' are available to be penetrated and known by her owner.[40] This is not so clearly true of the Picturesque, where, at the level of fantasy, the consummation of ownership is perpetually denied. '[A]ctive curiosity' is maintained by an always elusive object of desire, and this irritable seeking after sensation produces a voyeuristic consumption of landscape, a soft-porn aesthetics some-

where between the predictable pleasures of beauty and the debili-
tatingly uncontrollable power of the Sublime: the Picturesque

is the coquetry of nature; it makes beauty more amusing, more varied, more
playful, but also,
    'Less winning soft, less amiably mild.'
Again, by its variety, its intricacy, its partial concealments, it excites that
active curiosity which gives play to the mind, loosening those iron bonds
with which astonishment chains up its faculties.[41]

Like Wollstonecraft, Picturesque theory reacts against Burke's
static binary categories. But Wollstonecraft could hardly be satisfied
with the image of femininity imagined here as bearer of a 'more
amusing, more varied' version of beauty: woman is still reduced to
circumscribed pleasures and denied participation in the rational
Sublime. What Wollstonecraft envisaged was heterosexual relations
as a disruptive blend of sublimity and beauty, in which the respect
inspired by rational women would mean that 'pain should be
blended with pleasure, and admiration disturb the soft intimacy of
love'.[42] She diagnoses the libertine aesthetic as in part a fear of just
such a disturbance of ease and mastery. The erotics of Picturesque
texts suggest a refinement rather than a disruption of Burkean
libertinism: rather than Wollstonecraft's radical rewriting of gender,
their liberal 'blend'[43] of beautiful and sublime effects takes only
limited risks with masculinist 'pleasure'.

At one level, then, the Picturesque's fantasy of perpetual desire,
'curiosity alive and unsatisfied', is a predictable trope which justifies
property by writing it as unfettered nature. But the unwillingness to
imagine possession, the move to voyeuristic rather than consum-
matory fantasies, also signals a crisis of mastery and masculinity
within a particular section of the ruling class.[44] In *Solitude and the
Sublime*, Frances Ferguson makes the important suggestion that the
Beautiful is actually more threatening to selfhood than the Sublime:
the domestic, social sphere (which is also, of course, the sphere of the
feminine and, increasingly during the century, of bourgeois moral
values) is the deceptive site of 'death and defeat', of a 'physical and
political entropy' which destroys (masculine) individual identity.
Thus the Sublime – and the Picturesque – in Martin Price's words,
'mark a revolt against the tyranny of beauty'.[45] Given a more specific
historical inflection in terms of class and gender, Ferguson's insight
helps illuminate the Picturesque of Price and Knight. Their response
to the crisis of the 1790s was to seek 'intricate' and tantalising

pleasures beyond the comfort and ease of the beautiful. Libertine control over aesthetic categories and sexual narratives is under threat, as beauty becomes the site of predictable bourgeois taste and moralised femininity. Through voyeuristic structures of fantasy, the Picturesque seeks to maintain control over definitions of the feminine and thus to perpetuate a landowning aesthetic and its equivalent masculinity. But male voyeurism also speaks of castration, of potential powerlessness. Through a textual erotics which explicitly reproduces the impossible structure of desire itself,[46] the Picturesque points up the precariousness of libertine definitions at a moment of cultural transition. Under revolutionary pressure, new formulations of gender become possible: the identity of the 'libertine imagination' is vulnerable not just to a growing bourgeois hegemony but also, briefly, to the 'rational creatures'[47] imagined by Wollstonecraft as the female inheritors of change.

This crisis of libertine masculinity is exploited in various ways in the fiction of the period, and I want now to turn to my three novels. This involves a shift not simply of genre but, at an overt level at least, of gender and class position: from the libertine and ultimately anti-bourgeois discourse of Knight and Price to woman-centred and woman-authored narratives, one of the main projects of which is to effect that alliance between old property and new money which the later Picturesque only defensively accommodates. Most eighteenth-century novels manifest this hegemonic shift in some way, and in the sexual plotting of, particularly, women's fiction, it is motivated by attraction to the forbidden aristocratic aesthetic. The classic seduction plot so powerfully realised in *Clarissa*, for example, in which the middle-class woman is abducted and ruined by a dastardly aristocrat, has often been read as an unproblematic bourgeois warning about the fall of the nation under unchecked aristocratic influence. But what makes that plot so compelling is the sexual/ aesthetic fascination exerted by the Lovelace figure, eliciting in response a female desire which is doubly illicit – in its very existence as well as its object – and anxiously acknowledged in recurrent arguments about the reformable rake. Popular fictions thus provide a confirmatory space in which the material benefits of upward social mobility can be consumed at the level of fantasy – but with the effect, as Wollstonecraft well understood, of encouraging women to collude in their own sexual objectification: 'With respect to superficial accomplishments, the rake certainly has the advantage; and of these females can form an opinion, for it is their own ground.'[48]

In the three novels I have chosen to deal with here, these questions of class, aesthetics, femininity and sexuality operate within a comedic paradigm: Charlotte Smith's *The Old Manor House*, Sydney Morgan's *The Wild Irish Girl* and Jane Austen's *Mansfield Park* are versions of the romance plot of discovery and inheritance, a plot which puts the identification woman/estate, woman/house – and, by extension, woman/nation – at the centre of the text. Variations on this theme recur throughout the century: in Sarah Fielding's *The History of Ophelia* (1755), Agnes Maria Bennett's *Anna; or Memoirs of a Welch Heiress* (1785) or Charlotte Smith's *Emmeline: The Orphan of the Castle* (1788), for example. In these particular cases, the process of improvement involves the heroine leaving her rural retreat and demonstrating her ability to survive in a wider social context (classically operative in Fanny Burney's *Evelina*), and often under economic hardships; she establishes her bourgeois credentials by surviving sexual assaults and/or managing to make a living, for which her reward is rescue into wealth, leisure and luxury for life.

The novels I am looking at are more topographically fixed. In the interests of symbolic identification, their heroines have for the most part to stay on the estate they will ultimately inherit, to await discovery and definition by the hero. But, with growing confidence, these novels and their increasingly self-conscious heroines refuse to collude with the proprietorial male gaze which reduces woman to a sexualised symbolic function – to, in effect, a Picturesque object. The revolutionary moment allowed the possibility of emancipation from imprisoning narratives of desire, as well as of new class configurations. In the novel, this is realised through experimental forms explicitly critical of 'the libertine reveries of men', which might nevertheless also endorse a more orthodox – even conservative – social resolution.[49] What I want to explore, then, is a textual dynamic which registers, from a different position, the instabilities of class and gender which I have argued are evident in Picturesque texts. On the one hand, these novels remain firmly within a reconciliatory comic form which uses marriage to enact and celebrate an alliance of bourgeois and gentry values. But within that, they suggest subtle shifts of emphasis as the romance plot begins to emancipate itself from subjection to libertine masculinity, as motivating object of desire and as controlling gaze.

Published in 1794, the same year as Knight's *Landscape* and Price's interchange with Repton, Charlotte Smith's *The Old Manor House* is similarly engaged with the Revolution debate, and from a cautiously sympathetic position. The house of the title is an 'ancient and splendid seat', 'which had not received the slightest alteration, either in its environs or its furniture, since... 1698', a decaying pile which, as one of the servants comments, '"will tumble about our ears... one day or nother, and yet my lady is always repairing it"'.[50] 'My lady' is the estate's almost equally ancient owner, Mrs Rayland, for whom, in Burkean phrase, 'the age of chivalry did not seem to be passed' (p. 249):[51] she refuses to settle her will in favour of her nephew's family, her only surviving relatives, because he married a woman 'who had nothing to recommend her but beauty, simplicity, and goodness' (p. 4). Incarcerated, like Wollstonecraft's Maria, in this representation of feudal pride and neglect is an alternative image of femininity in Monimia, the housekeeper's penniless niece, whose 'beauty, simplicity, and goodness' make the house into an object of desire for Orlando, the great-nephew who will eventually inherit. Absolute ruin threatens the Hall when, through the corruption of her aunt, Monimia is forced to leave: 'a low, hollow gust of wind rushed through the deserted rooms: it seemed loaded with the groans of all he [Orlando] had ever loved' (p. 399). But ultimately she and Orlando inherit and Rayland Hall is tastefully improved to accommodate both tradition and change: 'without spoiling that look of venerable antiquity for which it was so remarkable, [Orlando] collected within [Rayland Hall] every comfort and elegance of modern life' (p. 515). The political implications of all this are clear enough, and very close to a Foxite Whig reformism: England is saved, through a mixture of rural tradition and moral idealism, from the ruin threatened by the combined forces of aristocratic neglect and urban corruption.[52]

But what I want to focus on here is the novel's more problematic sexual dynamic, and the gendering of its narrative/reading position. Perhaps through strategic self-interest, Smith's text is in the third person,[53] and we register Monimia's symbolic status through Orlando's dominant point of view; she is constructed as the object of his (our) gaze:

his fancy... saw her the adored mistress of that house, where she had been brought up in indigence, in obscurity, almost in servitude; this gem, which he alone had found, was set where nature certainly intended it to have been placed – it was to him, not only its discovery, but its lustre was owing – he saw it sparkle with genuine beauty, and illuminate his future days… (p. 300)

The improvement of the Hall is prepared for by the improvement of Monimia under Orlando's tutelage. At one level, then, the novel could be seen as reproducing the essentially passive and objectified femininity of much landscape writing and to be doing so in order to validate the inheritance of that landscape by bourgeois respectability. At the end of the novel, Monimia is explicitly the domesticated and subordinate 'lovely wife' who dutifully bears Orlando a son. But the revolutionary moment briefly produces more complex possibilities out of the romance paradigm. Monimia's mode of femininity changes in the course of the novel, not simply from innocence to accomplished domesticity, but from the sexualised object of desire of landscape writers to the containing status of the middle-class matron. The way in which she receives her education is wonderfully unrespectable: the first half of the novel is obsessively concerned with the secret midnight visits which Orlando makes, like the prince in *Rapunzel*, to Monimia's 'turret', to give her a course of directed reading. He comes to her through secret side-doors – and not without some interesting difficulties:

Orlando, who like another Pyramus, watched with a beating heart the breach through which he now saw the light, forced away these slight barriers with very little difficulty; and then, setting his foot against the door, it gave way, and the remnant of tattered hanging made no resistance. He found himself in the room with Monimia, who from mingled emotions of pleasure and fear could hardly breathe. (p. 30)

Monimia's '*to-be-looked-at-ness*',[54] her 'gem'-like quality as aesthetic object, apparently gives way here to a fantasy of penetration. But it would be a mistake, I think, simply to dismiss this as the unfortunate fall of a female writer into a masculinised point of view. The sexual sub-text here is interesting in itself as a phenomenon in women's fiction (and there are examples in Smith's other novels of radical treatments of sexuality),[55] but it also raises more general issues. Recent critiques of earlier feminist theories of the gaze and of romance-reading stress the productive instability of gendered spectator-positions and the importance of fantasy:

fantasy…is a crucial part of our constitution as human subjects. It is not either the contents of original fantasy, nor even necessarily the position from which we imagine them that can, or ought, to be stigmatized. Rather it is consciousness of the insistent nature of those fantasies for men and women and the historically specific forms of their elaboration that need to be opened up. Our priority ought to be an analysis of the progressive or reactionary politics to which fantasy can become bound in popular expression.[56]

The illicit pleasures offered to an implicitly female audience in such passages from *The Old Manor House* problematise a fixed identification of femininity with passivity through a fantasy of sexual/economic possession. At a time when women were officially denied both, this has transgressive, though not necessarily progressive, significance.[57] Later in the novel, Monimia breaks out of Orlando's possessive idealisation in more explicitly economic terms when she insists on working to support the family, since he cannot. Authority begins to shift to the heroine: liberated by Orlando's initial instruction from the Gothic histories inculcated by her aunt, she reads current reality far more efficiently than he is able to do from a position of displaced masculinity.[58] But the novel ultimately deflects this critique of the hero: firstly in its growing focus on what is effectively a detective narrative – Orlando seeking to establish his right of inheritance; and then through the romance ending itself.

In *The Wild Irish Girl*[59] the narrative of discovery, identification with place and inheritance is conducted even more explicitly through the terms of Picturesque discourse, and from a context – Ireland just after the Act of Union – which immediately foregrounds that discourse as a mode of national as well as sexual appropriation. The novel's heroine Glorvina, who is, significantly, never so wild as the title suggests, is cultural other as well as aesthetic/desired object to the jaded, effete and initially cynical 'hero' Mortimer, whose letters to an M.P. friend in England make up the bulk of the novel. Paradigms from both Irish and romantic Gothic fiction come together here: 'the scene of encounter between the English and the "wild" Irish'[60] is rewritten from within the libertine imagination.

Mortimer first sees Glorvina in a ruined chapel where, in keeping with the Picturesque's decadent fascination with ruins, history and change are reduced to an aesthetic sensation:[61]

surely Fancy, in her boldest flight, never gave to the fairy vision of poetic dreams, a combination of images more poetically fine, more strikingly picturesque, or more impressively touching. Nearly one half of the chapel of Inismore has fallen into decay, and the ocean breeze, as it rushed through the fractured roof, wafted the torn banners of the family which hung along its dismantled walls. (p. 37)

The same is true of Mortimer's construction of Glorvina herself as the embodiment of tantalising contradictions: like all good Picturesque landscapes she is 'without a very perfect regularity of feature', yet she 'possesses that effulgence of countenance…which poetry assigns to the dazzling emanations of divine beauty'; she is an accommodating blend of social categories, speaking 'the language of a court' whilst 'she looks like the artless inhabitant of a cottage'; and, being the thing itself, she is poor only at painting: 'the rules of the art of design are not sufficiently connected with those lively and vehement emotions of the soul she is so calculated to feel and to awaken. She was created for a musician' (pp. 56, 61, 78). The 'partial concealment' of her intellectual qualities presents more of a threat to Mortimer's power over definitions: 'sometimes when I think I am trifling with a child, I find I am conversing with a philosopher' (p. 83).

It is difficult – and, I would argue, distinctly unwise – to take Mortimer's idealising view entirely seriously. The parodic extravagance of the first-person narrative is pointed up by the hero's comic passivity, his inability to play his part adequately in the romance to which he is so self-consciously committed. The novel can be read as a piece of fictional propaganda, supporting the Act of Union by making Ireland attractive for an English audience.[62] But far from simply 're-processing the barbaric as the picturesque' by inviting its readers to share Mortimer's growing enthusiasm for things Irish, the novel undermines precisely such complacent political voyeurism.[63] As Claire Connolly has demonstrated, the novel actually refuses the 'absorption' which the Act of Union represented for many contemporary commentators,[64] and it exploits and develops the problematisation of the hero by post-revolutionary women's fiction in order to do so.

In *The Old Manor House*, the frame of masculine definition is broken by testing Orlando's romantic desire to fix Monimia in 'gem'-like stasis against economic necessity. In *The Wild Irish Girl*, the suspended voyeuristic moment is disrupted more directly: in a wonderfully comic scene, Mortimer penetrates Glorvina's apartment which he has been peering into – but only by falling off his perch on the 'mouldering' woodwork and 'loose stones' which he finds so aesthetically satisfying:

Oh! could I but seize the touching features – could I but realize the vivid tints of this enchanting picture, as they then glowed on my fancy!... as if the independent witchery of the lovely minstrel was not in itself all, all-sufficient, at the back of her chair stood the grotesque figure of her antiquated nurse. O the precious contrast! – and yet it heightened, it finished the picture.

While thus entranced in breathless observation, endeavouring to support my precarious tenement, ... the loose stones on which I tottered, gave way under my feet... (pp. 43–4)

Mortimer literally breaks the frame of his own 'finished' Picturesque composition. And he does so by falling off the ruin for which he, or at least his absentee family, is responsible. Far from endorsing the English male gaze, then, Morgan's text uses the first-person narrative to satirise it.

For the rest of the novel, Mortimer is forced to acknowledge the various histories occluded by his Picturesque appropriation of the 'ruin' of Ireland, as Glorvina and her father, the objects of his sexual and aesthetic gaze, and of his ancestors' economic and cultural imperialism, speak back. Their voices, supported by Morgan's authoritative footnotes, constantly challenge the first-person narration until it disappears entirely in the final sections of the novel. At the end of this moral and historical education, Mortimer is redeemed by marriage to Glorvina, and satire makes way for political optimism. But not before exposing the limitations of the Picturesque as a discourse of historical change – and of libertinism as a mode of sexual politics.

Like the heroines in *The Old Manor House* and *The Wild Irish Girl*, Fanny in Austen's *Mansfield Park* comes to represent the house she problematically inhabits, and the familiar ground of Fanny's relation to Mansfield values and landscape theory is given a sharper focus read against female fiction's critique of proprietorial masculinity.[65] Austen's critique of masculine possession is much more sustained, effectively disempowering the 'libertine imagination' altogether. Far from objectifying her protagonist, Austen's free indirect narrative makes the identification heroine/house/nation a function of Fanny's subjectivity – as Wollstonecraft might have put it (though with a very different political agenda) – of her *'active* sensibility'.[66] Austen's text boldly appropriates the aesthetic discourse of the improvers, and turns it to moral and spiritual account by locating its generalising power within Fanny's consciousness. It is the female gaze which now defines a mental landscape and, like Glorvina, articulates its threatened histories: the dependent heroine of romance fiction is the one who now 'blends' 'convenience' and 'ornament', past and present, suffering and consolation – and relocates inheritance not in the public material benefits of the big house, but in the private, spiritual satisfactions of the Parsonage.

Like Monimia, Fanny is mainly confined indoors, but Fanny's room of her own becomes an image not of her body, but of her consciousness. Disturbed by the threat of the theatricals, she seeks comfort from the East Room, into which she 'had so naturally and artlessly worked herself... that it was now generally admitted to be her's':

She could go there after anything unpleasant below, and find immediate consolation... Every thing was a friend, or bore her thoughts to a friend; and though there had been sometimes much of suffering to her... though she had known the pains of tyranny, of ridicule, and neglect, yet almost every recurrence of either had led to something consolatory;... and the whole was now so blended together, so harmonized by distance, that every former affliction had its charm.[67]

The consolatory process here depends, like Fanny's emotional, ideological and spiritual well-being throughout the novel, on the workings of memory. And the aesthetic vocabulary – 'Blended together'; 'harmonized by distance'; 'charm' – makes explicit the relationship between this passage and the arguments about landscape and improvement elsewhere in the text. Fanny constructs comfort out of suffering just as Picturesque taste produces pleasure out of 'roughness', ugliness or poverty. But hers is a moralised aesthetic of historical awareness and local attachment, more consistently Burkean than Price's fascination with 'accident and neglect'. We see this in another context when Fanny reflects on the shrubbery at the Parsonage:

'Every time I come into this shrubbery I am more struck with its growth and beauty. Three years ago, this was nothing but a rough hedgerow along the upper side of the field, never thought of as any thing, or capable of becoming any thing; and now it is converted into a walk, and it would be difficult to say whether most valuable as a convenience or an ornament; and perhaps in another three years we may be forgetting – almost forgetting what it was before. How wonderful, how very wonderful the operations of time, and the changes of the human mind!'...

Miss Crawford, untouched and inattentive, had nothing to say... (pp. 208–9)

That break in the syntax ('forgetting – almost forgetting') signals the vertiginous threat of change made meaningless by a failure of memory; at the same time ('*almost* forgetting'), it enacts the moral effort of recuperation, of memory self-consciously at work to make history manifest. Most immediately, that effort is needed to resist the commercial, Reptonian project represented by the very different femininity of the 'untouched and inattentive' Mary Crawford. But it is also central to the survival of the gentry position with which Fanny identifies, a position very close to that of Price and Knight: through a feminine '*active* sensibility' working on history, the anxious stasis which characterises the Picturesque's aestheticisation of transience is returned to narrative form.[68]

That form is, of course, the domestic romance and, in spite of Austen's immediate class affiliation, it appears here in a more securely bourgeois manifestation than in earlier fictions. In the more obviously radical novels of Smith and Morgan, the compromise endings are residual versions of reforming the rake: the sexual fascination with aristocratic masculinity survives at the level of plot as Orlando and Mortimer are subjected to a feminising re-education. In *Mansfield Park*, the libertine is explicitly excluded. Fanny's most heroinic moment is her refusal of Henry Crawford's proposal. Thereafter, she has to wait for confirmatory definition from Edmund, the domesticated Austenian 'new man', in that passage of desperately understated romantic closure which at once acknowledges and checks the fulfilment of female desire: 'exactly at the time when it was quite natural that it should be so, and not a week earlier, Edmund did cease to care about Miss Crawford, and became as anxious to marry Fanny, as Fanny herself could desire' (p. 470). In her subtle, but sometimes misguided, reading of *Mansfield Park* as engaged in 'progressive, though muted, social criticism', Claudia Johnson suggests that the moral failure of Sir Thomas and Lady Bertram, embodiments of the Sublime and the Beautiful, represents the bankruptcy of Burkean aesthetic/political values, of the conservative myth of the family.[69] Burke's libertine definitions of gender are very clearly rejected in *Mansfield Park*, but Johnson underestimates the conservative power of Austen's post-revolutionary appropriation of the Wollstonecraftian critique.[70] Through Fanny, a woman and a social outsider, the revolutionary possibilities manifest, in different ways, in Picturesque theory and women's fiction at the turn of the century are recuperated for a modified Burkean ideal: the possibilities for transgressive fantasy offered by the decadent libertine aesthetic of the Picturesque and the shifting subject-positions of the earlier novels are ruthlessly minimised.

NOTES

1 Early influential studies in this area are: Marilyn Butler, *Jane Austen and the War of Ideas* (Oxford: Clarendon Press, 1975); Gary Kelly, *The English Jacobin Novel* (Oxford: Clarendon Press, 1976); Mary Poovey, *The Proper Lady and the Woman Writer: Ideology as Style in the Works of Mary Wollstonecraft, Mary Shelley, and Jane Austen* (University of Chicago Press, 1984) and 'Ideology and *The Mysteries of Udolpho*', *Criticism*, 21 (1979), 307–30. More recent studies include: Claudia Johnson, *Jane Austen: Women, Politics, and the Novel* (University of Chicago Press, 1988); Gary Kelly, *English Fiction of the Romantic Period 1789–1830* (London and New York: Longman, 1989); Patricia Meyer Spacks, *Desire and Truth: Functions of Plot in Eighteenth-Century English Novels* (University of Chicago Press, 1990); Janet Todd, *The Sign of Angellica: Women, Writing and Fiction 1660–1800* (London: Virago, 1989); Nicola Watson, 'Purloined Letters: Revolution, Reaction and the Form of the Novel, 1790–1825', unpublished D.Phil. thesis, University of Oxford, 1990, forthcoming as *Purloined Letters* from Oxford University Press, 1993–4.

2 Mary Wollstonecraft, *A Vindication of the Rights of Men*, in Janet Todd and Marilyn Butler (eds.), *The Works of Mary Wollstonecraft* (London: William Pickering, 1990), vol. v, p. 46.

3 On the discursive complexity of the term 'Gothic', see Robert Miles, 'The Gothic Aesthetic: The Gothic as Discourse', *The Eighteenth Century*, 32 (1991), 39–57. See also Harriet Guest, 'The Wanton Muse: Politics and Gender in Gothic Theory After 1760', in Stephen Copley and John Whale (eds.), *Beyond Romanticism: New Approaches to Texts and Contexts 1780–1832* (London and New York: Routledge, 1992), pp. 118–39. For a discussion of Gilpin, see the essay in this volume by Ann Bermingham (pp. 81–90).

4 On the Price/Repton/Knight controversy see, for example, Edward Malins, *English Landscaping and Literature* (London, New York and Toronto: Oxford University Press, 1966), pp. 123–41, 147–53.

5 On the politics of the Picturesque see: Ann Bermingham, *Landscape and Ideology: The English Rustic Tradition, 1740–1860* (London: Thames and Hudson, 1987), pp. 57–87; Alan Liu, *Wordsworth: The Sense of History* (Stanford University Press, 1989), pp. 61–137; Kim Ian Michasiw, 'Nine Revisionist Theses on the Picturesque', *Representations*, 38 (1992), 76–100; Sidney K. Robinson, *Inquiry into the Picturesque* (Chicago University Press, 1991), especially pp. 47–89. Liu defines the Picturesque 'not in terms of the subject–object dialectic but of desire and violence', and suggests that: 'The full experience of the picturesque...must arise

from the lamination of eroticism and sadism, intricacy and roughness',
but does not pursue the gender politics of these definitions (Liu,
Wordsworth, pp. 85, 64).

6 William Gilpin, *Three Essays: On Picturesque Beauty; On Picturesque
Travel; and On Sketching Landscape*, second edition (London, 1794), p. 48.

7 *Ibid.*

8 Cf. Bermingham, *Landscape and Ideology*, pp. 66–72.

9 Richard Payne Knight, *The Landscape, A Didactic Poem* (London, 1794),
pp. 13–14. For further discussion of Knight see the essay in this volume
by John Whale (pp. 188–91).

10 Michasiw, 'Nine Revisionist Theses', 84.

11 'Curiosity' and 'irritation' are terms which recur in Price's definitions of
the Picturesque. See, for example, Uvedale Price, *An Essay on the
Picturesque, as Compared with the Sublime and the Beautiful*, 'A New Edition'
(London, 1796), pp. 26, 144, and cf. p. 146: 'Irritation is indeed the
source of our most active and lively pleasures'.

12 Robinson, *Inquiry*, p. 119.

13 Martin Price, *To the Palace of Wisdom: Studies in Order and Energy from
Dryden to Blake* (London and Amsterdam: Feffer and Simons, 1964), p.
362, cited by Frances Ferguson, *Solitude and the Sublime: Romanticism and
the Aesthetics of Individuation* (New York and London: Routledge, 1992),
p. 45. I shall be returning to Ferguson's reading of Burkean beauty.

14 Knight, *Landscape*, p. 37.

15 For example by Malcolm Andrews, *The Search for the Picturesque:
Landscape Aesthetics and Tourism in Britain, 1760–1800* (Aldershot: Scolar
Press, 1989), p. 36. On Knight's resistance to classicism in his own
gardening practice, see Nicholas Penny, 'Architecture and Landscape at
Downton', in Michael Clarke and Nicholas Penny (eds.), *The Arrogant
Connoisseur: Richard Payne Knight 1751–1824* (Manchester University Press,
1982), pp. 43–5.

16 Competing constructions of femininity were a significant element in the
revolutionary propaganda war: respectable English matrons versus
French whores; Britannia versus a caricatured Marianne. In this
context, the seductive, self-conscious but innocent 'nymphs' of Price and
Knight, though they might be predictable fantasy figures, do represent
a kind of transgression. Knight's 'cunning nymph' makes an interesting
comparison with, for example, Helen Maria Williams's sympathetic
characterisation of French liberty: 'adorned with the freshness of youth',
and 'loved with the ardour of passion' (Williams, *Letters Written in
France, in the Summer of 1790* (Oxford: Woodstock Books, 1989), p. 71).

17 See Robinson, *Inquiry*, pp. 79–80, and particularly Liu, *Wordsworth*, pp.
103–13. '[T]rue Whiggish liberty': Liu, *Wordsworth*, p. 109; 'Jacobinism
of taste': Anna Seward commenting on Knight, quoted by Liu,
Wordsworth, p. 111.

18 Knight, *Landscape*, pp. 73, 75n.

19 *Ibid.*, pp. 25, 54, 57. For a very clear political interpretation of this material, including a reading of the poem and footnote as representative of, respectively, an early and late Foxite position, see Alan Liu, *Wordsworth*, pp. 109–13.

20 As Liu tends to do, *ibid.*, p. 110.

21 Knight, *Landscape*, p. 73n.

22 Price, *Essay*, pp. 39–40n.

23 Uvedale Price, *A Letter to H. Repton Esq. On the Application of the Practice as well as the Principles of Landscape-Painting to Landscape-Gardening* (London, 1795), pp. 92–3.

24 Bermingham, *Landscape and Ideology*, pp. 66–9; and cf. Michasiw, 'Nine Revisionist Theses', 92–3.

25 Price, *Letter*, p. 37.

26 Price, *Essay*, p. 40.

27 Edmund Burke, *Reflections on the Revolution in France*, in L. G. Mitchell (ed.), *The Writings and Speeches of Edmund Burke*, vol. VIII (Oxford: Clarendon Press, 1989), p. 127; and cf. Robinson, *Inquiry*, p. 24: 'Burke's appeals to the singular significance of real events accumulating without apparent plan would seem to parallel the picturesque ideal of composition.'

28 Humphry Repton, *Mr Repton's Letter to Mr Price*, Price, *Letter*, p. 10; Liu, *Wordsworth*, p. 107.

29 Burke, *Reflections*, p. 112.

30 *Ibid.*, p. 137.

31 *Ibid.*, p. 216.

32 Price, *Letter*, p. 93.

33 Wollstonecraft, *Rights of Men*, p. 46.

34 *Ibid.*, p. 10.

35 *Ibid.*, p. 48.

36 Cf. Miles, 'The Gothic Aesthetic', 51–3, and Wollstonecraft: 'if there is any thing like argument, or first principles, in your [Burke's] wild declamation, behold the result: – that we are to reverence the rust of antiquity, and term the unnatural customs, which ignorance and mistaken self-interest have consolidated, the sage fruit of experience... These are gothic notions of beauty – the ivy is beautiful, but, when it insidiously destroys the trunk from which it receives support, who would not grub it up?' (Wollstonecraft, *Rights of Men*, p. 10).

37 *Ibid.*, pp. 45–6, 56, 9.

38 Price, *Essay*, p. 26n.

39 *Ibid.*, pp. 268, 142.

40 Carole Fabricant, 'Binding and Dressing Nature's Loose Tresses', *Studies in Eighteenth-Century Culture*, 8 (1979), 112, 121–3.

41 Price, *Essay*, pp. 105–6.

42 Wollstonecraft, *Rights of Men*, pp. 45–6.

43 'Blend' is a recurrent term in Picturesque writing. Cf. Knight's 'Well

mix'd and blended in the scene', quoted above (Knight, *Landscape*, p. 14).

44 By suggesting that voyeurism is symptomatic of crisis, I am not intending to endorse Freud's prescriptive view that scopophilic pleasure 'becomes a perversion ... if, instead of being *preparatory* to the normal sexual aim, it supplants it' (Sigmund Freud, *On Sexuality*, The Pelican Freud Library, vol. VII (Harmondsworth: Penguin, 1977), p. 70). Within the libertine context, however, perpetuation of desire through voyeurism rather than successive conquests represents a significant change.

45 Ferguson, *Solitude and the Sublime*, pp. 51, 52 and *passim*, and cf. above, n. 13.

46 Cf. Christian Metz, 'The Imaginary Signifier', *Screen*, 16 (1975), 61: 'If it is true of all desire that it depends on the infinite pursuit of its absent object, voyeuristic desire, along with certain forms of sadism, is the only desire whose principle of distance symbolically and spatially evokes this fundamental rent.' On scopophilia as evoking and containing the fear of castration, see Laura Mulvey, 'Visual Pleasure and Narrative Cinema', in *Visual and Other Pleasures* (Basingstoke and London: Macmillan, 1989), pp. 21–2.

47 Mary Wollstonecraft, *Vindication of the Rights of Woman*, in Todd and Butler (eds.), *Works*, vol. V, p. 75.

48 *Ibid.*, p. 188.

49 In a review of Elizabeth Inchbald's novel *A Simple Story*, Wollstonecraft complained that 'all female writers, even when they display their abilities, always give a sanction to the libertine reveries of men' (Todd and Butler (eds.), *Works*, vol. VII, p. 370).

50 Charlotte Smith, *The Old Manor House* (1794), ed. Anne Henry Ehrenpreis, new introduction by Judith Phillips Stanton (Oxford University Press, 1989), pp. 3, 7, 248. Hereafter, page references will be included in the text.

51 Cf. Burke, *Reflections*, p. 127: 'But the age of chivalry is gone.'

52 Orlando is explicitly committed to an ideal of rural retirement: '"How happy should I be to be allowed to cultivate one of the smallest of those farms which belong to the Rayland estate, and, comprising in thy society and that of my family all my felicity, have no wish but to live and die without reading that great book which they call the world!"' (p. 160).

53 Nicola Watson has drawn attention to the dangerously radical implications of epistolary and first-person narratives in women's fiction of this period. See Watson, 'Purloined Letters', especially Introduction, chapters 1, 2.

54 Mulvey, 'Visual Pleasure', p. 19.

55 In *Emmeline: The Orphan of the Castle* (1788), for example, a woman who has an illegitimate child is rehabilitated; and in *Desmond* (1792), the hero has an affair with a married woman, who becomes pregnant, when he is in love with the heroine.

56 Cora Kaplan, '*The Thorn Birds*: Fiction, Fantasy, Femininity' in *Sea Changes: Essays on Culture and Feminism* (London: Verso, 1986), p. 146. For a useful survey of recent critiques of Mulvey, see Patricia Erens (ed.), *Issues in Feminist Film Criticism* (Bloomington and Indianapolis: Indiana University Press, 1990), pp. xix–xxi.

57 On modern romance reading as transgressive rather than progressive, see Alison Light, '"Returning to Manderley" – Romance Fiction, Female Sexuality and Class', *Feminist Review*, 16 (1984), 7–25.

58 The distribution of virtues and capabilities between Orlando and Monimia can be seen as supporting Patricia Meyer Spacks's argument that 1790s fiction effects a 'mediation' between polarised gender qualities. See Spacks, *Desire and Truth*, chapter 7.

59 Sydney Morgan, *The Wild Irish Girl* (1806; London and New York: Pandora, 1986). Hereafter, page references will be included in the text.

60 Siobhan Kilfeather, 'Beyond the Pale: Sexual and National Identity in Early Irish Fiction', *Critical Matrix*, 2 (1986), 14. On the novel's evocation of traditional representations of Ireland's colonial relationship with England in sexual terms, see: Robert Tracey, 'Maria Edgworth and Lady Morgan: Legality versus Legitimacy', *Nineteenth-Century Fiction*, 40 (1985), 19–22; J. Th. Leerssen, 'How *The Wild Irish Girl* Made Ireland Romantic', *Dutch Quarterly Review of Anglo-Irish Letters*, 18 (1988), 210.

61 Cf. Anne Janowitz, *England's Ruins: Poetic Purpose and the National Landscape* (Oxford: Basil Blackwell, 1990), p. 56: 'what we often overlook in picturesque taste is the price exacted...the alteration of the presentation of the ruined castle as the site of historical event and succession into its presentation as a piece of nature conforms to a desire to master the content of the past while unfettering its form'.

62 For a reading of the novel as endorsing the Act of Union, see Barry Sloan, *The Pioneers of Anglo-Irish Fiction 1800–1850* (Gerrards Cross, Bucks. and Totowa, N.J.: Colin Smythe and Barnes and Noble, 1986), pp. 7–15. For a more subtle treatment of Morgan's politics, see Tom Dunne, 'Fiction as "the best history of nations": Lady Morgan's Irish Novels', in Tom Dunne (ed.), *The Writer as Witness: Literature as Historical Evidence* (Cork University Press, 1987), pp. 133–59.

63 Though that was precisely how the novel, and Morgan herself, were consumed by an English audience. On the Glorvina cult see, for example, Mary Campbell, *Lady Morgan: Life and Times of Sydney Owenson* (London, Sydney, Wellington: Pandora, 1988), pp. 71–2. '[R]e-processing the barbaric': Watson, 'Purloined Letters', p. 201.

64 Claire Connolly, 'The Politics of Love in *The Wild Irish Girl*', unpublished paper, Conference of the International Association for the Study of Anglo-Irish Literature, Trinity College, Dublin, July 1992.

65 The best discussion of the politics of landscape in *Mansfield Park* is still Alistair M. Duckworth, *The Improvement of the Estate: A Study of Jane*

Austen's Novels (Baltimore and London: Johns Hopkins Press, 1971), pp. 35–80. On Jane Austen and the Picturesque more generally see Michasiw, 'Nine Revisionist Theses', 95–6. On Austen's relationship with contemporary women's fiction and its politics see: Johnson, *Jane Austen*; Gary Kelly, 'Jane Austen and the English Novel of the 1790s' in Mary Anne Schofield and Cecilia Macheski (eds.), *Fetter'd or Free? British Women Novelists 1670–1815* (Athens, Ohio and London: Ohio University Press, 1986), pp. 285–306.

66 Mary Wollstonecraft, *The Wrongs of Woman: or, Maria. A Fragment*, in Todd and Butler (eds.), *Works*, vol. I, p. 144.

67 Jane Austen, *Mansfield Park*, R. W. Chapman (ed.), *The Novels of Jane Austen*, vol. III (Oxford University Press, 1966), pp. 151–2. Hereafter, page references will be included in the text.

68 On the Picturesque as a form of 'arrest', see Liu, *Wordsworth*, pp. 61–90.

69 Johnson, *Jane Austen*, pp. 99–100.

70 On the conservative implications of the domestic novel which, I have argued, *Mansfield Park* exemplifies, see Nancy Armstrong, *Desire and Domestic Fiction: A Political History of the Novel* (Oxford University Press, 1987). Austen's position in *Mansfield Park* is actually much closer to the conservative Hannah More than to Wollstonecraft.

CHAPTER 6

Picturesque figure and landscape: Meg Merrilies and the gypsies

Peter Garside

Guy Mannering (1815), Scott's second work of fiction, is filled with Picturesque scenery, much of it centred on the North Solway landscape of Ellangowan, which is seen at different seasons and plays an integral part in the story's pattern of rediscovery and redemption. Yet for all the conscientious effort on Scott's part, contemporary reviewers made only passing reference to this aspect of the novel, preferring instead to concentrate on one outstanding figure, the gypsy Meg Merrilies. This tendency is best encapsulated in an anonymous notice in the *Augustan Review*. Like so many reviews it singles out Meg Merrilies as 'the great agent' in the story ('an object at once original and exalted'), and like others it quotes her now famous speech to Godfrey Bertram, the Laird of Ellangowan, a powerful protest against eviction ('"Ride your ways," said the gypsy, "ride your ways, Laird of Ellangowan..."'). Noticeably, however, the quotation begins with a description of Meg on a high bank, and the reviewer's lead-in focuses on her not only as a rhetorician but also as a *visual* figure: 'The speech she makes to the old Laird of Ellangowan immediately after the expulsion of the gypsies from their dwellings, is filled with wild pathos, while the image of the heart-struck sybil is highly picturesque.' This sense of the figure's Picturesqueness is echoed, albeit in a more pejorative tone, in a contemporary letter by Wordsworth: 'the characters, with the exception of Meg Merrilies, excite little interest. In the management of this lady the author has shown very considerable ability, but with that want of taste, which is universal among modern novels... I allude to the laborious manner in which everything is placed before your eyes for the production of picturesque effect.'[1]

In the last instance it is tempting to point to a shift in the use of the word 'picturesque', from its heyday as a golden rule in the 1790s, to something more like 'showily picture-like'. More particularly, the sharply drawn Meg of the reviewers apparently clashes with the notion that in the Picturesque the figure has only a subordinate function. In the terms of William Gilpin's essay 'On Sketching Landscape', 'Their chief use is, to mark a road – to break a piece of foreground – to point out the horizon in a sea-view.'[2] Yet it is easy to underestimate the extent to which figures themselves (not least gypsies) were considered by Gilpin, Payne Knight and Uvedale Price as capable of creating distinct Picturesque effects. In his *Tour* of the Lake District (1786), Gilpin distinguishes between figures of a 'negative nature', who 'are at best only *picturesque appendages*', and those more suited to '*scenes* of grandeur...such as impress us with some idea of greatness, wildness, or ferocity': 'Figures in long, folding draperies; gypsies; banditti...are all marked with one or other of these characters.' Gilpin's purpose is to show that figures should not be tainted by any association with work, though to some degree his examples take over from the thesis, especially when he quotes Philip Thickness's account of the 'genuine breed' of gypsies as seen in Spain: 'They are extremely swarthy, with hair as black as jet; and form very picturesque groups under the shade of the rocks and trees of the Pyrænean mountains.'[3] As part of the same argument Gilpin recommends Salvator Rosa's 'book of figures' (the Figurine series) as a repository of models, thus reiterating his earlier eulogium of Rosa as a figurist in *An Essay upon Prints* (1768): 'His figures, which he drew in exquisite taste, are graceful, and nobly expressive, beautifully grouped, and varied into the most agreeable attitudes.'[4]

Similar concerns are found in the work of both Payne Knight and Uvedale Price. When in *An Analytical Inquiry into the Principles of Taste* (1805) Knight eventually tackles the Picturesque directly, it is to the human figure that he turns in illustration of Price's 'great fundamental error' in 'seeking for distinctions in external objects, which only exist in the modes and habits of viewing and considering them'. One of the most forceful images given is that of the female gypsy. 'The dirty and tattered garments, the dishevelled hair, and general wild appearance of gypsies and beggar girls are often picturesque.' This image, however, is immediately qualified as 'merely *picturesque*; that is, they have only the painter's beauties of harmonious variety of tint, and light and shade, blended with every thing else, that is disgusting'.[5] The 'merely' echoes Price's reference to gypsies in *An Essay on the Picturesque*:

In our own species, objects merely picturesque are to be found among the wandering tribes of gypsies and beggars; who, in all the qualities which give them that character, bear a close analogy to the wild forester and the worn-out cart-horse, and again to old mills, hovels, and other inanimate objects of the same kind.[6]

Notwithstanding Price's continuing insistence on an interchangeability of landscape, trees, buildings, animals, figures and faces, the image of the gypsy recurs throughout the *Essay*. One instance emerges as he locates the Picturesque between the beautiful and deformed in the human face: 'conceive the eyebrows *more* strongly marked, the hair rougher in its effect and quality, the complexion more dusky and gipsy-like'.[7] An apotheosis of sorts is found in 'A Dialogue on the Distinct Characters of the Picturesque and the Beautiful', where a gypsy encampment serves as a testing-ground for the aesthetic responses of Mr Hamilton (a surrogate of Price), the Knightian Mr Howard, and an uninitiated Mr Seymour: 'They talked in raptures of every part; of the old hovel, the broken ground, the blasted oak, gipsies, asses, panniers, the catching lights, the deep shadows, the rich mellow hints, the grouping, the composition, the effect of the whole'.[8] Elizabeth Manwaring notes the presence of 'Salvatorial adjuncts of gloom and ruined oak',[9] a touch of 'grandeur' again evident in the 'Dialogue' when the disputants discuss the figure of a 'foreign'-looking man seen on the open heath shortly after leaving the camp: 'what eyebrows! how they, and his black raven hair, hung over his eyes, and what a dark designing look in those eyes! then the slouched hat that he wore on one side, and the sort of cloak he threw across him, as if he were concealing some weapon!'[10] In spite of doctrinal differences, Price and Knight shared with Gilpin a sense of Rosa as a master of the 'picturesque' figure. 'Among painters', Price writes in his *Essay*, 'Salvator Rosa is one of the most remarkable for his picturesque effects: in no other master are seen such abrupt and rugged forms – such sudden deviations both in his figures and his landscapes.'[11]

One should not underestimate the extent to which Scott's own understanding of the Picturesque centred on *figures*. The much-quoted *locus classicus*, from his Ashestiel 'Memoirs' (1808–11), is usually taken to indicate a move from aesthetic theory and practice to a more historically grounded sense of place:

I do not by any means infer that I was dead to the feeling of picturesque scenery; on the contrary few delighted more in its general effect. But I was unable with the eye of a painter to dissect the various parts of the scene, to comprehend how the one bore upon the other or to estimate the effect which various features of the view had in producing its leading and general effect... But shew me an old castle or a field of battle and I was at home at once, filled it with its combatants in their proper costume and overwhelmed my hearers by the enthusiasm of my description!... I mention this to show the distinction between a sense of the picturesque in action and in scenery.[12]

Two points are worth noting here: the almost pastiche-like character of Scott's usage of the discourse of the Picturesque, even when claiming ineptitude; and his awareness (obtrusive in the last sentence quoted) of two branches in the theory, and personal prioritising of the Picturesque in action. Alexander M. Ross has argued a connection between Gilpin's association of the Picturesque with '*very spirited action*' and a Scottian *historical picturesque* 'in which stress is upon vivid pictorial detail, exciting historical action, and the emotions of characters caught up in the rush of resulting circumstances'.[13] Marcia Allentuck has also pointed to a close affinity *circa* 1810/11 with the writings of Price and Knight, a subject to which I will return later.[14]

If Scott's later comments on the Picturesque are sometimes coloured with an air of parody, his terms of reference remain uncannily accurate. 'The Rectors horse is *beautiful* – the curates is *picturesque*': this axiom in a letter of 1822,[15] playfully developing a suggestion by Lord Montagu that a delay in Scott's sitting for his portrait would make him more 'picturesque', matches with some precision both Gilpin's and Price's celebrations of the ass as the Picturesque animal *par excellence*.[16] Jocularity is less in evidence in Scott's fairly frequent invocations of Salvator Rosa, which almost invariably focus on figures. Not untypical is his concern for the 'Gothic Borderers' of *The Lay of the Last Minstrel* (1805) at the hands of the neo-classical artist John Flaxman: 'Would there not be some risk of their resembling the antique of Homer's heroes, rather than the iron race of Salvator?'[17] Visiting the Louvre, on a post-Waterloo trip to Paris, Scott gave pride of place to Rosa's *Saul and the Witch of Endor*, a choice perhaps guided by Knight's terms in praising the artist's disposition of his 'figures' in the same piece: 'the mixture of horror and frenzy in the witch, of awe and anxiety in the monarch, and of terror and astonishment in the soldiers, are expressed, both in their countenances and gestures, with all the... dignity and elevation of poetry'.[18]

Conventionally Scott criticism has interpreted Meg Merrilies as emblematic of an older 'feudal' culture, based on man-service and mutual obligation, as opposed to a 'new' commercial society operating through the strict letter of the law: the ejection of the gypsies from their homes at Derncleugh, followed by the supplanting of Godfrey Bertram by the corrupt lawyer Glossin, offering a microcosm of dubious Scottish 'progress' during the eighteenth century. Two recent writers have claimed a sharper relevance, pointing to a number of parallels with the Highland Clearances (e.g. the unroofing of cottages) to argue in favour of a displaced version of contemporary events.[19] In either case, Meg's gypsyhood is diminished – either to exotic peculiarity, or a camouflage – effectively placing *Guy Mannering* outside 'the increasingly powerful Western symbolism developed around the Gypsies' graphed by Katie Trumpener in the literature of the eighteenth and early nineteenth centuries.[20] As Trumpener indicates, however, the gypsy plot in *Guy* feeds on a number of well-established literary tropes (such as the child stolen by gypsies). In contemporary art, too, a correlation is observable between Meg's experiences and the three types of 'gypsy' painting most commonly exhibited in Britain: the gypsy encampment in the countryside; the moving caravan (an early example, Callot's 'Les Bohémiens' is directly alluded to by Scott); and the solitary figure of the gypsy, usually female.[21]

If there is a problematic factor in Scott's appropriation of these in *Guy Mannering*, it occurs in connection with the third type, where Knight's eminently patronisable 'gypsies and beggar girls' are hardly matched by the angular and isolated figure of Meg after the expulsion. To a point, it can be argued that Scott has tapped into some of the more 'dignified' characteristics granted by Price and Knight to 'a Marius in age and exile' or 'the warriors of Salvator Rosa'.[22] But this still leaves open the question of the gap, half suggested by the early reviews, which lies between the figure of Meg and the novel's more conventional description of landscape. Beyond that, there is the broader issue of the whole cult of the portentous gypsy (a kind of 'Meg-mania') which rapidly developed amongst Scott's earliest readers. In the main body of this essay, I wish to discuss the significance of Meg Merrilies as a 'Picturesque' figure, in the light of Regency culture, and with particular reference to her representation by some of Scott's earliest illustrators.

Fig. 6.1   Samuel de Wilde, *Mrs Egerton as Meg Merrilies.*

It was not long before the reviewers' *objectification* of Meg was matched by her actual portrayal as a figure. Mary Ann Flaxman's 'Meg Merrilies and the Domini Sampson, in the Kaim of Derncleugh', exhibited at the Royal Academy in 1818, is the first identifiable narrative painting to be based on a Waverley novel. Portraits of 'Meg Merrilius' by John Partridge and Samuel Drummond also appeared at the British Institution in 1816, followed by Sir William Beechey's 'Meg Merrylies' in 1818. None of these pictures are now traceable, though Claire Lamont[23] has recently drawn attention to the survival of a study by Samuel de Wilde (dated 1816) of Meg Merrilies as played by Mrs Sarah Egerton in Daniel Terry's highly successful *Guy Mannering; or the Gipsey's Prophecy*, which opened at the Theatre-Royal, Covent Garden, on March 12 1816. De Wilde's drawing (figure 6.1), in water-colour and chalk, shows Mrs Egerton in full length, apparently facing the audience, with a long stick in her right hand and gesturing in the opposite direction with the left (the stick, *pace* Lamont, is unlikely to relate to her denunciation of Godfrey Bertram, since the action of the play is limited to Scott's 'second generation' plot).[24] On her head the stage Meg wears a large turban-like object, held in place by a chin-strap, and three different kinds of tartan are hung over her shoulders, along with a theatrical rosy-pink cape. For the mixture of Eastern and Scottish elements some justification can be found in the text, as will be seen later. But one doubts whether Scott could have approved of the Highland touches, in view of his protests against the common English error of tartanising Southern Scotland. (Another actress, Sarah Smith, was advised by him to 'drub your management out of the general blunder of dressing the Scottish borderers in Tartan'.)[25] If the turban is meant to suggest an oriental ambience, it is hardly matched by Egerton's dyspeptic expression and fair skin, and like the tartans (and a sporran-like purse!) one suspects it is there partly for its frisson in reflecting fashionable dress.[26]

Much fuller representations of Meg are found in two of the earliest sets of engravings designed to accompany the Waverley novels, based respectively on the drawings of the Scottish artist, William Allan (1782–1850), and the prolific London illustrator, Richard Westall (1765–1836). *Illustrations of the Novels and Tales of the Author of Waverley, from the Designs of William Allan* (1820) consists of twelve plates, with no more than two accompanying any one novel. Allan's illustrations of *Guy Mannering* both involve Meg as the prominent figure: 'Meg Merrilies predicting the Fall of the House of Ellangowan' and 'Meeting of Meg Merrilies, Brown, and Dinmont, at the Ale-House in Cumberland'. These same incidents are duplicated in *Illustrations of Guy Mannering… Engraved by Charles Heath, from the*

Drawings of Richard Westall (1821), which contains six plates plus a vignette title-page; additionally, three of Westall's remaining plates feature 'Meg Merrilies Attending upon the Dying Smuggler', 'The Sudden Appearance of Meg Merrilies on Gibbie's-Knowe', and 'The Death of Meg Merrilies'.

This overlap in representing Meg is all the more remarkable in view of the different directions from which the two artists approached their project. Allan's *Illustrations*, commissioned by the Scottish publisher Archibald Constable in spring 1819, almost certainly came as a result of prompting by Scott. Allan had returned to Edinburgh in 1814 after a long period in Russia and the Near East, specialising in Turkish and Circassian figures, and by 1818 was being actively promoted by Scott as a leading Scottish painter. Letters between Constable & Co. and their London partners Hurst, Robinson & Co. reflect Allan's painstaking progress, broken by patches of illness, his refusal to be hurried and a series of complaints levelled at the London engravers. No direct mention is made of the two *Mannering* drawings, but it is deducible that they formed part of a batch of three studies dispatched from Edinburgh on 15 January 1820. While there is no clear evidence that Scott intervened directly, his growing friendship with Allan makes it likely that he fulfilled in some degree an earlier-stated ambition to be at John Flaxman's 'elbow when at work'.[27] Scott was also instrumental in Allan's conversion from exotic subject-matter to Scottish history, and the commissioning of the Waverley illustrations coincides with comments on Allan's sketch of the 'Murder of Archbishop Sharpe' indicative of Scott's idea of the 'historical picturesque': 'The savage ferocity of the assassins crowding one on another … contrasted with the old mans figure and that of his daughter endeavouring to interpose … are all amazingly well combined in the sketch.' Scott doubted whether a painting could preserve the same immediacy, but when the finished version was exhibited in 1821 he expressed admiration for its fidelity to Scottish 'manners': 'The faithful turn of the Scottish visages so different from the fantastic vision which an Englishman might have introduced of plaids & tartan & highland sergeants strikes every one.'[28]

If Allan enjoyed something like the reputation of official artist to the Waverley novels, Richard Westall was regarded by Scott and his coadjutors more as a necessary evil, a means of propagating a popular image of the poems and novels and squeezing an extra margin of profit out of sales. His illustrations of *The Lay of the Last*

Minstrel, in 1809, were the first to be based on Scott's poetry. Similar sets followed, some in competition with rival publications, though by the time of *The Lord of the Isles* (1815) Westall seems to have been operating on a semi-official basis and receiving cantos as they were printed. Work on the fiction began with *Ivanhoe* (1819), followed by illustrations in 1821 to *The Monastery* and *Guy Mannering*, all of which were commissioned by Hurst, Robinson & Co. In providing illustrations for the poems, Westall had written at least twice to Scott seeking approval for his choice of subject, though there is nothing to indicate that he received anything other than bland assurances in return. Scott's fears for his 'highland figures' in *The Lady of the Lake* (1810) indicate little faith in Westall's ability to interpret Scottish subjects: 'I expect to see my chieftain Sir Roderick *Dhu*...in the guize of a recruiting serjaint of the Black Watch and his Bard the very model of Auld Robin Gray upon a japand tea-tray.'[29]

Scott nevertheless conceded that he was dealing with a man of talent, and when taking on the commission Westall was close to the apogee of a fairly distinguished career. The *Catalogue* of an exhibition of paintings and drawings held at his home in Upper Charlotte Street in 1814 reveals a variety of subjects and styles, ranging through allegorical paintings, biblical subjects and the 'cottage' Picturesque. Two paintings in the latter mode – *An old Peasant smoking at a Cottage Door* and *An old Peasant in a Storm* – are both marked as owned by R. P. Knight Esq. In his *Analytical Inquiry* Knight praised 'Mr Westall's Storm in Harvest' as one of three studies 'in...which the pathos is much improved, without the picturesque effect being at all injured, by the characters and dresses being taken from common familiar life'. The distance between Westall and Allan at this stage is reflected in their Academy exhibits in 1815, when Allan's *A Circassian Prince on Horse-Back, Selling Two Boys of His Own Nation, to a Cossack Chief of the Black Sea* (one of three of its kind) appeared along with Westall's *Wife and Children of a Drowned Fisherman Finding His Body on the Beach after a Storm*.[30]

Considering all these differences, it is perhaps surprising that the two sets of pictures at first sight should look so similar. One contributory factor is the flattening effect of contemporary engraving, with its linear rather than tonal character. Moreover, Scott's way of 'picturing' Meg was tailor-made for the broad figural approach adopted by each artist. The word 'figure' (in the sense of 'shape' or 'outline') appears about forty times in *Guy Mannering*, at least twelve occurrences relating directly to Meg, in six of the nine incidents where she features prominently. Most often she appears suddenly, evoking a reaction of surprise from the startled or amazed on-looker(s). Twice she is viewed from a position of concealment, forming a tableau: first, when Colonel Mannering as a young man views her through the walls of the old Bertram Castle; again, when the returned Brown (actually Bertram, the lost heir of Ellangowan) looks through another 'aperture' at her attendance on a dying smuggler (the subject of one of Westall's illustrations). Articles of dress feature in all but two instances, usually with an emphasis on their bizarre or variegated nature. Even in the initial still-frames there is a sense of agitation; alternatively, in more complex sequences, Meg springs into animated action, as when noticing Brown's presence in the second incident noted above. All this was grist to the mill for Westall, who had earlier flattered Scott for 'the picturesque skill with which you have wrought every important scene in your works'.[31]

Ultimately, however, it is the *dissimilarities* between the two artists that are most telling. Some derive from stylistic conventions already touched on. Allan's shift to Scottish subjects brought him closer to the domestic genre painting of David Wilkie; Westall's Reynoldsian training is evident in an emphasis on composition and stylistic patterning. Most striking of all, though, is a marked difference in the depiction of Meg Merrilies. Both artists clearly want to show a tall, impressive woman – but their gypsies are otherwise essentially distinct in dress, mannerism and (apparently) ethnic origin.

Before discussing the two artists' depiction of Meg Merrilies delivering her famous speech to the Laird of Ellangowan, it is worth recalling the novel's set-piece description of her figure in the wake of the departure of the gypsy caravan:

She was standing upon one of those high banks, which, as we before noticed, overhung the road; so that she was placed considerably higher than Ellangowan, even though he was on horseback; and her tall figure, relieved against the clear blue sky, seemed almost of supernatural height. We have noticed, that there was in her general attire, or rather in her mode of adjusting it, somewhat of a foreign costume, artfully adopted perhaps for the purpose of adding to the effect of her spells and predictions, or perhaps from some traditional notions respecting the dress of her ancestors. On this occasion, she had a large piece of red cotton cloth rolled about her head in the form of a turban, from beneath which her dark eyes flashed with uncommon lustre. Her long and tangled black hair fell in elf locks from the folds of this singular head gear. Her attitude was that of a sybil in frenzy, and

Fig. 6.2 Engraving by Charles Heath, after Richard Westall, title-page vignette illustrating Meg Merrilies.

she stretched out, in her right hand, a sapling bough which seemed just pulled. (I, 122–3)[32]

Westall's vignette illustration (figure 6.2) places Meg on a bank of crag-like proportions, with a Highlandish mountain range in the distance. Both elevation and gesture are reminiscent of Gray's *The*

Bard, a popular source for two generations of painters from Thomas Jones (1774) to John Martin, whose version was exhibited at the Royal Academy in 1817. Meg herself appears in a long dress, with a dramatically flowing shawl, and a hat of indeterminate nature through which appear to be poking Westall's version of 'elf locks'. The cane-like object held aloft considerably extends the line of the figure. In most respects, accuracy of costume and Meg's gypsyhood are sacrificed in favour of linear design. If Westall manages a 'picturesque' effect, in conventional terms, it is mostly through implied physical movement. 'The more it's *smooth surface* is *ruffled*', Gilpin had argued when discussing 'the human form' in 'On Picturesque Beauty', 'the more picturesque it appears. When it is agitated by passion, and it's muscles swoln by strong exertion, the whole frame is shewn to the most advantage.'[33]

Even taking into consideration the opportunities allowed by a full plate, Allan's different way of handling his figures (figure 6.3) is immediately apparent. Compared with Westall's quasi-Shakespearean riders (a hangover from work as a young artist on Boydell's Shakespeare Gallery), Bertram and his groom are clothed more as men of their period and given facial expressions. Allan's greater attention to detail is again manifest in the caravan of gypsies, whose brimmed hats and panniered asses are just perceptible in the middle distance. The comparative closeness of the main grouping is made possible by the smallness of the eminence where Meg stands, itself more in keeping with the Solway coastline and the 'small hillock' (III, 134) later noted by Scott. In outline the figure of Meg is squatter and less stylised, though still dominating the two horsemen beneath. Allan's gypsy also grasps a much smaller sapling; her face is noticeably darker than the other protagonists; and on her head she wears a turban.

Clearly this is more than just a matter of 'right' and 'wrong' interpretations, since both artists might be said to have picked out strands from Scott's over-determined rhetoric. Westall could point to more than a hint of sublimity in the repeated stress on Meg's stature and elevation ('high banks, which...overhung the road', 'placed considerably higher than Ellangowan', 'her tall figure...almost of supernatural height'). In terms of graphic detail, however, Allan is more faithful. The text's emphasis on the darkness of Meg's features is clear-cut. Scott also seems to go out of his way to observe the 'foreign' nature of the dress adopted, and effectively offers his readers

Fig. 6.3   Engraving by H. Cook, after William Allan, *Meg Merrilies predicting the Fall of the House of Ellangowan.*

a lesson on how native Indian turbans are made ('a large piece of red cotton cloth rolled about her head in the form of a turban'). Even Allan's mixture of Eastern and Scottish elements (a plaid hangs over one shoulder) could claim authority from an earlier description of Meg in the old Tower of Ellangowan, 'Equipt in a habit which mingled the national dress of the Scottish common people with something of an eastern costume' (I, 64).

One important break with the stereotypical 'picturesque' gypsy is apparent, however, and survives in both pictures. Rather than being

Fig. 6.4   Engraving by Chas. Warren, after William Allan, *Meeting of Meg Merrilies,*
Brown and Dinmont, at the Ale-House in Cumberland.

subservient to the landscape, or reflective of its grandeur, Meg stands
separate and gazes *towards* the proprietorial figures of Bertram and
groom. The process reverses Mannering's first full viewing of her
figure, which comes as an end-point *after* a sweeping visual 'tour' of
Ellangowan, taking in cultivated vales, straggling hedgerows, a
seascape corresponding 'in variety and beauty', the 'well situated'
New Place of Ellangowan, and finally 'the ruined castle' (1, 58–62).
Scott's account of Derncleugh (*anglice*, a hidden ravine), similarly
employs a number of metaphors familiar in the Pricean Picturesque.

Conversely, Bertram's intervention, an over-zealous exercise of power expressed in terms of enclosure and prohibition, mirrors the devastation caused by Price's insensitive 'improver' ('in a few hours, the rash hand of false taste completely demolishes what time only, and a thousand lucky accidents can mature'). Even the 'hollow way' where the confrontation takes place in some respects represents a bleaker northerly version of the 'hollow-lanes and by-roads' favoured by Price, in which might be nurtured 'the slender elegant form of a young beech, ash, or birch'.[34] In this case, however, Meg stands starkly on the *edge* of the bank, holding the broken bough of an ash. In Allan's interpretation, too, there are signs of a transposition to another kind of figure, the enigmatic Romantic gypsy.

The 'Meeting of Meg Merrilies, Brown, and Dinmont', where Westall and Allan are both working in a similar frame, relates to the first appearance of Meg after a time-shift of some twenty years. Brown (unaware of his origins) stops at an ale-house in Cumberland on a Northern walking tour, and there meets the Border hill farmer, Dandie Dinmont. The incident chosen is Meg's reaction on over-hearing of the death of Godfrey Bertram: '"Dead!" – said the old woman, dropping her pipe, rising and coming forward upon the floor – "dead! – are ye sure of that?"' (II, 15). Since the text is primarily dialogic here, both artists draw on material from the surrounding passages to set the scene. Allan (figure 6.4), for instance, latches onto previous mention of Dinmont's 'saddled horse' in a shed, extending the anecdotal range of his picture. He also manages to translate Scott's 'tall, stout, country-looking man, in a large jockey great-coat' (II, 9) into a suitably burly and bucolic figure. The clutter of the wardrobe, though all Allan's, is defensible as an extrapolation from earlier indications of the 'rudeness' of the inn; and, together with the random articles on the floor, has the effect of enclosing all the figures in a kind of picturesque dishevelment.

Westall's composition (figure 6.5) belongs almost exclusively to its figures. Apart from the broken pipe, there are few still-life details to indicate disorder – the latticed window, in fact, gives more of a sense of a safe haven. The figures in the left of the picture – an effete, almost dandified Brown, with Dinmont as if in attendance – exude an air of contentment. Even the stolid-looking landlady lends an element of calm. Dominating the other half of the frame is the agitated figure of Meg. For her facial features and body movement Westall probably

Fig. 6.5   Engraving by Charles Heath, after Richard Westall, *The Meeting of Meg Merrilies, Brown and Dinmont.*

drew on a fuller description at the beginning of the next chapter, where Brown stares at Meg in a state of half-recognition:

he could not avoid repeatedly fixing his eyes on Meg Merrilies. She was, in all respects, the same witch-like figure as when we first introduced her at Ellangowan-Place. Time had grizzled her raven locks, and added wrinkles to her wild features, but her height remained erect, and her activity was unimpaired. It was remarked of this woman, as of others of the same description, that a life of action, though not of labour, gave her the perfect command of her limbs and figure, so that the attitudes into which she most naturally threw herself, were free, unconstrained, and picturesque. (II, 20–1)

Once again Scott proves an accurate practitioner of the discourse of the Picturesque – the 'unconstrained' movement matches Knight's advocacy of 'certain postures, in which the body naturally throws itself'[35] – and this passes straight into Westall's animated, if angular figure. In the two halves of the frame, however, one senses a more disruptive division between the sanitised cottage Picturesque and a more alarming image of cultural alienation.

In contrast, Allan's Meg stands firmly near the centre, her bare feet again making contact with the ground, and in a posture suggesting both responsiveness and a capacity to reveal knowledge. Above all, she remains the same mysterious hybrid of Eastern and Scottish characteristics, though the text here offers little to encourage this interpretation. Even the sparse details given about Meg before her intervention – 'a tall woman, in a red cloak and slouched bonnet, with the appearance of a tinker or beggar' (II, 9) – work in Westall's favour. The only possible support for Allan occurs in a brief paragraph, describing the reaction of Brown immediately following on the description of Meg's 'witch-like figure' quoted above. In particular it is worth noting that Brown is a professional soldier, just returned from service with the East India Company:

On his part, he was surprised to find that he could not look upon this singular figure without some emotion. 'Have I dreamed of such a figure?' he said to himself, 'or does this wild and singular-looking woman recal to my recollection some of the strange figures I have seen in our Indian pagodas?' (II, 21)

Why should Allan persist with this image of an Eastern-looking Meg? A possible linking point can be found in a letter of Scott's of June 1821, describing how he had taken Allan to see a gypsy at first hand: 'Yesterday I hunted out for him an old gypsey woman whose figure and features I was much struck with as I passed her on the road. As I found the artist studying a sketch of the recovery of a child which had been stolen by gipsies my old woman was quite a wind-fall...'[36] Among other things, the incident points to a fairly long-standing interest in gypsies on both sides (Allan had exhibited 'A Gypsy Boy and Ass', reportedly in the style of John Opie, before sailing to Russia in 1805).[37] In discussing Allan's travels, Scott and Allan are almost bound to have touched on the subject of gypsies, who had long been held to have entered Europe from the East in the early fifteenth century. It is not impossible that Allan had seen living examples himself. Travelling bands of gypsies feature in a number of popular travel books of the period. The first volume (1810) of Edward Daniel Clarke's *Travels in Various Countries*, for example, expands interestingly on its vivid account of a troupe of gypsy dancers in Moscow:

This extraordinary people, found in all parts of Europe, were originally one of the *casts* of India, driven out of their own territory, and distinguished among Indian tribes by a name which signifies Thieves... The extraordinary resemblance of the female gipsies to the women of India, was remarked by our officers and men in Egypt, when General Baird arrived with his army to join Lord Hutchinson.[38]

The odd montage of British, Indian and gypsy elements in the last part of the quotation is uncannily close to Brown's reaction to Meg Merrilies at the Cumberland ale-house.

In fact, the idea that the gypsies had emigrated from India (rather than from Egypt or Bohemia) was gaining ground as Clarke was writing. As a theory it first gained credence through the work of the German scholar, Heinrich Grellmann, whose *Dissertation on the Gipsies* (1783) was translated into English in 1787. Grellmann based his argument on an alleged similarity between the gypsy language and Hindustani, and also located the gypsies in the Indian caste system, identifying them with 'the lowest class of Indians, namely, *Parias*'.[39] Undoubtedly, too, the idea gained wider currency as officers employed by the East India Company made their own linguistic researches, or drew wider comparisons based on their Indian and British experiences. An interesting example is Captain David Richardson's 'An Account of the Bazeegars', which appeared in the seventh volume of *Asiatick Researches*, published in Calcutta in 1801. Richardson reported a number of similarities between the European gypsies and a special group in India, noted for their skill at juggling, 'adept in astrology', and occupying 'temporary huts'.[40] By the time of John Hoyland's *Historical Survey of the Gypsies* (1816), which carried a response by Scott on the Selkirkshire gypsies, the idea had evidently achieved the status of a *donné*.[41] A shift from the old tropes of child-kidnapping and carnivalesque democracy, to more exoticised images of gypsy alterity, is also apparent in the imaginative writing of John Leyden, James Hogg and Hazlitt, all of whom pointed to an Eastern origin.[42]

If Allan's knowledge of the debate is an unknown factor, there can be little doubt that Scott was aware of these issues when writing *Guy*

Mannering and that he was well on his way to accepting the Indian theory. His brief answer to Hoyland's questionnaire shows a reluctance to apply it to the vagrants in his own region: 'I do not conceive them to be the proper Oriental Egyptian race, at least they are much intermingled with our own national out-laws and vagabonds.'[43] More positive is a sequence of articles in *Blackwood's Magazine*, 'Notices Concerning the Scottish Gypsies', the first of which (April 1817) contains large sections by Scott. One passage which can be identified as his tangles with the question of whether there is a distinct gypsy language: 'A lady who had been in India addressed some gypsies in the *Hindhustanee* language, from the received opinion that it is similar to their own. They did not apparently understand her, but were extremely incensed at what they conceived a mockery; so it is probable that the sound of the language had an affinity to that of their own.'[44] Any lingering doubts had been dispelled by the time of two notes written for the 'Magnum Opus' edition (1831) of *Quentin Durward*, which together embrace the twin branches of the Indian theory: the proximity of the Romani and 'Hindostanee' languages; and the affinity between the gypsies and Indian Pariahs. Both notes relate to contexts in the novel where gypsies appear wearing turbans.[45]

Also familiar with turbans is Colonel Mannering, an amateur artist, who at one point is observed by his daughter, Julia, adjusting 'the folds of a Mahratta's turban' on a sketch intended to illustrate 'the peculiar notions and manners of a certain tribe of Indians' (II, 131, 129). In comparison with Meg's opaque Eastern ambience, the past experiences of the novel's East Indians are surprisingly clear and graphic. The tight chronology of the main action in *Guy*, set 'near the end of the American war' (II, 255) and almost certainly in November/December 1782, places Mannering's military career in close conjunction with a series of dramatic engagements involving the main British settlements in India between 1780 and 1782. Glimpses of the conflict surface in unexpected guises. While Mannering elaborates turbans, imperial occupation and the world of fashion are conflated as Julia smudges 'Turks' heads' on visiting cards: 'I assure you I succeeded in making a superb Hyder-Ally last night' (II, 134). Even in Scott's earlier account of the Derncleugh gypsies ('the *Parias* of Scotland, living like wild Indians among European settlers' (I, 103)) there are suggestions of the Bengal system of land occupancy, whose deleterious effects (which included the creation of landless

Fig. 6.6   Engraving by Charles Heath, after Richard Westall, *The Sudden Appearance of Meg Merrilies on Gibbie's-Knowe.*

labourers as a result of villages being parcelled together into larger estates) came under critical scrutiny in the public debate over the renewal of the East India Company's charter (which lapsed in 1813) in the years immediately preceding *Guy Mannering*.[46]

Only in the closing stages of the story, at Ellangowan, does Meg appear as a tangible *figure* again. In the absence of a contribution from Allan, one is left with Westall's two last plates as the earliest surviving contemporary illustrations.[47] 'The Sudden Appearance of Meg Merrilies on Gibbie's-Knowe' (figure 6.6) conflates elements from three equally stark manifestations, Meg's appearance being drawn mainly from a slightly earlier incident involving the young

Fig. 6.7   Engraving by Charles Heath, after Richard Westall, *The Death of Meg Merrilies*.

aristocratic Charles Hazlewood: 'He looked up; the spokes-woman was very tall, had a voluminous handkerchief rolled round her head, her grizzled hair flowing in elf-locks from beneath it, a long red cloak, and a staff in her hand, headed with a sort of spear point – it was, in short, Meg Merrilies' (III, 148–9). Westall's picture incorporates a number of familiar stylistic features. The beckoning figure dominating one side of the frame is kept sharply distinct from the group of fashionably dressed young people, especially the two female figures. Meg's headgear presumably represents another attempt at a rolled handkerchief with elf locks rampant, but the addition of a chin-strap is more reminiscent of Mrs Egerton. Similarly, the theatrical spear exceeds the pointed 'staff' first seen by Hazlewood. At the same time, the outlandishness of the figure is not entirely inapposite to the narrative at this stage. Leading Brown–Bertram and Dinmont away along the path of revisitation, Meg seems curiously spectral and disconnected from a nascently 'Picturesque' landscape:

> Her tall figure moved across the wintry heath with steps so swift, so long, and so steady, that she appeared rather to glide than to walk…She proceeded straight across the common, without turning aside to the winding path, by which passengers avoided the inequalities and little rills which traversed it in different directions…Her way was as straight, and nearly as swift, as that of a bird through the air. (III, 267–8)

Westall's last illustration ('The Death of Meg Merrilies': figure 6.7) shows the struggle in the smuggler Dirk Hatteraick's cave as Dinmont, Brown and Hazlewood rush at their diabolical foe. Meg, who has been mortally wounded, dominates the near foreground; but the eye is nevertheless directed to the pillar of smoke, the mixture of light and shade and the decisive onslaught on Hatteraick.[48] In crawling into the cave Hazlewood had earlier tugged at Dinmont's leg, as a sign that he was joining the group, thus metaphorically linking himself with the yeomanry and an older aristocracy. Faced with such a union of patriarchal interests, Meg fades into something of an irrelevance – in Westall's interpretation, effectively, into the ground. The last faint hint of a potent alterity occurs in a (safely misunderstood) request about her last resting position ('Na, na! not that way, not that way, the head to the east' (III, 301)); otherwise voice and figure are lost in the pieties of an attending minister and the acclamation of Bertram–Brown's disembodied tenantry. The novel ends in an orgy of planning: a 'cottage at Derncleugh', a 'Bungalow' for Mannering, and 'a large and splendid house…to be built on the scite [sic] of the New Place of Ellangowan, in a style corresponding to the magnificence of the ruins in its vicinity' (III, 352, 353, 358). The overall effervescence is captured in the facetiousness of the Edinburgh lawyer, Pleydell, and in Mannering's response:

> 'tower in the centre to be in imitation of the Eagle Tower at Caernarvon – *corps de logis* – the devil! – wings – wings? why, the house will take the estate of Ellangowan on its back, and fly away with it!'
> 'Why, then, we must ballast it with a few bags of Sicca rupees.' (III, 355–6)

* * *

'…I have made the old farm-house my *corps de logis*, with some outlying places for kitchen, laundry, and two spare bed-rooms, which run along the east wall of the old farm-court, not without some picturesque effect'.[49] Scott's letter to Daniel Terry, written as he was nearing the end of *Guy Mannering*, offers a sharp glimpse at the almost symbiotic relationship which existed between the writing of the early Waverley novels and the construction of Abbotsford. The original estate (Newarthaugh), consisting of a small farmhouse overshadowed by its barn, 110 acres of almost unwooded ground, and only the nearby Tweed as an indication of its 'picturesque' potential, had been purchased from Dr Douglas, the Galashiels minister, in 1811. Almost immediately Scott turned to Uvedale Price ('I am of course busy with Price and all manner of essays on picturesque scenery'); and it must have been with reference to essays such as 'On Architecture and Buildings' that the decision was made to build a new 'cottage', with a garden close by, integrating the existing buildings in the form of offices. By November 1816, buoyed up by profits from the novels, the scheme was revived in the form of an interlinking building between the farmhouse and out-houses, with Scott relishing the prospect of the irregularity such a spontaneous development would allow:

when the cottage enlarges itself and grows out of circumstances which is the case at Abbotsford the *outs* and *inns* afford without so much variety and depth of shade and within give such an odd variety of snugg accommodation that they far exceed in my estimation the cut-lugged bandbox with four rooms on a floor and two stories rising regularly above each other.[50]

From the earliest stages, too, Scott began planning his 'plantations'. 'Forest trees flourish with me at a great rate', Lady Abercorn was told in 1813, 'and of my whole possession of 120 acres I have reduced about 70 to woodland both upon principles of taste and œconomy. I have been studying Price with all my eyes and [am] not without hopes of converting an old gravel-pit into a bower and an exhausted quarry into a bathing-house. So you see my dear Madam how deeply I am bit with the madness of the picturesque'. Price also surfaces in another letter, written two days earlier to Joanna Baillie, in which Scott describes John Winnos (Waynes), his factotum in such operations: 'I cannot help singing his praises at this moment because I have so many odd and out of the way things to do that I believe the conscience of many of our jog-trot Countrymen would revolt at being made my instrument in sacrificing good corn land to the visions of Mr

Price's theory.' By 15 January 1815, just as *Guy* was being completed, Scott was able to tell Terry that 'the young wood upon the bank begins to appear hérissé & tufty even at some distance'; and, in the same year, he started purchasing adjoining territory (beginning with Kaeside), some of which, like Dick's Cleugh (renamed the Rhymer's Glen), brought with it more natural Picturesque effects. Scott's letter to Terry informing him about the second acquisition is filled to overspilling with Price, and all the more remarkable for placing a not unfamiliar figure in a 'deep ravine' (Derncleugh?): 'did I tell you that I have acquired a new glen near the lake? a quiet invisible sort of dell where a witch might boil her kettle in happy seclusion among old thorn trees & scathed oaks in a deep ravine totally out of sight unless you fall on it by accident.'[51]

In this way, Meg Merrilies might be said to have found a resting place at Abbotsford, at least in Scott's imagination. When next invoking Price, in two articles on 'Planting Waste Lands' and 'Landscape Gardening' in 1827/8, Scott had developed a full-scale programme for national afforestation, capable in his eyes of supporting 'a hardy and moral population...naturally attached to the soil'.[52] While it is inviting to look for overlaps between Knight's and Price's Whiggism, with its hostility to 'levelling', whether by democrats or despots, and Scott's anti-Reformism, especially in the 1820s, important distinctions need to be noted. At one point in the *Essay on the Picturesque* Price acknowledges the superior claims of agriculture over the unproductively Picturesque: 'The painter may indeed lament, but that science which of all others most benefits mankind, has a right to more than forgiveness, when wild thickets are converted into scenes of plenty and industry, and where gipsies and vagrants give way to the less picturesque figures of husbandmen and their attendants.'[53] Yet for much of the rest of the *Essay* there is an implicit suggestion that this will not (and perhaps *should not*) always be the case: the operation of those key elements, 'accident and neglect' and 'age and decay', is at least partly contingent on a condition of 'plenitude', to use Sidney K. Robinson's term, and 'the exercise of less control than one has access to'.[54] Control was never far from the surface at Abbotsford, and plenitude wore a coat of different colour. The sense of 'over-population' propagated by the myth of the laird of Abbotsford is not reflected in the personnel employed during the early improvements. No witch (or equivalent) would ever shelter in the Rhymer's Glen; the only human presence there in 1816 being an unemployed parishioner constructing a path to where Scott would later commission a cascade and rustic bridge. Scott's actual way of dealing with gypsies, as reported to Hoyland, is not remote from the elder Bertram's, and has more than a smack of the modern residents' association: 'Mr Riddell, Justice of Peace for Roxburghshire, with my assistance and concurrence, cleared this country of the last of them, about eight or nine years ago. They were thorough desperadoes, of the worst class of vagabonds.'[55]

Robinson also points to a dissipation of Picturesque theory through bourgeois appropriation, a concentration on surface meaning and 'rejection of the public realm'.[56] Scott's move to Abbotsford – and the eventual realisation of the 'cottage' as a baronial mansion – can be interpreted as an attempt to balance estate culture with professional values in Edinburgh, where Scott inhabited a Georgian terrace house during legal terms. His main entrée to the country gentry nevertheless was provided by profits from the book trade (a paper equivalent of Mannering's rupees), and the burgeoning house matched a wider proliferation of villas and cottages in accessible areas like Tweeddale, encouraged by the fall of land prices after the war and the building boom in the 1820s. In spite of claims of organic development, there was a frantic side to Scott's incorporation of 'oldness' and exotic variety: '*debris* from Melrose Abbey' for the well; bits rescued from 'the old Tolbooth of Edinburgh'; contrastive suits of Indian and 'Gothic' armour (where Allan was needed as a consultant).[57] In one respect, there remains something inherently more 'Picturesque' in Godfrey Bertram's 'cut-lugged bandbox' of a house, when seen in relation to the variegated terrain at Ellangowan and half-stationary residents at Derncleugh, than in all the hectic planning at the end of *Guy Mannering*. As Scott states in a well-known passage from the Magnum Opus Introduction to *The Fortunes of Nigel*: 'the most picturesque period of history is that when the ancient rough and wild manners of a barbarous age are just becoming innovated upon'.[58] The true Picturesque, then, can only be predicated on the past, and a past in a perilously transitional situation.

A final feature of Abbotsford takes us back to figures, while suggesting another shift in the Picturesque in Regency Britain. One source for the myth of gregarious over-population can be found in Scott's habit of 'dressing up' workers and guests in 'picturesque' guises. Thus John Waynes, when not 'ploughing harrowing and overseeing all my premises', was encouraged to follow his 'natural'

inclination as a poacher: 'he solemnly exchanges his working jacket
for an old green one of mine and takes the air of one of Robin Hoods
followers'. The process rebounded on Scott, to his evident pleasure,
in David Wilkie's painting 'The Abbotsford Family', which originated from a visit to Abbotsford in October 1817. 'The idea', Scott
recalled to Adam Ferguson in 1827, 'was to represent our family
group in the garb of South country peasants supposed to be
concerting a merry-making, for which some preparations are seen.
The place is the terrace near Kayside, commanding an extensive
view towards the Eildon Hills.' (Ferguson himself – soon to be taking
up his post as Deputy Keeper of the Scottish Regalia – is depicted as
'a country wag, addicted to poaching'.)[59] The finished picture, when
exhibited at the Royal Academy in 1818, was described by the
Catalogue in the following terms:

In the centre is Mr Scott seated on a bank, at his left hand is his friend Capt.
A Ferguson,... and behind them is an old dependant of the family. On the
right is Mrs Scott, attired as a cottage matron, with her daughters as ewe-
milkers. In front of the picture is Mr Scott's gigantic stag greyhound, of the
ancient Highland race now almost extinct, and in the distance is a view of
the Tweed, and the town and abbey of Melrose, and the top of
Cowdenknows.[60]

The same *Catalogue* itemises Miss M. A. Flaxman's 'Meg Merrilies
and the Domini Sampson, in the Kaim of Derncleugh'. It would be
hard to think of a more succinct illustration of the capacity of the
Picturesque to embody both imagined old and tangibly new figures
in the landscape.

NOTES

1 *Augustan Review*, vol. 1 (July 1815), p. 232; William Wordsworth to R. P.
   Gillies, 25 April 1815, *The Letters of William and Dorothy Wordsworth*, ed.
   Ernest de Selincourt, second edition, 6 vols. (Oxford: Clarendon Press,
   1967–82), vol. III, p. 232. The quoted passages also appear in John O.
   Hayden (ed.), *Scott: The Critical Heritage* (London: Routledge and
   Kegan Paul, 1970), pp. 86–9.
2 William Gilpin, *Three Essays: On Picturesque Beauty; On Picturesque
   Travel; and On Sketching Landscape*, third edition (London, 1808), p. 77.
3 William Gilpin, *Observations Relative Chiefly to Picturesque Beauty, Made in
   the Year 1772, on Several Parts of England; Particularly the Mountains, and
   Lakes of Cumberland and Westmoreland*, 2 vols. (London, 1786), vol. II, pp.
   45–7. For Thickness's full account, see *A Year's Journey through France, and
   Parts of Spain*, 2 vols. (London, 1777), vol. I, pp. 277–8. For a discussion

of Gilpin's attitude to work and the Picturesque, see Stephen Copley's essay in this volume.

4 William Gilpin, *An Essay upon Prints*, third edition (London, 1781), p. 80. Rosa's 'almost obsessive desire to be known as a master of the human figure in all its aspects rather than [as] a landscape artist' is noted in the catalogue to an exhibition of his works held at the Hayward Gallery, London, 1973 (*Salvator Rosa*, Arts Council, 1973, p. 50).

5 Richard Payne Knight, *An Analytical Inquiry into the Principles of Taste* (London, 1805), pp. 194, 152.

6 Uvedale Price, *An Essay on the Picturesque, as Compared with the Sublime and the Beautiful*, in Sir Thomas Dick Lauder (ed.), *Sir Uvedale Price on the Picturesque* (Edinburgh, 1842), p. 87.

7 *Ibid.*, p. 155.

8 Uvedale Price, 'A Dialogue on the Distinct Characters of the Picturesque and the Beautiful', in Lauder (ed.), *Price on the Picturesque*, p. 506.

9 Elizabeth Wheeler Manwaring, *Italian Landscape in Eighteenth Century England* (New York: Oxford University Press, 1925), p. 55.

10 Price, 'Dialogue', p. 511.

11 Price, *Essay*, p. 88.

12 In David Hewitt (ed.), *Scott on Himself* (Edinburgh: Scottish Academic Press, 1981), p. 37.

13 Alexander M. Ross, *The Imprint of the Picturesque on Nineteenth-Century British Fiction* (Waterloo: Wilfrid Laurier University Press, 1986), p. 41. For Gilpin on the 'picturesque in action', see 'On Picturesque Beauty' (*Three Essays*, p. 13).

14 Marcia Allentuck, 'Scott and the Picturesque: Afforestation and History', in Alan Bell (ed.), *Scott Bicentenary Essays* (Edinburgh: Scottish Academic Press, 1973), pp. 188–98.

15 *The Letters of Sir Walter Scott*, ed. H. J. C. Grierson, 12 vols. (London: Constable, 1932–7), vol. VII, p. 97.

16 See Gilpin in 'On Picturesque Beauty', where the ass is preferred to 'the pampered horse' (*Three Essays*, p. 14). Compare Price: 'The ass is generally thought to be more picturesque than the horse...' (*Essay*, p. 85).

17 *Letters*, vol. I, pp. 226–7.

18 Knight, *Analytical Inquiry*, p. 302. Scott's admiration for 'the celebrated picture of the Witch of Endor' is recorded by John Scott, in *Journal of a Tour to Waterloo and Paris, in Company with Sir Walter Scott in 1815* (London, 1842), p. 159.

19 Graham McMaster, *Scott and Society* (Cambridge University Press, 1981), pp. 158–61; Elaine Jordan, 'The Management of Scott's Novels', in Francis Barker *et al.* (eds.), *Europe and its Others*, 2 vols. (Colchester: University of Essex, 1985), vol. II, pp. 146–52.

20 Katie Trumpener, 'The Time of the Gypsies: A "People without History"', *Critical Inquiry*, 18 (1992), 843–84, 849.

21 The continuing currency of these types is reflected in the following works
exhibited at the British Institution in the years immediately surrounding
Guy Mannering: *Gipsies Regaling Themselves* by Sir William Beechey in
1814; *Travelling Gypsies* by Thomas Barker in 1815; and *A Gipsey Girl* by
John Boaden in 1818. The suitability of the first two for 'picturesque'
illustration is evident in two plates of 'Gypsies' drawn and etched by W.
H. Pyne, featuring 1) three studies of gypsies in transit, and 2) two
studies of gypsy encampments (see *Microcosm: or, A Picturesque Delineation
of the Arts, Agriculture, Manufactures, &c. of Great Britain*, second edition, 2
vols. (London, 1806), plates opposite vol. I, pp. 10, 17). A coloured
engraving concentrating on a single gypsy figure is found in Plate xxxvII
in *Picturesque Representations of the Dress and Manners of the English* (London,
1814), where a youngish woman holding a child lags behind a caravan
of gypsies, looking backwards in the direction of the viewer. The picture
sits oddly next to a prose commentary which in a detached tone points
to the gypsies' diminishing numbers, a pattern still more evident in the
contrast between Pyne's illustrations and the Malthusian text supplied
by C. Gray to *Microcosm*. For a discussion of the relationship between
pictures and commentary in the latter, see John Barrell's chapter,
'Visualising the Division of Labour: William Pyne's *Microcosm*', in *The
Birth of Pandora and the Division of Knowledge* (London: Macmillan, 1991),
pp. 89–118.

22 Price, *Essay*, p. 87; Knight, *Analytical Inquiry*, p. 152.

23 Claire Lamont, 'Meg the Gipsy in Scott and Keats', *English*, 36 (1987),
141. De Wilde's drawing is in the British Museum, English Drawings,
L.B.9. I am indebted to Miss Lamont for allowing me to see an earlier
and fuller version of her essay. For a general account of illustrations of
Scott, see Catherine Gordon, 'The Illustration of Sir Walter Scott:
Nineteenth-Century Enthusiasm and Adaptation', *Journal of the Warburg
and Courtauld Institute*, 34 (1971), 297–317.

24 For a record of early performances of the play (the first to be based on
a Scott novel), see H. Philip Bolton, *Scott Dramatized* (London: Mansell,
1992), pp. 56–60. A more likely origin of the stick is the 'goodly sloe-
thorn cudgel' carried by Meg on her first appearance in the novel.

25 *Letters*, vol. II, p. 471. In the same letter (5 April 1811), Scott recommends
the description of Wat of Harden in 'a very picturesque ballad by a
living borderer [James Hogg's "Gilmanscleuch"]' as a guide to ancient
Border dress.

26 Ladies' turbans, made from various materials and particularly gauze,
were 'almost *de rigueur* in the evening for the first twenty years of the
century' (James Laver, *Fashions and Fashion Plates 1800–1900* (London:
Penguin Books, 1943), p. 9). For a fuller discussion of women's fashions
and the Picturesque, see Ann Bermingham's essay in this volume
(turbans are mentioned specifically on p. 101).

27 *Letters*, vol. I, p. 227.

28 *Ibid.*, vol. v, p. 350; vol. vi, p. 393.

29 *Ibid.*, vol. ii, p. 321.

30 *A Catalogue of an Exhibition of a Selection of the Pictures and Drawings of Richard Westall, R.A.* (1814); Knight, *Analytical Inquiry*, p. 305; *The Exhibition of the Royal Academy MDCCCXV*, items 166, 102.

31 National Library of Scotland, MS 3877, f. 108v (Westall to Scott, 5 August 1808).

32 All references to *Guy Mannering* refer to the first edition (1815), and are given by volume and page number in parenthesis within the main text.

33 Gilpin, *Three Essays*, p. 12.

34 Price, *Essay*, pp. 73, 70–1.

35 Knight, *Analytical Inquiry*, p. 205. Meg's wrinkles and 'grizzled' locks likewise echo Gilpin on the 'patriarchal head' as an exemplar of the 'picturesque' in facial features ('On Picturesque Beauty', *Three Essays*, p. 10).

36 *Letters*, vol. vi, p. 469.

37 Allan's career as an artist is described in David and Francina Irwin, *Scottish Painters at Home and Abroad, 1700–1900* (London: Faber and Faber, 1975), pp. 207–13. For a racy account of his memento-packed studio, 'the most picturesque painting-room I fancy, in Europe', see John Gibson Lockhart, *Peter's Letters to his Kinsfolk* (1819), ed. William Ruddick (Edinburgh: Scottish Academic Press, 1977), p. 116.

38 *Travels in Various Countries of Europe, Asia and Africa*, 6 vols. (London, 1810–23), vol. i, p. 63.

39 Heinrich Grellmann, *Dissertation on the Gipsies, Being an Historical Enquiry, Concerning the Manner of Life ... of these People in Europe, and their Origin* (London, 1787), p. 168.

40 *Asiatick Researches* vol. vii (1801), pp. 457–63.

41 John Hoyland, *A Historical Survey of the Customs, Habits, and Present State of the Gypsies* (York, 1816), pp. 122–6, 228.

42 Leyden's 'Scenes of Infancy' (1803) suggests an African origin for the Border Yetholm gypsies (*Poems and Ballads* (Kelso, 1858), pp. 186–7); Hogg's 'The Gipsies' (1816?) plays on a legend of an Arabian tribe, exiled for helping the Crusaders (*Poetical Works*, 4 vols. (Edinburgh, 1822), vol. iv, pp. 281–3). William Hazlitt's juxtaposition of gypsies and 'Hindoos', each possessing more grace than the English, indicates knowledge of the 'Indian' explanation ('On Manner', 1815, *Collected Works*, 2 vols. (London, 1902), vol. i, pp. 45–6).

43 In Hoyland, *Historical Survey*, p. 95.

44 *Blackwood's Edinburgh Magazine*, vol. i (April 1817), p. 57.

45 *Waverley Novels*, 48 vols. (Edinburgh, 1829–33), vol. xxxi, pp. 116, 314, 96, 291.

46 *Copy of the Fifth Report from the Select Committee of the House of Commons on the Affairs of the East India Company* (London, 1812), *passim*.

47 A slightly later drawing by C. R. Leslie, engraved by J. Romney,

depicting 'Meg Merrilies compelling Dominie Sampson to eat', appeared as the frontispiece to vol. III of the 18mo edition of *Novels and Tales of the Author of Waverley*, 12 vols. (Edinburgh, 1823). Leslie emphasises the comic element in the incident, and there is little sense of the 'picturesque' in the uniformity of his figures.

48 For a fuller commentary on 'the picturesque properties' of this scene, see Frank Jordan, 'The Vision of Pandemonium in Scott's Novels' *Scottish Literary Journal*, 19 (1992), 24–35, 30.

49 *Letters*, vol. III, p. 514.

50 *Ibid.*, vol. XII, p. 329; vol. IV, p. 301.

51 *Ibid.*, vol. III, pp. 240, 237; vol. IV, pp. 8, 328.

52 'On Planting Waste Lands' (originally published in the *Quarterly Review*, October 1827), in *The Prose Works of Sir Walter Scott*, 30 vols. (Edinburgh, 1834–71), vol. XXI, p. 74.

53 Price, *Essay*, p. 204.

54 Sidney K. Robinson, *Inquiry into the Picturesque* (University of Chicago Press, 1991), pp. 8, 78.

55 In Hoyland, *Historical Survey*, p. 95.

56 Robinson, *Inquiry*, pp. 148–9.

57 *Letters*, vol. III, p. 154; vol. IV, pp. 289, 338, 422; vol. V, p. 171.

58 *Waverley Novels*, vol. XXVI, p. vi.

59 *Letters*, vol. III, p. 237; vol. X, pp. 168–9. For a fuller account of the history of Wilkie's piece, see Francis Russell, *Portraits of Sir Walter Scott, A Study of Romantic Portraiture* (London: Printed for the Author, 1987), pp. 90–1.

60 *The Exhibition of the Royal Academy MDCCCXVIII*, p. 10.

CHAPTER 7

Romantics, explorers and Picturesque travellers
John Whale

Tour, Journey, Voyage, Lounge, Ride, Walk,
Skim, Sketch, Excursion, Travel-talk-
For move you must! 'Tis now the rage,
The law and fashion of the Age.
. . .
Of all the children of John Bull
With empty heads and bellies full,
Who ramble East, West, North and South,
With leaky purse and open mouth,
In search of varieties exotic
The usefullest and most patriotic,
And merriest, too, believe me, Sirs!
Are your Delinquent Travellers![1]

In this essay I wish to exploit the pervasiveness of travel writing in the late eighteenth and early nineteenth century and, by exposing its permeation through 'Romantic' literary texts, to raise questions about the supposedly self-enclosed, autonomous aesthetic realm of the Romantic canon. By juxtaposing the texts of poets, explorers and Picturesque theorists, I hope to achieve an insight into the nature of the Romantic self: in particular, this figure's capacity to double between weakness and power, violence and annihilation. I am particularly interested in the nature of Romantic disappointments – a version of what Conrad was later to formulate as 'the horror, the horror'. By taking advantage of the incapacities of many of these texts, their slippages between the familiar and the exotic, the way they flip dangerously from destination to source, I hope to investigate from a new angle the recurrent problem of Romantic origins and identity.

In the context of slippage between selves, genres and cultural counters, the Picturesque, particularly in the very different examples of William Gilpin and Richard Payne Knight, offers an opportunity to explore an aesthetic discourse which attempts to accommodate exotic specimens within an English climate, and which struggles anxiously to mix cultural relativity with English patriotism.

To compare Romantic poets with explorers is familiar enough. The figure of the poet is frequently constructed through identification with outcasts, pariahs and wanderers, who are the victims of compulsive idealism and of their own irritable wanderlust. But it might be useful to enquire a little more closely into the make-up of what has often rather glibly been taken for granted as 'Romantic wanderlust' by comparing it with the Picturesque. For example, Byronic 'mobility' or '*mobilité*', consisting of 'an excessive sus-ceptibility of immediate impressions – at the same time without *losing* the past',[2] immediately suggests an interesting comparison with the Picturesque which, as we shall see, in many of its articulations combines the pleasures deriving from irritations of sense perception with a capacity to register a process of time: of decay, ruination and various forms of 'naturalisation'.

* * *

The first source of amusement to the picturesque traveller, is the *pursuit* of his object – the expectation of new scenes continually opening, and arising to his view. *We suppose the country to have been unexplored* [my italics]. Under this circumstance the mind is kept constantly in an agreeable suspence. The love of novelty is the foundation of this pleasure. Every distant horizon promises something new; and with this pleasing expecta-tion we follow nature through all her walks. We pursue her from hill to dale; and hunt after those various beauties with which she every where abounds.[3]

Gilpin suggests that the Picturesque traveller is a surrogate explorer. Appetite is here promiscuous, roving, pluralistic – a libertine freedom which seems to lack the compulsive, and potentially tragic, quest for origins and consequent terminations, which are to be found in Romantic poetry. We seem to be in the safety of native pleasure-grounds, inside a decidedly male make-believe aesthetic which has tamed, or turned its back on, the terrible threat of cultural otherness. Indeed, the Picturesque has often been considered as a safe middle-ground, a compromise category, happily mediating the dangerous Burkean opposites of the Sublime and the Beautiful. It has been thought of as offering a particularly English aesthetic of landscape and even as playing a formative role in the construction of a particular kind of Englishness.[4]

It was Gilpin, the writer of tours to various parts of Britain, who provided the opportunity for the mass consumption of the Picturesque. In so doing, as Ann Bermingham suggests, he jeopardised the scarce cultural commodity he had done so much to expound.[5] The very rarity value of the Picturesque would be lost once the roads were jammed with bourgeois tourists. If the Picturesque represented a particularly English form of landscape aesthetic to rival that of the Continent, this does not mean, of course, that it ruled out a sense of the exotic. The self-conscious make-believe evident in Gilpin's 'we suppose the ground to be undiscovered' not only raises the spectre of looking at certain parts of Britain with the imperial eyes of a leisured aesthetic ('discovering' North Wales, for example), but also gestures towards a rewriting of the landscape, a 'making it strange'. Ann Bermingham's valuable suggestion that: 'The picturesque, by restricting itself to humble English rural scenery, represented a landscape both familiar and accessible' is immediately followed by her conclusion that: 'It thus could be widely *consumed*, and with all the more enthusiasm in that the landscape it celebrated was beginning to vanish.'[6] Clearly, the precariousness of the Picturesque pertains as much to its consumption as to its definition; and in both cases it proves to be an elusive object.

Gilpin repeatedly claims that 'roughness' is the defining characteristic of the Picturesque: 'we do not scruple to assert, that *roughness* forms the most essential part of difference between the *beautiful*, and the *picturesque*'.[7] 'Roughness' may be seen as the source of Gilpin's picturesque energy – an equivalent in some ways, as we shall see, to the 'irritation' on which Richard Payne Knight also bases his theory. But this 'roughness' is as likely to be read as an effect of the Picturesque as its cause. Typically, Gilpin only flirts modestly with the origins of his Picturesque, partly as a reaction away from the materialist sensationism of Burke's theory of the Sublime and the Beautiful and partly because of a mistrust of abstract theorising itself. For example, the very logic and justification of the essay 'On Picturesque Travel' is to evade origins: 'Enough has been said to shew the difficulty of *assigning causes*: let us then take another course, and amuse ourselves with *searching after effects*. This is the general intention of picturesque travel. We mean not to bring it into competition with any of the more useful ends of travelling.'[8] Gilpin's tactic is to minimise his investment in the Picturesque, to play down its significance. For him, it is modest: a mere amusement. At the beginning of the essay on Picturesque travel he hypothesises only briefly on the morality of his aesthetics:

we have scarce ground to hope, that every admirer of *picturesque beauty*, is an admirer also of the *beauty of virtue*; and that every lover of nature reflects, that
    Nature is but a name for an *effect*,
    Whose *cause* is God –.
If however the admirer of nature can turn his amusements to a higher purpose; if it's great scenes can inspire him with religious awe; or it's tranquil scenes with that complacency of mind, which is so nearly allied to benevolence, it is certainly the better. *Apponat lucro.* It is so much into the bargain; for we dare not *promise* him more from picturesque travel, than a rational, and agreeable amusement. Yet even this may be of some use in an age teeming with licentious pleasure; and may in this light at least be considered as having a moral tendency.[9]

This modest disclaimer provides the introduction to Gilpin's fantasy of the explorer engaged in the pursuit of his Picturesque quarry. The text has slipped disarmingly from moral causes to stimulating effects.

It has long been recognised that Gilpin's confused and confusing definitions of the Picturesque depend upon a paradox.[10] The further he travels towards nature, the more he must admit artifice; the more he defines his idea of beauty, the further he flies from nature. Gilpin's definition of the Picturesque, like many an aesthetic definition, operates like a structure of desire. As a Picturesque traveller, Gilpin is in pursuit of a spirit of nature which always escapes the materiality of beautiful objects. Like Wordsworth's 'something ever more about to be', or the Rousseauistic idea of the unattainable object of desire, it defies self-presence or satisfying consummation. The paradox of Gilpin's Picturesque means literally that it cannot define itself: it falls between nature and art. Either the pursuing Picturesque traveller is disappointed, or the artist must improve upon nature. Ultimately, the practical solution or artistic manifestation of the Picturesque for Gilpin – the sketches of the artist or the memories of the traveller – is more like a compromised reassemblage of parts than an actual discovery.

At least in Gilpin's version of the Picturesque, there seems to be no ultimate preference, no still point, only an unresolved oscillation between nature and art. The Picturesque traveller might attempt to reassemble the variously disposed and dispersed body of woman in the landscape,[11] but even the rough strokes of the Picturesque artist cannot make her into an object. It is as if she slips between one scene and another, between expectation, vision, sketch and memory. Picturesque beauty, for Gilpin, lies more in the expectation than the attainment. He concentrates to an extraordinary extent on the pleasures of the chase.

Malcolm Andrews sees Gilpin's articulation of the energy of the Picturesque as a controlling mechanism. He reads Gilpin's use of the hunting analogy – 'we pursue her from hill to dale' – as an attempt to substitute the corporeal licentiousness of the English squire with a more refined (and more moral) quest.[12] As we have seen, in his essay on Picturesque travel, Gilpin laments the pressures of a licentious age and appears to be a reluctant theoriser. Nevertheless, his search for the Picturesque seems to be about a manifestation as well as a channelling of energy. At least, there is an energy at the heart of the Picturesque which makes for an interesting instability; it is not just the fluidity of a carelessly or variously defined aesthetic. This energy needs greater definition and can be usefully compared with other forms of aesthetic energy,[13] or mobility, in the period. The appetite for novelty in Gilpin's Picturesque can thus be measured against the obsessive questing of the actual explorer and the wanderlust of the Romantic poet.

Coleridge's lecture notes on *Hamlet* contain a classic articulation of what we have come to know as Romantic sensibility and 'the Romantic predicament'. This is where he makes the by now familiar suggestion that Hamlet is a procrastinating genius with a flawed will. In case we forget, Coleridge is here diagnosing what he takes to be a particularly sick self. At the very point where he highlights the deranged nature of Romantic subjectivity he draws on what must have been a very familiar experience for an age besotted with Picturesque travel:

The effect of this overbalance of the imaginative power is beautifully illustrated in the everlasting broodings and superfluous activities of Hamlet's mind, which, unseated from its healthy relation, is constantly occupied with the world within, and abstracted from the world without, – giving substance to shadows, and throwing a mist over all common-place actualities. It is the nature of thought to be indefinite; – definiteness belongs to external imagery alone. Hence it is that the sense of sublimity arises, not from the sight of an outward object, but from the beholder's reflection upon it; – not from the sensuous impression, but from the imaginative reflex. Few have seen a celebrated waterfall without feeling something akin to disappointment: it is only subsequently that the image comes back full into the mind and brings with it a train of grand or beautiful associations. Hamlet feels this; his senses are in a state of trance, and he looks upon external things as hieroglyphics. His soliloquy –

"O! that this too too solid flesh would melt," &co. –

springs from that craving after the indefinite – for that which is not – which most easily besets men of genius...[14]

At the same time as he confirms the escape from eighteenth-century materialism Coleridge is quick to diagnose the problems of idealism. Faced with the threat of alienation in the figure of Hamlet he performs something akin to a Wordsworthian act of consolation or 'recompense'. The handy illustration of a tourist's disappointment might seem like a glib comparison, but it serves to prove the mind's metamorphic, restorative power. The only problem is that Hamlet is credited with having already seen the recompense – 'Hamlet feels this' – yet it does not release him from his predicament. If this is Coleridge curing the Romantic dilemma he seems, as ever, strangely attracted to the disease. One might even go so far as to suggest that the passage could be read the other way round, with Coleridge here fending off the terrible threat of material disappointments and seeing a power in the genial indefiniteness of the mind. From this point of view an 'overbalance of the imaginative power' might actually be considered 'beautiful'. The sublime experience might actually be a rather useful and self-supporting form of evasion.

If Coleridge's description of this consoling or restorative 'imaginative reflex' is ambiguous in the way that I have suggested, then perhaps he is not interested in Wordsworthian recompense at all. The props and supports which keep hope alive for Coleridge depend upon an agonised self-consciousness which can actually make a virtue out of weakness. The more famous imaginative reflex of the Snowdon episode in *The Prelude* is double in nature, rendered both as the narrative of the journey and as abstract symbolical interpretation. But this superfluity is on the positive side. Where disappointment is concerned, the crossing of the Alps in Book VI is a more pertinent 'event' – if such it can be called. For here there is only a gap where there should be an event, followed by a narrative of going down the Simplon in retrospect; and the mighty invocation of imagination which follows is badly needed at this moment of crisis. Once solaced by the 'unfather'd vapour' of imagination the mind is quietly confident – 'Strong in itself, and in the access of joy/Which hides it like the overflowing Nile'.[15] Secure in the presence of this 'Power' Wordsworth can thrill to the kind of baptismal overflow which might otherwise threaten annihilation.

Such a confident resource of faith is required to contemplate the prospect which the Wanderer confronts in Book III of *The Excursion* when he makes a brief foray into comparative religion. The horror contemplated here is more than touristic disappointment. Describing the vision of life according to Hindoo philosophy, he presents us with a typical Wordsworthian binary of either harmonious absorption or arid extinction. For this most alluvial of poets the religion of the 'holy Ganges' offers the following split:

> That our existence winds her stately course
> Beneath the sun, like Ganges, to make part
> Of a living ocean; or, to sink engulfed,
> Like Niger, in impenetrable sands
> And utter darkness: thought which may be faced,
> Though comfortless![16]

Wordsworth's powerful appropriation of exotic geography to a shared vision of life appears to be a more spectacular manifestation of a Romantic dilemma than Coleridge's disappointment with waterfalls. But Coleridge's commentary on *Hamlet* presents us with a classic example of the way in which the Romantic sublime can be made to trump the Picturesque. Imaginative reflex is more important than immediate impression and the forms of nature need translating into a higher meaning: 'external things' are 'hieroglyphics'. And in its description of a 'craving after the indefinite' the commentary also suggests that this questing self-consciousness has been set in motion, as one might expect from the figure of Hamlet, by an unaccountable motive which lies close to home.

This unexpected connection between Romantic exploration and the Picturesque is examined in Alan Liu's *Wordsworth: The Sense of History* (1989). Working from the proposition that 'the literary text is not just the displacement but the overdetermined and agonic denial of historical reference',[17] Liu exhaustively writes the history which lies buried in Wordsworth's 'disappointment' at crossing the Alps in the Simplon Pass episode of *The Prelude*. More particularly, Liu's opening strategy is to question the link between exploration and the Romantic self by substituting a model of exploration with one of tour and thereby replacing the quest for goals with a sense of passage. In a tour, Liu argues, 'any sense of completion posited at the terminus can only appear a gap, an absence'.[18] His claim for the distinct nature of touristic travel has important implications for the difficult economies of desire which lurk in Picturesque, Romantic and exploration texts: 'Tours, as opposed to journeys or explorations, always seem undermotivated; they always seem to be impelled by someone else's motive. A tour's conventional motivation, perhaps, always represses something indescribable at home – whether ennui or something stronger'.[19] This suggestion offers a good basis from which to assess the precariousness of the Picturesque. In the accounts of the two explorers – James Bruce and Mungo Park – which we will examine in the next section, there are moments which combine, as one might expect, discovery with disappointment. At such moments, the disproportionate energy invested in exploration finds its reflex in a bathetic or self-parodic return to home. These points of cultural collapse provided a further point of orientation with the seeming repose, or the arrested narrative,[20] of the English Picturesque.

In her recent *Imperial Eyes* Marie Louise Pratt categorises the narratives of Bruce and Park as 'sentimental'. Such experiential, heroic and affective texts were, she claims, supplanted by the 1860s with a more informational kind of writing which aspired to scientific status and which is, in her terms, 'unheroic, unparticularised, without ego, interest or desire'.[21] By reversing and refusing 'heroic priorities' such a 'scientific' text, she argues, 'narrates place and describes people'.[22] Pratt's account is valuable for its insight into the visual economy of ethnography and landscape in nineteenth-century exploration writing, but her historical classification of 'sentimental literature' is in danger of homogenising the differences, both within and between the respective accounts of Bruce and Park, both of whom attempt, in their singular ways, to negotiate between affective story and scientific observation. The difficulty in this genre is in deciding whether we are witnessing an actual separation of explorer, scientist and romantic sensibility. The more one considers it, the less a clear-cut separation appears possible, and one is tempted to agree instead with Pratt's more general belief in the 'discursive polyphony of travel writing'[23] and her daring claim that: 'Partly because it has never been fully professionalized or "disciplined", travel writing is one of the most polyphonous of genres.'[24] In the exploration texts of

Bruce and Park this babble of voices is suffused with ego, interest and desire.

'He will always be the poet, and his book the epic, of African travel writing' reads the entry in the *Dictionary of National Biography*.[25] James Bruce's own claim that the narrative of his travels 'is now come to fill a great chasm in the history of the universe'[26] is amply confirmed by the five volumes, running to more than 3,000 pages, of his *Travels to Discover the Source of the Nile in the Years 1768, 1769, 1770, 1771, 1772 and 1773*, written with the licence of considerable retrospect and published in 1790.

Despite the overriding direction of its title, Bruce's text is a confusion of voices: in his own terms it is literally 'abyssinian'. It combines *Boy's Own* adventure story with erotic fantasy, geological survey with military history. And, for all the supposed single-mindedness of his quest for the source of the Nile, the hero of his attenuated tale is captured repeatedly, encounters a lost tribe of Visigoths in the Sahara, is embroiled in an Abyssinian civil war, fires a tallow candle through a deal table, shoots kites straight out of the sky and forms a close relationship with the princess Ozoro Esther in the Ethiopian metropolis of Gondar.

Bruce's text is self-consciously an exhibition of male pleasure. The Harrow-educated Scottish laird glories in his identity as a private citizen with the liberty to roam. He is the gentleman amateur for all his academic and scientific pretensions:

It will be remembered likewise that one of the motives of my writing is my own amusement, and I would much rather renounce the subject altogether than walk in fetters of my own forging. The language is, like the subject, rude and manly. My paths have not been flowery ones, nor would it have added credit to the work, or entertainment to the reader, to employ in it a stile proper only to works of imagination and pleasure.[27]

Similarly, the terms of Bruce's justification for his quest, and what he admits to as his 'vain-glory', have more to do with the failed classical scholar, the military hero and the polite reader of Ovid's *Metamorphoses* than they have to do with a Royal Geographical Society or an African Association. For Bruce, the source of the Nile represents a classical, historical conundrum which has hitherto defeated all heroes.

Far in antiquity as history or tradition can lead us, farther still beyond the reach of either, (if we believe it was the first subject of hieroglyphics) begins the inquiry into the origin, cause of increase, and course, of this great river. It is one of the few phaenomena in natural history that ancient philosophers employed themselves in investigation, and people of all ranks seemed to have joined in the search with a degree of perseverance very uncommon; but still the discovery, though often attempted under the most favourable circumstances, has as constantly miscarried; it has baffled the endeavours of all ages, and at last come down, as great a secret as ever, to these latter times of bold and impartial inquiry.[28]

Even the scientific plain-style as described by Bruce seems no more than an excuse for heroic self-construction. The following sentence from his introduction immediately demonstrates how the supposedly objective discourse of scientific observation gives way to a sensational drama of the suffering and achieving self: 'To see distinctly and accurately, to describe plainly, dispassionately and truly, is all that ought to be expected from one in my situation, constantly surrounded with every sort of difficulty and danger.'[29]

Distracted and digressive as Bruce's text undoubtedly is, 'polyphony' hardly seems the right word to describe it. The narrative resolutely orientates itself around its suffering hero/narrator, even to the extent of effacing or dislocating the text's destination and *raison d'être*: the search for the source of the Nile. In this classic tale of failure the mere excuse of the experiencing subject perhaps has to fill the void left by its material goal. Bruce's narcissistic fantasy may be another kind of imaginative reflex.

Before we proceed to what, erroneously, Bruce took to be the source of the Nile, it is necessary to consider the way in which this 'source' is mediated in his text. I have already suggested that for all his resemblance to the Hollywood man-of-action, Bruce conceives his journey to the centre in classical textual terms. While these point to the poetic qualities inherent in his quest, they also highlight a cruder kind of empirical competition. Indeed, Bruce's version of the sublime might be said to be itself partially obscured by his own egotistical presence. For example, his rendering of the sublime moment at the great cataract of the Nile combines the infinite power of nature with the minute pettiness of the heroic explorer.

Bruce begins his account of the cataract in the usual sublime terms, proclaiming that it was 'the most magnificent sight' he ever beheld and that its effect was 'truly terrible' so that it 'stunned' him and made him 'for a time, perfectly dizzy'. But then he immediately proceeds to quibble about its size. He launches a savage attack on the account given previously by the Jesuit priest Jerome Lobo who had claimed to sit on a seat under the waterfall where he could view 'a number of rainbows of inconceivable beauty in this extraordinary prism'. However, anything but shared aesthetic pleasure is on Bruce's agenda at this point: the oblivion of his sublime moment clearly includes the attempted erasure of all rivals:

It was a most magnificent sight, that eyes, added to the greatest length of human life, would not deface or eradicate from my memory; it struck me with a kind of stupor, and a total oblivion of where I was, and of every other sublunary concern. It was one of the most magnificent stupendous sights in the creation, though degraded and vilified by the lies of a groveling, fanatic peasant.

... I measured the fall, and believe, within a few feet, it was the height I have mentioned, but I confess I could at no time in my life less promise upon precision; my reflection was suspended, or subdued and while in sight of the fall I think I was under a temporary alienation of mind; it seemed to me as if one element had broken from, and become superior to all laws of subordination; that the fountains of the great deep were extraordinarily opened, and the destruction of a world was again begun by the agency of water.[30]

Side by side with his desperate attempt to be original, Bruce contends well with a '*temporary* alienation of mind'. Aesthetic categories seem actually to confirm, by conventionalising, this 'event of place'. For all its anarchy, chaos and annihilation, the language of apocalypse speaks of quiet confidence and control.

When Bruce's text eventually arrives at its proclaimed destination the event turns out, not surprisingly, to be an extremely dislocating, destabilising and disorientating experience. It is anything but an untrammelled moment of joy, and the blankness it produces has some dizzying consequences. The moment of heroic affirmation, the laurel-wreathed victory he had long anticipated, soon turns to profound disappointment.

It is easier to guess than to describe the situation of my mind at that moment – standing in that spot which had baffled the genius, industry, and inquiry of both ancients and moderns, for the course of near three thousand years... Though a mere private Briton, I triumphed here, in my own mind, over kings and their armies; and every comparison was leading nearer and nearer to presumption, when the place itself where I stood, the object of my vain-glory, suggested what depressed my short-lived triumph. I was but a few minutes arrived at the sources of the Nile [when]...I found a

despondency gaining ground fast upon me, and blasting the crown of laurels
I had too rashly woven for myself. I resolved therefore to divert, till I could
on more solid reflection overcome its progress.[31]

Instead of reporting on 'a temporary alienation of mind' this
passage exhibits it. The place 'suggests', despondency 'gains ground'
and our hero is 'diverted'. Not only is the dawning realisation of
error present here: there is also an unnameable state of mind, what
the text refers to tentatively as 'some other thoughts, perhaps, still
nearer the heart'. What has been envisaged as a moment of
consummation and possession turns into a state of transference as one
failed origin is suddenly eclipsed by another:

I was, at that very moment in possession of what had, for many years, been
the principal object of my ambition and wishes: indifference, which from the
usual infirmity of human nature follows at least for a time, complete
enjoyment, had taken place of it. The marsh, and the fountains, upon
comparison with the rise of many of our rivers, became now a trifling object
in my sight. I remembered that magnificent scene in my own native
country, where the Tweed, Clyde, and Annan rise in one hill; three rivers,
as I now thought, not inferior to the Nile in beauty, preferable to it in the
cultivation of those countries through which they flow; superior, vastly
superior to it in the virtues and qualities of the inhabitants, and in the
beauty of its flocks; crowding its pastures in peace, without fear of violence
from man or beast. I had seen the rise of the Rhine and Rhone, and the more
magnificent sources of the Saône; I began, in my sorrow, to treat the inquiry
about the source of the Nile as a violent effort of a distempered fancy: –
    What's Hecuba to him, or he to Hecuba,
    That he should weep for her? –
Grief or despondency now rolling upon me like a torrent; relaxed, nor
refreshed by unquiet and imperfect sleep, I started from my bed in utmost
agony; I went to the door of my tent: everything was still; the Nile, at whose
head I stood, was not capable either to promote or to interrupt my
slumbers...[32]

Our bold military hero has suddenly been replaced by a brooding
Hamlet. Destruction by the 'agency of water' now has more to do
with the construction of his subjectivity than any river flowing past
his tent. Grief rolls upon him like a torrent just as despondency gains
ground upon him like a rival explorer. Bruce articulates what he
glibly refers to as 'the horrors' – the abyss of the explorer.[33]
    Mungo Park's *Travels in the Interior Districts of Africa* (1799) reveals
in its sub-title – 'Performed under the Direction and Patronage of the

African Association' – the difference from Bruce. Park assured Lord Camden that the objects which he would 'constantly keep in view' would be 'the extension of British Commerce and the enlargement of our Geographical Knowledge'.[34] And, almost inescapably, his text deals as much with physical as with – to use the language of the time – 'moral geography'. That is to say its ethnographic content would be read directly as a contribution to the debate on slavery. His status as employee is confirmed by the defensive introduction provided by a member of the Association. We are told that the talents of our hero 'were not brilliant, but solid and useful', that he is 'consistent and rational' and rarely 'indulged in conjecture, much less in hypothesis or speculation'.[35] Simple solid British truth is the order of the day and it is sanctioned by Providence.

The moment of achievement for Park – when he sees the river Niger ahead of him and solves the riddle of its termination – confirms the providential aspect of the narrative. And although his destination is imaged by its source, that source is not his Scottish hills, but the seat of English government:

one of them called out, *geo affilli*, (see the water) ; and looking forwards, I saw with infinite pleasure the great object of my mission; the long sought for majestic Niger, glittering to the morning sun, as broad as the Thames at Westminster, and flowing slowly *to the eastward*. I hastened to the brink, and, having drank of the water, lifted up my fervent thanks in prayer, to the Great Ruler of all things, for having thus far crowned my endeavours with success.[36]

Even at the nadir of his fortunes, Park's piety is unruffled. Robbed, stripped, 500 miles from the nearest European settlement and surrounded by lions, Park considers the possibility of despair:

I was indeed a stranger in a strange land, yet I was still under the protecting eye of that Providence who has condescended to call himself the stranger's friend. At this moment, painful as my reflections were, the extraordinary beauty of a small moss in fructification, irresistibly caught my eye. I mention this to shew from what trifling circumstances the mind will sometimes derive consolation; for though the whole plant was not larger than the top of one of my fingers, I could not contemplate the delicate conformation of its roots, leaves, and capsula, without admiration. Can that Being (thought I), who planted, watered, and brought to perfection in this obscure part of the world, a thing which appears of so small importance, look with unconcern upon the situation and suffering of creatures so formed after his own image? – surely not! Reflections like these, would not allow me to despair.[37]

As one might suspect, the greatest disturbance to the myth of this text's virtuous, even pious, transparency is provided by its first-person narrative which creates a parodic portrait of its suffering hero. Park is made to play the part of Gulliver extremely well. He may well avoid sublime extremities, but as Pratt puts it: 'The subject here is split simply by virtue of realizing itself as both protagonist and narrator, and it tends to split itself even further... the self sees, it sees itself seeing, it sees itself being seen. And always it parodies both itself and the Other.'[38]

The work of Richard Payne Knight, particularly in his couplet poem *The Landscape* (1794) and his *An Analytical Inquiry into the Principles of Taste* (1805), offers an interesting example of the complex and culturally fraught combinations that go to make up the excessively mixed category of the Picturesque. In both texts (and particularly the first) the context suggests anything but safety, being significantly formed by the French Revolution and, in particular, by the horrors of the French Terror. (An extensive footnote on this subject at the end of *The Landscape* is in danger of dominating the whole book.) Frequently, Knight is at pains to reinterpret the Burke of the *Enquiry into Our Ideas of the Sublime and the Beautiful* so as to fit in with the Burke of the *Reflections on the Revolution in France*. He wages a fierce onslaught on what he takes to be the dangerously empiricist, mechanistic/aesthetic categories of the earlier book and offers up, instead, an élitist individualism which has the 'grace' – what is also considered as 'soul' or 'imagination' – to appreciate those 'happy arts of peace' which represent the possibility of human improvement through their civilising effect. The emphasis is on a form of moderation which is haunted by the spectre of revolutionary France.[39] The Republic's rationalist uniformity would spell disaster for the diverse pleasures of a man of leisure. Knight's definitions of the Picturesque are thus caught between a politically necessary variety and the chaotic gracelessness of modern effete improvers. But this overview does no more than restate the overt polemic of Knight's texts. The difficulty and the contradictions with which they negotiate this politically 'safe' path are more illuminating.

According to Knight, the Picturesque 'ought to signify that middle style, which is not sufficiently smooth to be beautiful, nor sufficiently rough and elevated to be sublime'[40] and it should be composed not just of 'opposite kinds', but of 'opposite extremes of the same kind'[41]

– a revision of Price which suggests not just compromise, but inherent conflict. Knight combines a strong sense of universals with a strong sense of difference. The dynamic basis of his ideas on the Picturesque is certainly not as corporeal as Burke's. The source of pleasure, for Knight, lies at a slight but significant remove from the physical body: 'Change and variety are, therefore, necessary to the enjoyment of all pleasure; whether sensual or intellectual: and so powerful is this principle, that all change, not so violent as to produce a degree of irritation in the organs absolutely painful, is pleasing; and preferable to any uniform and unvaried gratification.'[42]

As critics such as Ann Bermingham and Anne Janowitz have pointed out, the Picturesque is peculiarly concerned with, and susceptible to, time;[43] and in particular, with the processes of decay, loss and ruination. Similarly, Ronald Paulson hypothesises that Ruskin 'made the pertinent distinction that the picturesque is a function... of time, of nature itself – of organic change, decay, and collapse'.[44] In *The Landscape* Knight insistently draws attention to the process of 'naturalisation'. He urges his readers, in this most didactic of poems, to refrain from indulging in the 'infinite variety' of exotic imports and to concentrate instead on native plants.[45] By so doing they will avoid the shock or revolutionary disturbance of 'premature decay'.[46] He advocates 'Walls, mellowed into harmony by time'[47] and is generally fascinated by the paradoxical achievement of identity through decay: how foreign objects may be 'nat'raliz'd by use'.[48]

In his commentaries on Picturesque architecture Knight embraces diversity. 'The best style of architecture,' he argues '...admits of all promiscuously...in a style professedly miscellaneous'.[49] More generally, he suggests that there can be nothing 'blamable' in 'uniting the different improvements of different ages and countries in the same object...'.[50] But at the same time he is desperate to celebrate the transhistorical power of the Greeks, and of Homer in particular. Systems and empires may fall into ruin, decay and oblivion, but the classical spirit of 'grace' remains.[51]

In order to define this 'celestial grace'[52] in *The Landscape*, Knight invokes an image of the noble savage endowed with 'native energy and native sense'.[53] In a footnote to his poem, he endorses the President of the Royal Academy's comparison between the Apollo Belvedere and Mohawk warriors.[54] In contrast to this combination of classical/Enlightenment universalism, he provides us with a desperate attempt at cultural relativity at the beginning of his book on

Taste. His footnote here refers us to Park's *Journey to the Niger.*[55] The classical confidence seems to have diminished, but two fraught kinds of voyeurism remain:

The sable Africans view with pity and contempt the marked deformity of Europeans; whose mouths are compressed, their noses pinched, their cheeks shrunk, their hair rendered lank and flimsy, their bodies lengthened and emaciated, and their skins unnaturally bleached by shade and seclusion, and the baneful influence of a cold humid climate.* Were they to draw an image of female perfection, or a goddess of love and beauty, she would have a broad flat nose, high cheeks, woolly hair, a jet black skin, and squat thick form, with breasts reaching to her navel. To us imagination can scarcely present a more disgusting mass of deformity; but perhaps at Tombuctoo the fairest nymph of St James's, who, while she treads the mazes of the dance, displays her light and slender form through transparent folds of muslin, might make the same impression; and who shall decide which party is right, or which is wrong; or whether the black or the white model be, according to the laws of nature, the most perfect specimen of a perfect woman?[56]

* See Park's Journey to the Niger.

For Knight, even the word 'picturesque' is still in the process of achieving cultural identity. Its common, imprecise usage is typical, he argues, of foreign words which have entered 'our own tongue'.[57] On the basis of Johnson's *Dictionary*, he is quick to claim that the word 'has not been considered as perfectly naturalized among us'.[58] For all the confident invocation of 'British genius' in *The Landscape*, Knight is never quite at home with the Picturesque. He might reject the Sublime's binary oppositions of presence and annihilation, but his is another kind of displacement. He implores others not to wander, but is himself for ever on the move. His 'irritation' may not be the high anxiety of the Sublime and the question of identity, for him, may not turn on blankness, annihilation, indifference, the 'horrors' or fractured self-parody. His aesthetic solution may not be able to overcome the monotony, fixity and terror of the Sublime and Beautiful. But the 'confinement' of his pleasures produces anything but ease. 'Irritation' gives no possibility of release from disquieting juxtapositions and the dizziness of perpetual motion.

The energy within the Picturesque has itself, until recently, been only latent or partly hidden within accounts of the subject. When Martin Price claims that the Picturesque 'offers its witty complexity and playfulness as an appeal to the energy of man's mind'[59] he suggests that there is much more to this aesthetic category than literally meets the eye. In his brief suggestion of the hidden energy implicit in the Picturesque, he touches on its motive force. And it is this peculiar energy which enables him to propose that Gilpin and Knight share 'a humanism that finds order and rhythm inherent in our loose, instinctive movements'.[60] As a result of this underlying energy, the Picturesque, for Price, is able to stand as a valuable 'counterpoint' to Sternian expressive gesture.

Sidney K. Robinson's idea of an underdeployment of assumed power in the Picturesque[61] – the plenitude which lies behind its strategic casualness – offers an interesting alternative to accounts, such as those of Janowitz and Bermingham, which stress its mystificatory capacity. However, while he is painfully aware of the precarious and paradoxical mixture of the Picturesque, Robinson depends upon a limiting proprietorial assumption which means that his definition cannot accommodate the touristic or the imperialistic Picturesque, both of which would find more of a problem in happily matching aesthetic effects with plenitude and possession. As we have seen in the case of Gilpin, the Picturesque, as a form of travel, is likely to find the idea of plenitude disturbed and the very possibility of repose unlikely. There is a world of difference, as Kim Ian Michasiw points out, between 'the disempowered traveller' and 'the improving landowner'.[62]

Compared with the spectacular polarities of Romantic subjectivity and the exoticism of actual exploration, the energy of the Picturesque may seem tame, even safe. But, as we have seen, it contains its own disturbing complexities. It too has problems in facing up to origins and may be seen as a displacement or manifestation of desire. It also contains an energy capable of permeating Romanticism and exploration, and of providing a widespread and popular aesthetic consumerism.

NOTES

1 S. T. Coleridge, 'The Delinquent Travellers', lines 18–21, 120–7, in *Poetical Works*, ed. Ernest Hartley Coleridge (London and New York: Oxford University Press, 1969), pp. 445–7.

2 Lord George Byron, *The Complete Works*, ed. Jerome J. McGann, vol. v, *Don Juan*, (Oxford: Clarendon Press, 1989), p. 769. For an account of Byron's historical imagination in terms of 'oceanic feeling' and a retreat from struggle and difference, see Anne Janowitz, *England's Ruins: Poetic Purpose and the National Landscape* (Oxford: Basil Blackwell, 1990), pp. 49–53.

3 William Gilpin, 'On Picturesque Travel', in *Three Essays: On Picturesque Beauty; On Picturesque Travel; and On Sketching Landscape: To Which is Added a Poem, On Landscape Painting*, second edition (London, 1794), pp. 47–8.

4 See Ann Bermingham, *Landscape and Ideology: The English Rustic Tradition 1740–1860* (London: Thames and Hudson, 1986), pp. 57, 73–83; Malcolm Andrews, *The Search for the Picturesque: Landscape Aesthetics and Tourism in Britain, 1760–1800* (Aldershot: Scolar Press, 1989), pp. 3–23; Janowitz, *England's Ruins*.

5 See Bermingham, *Landscape and Ideology*, pp. 63–6.

6 *Ibid.*, p. 85.

7 Gilpin, *Three Essays*, p. 6.

8 *Ibid.*, p. 41.

9 *Ibid.*, p. 47.

10 See Bermingham, *Landscape and Ideology*, p. 65: 'Gilpin's notion that "nature is the archetype" had some interesting consequences. If nature prefigures the picturesque, then there must exist in nature a purely picturesque landscape, one that is all roughness, irregularity, and variousness. Yet if there were such a landscape, the hand of art, unable to improve it, would become secondary and even superfluous'; and Carl William Barbier, *William Gilpin: His Drawings, Teachings, and Theory of the Picturesque* (Oxford: Clarendon Press, 1963), pp. 102–6; and Walter J. Hipple, *The Beautiful, the Sublime and the Picturesque in Eighteenth-Century British Aesthetic Theory* (Carbondale: Southern Illinois Press, 1957), pp. 198–9: 'There is a paradox here: a system which isolates a certain property of nature for admiration [picturesque beauty], a property defined by its excellence as a subject for art, comes at last to reject the art for the nature which was at first only its subject.'

11 I am thinking of lines 2–3 and 311 ff. from Gilpin's poem 'On Landscape Painting' (1794): 'to combine/ In one harmonious whole her scattered charms' (2–3); 'so must thou cull/ From various scenes such parts as best create/ One perfect whole. If Nature ne'er arrayed/Her most accomplished work with grace compleat,/ Think, will she waste on desert rocks, and dells,/What she denies to Woman's charming form?'; in Gilpin, *Three Essays*, pp. 99, 110.

12 Andrews, *The Search for the Picturesque*, pp. 67–8.

13 For an exploration of the word 'energy' in relation to French Romantic writing and travel, see C. W. Thompson, 'French Romantic Travel and the Quest for Energy', *Modern Language Review*, 87 (1992), 307–19.

14 S. T. Coleridge, *Coleridge's Essays and Lectures on Shakespeare* (London and New York: J. M. Dent, 1909), p. 137. For other versions and transcriptions of this lecture, see *Coleridge's Shakespearean Criticism*, ed. Thomas Middleton Raysor (London: Constable, 1930), vol. II, p. 273; and S. T. Coleridge, *Lectures 1808–1812: On Literature*, ed. R. A. Foakes (London

and Princeton: Routledge and Kegan Paul/ Princeton University Press, 1987), *The Collected Works of S. T. Coleridge 5*, vol. I, pp. 536–46.

15 William Wordsworth, *The Prelude or Growth of Poet's Mind* (Text of 1805), Book VI, lines 547–8, ed. Ernest de Selincourt, revised impression (Oxford University Press, 1969), p. 100.

16 William Wordsworth, *The Excursion* Book III, lines 258–63, in *The Poetical Works of William Wordsworth: The Excursion, The Recluse*, ed. Ernest de Selincourt and Helen Darbishire (Oxford University Press, 1972), p. 83.

17 Alan Liu, *Wordsworth: The Sense of History* (Stanford University Press, 1989), p. 47.

18 *Ibid.*, p. 4.

19 *Ibid.*, p. 7.

20 *Ibid.*, pp. 75–88.

21 Marie Louise Pratt, *Imperial Eyes: Travel Writing and Transculturation* (New York and London: Routledge, 1992), p. 143.

22 *Ibid.*, p. 146.

23 *Ibid.*, p. 141.

24 *Ibid.*, p. 160.

25 Richard Garnett, entry on James Bruce in *Dictionary of National Biography*, ed. Leslie Stephen (London, 1886), vol. VII, p. 102.

26 James Bruce, *Travels to Discover the Source of the Nile in the Years 1768, 1769, 1770, 1771, 1772 and 1773*, 5 vols. (Edinburgh and London, 1790), vol. I, p. lxvii.

27 *Ibid.*, p. lxvi.

28 *Ibid.*, vol. III, pp. 603–4.

29 *Ibid.*, vol. I, p. lxvi.

30 *Ibid.*, pp. 426–7.

31 *Ibid.*, pp. 597–8.

32 *Ibid.*, pp. 640–1.

33 *Ibid.*, p. 437.

34 Mungo Park, *Travels in the Interior Districts of Africa; Performed under the Direction and Patronage of the African Association*, second edition (London, 1799), p. xxix.

35 *Ibid.*, p. lxxxvii.

36 *Ibid.*, pp. 194–5.

37 *Ibid.*, pp. 243–4.

38 Pratt, *Imperial Eyes*, p. 151.

39 For an analysis of this aspect of the politics of the Picturesque see: Bermingham, *Landscape and Ideology*, pp. 73–83; Liu, *Wordsworth*, pp. 61–137; and Sidney K. Robinson, *Inquiry into the Picturesque* (University of Chicago Press, 1991), pp. 47–89.

40 Richard Payne Knight, *An Analytical Inquiry into the Principles of Taste* (London, 1805), pp. 151–2.

41 *Ibid.*, p. 152.

42 *Ibid.*, pp. 425–6.

43 Bermingham, *Landscape and Ideology*, p. 69; Janowitz, *England's Ruins*, p. 57.

44 Ronald Paulson, *Representations of Revolution 1789–1820* (New Haven and London: Yale University Press, 1983), p. 177.

45 Knight, *The Landscape: A Didactic Poem in Three Books* (London, 1794), Book III, lines 37–42, p. 53.

46 *Ibid.*, line 35, p. 2.

47 *Ibid.*, Book II, line 69, p. 26.

48 *Ibid.*, lines 284–5, p. 37.

49 Knight, *Inquiry into Taste*, pp. 218–19.

50 *Ibid.*, p. 216.

51 *Ibid.*, pp. 204–5.

52 Knight, *The Landscape*, Book II, line 337.

53 *Ibid.*, Book I, line 45.

54 The footnote reads: 'It has been frequently observed by travellers, that the attitudes of savages are in general graceful and spirited; and the great artist who now so worthily fills the President's chair in the Royal Academy, assured me, that when he first saw the Apollo of the Belvidere, he was extremely struck with its resemblance to some of the Mohawk warriors whom he had seen in America. The case is, that the Mohawks act immediately from the impulse of their minds, and know no acquired restraints or affected habits' (Knight, *The Landscape*, p. 3).

55 The footnote also contains the following observations, which form an interesting comparison with the description of Mohawk warriors in *The Landscape*: 'Mr Hearne, who resided more than twenty years among the nations of the frozen regions of North America, says, "Ask a northern Indian what is beauty, he will answer, *a broad flat face, small eyes, high cheek bones, three or four black lines across each cheek, a low forehead, a large broad chin, a clumsy hook nose, a tawny hide, and breasts hanging down to the belt.*"
The same people were so far from thinking the whiteman of an European skin at all conducive to beauty, that it only excited in them the disgusting idea of dead flesh sodden in water till all the blood and juices were extracted.' (Knight, *Inquiry into Taste*, p. 14n.)

56 *Ibid.*, pp. 13–15.

57 *Ibid.*, p. 150.

58 *Ibid.*, p. 143.

59 Martin Price, 'The Picturesque Moment', in *From Sensibility to Romanticism: Essays Presented to Frederick A. Pottle*, ed. Frederick W. Hilles and Harold Bloom (New York and London: Oxford University Press, 1965), p. 275.

60 *Ibid.*, p. 280.

61 Robinson, *Inquiry into the Picturesque*, p. 78 and *passim*.

62 Kim Ian Michasiw, 'Nine Revisionist Theses on the Picturesque', *Representations*, 38 (1992), 76–100, 84–5. Michasiw writes: 'The traveler, by contrast, has no authority or control and can be drawn from him or

herself by the Other, whether that other is the grand projection of the tasteful proprietor...or the less grand but as alluring call of the marginal... The possibility of seduction is most powerful when the Other is so culturally – that is, when the picturesque being is not a marginalized portion of the observer's own culture but is, or represents, a wholly separate cultural formation.' For further discussion of Gilpin and Knight, see the essays in this volume by Ann Bermingham (pp. 81–90), Stephen Copley, and Vivien Jones (pp. 120–30).

CHAPTER 8

The legacy of the Picturesque: landscape, property and the ruin

Raimonda Modiano

In this essay I investigate the role of the destitute in Picturesque aesthetics. I argue that destitutes, be they rustics, beggars or gypsies, are salvational figures for the practitioners of the Picturesque, embodying the landed gentry's ideals of self-sufficiency and independence. The idealisation of rustic life in this period has certainly been discussed many times and has been the object of intense ideological controversies. John Barrell, for example, exposed John Constable for his perversely idealistic portrayal of rustics that misrepresents the actual conditions in which they lived.[1] In my view, an ideological critique may explain how destitutes are used but does not resolve the mystery of why they appear with such astonishing frequency in the literature and art of the period. By means of a psychological model derived from Freud and Melanie Klein, I show that destitutes function as narcissistic ego ideals, as figures of undisturbed self-sufficiency and self-absorption. They become the repository of narcissistic desire without eliciting envy, for their very ordinariness and state of decay affiliates them not with a monument of perfection but with the ruin, a perennial emblem of the vanity of human achievements. Destitutes capture the fear of monumentality that is particularly acute in this period, which is due in large measure to the unsettling violence unleashed by the French Revolution and the momentous execution of the king, previously regarded to have otherworldly perfection and divine authority. Destitutes are the very antithesis of the king: already sacrificed, they cannot be sacrificed again and can thus constitute an ideal safe from the threat of violence. Furthermore, destitutes embody a strong anti-proprietary code of ethics which counteracts the prevalent tendency, in this period of vast agricultural reform, to treat landscape as property. They highlight the coexistence of two opposed ideologies within the Picturesque, one proclaiming the insignificance of private property, the other honouring the rights of real or symbolic ownership. I will show that it is precisely the ambiguity generated by the double desire to own and renounce property that accounts for the absence of gift exchange in Picturesque art and literature. Hence, the objects typically featured in the Picturesque are not objects owned or acquired through gift transfers but those which fall under the category of 'the found object'. The ruin forms a special class of such objects due to its association with sacrifice.

'Sometimes when I earnestly look at a beautiful Object or Landscape', Coleridge wrote in a notebook entry, 'it seems as if I were on the *brink* of a Fruition still denied – as if Vision were an *appetite*: even as a man would feel, who having put forth all his muscular strength in an act of prosilience, is at that very moment *held back* – he leaps & yet moves not from his place.'[2] Coleridge's note, although referring specifically to the Beautiful, identifies a central feature of the economy of desire in the Picturesque tradition, namely its inability to move beyond itself toward the acquisition of an object. The birth of desire in this note is simultaneously the point of its blockage; hence motion which is characteristic of desire is entirely arrested. The speaker experiences an imaginary leap forward carried on with utmost physical exertion, but in fact he remains fixed in the same spot, 'held back' by the very intensity of a desire which generates its own irrevocable inhibition. When desire is thus barred from its object, vision itself becomes appetite. I would like to suggest that the Picturesque traffics heavily in the erotics of denied desire, relegating appetite to the exclusive realm of vision which at once limits and sustains it. The Picturesque abounds in 'wistful gazes toward untouchable objects', and features perpetual brides and bridegrooms who never consummate their 'affair with landscape', as Alan Liu well puts it.[3]

But it is important to note that the Picturesque misses the anguished intensity present in Coleridge's entry. Coleridge was in fact accurate in labelling his experience as one pertaining to the Beautiful and not the Picturesque, for the painful immobility he describes arises from the reversal of an expectation which the Beautiful amply promises, namely the possibility of reaching the object of desire, usually located in close proximity to the observer. By contrast, the Picturesque characteristically places objects at a far remove from the observer, making access to them difficult if not impossible.[4] By this strategy the Picturesque systematically avoids the painful disappointment rendered by the failure of the Beautiful as represented by Coleridge. It cancels in advance all illusions of attaining the object of desire, and thus it protects the observer from falling into the trap of potentially tragic experiences. Playfulness, after all, and not tragedy is the choice province of the Picturesque.

In this context it is worthy of remark that the term 'arrested desire' which Liu uses in connection with the Picturesque (pp. 60–1) is accurate insofar as it designates the observer's unconsummated 'affair with landscape', but it is also a misnomer. Coleridge's note allows us to see the difference between 'arrested desire' in a true sense, i.e. desire that becomes completely immobilised, and a different type of desire characteristic of the Picturesque, which is not so much arrested as it is not fixated on any single object. By virtue of its paramount insistence on variety and intricacy, the Picturesque confronts the observer with a dazzling multiplicity of objects which renders attachment to any one of them impossible. Hence, in the Picturesque desire remains eminently free. Its most distinguishing feature is not its immobility but its infinite mobility.[5] The observer of the Picturesque is always in a position of mastery, never dependent on an object, however desirable, and free to seek yet another sight. We might say that the observer of the Picturesque plays at the game of love but is never a lover and never in love.

Love is actually the domain of the Beautiful and not of the Picturesque, as Burke showed. According to Burke, the Beautiful is 'that quality…in bodies by which they cause love, or some passion similar to it'.[6] By love Burke means something distinct, though not entirely separable from lust, that 'energy of the mind, that hurries us on to the possession of certain objects' irrespective of their aesthetic or social qualities (p. 91). Perhaps the best description of Burke's concept of love is to call it preferential lust. Unlike the brutes who are satisfied with any mates as long they are available, men become attached to women through the mediation of the Beautiful which enables a preferential fixation on the objects of desire. Such objects share two fundamental qualities: they are always in close proximity to the speaker (as Burke puts it, 'we like to have' beautiful objects, be they people or animals, 'near us, and we enter willingly into a kind of relation with them' ((p. 43)); and they pose no threat to the observer, but willingly acknowledge his superior might. We only love, Burke states, 'what submits to us' whereas 'we submit to what we admire', i.e. the Sublime (p. 113). The Beautiful thus seems to secure for the observer a comfortably stable power relationship and the enviable position of complete mastery. But this position is in fact illusory, as Burke himself is forced to admit in a passage which is especially revealing: 'But if you listen to the complaints of a forsaken lover,' Burke writes, 'you observe, that he insists largely on the pleasures which he enjoyed, or hoped to enjoy, and on the perfection of the object of his desires; it is the *loss* which is always uppermost in his mind.' Furthermore, Burke notes that the impressions caused by love can be so 'violent' and entail such an intense concentration on an object to the exclusion of all others, that it 'is capable of producing very extraordinary effects' including madness (pp. 40–1).

The problem with love, in Burke's formula, is that by engaging social affections it creates a structure of mutual dependencies, and by being a 'mixed passion', at once sexual and social, it enslaves the observer to the very objects that seemed so willing to submit to his power. The statement above makes a mockery of all illusions of mastery that the Beautiful seemed to guarantee. Precisely because possession of an object is so important to a lover, its loss 'is always uppermost in his mind', haunting him to the point of mental breakdown.

In reviewing the tradition of the Picturesque it is striking to see how carefully its practitioners obstruct the intrusion of Burke's distempered lover. The preference for the unattached observer is evident in the most widely shared standards brought into circulation by the Picturesque. Thus it would be hard to find a more obvious and prominent marker of the Picturesque than the emphasis on variety.[7] Price was especially insightful when he pointed out that the main function of variety is to allow utmost freedom of expression by exciting curiosity 'which gives play to the mind, loosening those iron bonds with which astonishment chains up its faculties'. As Price makes clear, it is enchainment which most threatens the writers of the Picturesque, be it the mind's surrender to a single object of such fearful proportions and power that 'it cannot entertain any other', as in Burke's Sublime, or the more innocuous yet equally confining passion for the Beautiful (p. 98).

If variety disperses desire among numerous objects that claim equal attention from the viewer, the substitution of objects that are old, decayed and even grotesque for those that evoke the beauty and freshness of youth undoubtedly takes the sting, or I should say the itch, out of any erotic longings. As Price puts it, 'in real life, I fancy, the most picturesque old woman, however her admirer may ogle her on that account, is perfectly safe from his caresses' (p. 91). Price's old woman is undoubtedly safe from her admirer's caresses in real life, but precisely for that reason her appearance in Picturesque art fulfils an important function: it undercuts the spectator's erotic inclinations, separating vision from appetite. Yet even when the human figures are selected from among those who do not naturally repel desire by their old, disfigured and tattered appearance, they resist appropriation as adamantly as Price's old woman. Characteristically such figures, be they shepherds or other types of rustics, are thrown into a landscape of such complexity that they become barely distinguishable even if they are placed in the foreground. Often figures have their backs turned to the viewer, as in Gainsborough's *Road through a Wood* (1747),[8] or are thrown into the middle or far distance to the point of dissolving into the natural environment that contains them, as in some of Constable's later landscapes.[9]

To a large extent this practice reflects the suspicion of theatricality which, according to Michael Fried, was paramount in the eighteenth century, leading to an assault on art as an intrinsically deceptive medium due to its dependence on the spectator's gaze.[10] In a provocative chapter on the Picturesque Frances Ferguson proposes that we look at this tradition as a major participant in the denial of theatricality in this period. From this perspective the aggressive turn toward nature and the rejection of society can be seen as the choice of a milieu in which one's definition of self does not depend on the kind of self-consciousness that develops from being watched by another, a self-consciousness which is unavoidably theatrical. Nature, which by definition neither watches nor responds to one's reactions, allows for the formation of an individuality that is self-referential and entirely natural 'like the forced product of nature's coercive force'.[11]

The ideal of naturalness, the antithesis to theatricality, makes its appearance not only in art, aesthetic treatises and poetry, but also in books of manners. The ideological implications of the eighteenth century's wholesale adoption of this ideal have been amply and judiciously explored by Ann Bermingham in *Landscape and Ideology* and I have nothing to add on this score. I am interested, however, in deepening the psychological profile of the Picturesque's rejection of theatricality, and for this I shall turn to the work of Freud and Melanie Klein.[12] The point I wish to make here is that the figure in

Picturesque landscape is anti-theatrical by virtue of its narcissism, and that the writers of the Picturesque are attracted to an unusual degree to prototypes that display narcissistic behaviour.

In his 1914 essay on narcissism Freud develops an important distinction between ego libido and object libido which extends his hypothesis about the existence of two separate instincts within the self, namely ego instincts and sexual instincts.[13] Ego libido is essentially the state of primary narcissism when the child finds all perfection within itself and, like primitive people, overestimates 'the power of wishes and mental processes, the "omnipotence of thoughts"' (p. 106). Unlike the child, the adult in the process of growth renounces part of his narcissism in favour of love objects but this renunciation is never complete. In fact, as Freud shows – and this is the point that will become especially pertinent to this discussion – the adult attaches himself exclusively to objects that have retained the narcissism he has been forced to abandon. It is for this reason that women who, as Freud states, 'love only themselves with an intensity comparable to that of the man's love for them' are so appealing. Similarly, the 'charm of a child lies to a great extent in his narcissism, his self-sufficiency and inaccessibility, just as does the charm of certain animals which seem not to concern themselves about us, such as cats and the large beasts of prey' (p. 113). The development into adulthood is then not a loss of narcissism but merely a displacement of primary narcissism onto an ego ideal, that is, an object which 'like the infantile ego, deems itself the possessor of all perfections' (p. 116).

The formation of ego ideals is not, however, an activity without risks, not only because as Freud shows, the ideal ego is censorious like conscience, imposing 'severe conditions upon the gratification of libido through objects', but because ego ideals always remind the self of what it lacks. Idealisation of another thus goes hand in hand with self-humiliation which ultimately causes rage and a desire to destroy the very object that gained supreme esteem. For this aspect we need to turn to Klein's analysis of the infant's relationship to the mother's breast. In *Envy and Gratitude* Klein shows that even under the best nursing and caring conditions the infant develops not merely an appreciation for the so called 'good breast' which represents the mother and through her the world at large, but also envy which 'spoils the primal good object' giving rise to 'sadistic attacks' on it.[14] As Klein points out, it is not just the ungenerous 'bad' breast which does not meet the child's feeding demands that becomes the object of destructive impulses, but predominantly the 'satisfactory breast'. 'The very ease with which the milk comes – though the infant feels gratified by it – also gives rise to envy because this gift seems so unattainable' (p. 11). The breast for Klein is in essence equivalent to the Freudian ego ideal: it is, as Klein puts it, 'inexhaustible' and 'ever-present', a compelling symbol of self-sufficiency that reveals dramatically the child's lack of self-sustenance. As Doug Collins aptly explains, in Klein's model the child is both 'fascinated by the mysterious source of nourishment' and its 'awesomely autonomous powers' as well as 'enraged because of the ontological imbalance it creates between its own feelings of radical insufficiency and the seemingly opposed imagery offered by the mother'. The child is thus tempted to destroy this figure of self-sufficiency in order to appropriate its place and become 'the glorious thing that it appears to be'. But precisely because the child remembers the rage it felt in relation to the breast it abandons this goal, understanding that if it were to realise it, 'it could itself expect to become a target of violence of the resentful other', that same violence that the 'hyper sufficient breast' had originally triggered in it. Hence the movement to identify with the ego ideal which 'incarnates impossible happiness' is followed by the counter-movement of non-identification, since 'the murder of the insulting perfection is always automatically imagined'.[15]

The double movement of identification with and withdrawal from an idealised self-sufficient object is beautifully illustrated by Freud's essay 'On Transience', one of the few works in which he explicitly tackles the subject of aesthetics. In this essay Freud reports taking a walk through a 'smiling countryside' together with a friend and a young poet, probably Rilke. He is struck by the poet's melancholy response to the landscape and his inability to enjoy it because of his awareness that 'all this beauty was fated to extinction, that it would vanish when winter came, like all human beauty and all the splendour that men have created or may create'. Freud's purpose is to show that the poet is profoundly mistaken, that in fact it is on account of their transience that objects become beautiful to us. The Beautiful consists in the liberation of desire from objects and its return to the ego. The psychology of the aesthetic is then the very reverse of the psychology of mourning. In the latter 'libido clings to its objects and will not renounce those that are lost even when a substitute lies ready to hand'; in the former, the loss of an object or the consciousness of its transience lends it 'a fresh charm' and enables desire to become attached to other objects or return to the self.[16]

Freud's essay allows us to understand the psychological mechanism that informs the pleasurable realm of Picturesque aesthetics where, as I have already argued, the viewer's attachment to objects is rendered transitory by their very multiplicity and his desire remains free to return to the self. More importantly, Freud's analysis of ego ideals and especially Klein's model of envy enable us to gain a much more cogent comprehension of the startling preference for dispossessed and destitute figures in the Picturesque. The rustics, gypsies and beggars that litter the Picturesque landscape function as ego ideals in a Freudian sense. They are characteristically represented as eminently self-sufficient and self-subsistent like the natural environment into which they are placed. Despite their position of marginality in society, or rather because of it, they are masters within their world, having renounced all dependence on possessions or any other worldly ideals such as beauty itself. The writers of the Picturesque anticipate George Bataille's belief that the true master is not the chief or king who in potlatch festivities makes a display of his power by destroying vast amounts of wealth, but the destitute, who insults all wealth by his or her complete renunciation of it and moreover by his or her ability to renounce it without seeking any recognition for doing so, thus by-passing the Hegelian master–slave dialectic in which the king is inevitably trapped.[17] The destitute, moreover, has an advantage for the writers of the Picturesque, over a figure of political prestige: he or she is a pre-sacrificed figure who by his or her ordinariness prevents the formation of envy and its subsequent violent course.[18] The destitute at once invites identification due to his or her embodiment of narcissistic self-sufficiency but also liberates desire to return to the self by being in fact a ruin rather than an embodiment of a glorious perfection.

I shall illustrate these points by turning to two texts, Ruskin's essay 'Of the Turnerian Picturesque', and Wordsworth's 'Resolution and Independence'. In his essay Ruskin takes up the subject of ruins which he feels is the most significant contribution of the Picturesque as well as 'the most suspicious and questionable of all the characters distinctively belonging to our temper'.[19] Ostensibly Ruskin's purpose is to criticise what he calls 'the lower Picturesque' for its 'heartless' exploitation of ruins for purely aesthetic effects in order to show Turner's sensitivity to human suffering in his incomparably more humane treatment of the same motif. The sight of a ruin, Ruskin contends, ought to evoke regret, pity or melancholy and yet the lover of the Picturesque regards it with as much pleasure as if 'it were a fruit-tree in spring blossom' (pp. 19–21). What angers Ruskin is not only the mishandling of the ruin in this particularly offensive way from an ethical standpoint but also the further offence of its importation into a culture that is temperamentally at odds with it. The English, unlike the people on the Continent, cannot tolerate signs of decay or neglect in an environment, being entrenched in a mentality that values newness, cleanliness and trimness. Hence the ruin becomes a mere fashionable ornament in the middle of a 'green shaven lawn', a 'mere *specimen* of the middle ages put on a bit of velvet carpet to be shown' to the world. While abroad all habitations make 'some confession of human weakness' and their appearance is in tune with the fate of the people living or dying in them, 'with us', Ruskin claims, 'let who will be married or die, we neglect nothing. All is polished and precise again next morning; and whether people are happy or miserable, poor or prosperous, still we sweep the stairs of a Saturday' (pp. 15–16). Against the intolerance for waste and decay and the artificiality of the cult of ruins in the Picturesque, Ruskin sets up the example of the old tower of Calais which epitomises the difference between the genuine and the inauthentic ruin, between the 'noble' and the 'surface' Picturesque. I am quoting at length from Ruskin's description of the Calais tower as it represents perhaps the strongest evidence I can offer here concerning the narcissistic ideals that are tied to images of destitution in the Picturesque:

I cannot find words to express the intense pleasure I have always in first finding myself, after some prolonged stay in England, at the foot of the old tower of Calais church. The large neglect, the noble unsightliness of it; the record of its years written so visibly, yet without sign of weakness or decay; its stern wasteness and gloom eaten away by the Channel winds, and overgrown with the bitter sea grasses; its slates and tiles all shaken and rent, and yet not falling; its desert of brickwork full of bolts, and holes, and ugly fissures, and yet strong, like a bare brown rock; its carelessness of what any one thinks or feels about it, putting forth no claim, having no beauty nor desirableness, pride nor grace; yet neither asking for pity; not, as ruins are, useless and piteous, feebly or fondly garrulous of better days; but useful still, going through its own daily work, as some fisherman beaten grey by storm, yet drawing his daily nets: so it stands, with no complaint about its past youth, in blanched and meagre massiveness and serviceableness, gathering human souls together underneath it... And thus in its largeness, in its permitted evidence of slow decline, in its poverty, in its absence of all pretence, of all show and care for outside aspect, that Calais tower has an infinite of symbolism in it, all the more striking because usually seen in contrast with English scenes expressive of feelings the exact reverse of these. (pp. 12–14)

This is a memorable description which a reader of Ruskin is unlikely to miss. Its full symbolism can be grasped only in conjunction with a later and equally powerful passage in which Ruskin defines the category of the noble Picturesque:

Now, I have insisted long on this English character, because I want the reader to understand thoroughly the opposite element of the noble picturesque; its expression, namely, of *suffering*, of *poverty*, of *decay*, nobly endured by unpretending strength of heart. Nor only unpretending, but unconscious. If there be visible pensiveness in the building, as in a ruined abbey, it becomes, or claims to become, beautiful; but the picturesqueness is in the unconscious suffering, – the look that an old labourer has, not knowing that there is anything pathetic in his grey hair, and withered arms, and sunburnt breast; and thus there are the two extremes, the consciousness of pathos in the confessed ruin, which may or may not be beautiful, according to the kind of it; and the entire denial of human calamity and care, in the swept proprieties and neatness of English modernism: and, between these, there is the unconscious confession of the facts of distress and decay, in by-words; the world's hard work being gone through all the while, and no pity asked for, nor contempt feared. And this is the expression of that Calais spire, and of all picturesque things, in so far as they have mental or human expression at all. (p. 16)

Here in a nutshell is a vivid depiction of an anti-theatrical ideal which, as Ferguson argues, is a quintessential marker of the Picturesque. Clearly the main difference between the ruin in the surface Picturesque and the ruin in the noble Picturesque is that the former is theatrical whereas the latter is not. While the former makes a display of its dejected state, pointing to the monument it once was, the latter relinquishes all claims to monumentality; it is not 'garrulous of better days' and it makes no 'complaint about its past youth'. While the ruin of the surface Picturesque in a typically theatrical manner demands the viewer's attention, relying on his or her pity for full effect, the Calais tower stubbornly turns its back on the viewer, refusing to put on a spectacle of any sort and remaining entirely indifferent to 'what any one thinks or feels about it'. Its exclusion of the viewer is all the more radical because the tower of Calais, unlike the 'piteous' and 'garrulous' ruin, expresses no desire for anything and in its 'unsightly', wasted, and neglectful appearance, is meant to evoke no desire. The tower of Calais is the prototypical undesirable object. But unlike Shelley's 'Sensitive Plant', which suffers on account of its undesirability and 'desires what it has not – the Beautiful', the tower of Calais cuts itself off completely from the Beautiful or from love with which the Beautiful is so strongly associated in Shelley's poem. The tower of Calais desires nothing, 'putting forth no claim, having no beauty nor desirableness, pride nor grace'. For this reason it is also invulnerable, for despite the unseemly evidence of decay, its 'shaken and rent' tiles, its many 'holes and ugly fissures', the Calais tower is the epitome of durability and tenacity. It is as strong as a 'bare brown rock'.

It is easy to see that in an important respect the Calais tower fulfils the conditions of a Freudian ego ideal: it is after all the embodiment of narcissistic self-sustenance, needing nothing and no one, having everything it desires within itself, manifesting no consciousness of lack of any sort. As such it can easily lend itself to becoming a mobilising force of group identity, and Ruskin hints as much when he suggests that the Calais tower gathers 'human souls together underneath it'. But in one important respect the tower of Calais escapes the fate of mob identification, a dangerous situation which can often result in the outburst of sacrificial violence. It refuses to become an object of fetishistic worship. It draws as little attention to itself as the old and withered labourer who, unlike Prufrock, a prime theatrical figure, knows nothing about the pathos of his grey hair or the scope of his misery. As such it remains as safe from idolatry as from the assault of sadistic impulses, in Klein's terms, for surely the tower of Calais is a damaged object already. Another crack in its already gaping fissures would make little difference.

Ruskin's assessment of the noble Picturesque reads like a gloss to Wordsworth, and I have wondered whether a poem like 'Resolution and Independence' was not on Ruskin's mind when he composed the essay on the 'Turnerian Picturesque'. The connection between them is all the more revealing in that in their adamant opposition to this tradition, they articulate its concerns most vividly. While Ruskin rejected only the 'surface picturesque', Wordsworth rejected the Picturesque wholesale as early as 1793. But Wordsworth owes more to the tradition of the Picturesque than his outspoken rejection might indicate, as several critics have pointed out.[20] What he owes in particular, and what has not been emphasized by critics, is the use of the self-sufficient narcissistic figure, who is at once ordinary and enigmatic in his or her untheatrical self-absorption.

'Resolution and Independence' opens with a description of nature that abounds in narcissistic images, as exemplified by the Stock dove brooding over 'his own sweet voice' or the self-delighted hare whose mirth is so catching that nature itself follows, the mist running 'with her all the way, wherever she doth run'. The centre of the poem, however, is occupied by a much sterner image of narcissism which is embodied in the figure of the leechgatherer. The leechgatherer, who is first perceived hyperbolically by the speaker's overheated imagination as akin to a stone in its inert and immobile appearance, shares with nature a fundamental quality, namely lack of self-consciousness. He is as unaware of his suffering as the hare in the opening landscape is unaware of her mirth. He becomes the perfect example of the noble Picturesque in Ruskin's definition; having lost his wife and ten children, as Wordsworth makes clear in an earlier version, being reduced to almost impossible self-subsistence through the scarcity of the leeches which provide his ignoble livelihood, he bears his poverty with 'unpretending strength of heart' and 'not only unpretending, but unconscious'. The leechgatherer asks for no pity and certainly confesses 'the facts of distress and decay, in by-words' (to cite Ruskin again), at least in the final version of the poem. (He was certainly more 'garrulous' in an earlier version.)[21] The leechgatherer represents the speaker's salvation in this poem precisely because he is pitted against a theatrical model of self-consciousness, that of the dejected poet in which Wordsworth implicates himself but most particularly Coleridge. Certainly one of the most glaring features of 'Dejection: An Ode', particularly its earlier version known as the 'Letter to Sara', is the speaker's self-indulgent display of grief and domestic woes, his appeal to pity and his need for self-aggrandisement based on loss. The poem is a prime example of the 'piteous ruin' of Ruskin's surface Picturesque, 'feebly or fondly garrulous of better days'. By contrast, the uncomplaining figure of the leechgatherer who has suffered incomparable losses, stands as an admonishment to self-indulgence; moreover, it saves the poet from potential tragedy such as befell the poet Chatterton. The leechgatherer is beyond tragedy. Like the tower of Calais he is a pillar of strength that remains undiminished in spite of decay. But the leechgatherer resists idealisation, also; his plain speech when he finally does speak deflates the poet's sense of his 'lofty utterance'. The comic relief at the end of the poem is a sign of a liberation that the speaker has earned; not only from the instability of a dramatic imagination but also from identification with the leechgatherer. The poet is free 'to think of the leechgatherer' in times of need without having to become the leechgatherer.

All this is to say that destitutes are salvational figures in the Picturesque. They represent the landed gentry's desire for self-sufficiency, even as they betray their anxieties about accomplishing this ideal during a period of vast economic and social transformations. From an ideological standpoint Ruskin's nobly Picturesque old labourer or Wordsworth's leechgatherer are subject to criticism, for one might say that as long as such destitutes are idealised, as long as they are represented as uncomplaining and unconscious of their suffering, no one would be inclined to change their social condition. Nonetheless, it is impossible to remain unmoved by Ruskin's description of the Calais tower or fail to appreciate the sheer efficacy of the strategy developed by the practitioners of the Picturesque in pinning their ideals onto destitute figures, for in a surprisingly modern way they resolve the problems of identification with ego ideals and the violence that this may bring forth. It is thus that they salvage for themselves an area where the mind can gloat in its freedom and enjoy the sheer playfulness of semi-erotic longings, without confronting the 'darker side of landscape', which the Sublime deepens to tragic proportions.

The use of the destitute figure also illuminates another controversial aspect of Picturesque aesthetics, namely the question of the re-lationship between landscape and property. By definition the destitute has renounced all claims on possessions and as a figure of idealisation projects a strongly anti-proprietary code of ethics. Yet commentators like Liu and Bermingham have emphatically drawn our attention to the fact that in the Picturesque the attachment to property is so strong that landscape itself comes to designate property just as property comes to designate landscape.[22] There is certainly no way of ignoring the fact that the major aestheticians of the Picturesque were wealthy landowners and that their ability to reserve vast amounts of land for the enjoyment of Picturesque views was made possible by the profits they drew from enclosures. But precisely because this is the case, it is all the more striking to see the strong resistance of the practitioners of the Picturesque to the equivalence between landscape and property and their effort to downplay or outspokenly reject the importance of private property. A comment from Addison regarding the possibility of transforming an estate into a garden 'by frequent Plantations' is particularly relevant in this respect: 'A man might make a pretty Landskip of his own Possessions'.[23] We can infer from Addison's remark that the transformation of possessions into landscape is also at the same time an abandonment of acquisitive interests to a different order, the order of nature which in a profound way can never be possessed. Raymond Williams is right in suggesting that it is exactly at the point of the rupture between possession and prospect, between control of land and the surrender to forces which cannot be controlled that a new view of nature emerges in this period, whereby nature is seen as a 'principle of creation, of which the creative mind is part, and from which we may learn the truths of our own sympathetic nature'.[24]

For the writers of the Picturesque the contrast between property and prospect is not absolute, and it leads to a number of ambiguous if not downright paradoxical formulations. Thus William Mason asserts that 'Great Nature scorns controul' and that at the same time it willingly gives itself to man to have its features adorned and mended.[25] This captures beautifully one of the main paradoxes of the Picturesque, to which several commentators have drawn our attention: namely the cult of the raw, uncultivated and mysterious nature on the one hand, and the need to improve and contain nature within a set of preestablished norms.[26] Moreover, the contrast between property and prospect does not always ensure the rejection of appropriative practices but merely a change in the form in which such appropriation takes place. The prospect which is no longer the landlord's property is a free space that allows for an imaginative appropriation by the viewer generally or the poet in particular. 'There is a property in the horizon', Emerson wrote, 'which no man has but he whose eye can integrate all the parts, that is, the poet.'[27] Or as the seventeenth-century poet John Norris put it,

> While you a spot possess with care
> Below the notice of the Geographer,
>   I by the freedom of my soul
>   Possess, nay more, enjoy the whole...
> I can enjoy what's yours much more than you.
>   Your meadow's beauty I survey
>   Which you prize only for its hay.

> There can I sit beneath a tree
> And write an ode or elegy.
> What to you care does to me pleasure bring;
> You own the cage, I in it sit and sing.[28]

It is not clear whether Norris understands the irony of his situation, which is fully revealed in the last line. The cage in which he sits and which mocks the idea of freedom flaunted earlier cannot be separated from the imprisonment caused by mimetic desire, to use René Girard's term, for clearly a sense of rivalry with the possessor of the meadow traps the poet in an equally possessive stance. Thus Norris articulates precisely the paradoxical position of the writer of the Picturesque who by virtue of a misrecognised imitative gesture ends up in the same position as the owner of property that he or she sought to displace. But against such mystification as well as conscious concealment of property in landscape[29] stands the figure of the destitute who rivals no one and desires nothing, who like Wordsworth's Old Cumberland Beggar lives 'but for himself alone,/ Unblam'd', as well as 'uninjur'd' (lines 165–6). The destitute cuts through all paradoxes for he makes a radical break with property, with power play and control. Like the ruin with which this figure is associated, he reminds one of the vanity of all human possessions. In his solitude, his estrangement from society and his utter indifference to audience, he becomes the sole master of the world, resilient to the point of humiliating all who are attached to worldly riches.

Given the renunciatory attitude toward property that the Picturesque embodies, one would expect to see in the literature and art of the period the prevalence of gift exchange, for gift economy survives to the extent that objects cease to be regarded as private property and the fulfilment of purely utilitarian ends and are passed on to others for the sake of securing social bonds. Despite the strong anti-utilitarian sentiments voiced by the practitioners of the Picturesque as a reaction to the agrarian revolution that was changing the face of the countryside, there is, as far as I have been able to determine, a conspicuous absence of gift exchange in Picturesque art which raises a number of interesting questions. As an example of gift exchange I have chosen a passage from Goethe which not only exhibits some of the essential requirements for gift exchange but also begins with a moment of 'arrested desire' (in Liu's terms) which is so prevalent in the Picturesque:

I lately had a present of a basket of fruit. I was in raptures at the sight of it, as of something heavenly, – such riches, such abundance, such variety, and yet such affinity! I could not persuade myself to pluck off a single berry: I could not bring myself to take a single peach or fig. Most assuredly this gratification of the eye and the inner sense is the highest, and most worthy of man: in all probability it is the design of Nature, when the hungry and thirsty believe that she has exhausted herself in marvels merely for the gratification of their palate. Ferdinand came and found me in the midst of these meditations. He did me justice and then said, smiling, but with a deep sigh, 'Yes, we are not worthy to consume these glorious products of Nature: truly it were a pity. Permit me to make a present of them to my beloved?' How glad was I to see the basket carried off. How did I love Ferdinand! How did I thank him for the feeling he had excited in me, for the prospect he gave me! Ay, we ought to acquaint ourselves with the beautiful: we ought to contemplate it with rapture, and attempt to raise ourselves up to its height. And, in order to gain strength for that, we must keep ourselves thoroughly unselfish: we must not make it our own, but rather seek to communicate it, indeed, to make a sacrifice of it to those who are dear and precious to us.[30]

Like Coleridge in the quotation with which I began this essay, Goethe is confronted with a spectacle of beauty which engages both 'vision' and 'appetite' and in which desire is barred from its object. But Goethe escapes from the painful predicament of the immobilised Coleridgean figure by first separating the pleasures of vision from appetite and finally, by willingly renouncing the object of desire in favour of gift exchange. We have in this quotation two moments of gift exchange. In the first instance Goethe is in the position of a receiver of the gift, in the second he takes on the role of the giver. As Marcel Mauss has shown, there is a clear advantage to being a donor, for one achieves thereby a considerable authority over the receiver who, from then on and until he or she returns the gift, will be subjected to the pressure of indebtedness.[31] In one sense it could be said that by refusing to eat the fruit given to him by the anonymous donor, Goethe violates the ethics of gift exchange, neglecting one of the three indispensable obligations that secure the ties between partners, namely the obligation to receive. The gift is not a gift until it has been accepted as a gift. Furthermore, the gift is, as Lewis Hyde remarked, '*property that perishes*', that must be consumed, 'eaten up' by the receiver so as not to become stored away like capital and turned into a profitable investment.[32] But on the other hand, by not eating the fruit, Goethe actually abides fully by the spirit of gift exchange for it is this which enables him to give the basket away as a present to another. Hence Goethe does not destroy but actually increases the value of the original gift by keeping it in motion.[33] It is clear that by resisting not only the temptation of eating the fruit but, more significantly, the more dangerous temptation of remaining trapped in an imaginative possession of its sheer visual beauty, trapped that is, in a mode of vision that is very much like the appetite it presumably supplanted, Goethe has gained the advantage of establishing a community of devotees of the Beautiful, who like him, will have learned to sacrifice selfish interests for the sake of enhancing the lives of those 'who are dear and precious' to them. We can infer from the enormous relief and rapturous ecstasy experienced by Goethe at the moment when he relinquishes the basket to Ferdinand that he has undergone a tortuous struggle for reasons not fully articulated in the text and that he regards his resolution of it as a significant victory.

In the Picturesque there are no signs of either Goethe's hidden torment or of his victory, and arrested desire is not released through gift exchange. This might have something to do with the ambiguous status of property in the Picturesque, which is both vigorously upheld and as vigorously denied, as the obsession with destitutes and ruins reveals. Pierre Joseph Proudhon once made a remark that might have a bearing on this subject. He mentioned that there are two kinds of property which do not lend themselves to exchange: one is private property which is essentially 'non-reciprocity' and equivalent to theft; the other is 'common ownership' which is likewise 'non-reciprocity, since it is the negation of opposing terms'.[34] It seems to me that the Picturesque falls into either of the two extremes and therefore leaves behind the world of exchange which, as Proudhon and Lévi-Strauss claim,[35] can happen only in the space between these two polarities. It endorses either the singular and mostly imaginative appropriation of a spot or,[36] alternatively, the view of a place as accessible to all, the vision of 'the national park', as Liu suggests. Furthermore, and this is the last point I want to make, the object typically featured in the Picturesque is not so much the object owned or acquired through gift transfers, but what I would call 'the found object'. The found object is a distinguishing marker of modern sensibility, as Collins has shown, but its appearance can be seen in earlier texts as well. It is characteristically an ordinary object which is not sought after but accidentally discovered. It is an object which has no known owner or if the owner is known, he or she is either unlocatable or out of reach. Because this object is not given by someone, a relationship with it incurs no obligation and fosters no dependency, as in gift exchange. On the contrary, this object guarantees the discoverer's independence for it asks for nothing and invites no attachments. It is precisely through such an object that the speaker of Coleridge's poem 'The Picture' finds his long sought freedom from the precarious condition of a Burkean lover. His long journey through nature's Picturesque places, which he seeks out as a rescue from passion but which he infects with his passion everywhere he goes, finally ends when he finds the ordinary picture left behind by his beloved, a picture of a child sleeping with a dog, rudely painted. For a moment the speaker is tempted to keep the painting and turn it into a fetishised object, worshipping it as he previously worshipped the watery idol of his phantasmagoric recreation of the beloved in the surface of the river. But instead, the speaker decides to return the painting to its owner whom he may or may not locate in the wood. Although the ending of the poem leaves this question unresolved, it is not a crucial dénouement for the speaker. Through the picture the speaker has already attained a degree of independence and self-control that he did not have before and which he is bound to carry over into a relationship with the beloved, if such a relationship were to occur.

The writers of the Picturesque delight in found objects, and court nature precisely because among its inexhaustible riches there lies 'some accidental rough object', as Gilpin put it, 'which the common eye would pass unnoticed'.[37] Such objects are in essence ordinary and non-monumental, but their ordinariness is often transitory and unstable. Unlike modern writers, the practitioners of the Picturesque oscillate between an attraction to the ordinary and to the extra-ordinary. Hence they maintain a foot in the Sublime even while they may vociferously reject it. Ruskin's tower of Calais, to return to one of my examples, is hardly an ordinary and inconspicuous object. However broken down and decayed it might be and however scornful of spectacle and desirability by others, it is rendered through Ruskin's passionate description a monument once again. Like Wordsworth's leechgatherer, its ordinariness is projected on a large scale. But despite such paradoxes, the practitioners of the Picturesque break the spell of the Sublime object and show us that to sustain an interest in the untheatrical object, divested of any claims on beauty or desirability, is perhaps the more difficult, if only tenuously realised achievement.

NOTES

1 John Barrell, *The Dark Side of the Landscape: The Rural Poor in English Painting 1730–1840* (Cambridge University Press, 1980), chapter 3.
2 *The Notebooks of Samuel Taylor Coleridge*, ed. Kathleen Coburn, Bollingen Series 50, vols. I and II (New York: Pantheon Books; London: Routledge and Kegan Paul, 1957, 1961); vols. III and IV (Princeton University Press, 1973, 1989), vol. III, no. 3767.
3 Alan Liu, *Wordsworth: The Sense of History* (Stanford University Press, 1989), chapter 3, p. 62. Liu's chapter on the Picturesque was a major influence on this essay, alerting me to the problematic status of private property in the Picturesque. In this chapter Liu makes two independent remarks which taken together highlight the conflicted desire to both assert and deny private property, which is prevalent among the practitioners of the Picturesque. He notes 1) that 'arrested desire' and its corollary 'arrested violence' are distinguishing features of the Picturesque (pp. 60–1); and 2) that the practitioners of the Picturesque 'saw scenery as identical with property' (p. 91). In my view 'arrested desire' conflicts directly with the treatment of landscape as property, signalling a renunciatory rather than an acquisitive approach to it. Furthermore, as I will show, the term 'arrested desire' is itself misleading, for in the Picturesque desire remains free and unattached, continuously disconnecting from specific objects in order to return to the self or move on to another object.
4 As John Barrell notes, 'in no other of the eighteenth-century landscape arts was the landscape kept so carefully remote from the observer'. *The Idea of Landscape and the Sense of Place 1730–1840* (Cambridge University Press, 1972), p. 48.
5 William Gilpin explicitly identifies freedom of desire and the avid search for new objects as the main incentive for Picturesque travel: 'The first source of amusement to the picturesque traveller, is the *pursuit* of his object – the expectation of new scenes continually opening, and arising to his view. We suppose the country to have been unexplored. Under this circumstance the mind is kept constantly in agreeable suspense. The love of novelty is the foundation of this pleasure. Every distant horizon promises something new; and with this pleasing expectation we follow nature through all her walks. We pursue her from hill to dale; and hunt after those various beauties, with which she everywhere abounds' (*Three Essays* (London, 1794), pp. 47–8).
6 Edmund Burke, *A Philosophical Inquiry into the Origin of Our Ideas of the Sublime and the Beautiful*, ed. James T. Boulton (University of Notre Dame Press, 1968), p. 91. The association between love and the Beautiful is also maintained by Erasmus Darwin in a more idyllic and less troubled

setting than in Burke. Darwin traces the origin of love to the infant's entirely satisfying relationship with the mother's breast which is at the same time the origin of its developing sense of the beauty of form. 'Hence', he notes, 'at our maturer years, when any object of vision is presented to us, which by its waving or spiral lines bears any similitude to the form of the female bosom... we experience an attraction to embrace it with our arms, and to salute with our lips... And thus we find, according to the ingenious idea of Hogarth, that the waving lines of beauty were originally taken from the temple of Venus' (*The Temple of Nature; or the Origin of Society: A Poem* (London, 1803), Notes to Canto III, pp. 101–2).

7 See e.g. Uvedale Price, *An Essay on the Picturesque, as Compared with the Sublime and the Beautiful* in *Sir Uvedale Price on the Picturesque...*, ed. Sir Thomas Dick Lauder (Edinburgh, 1842), p. 69: 'It seems to me that the neglect – which prevails in the works of modern improvers – of all that is picturesque, is owing to their exclusive attention to high polish and flowing lines – the charms of which they are so engaged in contemplating, that they overlook two of the most fruitful sources of human pleasure: the first, that great and universal source of pleasure, *variety* – the power of which is independent of beauty, but without which even beauty soon ceases to please; the second, *intricacy* – a quality which, though distinct from variety, is so connected and blended with it, that the one can hardly exist without the other.'

8 This painting is reproduced and discussed by Ann Bermingham in *Landscape and Ideology: The English Rustic Tradition, 1740–1860* (Berkeley and Los Angeles: University of California Press, 1986), p. 35.

9 It was precisely this practice that, according to Barrell, made it possible for Constable to idealise rustic life: 'Only by being kept at a distance are men in Constable's paintings able to be seen as at one with the landscape, and as emblems of the contentment and industry which ideally were the basis of England's agricultural prosperity...' (*The Dark Side of the Landscape*, p. 139).

10 Michael Fried, *Absorption and Theatricality: Painting and Beholder in the Age of Diderot* (Berkeley and Los Angeles: University of California Press, 1980).

11 Frances Ferguson, 'In Search of the Natural Sublime: The Face on the Forest Floor', in *Solitude and the Sublime: Romanticism and the Aesthetics of Individuation* (London: Routledge, 1992). I am grateful to Ferguson for sending me a copy of this chapter while still in manuscript.

12 For this portion of my paper I owe a large debt to my colleague Doug Collins from the Romance Languages and Literature Department at the University of Washington, who has lectured extensively and written on modernism, using the psychoanalytic model based on Freud and Klein to which I refer below. His book manuscript *The Found Object: The Representation of Indifference in Critical Theory*, parts of which I read, has also

been influential in focusing my attention on the preference among the practitioners of the Picturesque for accidental objects, which do not bind the observer in a relationship of dependence on them.

13 Sigmund Freud, 'On Narcissism: An Introduction' (1914), in *A General Selection from the Works of Sigmund Freud*, ed. John Rickman (New York: Liveright Publishing Corporation, 1957), pp. 104–123.

14 Melanie Klein, *Envy and Gratitude: A Study of Unconscious Sources* (New York: Basic Books, 1957), chapters 1 and 2. I am using Klein's theory of envy primarily as a heuristic model that illuminates the desire as well as difficulties of relating to objects that embody self-sufficiency and perfection. As to the origin of envy, I am more closely in alignment with René Girard than Klein. Envy, in my view, is based on mimetic desire; the mother's breast could become an object of envy only if it is perceived as being desired by another. It would seem, therefore, that envy requires a more developed child with greater social awareness than the infant at the breast. For a different use of Klein in relationship to the Picturesque see David Punter's stimulating essay 'The Picturesque and the Sublime: Two Worldscapes' in this volume. Punter uncovers in the Picturesque a structure of violent assault on nature which he relates to the child's assault on his or her parents, as described by Klein. This explains, Punter argues, the source of the predominant references to concealment and secrecy among the practitioners of the Picturesque. For a different reading of the sources of suppressed violence in the Picturesque from a new historicist rather than psychological perspective see Liu, *Wordsworth*, chapter 3.

15 Doug Collins, 'Banality and Repetition: The Critique of Power in Modern Aesthetic Culture'. Paper presented at the Symposium *Music and Power* held at the University of Washington, 4 and 5 May 1991.

16 Freud, 'On Transience' (1915); in *Complete Works*, ed. James Strachey, 24 vols. (London: Hogarth Press), vol. XIV (1957), pp. 305–7. I am grateful to Collins for bringing this essay to my attention.

17 For Bataille's view of 'potlatch' as a mere theatrical show of destruction of wealth in the sight of others, and of loss which 'brings profit to the one who sustains it', see *The Accursed Share: An Essay on General Economy*, trans. Robert Hurley, 2 vols. (New York: Zone Books, 1988), vol. I, pp. 63–77. For Bataille 'The true luxury and the real potlatch of our times falls to the poverty-stricken, that is, to the individual who lies down and scoffs. A genuine luxury requires the complete contempt for riches, the somber indifference of the individual who refuses work and makes his life on the one hand an infinitely ruined splendor, and on the other, a silent insult to the laborious lie of the rich' (pp. 76–7). For the importance in the Picturesque of the 'aesthetics of poverty' see Malcolm Andrews's informative essay 'The Metropolitan Picturesque' in this volume.

18 The fear of and containment of violence is paramount in the Picturesque and is best expressed in the period's obsession with ruins. The ruin is an

object which has sustained violence, be it the violence of man or simply the violence of time, but this violence is mitigated by being placed in a distant and unrecoverable past. One of the most evocative and little known documents which captures the period's typical response to ruins is Richard Payne Knight's journal of his expedition into Sicily (1777). (This journal was translated and published thirty years later by Goethe. The original was found by Claudia Stumpf in the Goethe- und Schiller Archiv and published in 1986.) Here Knight reports two arresting incidents. Being detained at Porto Palinuro due to bad weather, Knight and his two companions (Charles Gore and Jacob Phillip Hackert) take a casual walk on the coast which leads to the unexpected discovery of 'a cavern of very singular type'. What surprises the travellers is that the cavern is not made of petrified sea shells as in other parts of the coast, but 'of human bones' forming thick strata that 'seemed to go far into the Mountain, which is of considerable height'. The mountain speckled with human bones as far as the eye can see must have been a 'singular' sight indeed, far more conducive to moods of 'mountain gloom' than 'mountain glory'. And yet Knight's response to this monument of destruction is surprisingly serene. Knight remains unmoved by the fate of the victims whose anonymous annals of suffering are recorded in petrified form. Instead, he derives from this disturbing scene a saving consolation, observing that the infinite changes that take place on 'this globe' involve 'disorder as well as order, which perhaps regularly spring from each other'. Similarly, in the second incident, where Knight encounters the extraordinarily moving sight of the ruins of Celinus, with its 'magnificent Temples, all prostrate on the ground' he avoids even more stubbornly the disturbing implications of the spectacle of violence that these ruins evoke. As Knight well knows, the city of Celinus was destroyed by Annibal who, in addition to dismantling 'the most magnificent Edifices ever built', sacrificed 3,000 inhabitants at the tomb of his father and killed or sold the rest of them as slaves. But once again Knight inscribes an act that clearly speaks of man's 'wanton love of destroying' into a narrative that renders history supremely rational and just. Rather than mourning the destruction of the temples, Knight rejoices in the vestiges that still remain behind because their survival attests to the incontestable superiority of the political system that engendered them, specifically to the 'inestimable...blessing of Liberty, that enabled so small a State as Selinus...to perform what the mighty Lords of the Earth have scarcely equalled'. See *Expedition into Sicily*, ed. Claudia Stumpf (London: British Museum Publications, 1986), pp. 30, 39–42. For a comprehensive discussion of the response to ruins among the practitioners of the Picturesque see Malcolm Andrews, *The Search for the Picturesque: Landscape Aesthetics and Tourism in Britain, 1760–1800* (Aldershot: Scolar Press, 1989), chapter 3, pp. 41–50 and nn.

19 John Ruskin, 'Of the Turnerian Picturesque', in *Modern Painters*, 5 vols.

(New York: John W. Lovell, 1873), vol. IV, part V, pp. 11–26. For further discussion of Ruskin's essay see Andrews, 'The Metropolitan Picturesque'.

20 Some critics have underplayed the influence of the Picturesque on Wordsworth, following Wordsworth's own indictment of this tradition in Book XII of *The Prelude*. W. J. B. Owen, for example, notes that 'Wordsworth's debt to the Picturesque has probably been exaggerated' ('Wordsworth's Aesthetics of Landscape', *The Wordsworth Circle*, 7 (1976), 70). Martin Price also notes that for Wordsworth 'the picturesque moment had already passed', just as it was coming into prominence in the works of Price and Knight ('The Picturesque Moment', in *From Sensibility to Romanticism*, ed. Frederick W. Hines and Harold Bloom (New York: Oxford University Press, 1965), p. 289). Other critics have attributed a much more significant influence of this tradition on Wordsworth. For this view, see J. R. Watson, *Picturesque Landscape and English Romantic Poetry* (London: Hutchinson Educational, 1970), particularly pp. 93–107; Russel Noyes, *Wordsworth and the Art of Landscape* (Bloomington: Indiana University Press, 1986); and Matthew Brennan, *Wordsworth, Turner, and Romantic Landscape: A Study of the Traditions of the Picturesque and the Sublime* (Columbia, S.C.: Camden House, 1987), Appendix pp. 127–132.

21 For a discussion of the differences between the early and revised versions of the poem see Lucy Newlyn, *Coleridge, Wordsworth and the Language of Allusion* (Oxford: Clarendon Press, 1986), chapter 5, and Gene Ruoff, *Wordsworth and Coleridge: The Making of the Major Lyrics, 1802–1804* (New Brunswick, N.J.: Rutgert University Press, 1989), chapters 4 and 5.

22 Liu, *Wordsworth*, p. 91 and Bermingham, *Landscape and Ideology*, pp. 13–14.

23 Cited by Raymond Williams, *The Country and the City* (New York: Oxford University Press, 1973), p. 127.

24 *Ibid.*

25 Cited by Barrell, *The Idea of Landscape and the Sense of Place*, p. 62.

26 See e.g. Andrews, *The Search for the Picturesque*, p. 3; and Barrell, *The Idea of Landscape and the Sense of Place*, pp. 60–2.

27 Cited by James Turner, *The Politics of Landscape: Rural Scenery and Society in English Poetry, 1630–1660* (Oxford: Basil Blackwell, 1979), p. 195.

28 *Ibid.* For a discussion of the 'imaginary appropriation of landscape' among the practitioners of the Picturesque see Liu, *Wordsworth*, pp. 91–5.

29 On Knight's habit of concealing property in nature see Liu, *Wordsworth*, p. 91.

30 Johann Wolfgang von Goethe, 'Letters from Switzerland. Travels in Italy', in *The Complete Works of Johann Wolfgang von Goethe*, trans. Thomas Caryle *et al.*, 10 vols. (New York: P. F. Collier, n.d.), vol. IV, p. 10.

31 In *The Gift* (New York: Norton, 1967), Marcel Mauss places particular

emphasis on the obligation to return gifts which always retain a mystical link with the spirit of the giver. 'The obligation attached to a gift itself', he notes, 'is not inert. Even when abandoned by the giver, it still forms a part of him. Through it he has a hold over the recipient, just as he had, while its owner, a hold over anyone who stole it' (p. 10).

32 Lewis Hyde, *The Gift: Imagination and the Erotic Life of Property* (New York: Random House, 1979), pp. 8–11.

33 As Hyde emphasised, 'A gift that cannot move loses its gift properties' (*The Gift*, p. 8).

34 Cited by Claude Lévi-Strauss, *The Elementary Structures of Kinship*, trans. James Harle Bell, John Richard von Sturmer and Rodney Needham (Boston: Beacon Press, 1969), p. 490.

35 *Ibid.*

36 Liu, *Wordsworth*, p. 95.

37 William Gilpin, *Observations, Relative Chiefly to Picturesque Beauty, Made in the Year 1776, on Several Parts of Great Britain; Particularly the High-Lands of Scotland*, 2 vols. (London, 1789), vol. I, p. 49.

CHAPTER 9

The Picturesque and the Sublime: two worldscapes

David Punter

Ruskin said that probably no word in the language, exclusive of theological expressions, had been the subject of disputes so frequent or so prolonged as the word 'picturesque'.[1] He said that, of course, quite a long time ago, and at a time when, although the original 'disputes' might have died down, the overall controversy remained a very live issue. I am not sure that we can claim that today the issue is live, in the sense of one which directly informs painterly or literary practice; but on the other hand, in terms of cultural history, it would still be fair to say that 'the Picturesque' remains a 'contested site'. Hence, of course, this volume; and hence also the considerable body of work published on the Picturesque over the last three decades.[2]

I do not want to begin by rehearsing this history of dispute in any detail. The key definitional works we may take to be those by William Gilpin, Richard Payne Knight and Sir Uvedale Price.[3] Price, in fact, neatly sets up the difficulty of precision in the area when he seeks to establish the Picturesque as a third category alongside Burke's earlier identifications of the Beautiful and the Sublime, arguing that it holds a position midway between the two but in the same breath pointing out that, for that very reason, it 'perhaps, is more frequently, and more happily blended with them both'.[4] Walter Hipple has usefully pointed out the difficulties with Price's adaptation of Burke's physiological aetiology: Price's paraphrase of Burke agrees that the 'sublime produces astonishment by stretching the nervous fibres beyond their normal tone... [while] the beautiful produces love and complacency by relaxing the fibres below their natural tone', and then claims that the Picturesque cleverly does something midway between these: which, it would seem, can only be to keep our nervous fibres in precisely the condition they were in in the first place, which would, if true, make the effect of the Picturesque peculiarly difficult to discern.[5]

If we turn, as I would like to, more specifically to the contrast between the Picturesque and the Sublime, we find our paths attended by even more imps of unclarity. Malcolm Andrews, in his extremely engaging book on the search for the Picturesque, talks on several occasions of the ability of the Picturesque to modulate more or less swiftly into the Sublime, and ties this not only to qualities of scenery but also to specific difficulties facing the tourist with a wish to place him- or herself in the right position to apprehend these qualities, 'the sense of difficulty, even peril, in negotiating a way into the landscape'.[6] He attests to this by quoting anecdotes of numerous difficulties into which people plunged themselves when trying to find just the correct, but usually exceedingly damp, prospect from which to view, for example, Devil's Bridge in mid-Wales, where the local publican did a roaring trade in superannuated guides and general rest and recuperation.[7]

Hipple, more soberly, speaks at length of the ways in which sublimity and picturesqueness are defined largely by distinction from beauty and from one another.[8] Wylie Sypher argues for the Picturesque as 'a sentimentalised sublimity, the excitement of the sublime without its abandon'.[9] Blake Nevius talks of the Picturesque, by contrast with the Sublime, as a matter of 'cooler and more secular emotions'.[10] And on top of this we have to deal with changes in the apprehension of the Picturesque in particular, from the extreme simplicity of early approaches, through efflorescence, to the eventual and historically symmetrical reduction of the Picturesque to a mere bundle of clichéd conventions.[11]

Interestingly, although it might be said that such a movement towards the 'conventionalising' of a form has also attended the Sublime at certain moments in its cultural history, there are significant differences in the historical trajectories of the two terms. We need to notice in particular the way in which the Sublime has recently been readopted into the critical fold in the guise of the 'postmodern sublime'.[12] In a way, this recapitulatory moment might be seen as a starting point of my essay, if only because it has seemed over the years improbable that such a rehabilitation would come the way of the Picturesque, exiled as it has been to over-wallpapered drawing rooms and sentimental Christmas cards.

We can perhaps take this point further by enquiring into what it is about the Sublime which seems to be recapturing our attention. A recent book by Henry Sussman, called *Afterimages of Modernity*

(1990), is sub-titled 'Structure and Indifference in Twentieth-Century Literature', and his central effort is to distinguish between Modernism, as a school based on almost architectonic structure, and Postmodernism where, in his view, structure and meaning are subjugated to a kind of indifference in which forms and values dissolve into a continuing, endless web of discourse.[13]

I would like to connect this back to earlier definitions of the Sublime and the Picturesque. For example, Gilpin famously points out that 'picturesque composition consists in uniting in one whole a variety of parts; and these parts can only be obtained from rough objects'.[14] Or again, although very contentiously in view of the relations between art and nature in the Picturesque: 'the picturesque eye abhors art; and delights solely in nature: and that as art abounds with regularity, which is only another name for smoothness; and the images of nature with irregularity, which is only another name for roughness, we have here a solution of our question'.[15] We do not need to spell out what the question was in that particular case, if only because Gilpin does not seem to have been quite clear about it himself, but it does seem to me important and potentially illuminating that the notion of irregularity, here equated with roughness but perhaps as usefully synonymised with 'resistant material', crops up helpfully in some arguments from Jung which I shall be adducing later.[16]

To return to the point, however: against the presumed roughness and variety of the Picturesque is supposed, we are told, to stand the Sublime:

The picturesque is...distinct from the sublime, both in its characteristics and its causes. The sublime is great, often infinite or apparently so, often uniform, and is founded on awe and terror. The picturesque may be great or small, but, since it so depends on the character of boundaries, can never be infinite; it is various and intricate rather than uniform...[17]

Here, it seems to me, the infinity and uniformity of the Sublime lead us directly to the 'indifference' of Sussman's characterisation of the Postmodern, with, precisely, its continual 'sublimations' of overt structure – Sussman's prime example contrasts *Finnegans Wake* (1939) with *Ulysses* (1922) – although what is equally important here is the mention of boundaries, which we need to examine in greater detail.[18]

Andrews has a remarkable chapter in which he describes the

various 'knick-knacks', from pedometers to Claude glasses, with which the Picturesque traveller used to festoon his or her person, the better to appreciate the revealed prospect, and he comments astutely that with the aid of these 'knick-knacks' the Picturesque traveller, or artist, 'converts Nature's unmanageable bounty into a frameable possession'.[19] Clearly there are political dimensions here, of kinds which John Berger and John Barrell have variously pursued;[20] but I would like to look at the issue of boundaries and framing in a broader light. The Picturesque frames roughness and variety; the Sublime has to do with being overwhelmed, surprised, being taken out of one's frame by a scene which, in a parallel way, threatens its boundaries as well as our own. Gilpin uses the frequent analogy of stage design to claim that rivers, as aesthetic objects, have four elements which need to be considered: 'the area, which is the river itself; the two side-screens, which are the opposite banks, and mark the perspective; and the front-screen, which points out the winding of the river'.[21]

We could equally well pursue these remarks on framing from any number of Picturesque and/or high Romantic texts, including the opening of 'Tintern Abbey' (1798);[22] but I would prefer, in order to see their psychological implications more clearly, to turn to a poem which is not in any conventional way descriptive of natural landscape, Blake's 'The Tyger' (c. 1793). For 'The Tyger' is, seen from one angle, a poem entirely about the appeal and the problems of framing. 'What immortal hand or eye', we are asked in the first stanza, 'Could frame thy fearful symmetry?' And, by the end, this question has modulated to, 'What immortal hand or eye/Dare frame thy fearful symmetry?'[23]

I am not suggesting that 'The Tyger' is a poem consciously about the Picturesque, a term which Blake only uses twice, in uninteresting contexts,[24] although of course he makes very much more play with the Sublime and sublimity. But the question here, nevertheless, is clearly one to do with art and nature, and with what the effect is of making over the natural object into a framable, or indeed framed, picture. The 'tyger', we may say, stands for raw material in many senses of that term: the natural object in the outer world, but in the inner world the half-perceived point of origin which can only be seen, as it were, in a slanting vision, such that its stripes cannot be picked out from the jungle where it lurks.

The artist's job can be seen as to frame this elusiveness, to provide a boundary, because according to one way of thinking, whether psychological or sociological, it is only through the provision of a boundary that meaning can be transferred. Yet for Blake there is a deeper dialectic: we are working here with roughness, indeed, with irregularity and with raw, resistant material, and our framing is always in danger from the excess of vitality which jumps from our frame – as it does emblematically in Roy Fisher's poem 'The Supposed Dancer'[25] – and which in the end will, we might say, destroy the comfortable and comforting stage-set on which we try to place it.

I have mentioned Jung already, and thus it is perhaps obvious that I wish to try to see these matters from a psychoanalytic perspective: from this angle, what is being described here is the activity of the unconscious and the ambiguous fate of our efforts to render our drives, our primal substance, in manageable and negotiable form.[26] The Picturesque, I suggest, is tied into this same psychic constellation: nature is there to be improved upon, to be adapted to our picture and voice. With the Sublime, I suspect something very different, even opposite, is taking place, whereby the frame itself, the frame of the picture but also the frame of conscious experience, is being constantly threatened, precisely by the intimations of unmanageable infinity – Blake here talks of 'immortality' – which I mentioned earlier.

It may of course be said that framing is a constant and unavoidable activity. It is treated, to my mind, in an especially interesting way by analysts and also by therapists using the creative arts. An example can be found in an essay by Joy Schaverien, an art therapist: 'Framed experience is not a strange or unusual concept; there are many analogies to draw on. For various reasons we go to special places, spaces "set apart" for a particular purpose. One space "set apart" in this manner is the theatre'.[27] Here we find the theatrical analogy again, but with painting perhaps the matter is not quite so simple:

When an artist makes a mark on a piece of paper or canvas, that mark is framed immediately, in that the piece of paper, the canvas, has edges which are predetermined boundaries... [But] the artist may choose to accept these limitations, making marks within the boundaries of the paper. Alternatively she may reject these limitations, extending the edges in one of several possible ways.[28]

This, I think, is a very interesting argument to apply to the imaginary and endlessly deferred edges of the Sublime. Marion

Milner, another writer dealing with psychology and the creative arts, deepens the point in her discussion of therapeutic painting, a discussion which she describes as 'an attempt to discover, within the limits of a special field, something of the nature of the forces that bring order out of chaos'.[29] This could also be taken as a description of Blake's enterprise, and the reference to chaos and to what I take to be the ego's defences against chaos is also, I think, important. We might go back to look at Pope on what might be loosely defined as Picturesque technique in *Windsor-Forest* (1713):

> Not Chaos-like together crush'd and bruis'd,
> But, as the world, harmoniously confus'd:
> Where order in variety we see,
> And where, tho' all things differ, all agree.[30]

Or we might turn to Barbara Stafford's important essay on the taste for chaos in landscape at the end of the eighteenth century, where she claims that 'chaos has form, form of a special kind which existed before the overlay of sophisticated cultures'.[31] She is talking here about contemporary perceptions of wild scenery as partly concealed evidence of the divine hand, or failing that as a divine rubbish tip, but I think she is wrong to claim that chaos has form; or rather, in saying so she is acting out the recuperative work of the ego appalled and traumatised before the prospect of the truly chaotic, the uncontrollable.

Chaos is indeed the 'creature void of form', and Gilpin was not happy about it at all. The fenlands of East Anglia, he found, were by no means Picturesque for they have no boundary lines; he was, in fact, quite startlingly wrong about that. In his view, however, they are thus inferior to lakes, which provide their own margins and definitions and thus prefigure and act as guarantor for what Andrews calls the controlling of 'untamed landscapes'.[32]

What is at stake here in this discourse of boundaries and frames is, as always, a negotiation of the bounding line between self and other, whether the other be conceived in the outer world or the inner. And our best evidence of this comes from the discourse of the Picturesque itself, where there is a perpetual hovering as to whether the Picturesque is a property of given forms or a description of a transformational psychic process, a process which can only be narcissistic as the ego seeks to remodel the outer world in its own shape.[33] Narcissus, Gilpin would perhaps have believed, could not have seen his image accurately anywhere between Norwich and Kings Lynn, for no answering 'shape' could have been found.

The two worldscapes of my title, we might conveniently say, are those of inscape and escape. The Picturesque, in this opposition, represents the movement of enclosure, control, the road which moves securely and fittingly into the countryside, the comforting flanking of the 'side-screen' hills, roughness subjected to symmetry, the ego's certainty about the world it can hold and manage. The Sublime represents the movement outward, the sudden rush of air which deflates the ego in the face of the avalanche, the pleasurable abandon of control. I shall go into this at greater length a little later in the essay; but I should say that neither of these, in my view, represents real bypassing of the ego, which is in any case impossible: the former reproduces the tightness of narcissistic anxiety, the latter what has now come to be called regression in the service of the ego, and they both thus relate to childhood states and accompanying pathologies.[34]

The problems of narcissism I am trying to discuss have been brilliantly encapsulated by Norman Nicholson in his poem 'Thomas Gray in Patterdale' (1948), where he alludes to the technicalities of the Picturesque traveller and his mirrors and glasses, themselves, of course, devices of containment, and says:

> What if I listen? What if I learn?
> What if I break the glass and turn
> And face the objective lake and see
> The wide-eyed stranger sky-line look at *me*?[35]

Here framing, the perceiving eye, the ambiguity and violence – 'ambiviolence' in Stephen Heath's phrase[36] – of the gaze are all related around the singular image of the tourist who believes he can see the world more clearly by turning his back on it and manipulating the great forces of nature – time of day, the season, the weather – by the deployment of tinted lenses.

Wordsworth, of course, is not immune from this kind of process, as we see from poems like 'An Evening Walk' (1788–9).[37] Dorothy Wordsworth reinforces this point in a well-known extract from her journal of the 1803 tour of Scotland, when she records herself, Wordsworth and Coleridge travelling near Loch Lomond:

When we were within about half a mile of Tarbet, at a sudden turning, looking to the left, we saw a very craggy-topped mountain amongst other smooth ones; the rocks on the summit distinct in shape as if they were buildings raised up by man, or uncouth images of some strange creature. We called out with one voice, 'That's what we wanted!' alluding to the frame-like uniformity of the side-screens of the lake for the last five or six miles.[38]

J. R. Watson, who quotes this passage, comments that it has 'the authentic air of a picturesque experience' with its combination of the frame of the side-screens and the roughness of the mountain.[39] I would only want to add that I find a deeper mythic resonance in the cry of 'That's what we wanted!' This scene appears to be one version of what the eye might want because it is essentially confirmatory: it does not open avenues towards unconsoling experiences of the outer, but instead relates back direct to the past, to the possibility that the wishes harboured and imaged in the inner world were somehow all along not fruitless or the result of pointless and unenviable solitude; instead this shows that 'we' were on the right track, that the comforting and nostalgic images of an ordered, tamed universe had some primal connection with the way things really are, and thus the divided image of Narcissus can come together again, if only in a momentary experience of wholeness – and an experience, further-more, wherein the shards, the bits and pieces of undigested, rough experience, still *also* remain visible.

I think it is something like this that Coleridge is trying to express in the passage from *Biographia Literaria* (1817) where he tries for definitions of the Picturesque, the Grand, the Majestic and the Sublime. It is typical of Coleridge not to be content with the conventional aesthetic terms, typical also of him to end by producing more puzzles and conundrums than he started with. Here is his attempt on the Picturesque:

Where the parts by their harmony produce an effect of a whole, but where there is no seen form of a whole producing or explaining the parts, i.e. when the parts only are seen and distinguished, but the whole is felt.[40]

Characteristically, this is brilliantly suggestive; what I think Cole-ridge is talking about is the way in which the 'wholeness', the sense of impregnable organisation which we find in the Picturesque, is indeed only an illusion, and one which has been carefully manu-factured, if not by the Claude glass then by the ceaseless spidery – or claw-like? – workings of the ego; you only have to blink and the whole construct falls apart in the valley of dry bones, and for that very reason the sense of order is indefinably precious, and no less so for the fragility of its speciousness.

Above I mentioned 'pathologies', and I would now like to turn for a moment to a brief description of what I take the pathologies of the Picturesque and the Sublime to be. If we are talking about pathologies, then we are talking about constructs which have at best an ambiguous relation to time boundaries; and I have therefore chosen my examples not from the eighteenth or nineteenth centuries but from quite different areas. I want first to make some points, in connection with the Picturesque, about a brief passage from Beckett. It occurs in *From an Abandoned Work* (1958), and I think that in some ways it is a very obviously 'painterly' passage; but the more important thing, to my mind, is what it has to say about the inner functions of 'framing':

Up bright and early that day, I was young then, feeling awful, and out, mother hanging out of the window in her nightdress weeping and waving. Nice fresh morning, bright too early as so often. Feeling really awful, very violent. The sky would soon darken and rain fall and go on falling, all day, till evening. Then blue and sun again a second, then night. Feeling all this, how violent and the kind of day, I stopped and turned. So back with bowed head on the look out for a snail, slug or worm. Great love in my heart too for all things still and rooted, bushes, boulders and the like, too numerous to mention, even the flowers of the field, not for the world when in my right senses would I ever touch one, to pluck it. Whereas a bird now, or a butterfly, fluttering about and getting in my way, all moving things, getting in my path, a slug now, getting under my feet, no, no mercy. Not that I'd go out of my way to get at them, no, at a distance often they seemed still, then a moment later they were upon me.[41]

I wish to emphasise one or two details. The presenting pathology here is structured around an opposition between the moving, which is always construed as threat, and the still, onto which is projected all love. Therefore the world, for this paranoid subject, has to be cemented into place, if necessary by killing it; otherwise the risk of something escaping from the frame would be too great to be borne. That frame is already established in the opening image of the mother, which of course also opens us back onto the necessity betrayed here of fixing the origin, of penning the potentially and threateningly fertile into the space of the eye, precisely the movement whereby nature can be denaturalised, subjected to the framing and shuttering effect of the ego, or the lens, for the photographic image is now always with us when we discuss the Picturesque. The passage continues:

Birds with my piercing sight I have seen flying so high, so far, that they seemed at rest, then the next minute they were all about me, crows have done this. Ducks are perhaps the worst, to be suddenly stamping and stumbling in the midst of ducks, or hens, any class of poultry, few things are worse. Nor will I go out of my way to avoid such things, when avoidable, no I simply will not go out of my way, though I have never in my life been on my way anywhere, but simply on my way.[42]

I want to place the Picturesque traveller within this scenario: not merely as social exploiter, but also as the embodiment of the assertion of the ego's right to travel freely without let or hindrance. In many ways this may seem an admirable thing, and indeed on the surface what we may seem to have in the great late eighteenth-century tourists is a move towards desublimation, an attempt to visit and see, despite the problems they continually encountered of being seen as colonialists in their own land.[43] But I think that what is revealed here by Beckett is the difficulty of matching perception of the near and the far: there is some strange elision between the crows above and the poultry below, so that the terror of overarching flight becomes transmuted into an absolute unwillingness to respect ground-based territorial integrity. These hens and ducks are precisely what cannot be willed away by a deliberate uncluttering and arranging of the scenery. And finally, skipping a brief and awesome passage:

Then I raised my eyes and saw my mother still in the window waving, waving me back or on I don't know, or just waving, in sad helpless love, and I heard faintly her cries. The window-frame was green, pale, the house-wall grey and my mother white and so thin I could see past her (piercing sight I had then) into the dark of the room, and on all that full the not long risen sun, and all small because of the distance, very pretty really the whole thing, I remember it, the old grey and then the thin green surround and the thin white against the dark, if only she could have been still and let me look at it all.[44]

First, I would draw attention to the phrasing of 'saw my mother *still* in the window': what is undecidable here is whether we are dealing with the stillness of fixing or the stillness of always; in this worldscape they are indistinguishable because the prime need is to dispel the anxiety occasioned by the crows, by the unmanageable and the untamed, by that which might, in however remote a way, represent 'mother' nature. And then there is the ambiguity of the image of the mother herself, vivid in one way but 'so thin', as though all this framing has the effect of reducing the subject to a ghost – a useful comparison here would be with Dickens's extraordinary short ghost story 'The Signalman' (1866), where the action and indeed the eponymous signalman himself are crucially framed and disembodied by a railway cutting.[45] At this point, of course, one asks *which* subject, mother or son? For what is at stake here is a sense of vanishing, which would result unless some confirmation were available in what little thinness remains in the 'natural' scene.[46]

It is my contention that all this has to do with the problems of framing and thus of the Picturesque, which stem from the necessity for tight and incontrovertible boundaries; there is no space here for me to try to relate that to a more general cultural psychology of the period, but I think the lines along which such an enterprise might be begun are obvious enough, for boundaries, enclosures, possessions and dispossessions, what Gilles Deleuze and Felix Guattari refer to as deterritorialisations and reterritorialisations, or what, following Raimonda Modiano, we might refer to as institution and destitution, all these are deeply etched in the social history of the eighteenth century.[47] I will, however, mention another comment from Andrews, where he speaks of 'life accidentally imitating art' as 'the purest of Picturesque pleasures':[48] I believe I see what he means, but in the end what is being talked about is therefore de-natured, evasive, looking to invented structure because the organism is regarded as too fragile to survive. What is demonstrated, in analytic terms, is a fear of death, of obliteration unless a theatre, a frame, sufficiently firm can be found to contain what would otherwise inevitably and fruitlessly be spilled.[49]

In trying to provide a similar instance of the pathology of the Sublime my chosen text is J. G. Ballard's *The Unlimited Dream Company* (1979), which strikes me as peculiarly apposite because Blake is its hero. There is again no space to examine the text in detail, but I would like to quote the 'sublime' apotheosis of the ending, which self-consciously parallels the ending of Blake's *Jerusalem* (1804–20):

On all sides an immense panoply of living creatures was rising into the air. A cloud of silver fish rose from the river, an inverted waterfall of speckled forms. Above the park the timid deer ascended in a tremulous herd. Voles and squirrels, snakes and lizards, a myriad insects were sailing upwards. We merged together for the last time, feeling ourselves dissolve into this aerial fleet. Taking them all into me, I chimerised myself, a multiple of all these creatures passing through the gateway of my body to the realm above. Concourses of chimeric beings poured from my head. I felt myself dissolve within these assembling and separating forms, beating together with a single pulse, the infinitely chambered heart of the great bird of which we were all part.[50]

I hope the relation between this vision and the question of indifference, or at least of undifferentiation, is obvious, and also the megalomaniac implications of this uninterrupted channelling between upper and lower worlds, reminiscent of aspects of Freud's Schreber case.[51] Both of these loci seem to me to relate closely to the pathologically opened channels of the Sublime insofar as it offers the prospect of an unrestricted and unmarked life spent in communion with great forces, even if those forces seem uncomfortably frequently imaged in the archetypes of death, otherwise known in the undifferentiated merging signalised in the general chimera.

The mention of archetypes brings me to a further point. I want next to think for a moment about whether we can deepen our characterisation of the Picturesque and the Sublime through looking in a little more detail at a particular variant of Jungian psychology, and particularly at the work of a major neo-Jungian, the archetypal-analyst James Hillman.

I mentioned earlier on the Jungian connection with the Picturesque discourse of roughness and irregularity, and perhaps I should now make that clearer. Essentially, Jung claims that our sense of the irregular is, precisely, our irrepressible intimation of the other within us; so that, whenever we wish to see unclouded skies or an untroubled sea – or better, lake – we find ourselves inevitably encountering the misplaced rocks and shoals of the unconscious.[52] Interestingly, the theory of the Picturesque seems to be second-guessing this: whenever nature does, by some mischance, provide smoothness, then roughness must be conjured from nowhere to correct this punishable maternal bias, or threat of bliss. Yet in doing this, I would maintain, it is practising a sophisticated version of incorporation, such that a 'system' can be put in place which cannot be disturbed by other data. The work of Narcissus proceeds – which is also, emblematically, the work of projection whereby the inner world seeks to enforce its equivalents on the outer, and presses it into shape, the shape which possesses the imagining.

Thus far, these ideas are common to psychoanalysis in general; where Jung differs, of course, from Freud is in his insistence that the primary shapings of the outer are not massive reinscriptions of the sexual but are instead responsive to deeper formings in the psyche.

Jung calls these the archetypes, a term to which Picturesque theory, as it happens, also refers.[53]

Hillman goes further than this in his attempt to investigate and classify the archetypes, and over a long series of books from *The Dream and the Underworld* (1979) through *Facing the Gods* (1980) to *Healing Fiction* (1983) has tried to put forward the gods as the shapes in which we actually encounter – in the real world, which is conveyed to us in dream – the entities of which the Jungian archetypes are merely the schematisations.

In accordance with this, I would like to suggest a characterisation of the Picturesque and the Sublime in Hillman's terms. With the Sublime, I have no difficulty. Jung establishes as one of his archetypal positions the 'senex', the wise old man.[54] I think that if we consider for a moment the exemplary Sublime in the paintings of John Martin, we should have no difficulty in seeing that this is the constellation in whose presence we are.[55] The guiding god of the senex is Saturn: father of all the Olympians, child-eater, exemplar of cold and magical malevolence. Saturn signifies all that is beyond our powers: the cannibalistic urge, the 'man-eating', the power which controls the avalanche as well as that which afflicts us when we are asleep on the cold hillside. The position unconsciously taken by the artist of the Sublime is of that which is ancient but which survives, that which will dwarf and eventually murder the petty avatars of freedom and the future.

Death is the substance of Saturn; his joking facade, his saturnalia, are only meant as reminders of the doom, the collapse from the mountain, to which we all go down. His colours are the darkest, the most sombre, lit by the flashes of purple majesty which disclose only a face with a fixed and bloody grin, a death mask: these are the colours of Martin, and they are the fate we worship because, precisely, it brings with it indifference, undifferentiation, the potential disappearance of all human distinctness in the imminent night when all things will be as one.

But with the Picturesque, I have more of a problem. I offer you Hermes as its presiding god, but with some doubts. The possible aptness of Hermes may be summarised as follows.[56] He is guide, an escort, *pompos* or *psychopompos*; we see his figure preceding us over the already known landscape of the road winding between the hills. He stands for roads, as for boundaries, journeys, entryways: he allows us access to the projected picture of our psyche while uttering a warning that what we shall see is what we came to see; he stands at the door of every freakshow, every circus. He stands also, however, for thievery, trickery, wiles and deceit: what we shall see is not, in the end, really what we expected because we shall never know the teller of the tale, shall never see the painter in the picture (he is thus, of course, the god of criticism): we shall be subjected to the trickery of the consummate narrator, and shall never know whether the world of which he tells was there before him or is his own invention. He is the owner and wielder of the caduceus, by whose redoubled image we shall know the inseparability of the teller and the told: we shall see in this perfect symmetry, which is also the endless and deceptive symmetry of the serpent, an image which is, indeed, well arranged, well flanked, but offers no real security, only the certainty of a message which might, after all, be unsanctioned by the more real gods, might be the message we have been, for a long time, sending to ourselves. As opposed to the 'senex', although I am not sure Hillman would agree with this, Hermes has aspects of the 'puer', the endlessly young and refreshed, Narcissus fully bathed and smiling an ambiguous welcome.[57] The Picturesque, by its very clarity, by the apparent openness of its admiration, deceives us about the crucial borders between man and nature, between inner and outer; revelation and concealment are delicately locked, a point I shall go on to explore a little further below.

Throughout this essay, I have been alluding on occasion to 'mother' nature, and perhaps this is the moment to bring to the fore some of the gender assumptions behind this analysis of forms and stances. I can do so through two quotations. The first is from Knight, complaining about the encroachments of the landscape gardeners on a world which he regards, in a primordial fantasy, as having been previously ruled by the great mother:

> But ah! in vain: – See yon fantastic band,
> With charts, pedometers, and rules in hand,
> Advance triumphant, and alike lay waste
> The forms of nature, and the works of taste!
> T'improve, adorn, and polish, they profess;
> But shave the goddess, whom they came to dress.[58]

The castration symbolism here is obviously important, as the tourists of the Picturesque proceed to 'unman' that which is, on another scene, unmistakably female in the first place. The rhetoric is given a new slant by Ernest Tuveson:

Nature, obscured for centuries by the mists of scholastic ignorance, has once more been revealed in all her loveliness and majesty – a 'spreading' scene, the vastness of the prospect giving evidence of its purity. The newborn earth thus revealed is transfigured, clothed in a radiance that rises to touch the heavens in the great mountains and in the endless horizons of the sea.[59]

Do the Picturesque writers and painters come to clothe nature or to unclothe her? To proceed with this question, and also to conclude my essay, I want to move briefly to a quite different set of psychoanalytic principles and writings, based on the work of Melanie Klein. The question of the clothed and the unclothed has to do with concealment and secrecy, and we can find this motif of secrecy deeply inscribed on the Picturesque. Knight writes:

> But cautiously will taste its stores reveal;
> Its greatest part is aptly to conceal;
> To lead, with secret guile, the prying sight
> To where component parts may best unite,
> And form one beauteous, nicely blended whole,
> To charm the eye and captivate the soul.[60]

The 'secret guile', I suspect, is that of Hermes, and this perhaps lends an added ambiguity to the notion of 'discovering' the 'spreading scene';[61] Knight also refers to 'art clandestine, and conceal'd design'[62] and we must here surely wonder what designs on the mother goddess are being encoded, what childhood secrecies are being given the clothing and decencies of well-regulated landscape.

Whatever is going on here, in Kleinian terms it obviously has to do with a veiled assault on a parent conceived of as bearing secrets which will not be revealed except to the force of 'art' in its strongest, most *hermetic* sense. Klein's theory of art, and indeed of symbolism in general, is that it arises from precisely this sense of the need to pry secrets loose, for a particular reason. The small child, she argues from her unique early practice of infant analysis, in order to establish a free space in the world conducts fantasy attacks on his or her parents: the knowledge that these attacks have occurred is the source of future guilt, and the need to repair the fantasised consequences of these attacks results in the establishment of a system of symbolism in terms of which that which has been broken and forced apart, principally the parents' sexual relationship, can be put back together through the surrogate deployment of aesthetic form.[63]

Let us, in this light, consider one or two Picturesque comments. Here we find Gilpin complaining that he is so offended by the gable-ends of Tintern Abbey that he recommends they be fractured 'judiciously' with a mallet.[64] In greater detail, we find this comment:

A piece of Palladian architecture may be elegant in the last degree. The proportion of its parts – the propriety of its ornaments – and the symmetry of the whole may be highly pleasing. But if we introduce it in a picture, it immediately becomes a formal object, and ceases to please. Should we wish to give it picturesque beauty, we must use the mallet, instead of the chisel, we must beat down one half of it, deface the other, and throw the mutilated members around in heaps. In short, from a smooth building we must turn it into a rough ruin.[65]

'Beat down one half', 'deface the other', 'throw the mutilated members around in heaps'. I pointed out earlier on that the theorists of the Picturesque seemed frequently uncertain as to whether they were describing a set of given properties or a psychic process; I think these passages make it clear that the former is merely a mask for the latter. The Picturesque is not just a matter of perception and receptivity, as indeed we know: it describes an active 'doing to things', and this of a double kind. The attack on symmetry, the attack on authority, is violently present, as a presumably necessary ground-clearing so that nothing shall stand between Narcissus and his image; the destruction of the parent gods is a necessary precondition of the fantasised rebuilding of childlike, pastoral myth in which potential conflict is reduced to harmonious side-screens, the mother and father to a pair of beneficent divine onlookers.

The Sublime also, of course, has its destructive moment: 'Your organs of perception are hurried along and partake of the turbulence of the roaring waters. The powers of recollection remain suspended by this sudden shock; and it is not till after a considerable time, that you are enabled to contemplate the sublime horrors of this majestic scene'.[66] The difference here is that control is suspended by shock, something which happens *to* you rather than something you perform with mallet or whatever other tools – pen, paintbrush – happen to be around; although Price would nonetheless claim, even if only through a verbal confusion, that the two categories, the two worldscapes, are still undifferentiable: 'The limbs of huge trees shattered by lightning or tempestuous winds,' he says, 'are in the highest degree picturesque; but whatever is caused by those dreaded powers of destruction, must always have a tincture of the sublime'.[67]

If I were to try to summarise my argument, I would have to refer again to the image of the 'tyger' and to talk about the Picturesque and the Sublime as ways in which the ego tries to deal with troubling and unmanageable material; but perhaps it is better to avoid a summary, because, after all, that is a way of trying to put things into a frame; and frames are themselves, as I have hoped to show, ambiguous matters at best, open if we like to inspection even as we recognise that they implicate us as much in our destructive impulses as in the equally essential work of reparation of the shaping imagination.

NOTES

1 See John Ruskin, *The Seven Lamps of Architecture* (London: George Allen, 1880), p. 342.

2 On the Picturesque and related matters I am thinking of, e.g., Samuel Holt Monk, *The Sublime* (Ann Arbor: University of Michigan Press, 1962); John Dixon Hunt, *The Figure in the Landscape: Poetry, Painting and Gardening during the Eighteenth Century* (Baltimore, Md.: Johns Hopkins University Press, 1976); James Turner, *The Politics of Landscape: Rural Scenery and Society in English Poetry, 1630–1660* (Oxford: Basil Blackwell, 1979); John Barrell, *The Dark Side of the Landscape: The Rural Poor in English Painting, 1730–1840* (Cambridge University Press, 1980); Ann Bermingham, *Landscape and Ideology: The English Rustic Tradition, 1740–1860* (London: Thames and Hudson, 1987); Malcolm Andrews, *The Search for the Picturesque: Landscape Aesthetics and Tourism in Britain, 1760–1800* (Aldershot: Scolar Press, 1989).

3 See particularly William Gilpin, *Three Essays: On Picturesque Beauty; On Picturesque Travel; and On Sketching Landscape* (London, 1792); Richard Payne Knight, *The Landscape* (London, 1794); Uvedale Price, *Essays on the Picturesque As Compared with the Sublime and the Beautiful*, 3 vols. (London, 1810).

4 Price, *Essays on the Picturesque*, vol. I, p. 68.

5 Walter J. Hipple, *The Beautiful, the Sublime, and the Picturesque in Eighteenth-Century British Aesthetic Theory* (Carbondale: Southern Illinois University Press, 1957), p. 204.

6 Andrews, *The Search for the Picturesque*, p. 219.

7 *Ibid.*, pp. 148–50.

8 See Hipple, *The Beautiful, the Sublime, and the Picturesque*, pp. 3–10, 185–91.

9 Wylie Sypher, 'Baroque Afterpiece: The Picturesque', *Gazette des Beaux-Arts*, vol. XXVII (1945), p. 46.

10 Blake Nevius, *Cooper's Landscapes: An Essay on the Picturesque Vision* (Berkeley: University of California Press, 1976), p. 36.

11 See, e.g., Andrews, *The Search for the Picturesque*, pp. 239–40; Bermingham, *Landscape and Ideology*, p. 193.

12 See, e.g., Jean-François Lyotard, *The Postmodern Condition: A Report on Knowledge*, trans. G. Bennington and B. Massumi (Manchester University Press, 1984), pp. 77–81, as the origin of a continuing debate.

13 See Henry Sussman, *Afterimages of Modernity* (Baltimore, Md.: Johns Hopkins University Press, 1990), pp. 161–205.

14 Gilpin, *Three Essays*, p. 19.

15 *Ibid.*, pp. 26–7.

16 See, e.g., Jung, 'The Undiscovered Self (Present and Future)' (1957), in *Civilisation in Transition, The Collected Works of C. G. Jung*, ed. Sir Herbert Read *et al.*, 20 vols. (London: Routledge and Kegan Paul, 1957–79) vol. x, pp. 247–55.

17 Hipple, *The Beautiful, the Sublime, and the Picturesque*, p. 211.

18 On boundaries see, e.g., Freud, *Totem and Taboo* (1913), in *The Standard Edition of the Complete Psychological Works of Sigmund Freud*, ed. J. Strachey *et al.*, 24 vols. (London: Hogarth Press and the Institute of Psychoanalysis, 1953–73), vol. XIII, pp. 1–161; Ernst Kris, 'Notes on the Psychology of Prejudice' (1946), in *The Selected Papers of Ernst Kris*, ed. L. M. Newman (New Haven and London: Yale University Press, 1975), pp. 465–72.

19 Andrews, *The Search for the Picturesque*, p. 81.

20 See John Berger, *Ways of Seeing* (London: British Broadcasting Corporation and Penguin, 1972), pp. 83–108; John Barrell, *English Literature in History 1730–80: An Equal, Wide Survey* (London: Hutchinson, 1983), e.g. pp. 33–6, 74–9.

21 William Gilpin, *Observations on the River Wye, and Several Parts of South Wales, etc., Relative Chiefly to Picturesque Beauty; Made in the Summer of the Year 1770* (London, 1782), p. 8.

22 See Wordsworth, 'Lines Composed a Few Miles above Tintern Abbey, on Revisiting the Banks of the Wye during a Tour. July 13, 1798', lines 1–22, in *The Poems*, ed. J. O. Hayden, 2 vols. (Harmondsworth: Penguin, 1977), vol. I, pp. 357–8.

23 William Blake, 'The Tyger', lines 3–4, 23–4, in *Complete Writings*, ed. G. Keynes (London: Oxford University Press, 1966), p. 214.

24 See Blake, *A Descriptive Catalogue of Pictures …* (1809), in *Complete Writings*, p. 581; letter to Thomas Butts (22 November 1802), in *Complete Writings*, p. 814 (the latter in fact comprises a group of references).

25 See Roy Fisher, 'The Supposed Dancer', in *Poems 1955–1980* (Oxford University Press, 1980), p. 164.

26 See, e.g., Jung, *The Relations between the Ego and the Unconscious* (1945), in *Two Essays on Analytical Psychology, Collected Works*, vol. VII, pp. 210–24.

27 Joy Schaverien, 'The Picture within the Frame', in *Pictures at an Exhibition: Selected Essays on Art and Art Therapy*, ed. A. Gilroy and T. Dalley (London: Tavistock/Routledge, 1989), p. 148.

28 *Ibid.*, p. 151.

29 Marion Milner, 'The Ordering of Chaos' (1957), in *The Suppressed*

Madness of Sane Men (London and New York: Tavistock and the Institute of Psychoanalysis, 1987), p. 216.

30 Pope, 'Windsor-Forest', lines 13–16, in *Poetical Works*, ed. H. Davis (London: Oxford University Press, 1966), p. 37.

31 Barbara Stafford, 'Toward Romantic Landscape Perception: Illustrated Travels and the Rise of "Singularity" as an Aesthetic Category', *Art Quarterly*, NS 1 (1977), 98. I should say at this point that several of the citations I adduce in this part of the essay (and notably the quotation below from Norman Nicholson) are not original to me, but can be found in the various authorities already mentioned, although I hope that here they are reworked into a differently shaped argument.

32 Andrews, *The Search for the Picturesque*, p. 67.

33 See Freud, 'From the History of an Infantile Neurosis' [The Wolf Man] (1914), in *Standard Edition*, vol. XVII, especially pp. 110–11.

34 See, e.g., Ernst Kris, *Psychoanalytic Explorations in Art* (New York: George Allen and Unwin, 1952); also Roy Schafer, *Aspects of Internalisation* (New York: International Universities Press, 1968), pp. 56, 94, 109; and W. W. Meissner, *Internalisation in Psychoanalysis* (New York: International Universities Press, 1981), pp. 163–7.

35 Norman Nicholson, 'Thomas Gray in Patterdale', lines 18–21, in *Rock Face* (London: Faber, 1948), p. 31.

36 See Stephen Heath, *Ambiviolences: Notes pour la lecture de Joyce* (Paris, n.d.).

37 Wordsworth, 'An Evening Walk Addressed to a Young Lady', e.g. lines 331–8, in *Poems*, p. 86.

38 *Journals of Dorothy Wordsworth*, ed. Ernest de Selincourt, 2 vols. (London, 1941), vol. I, pp. 255–6.

39 J. R. Watson, *Picturesque Landscape and English Romantic Poetry* (London: Hutchinson Educational, 1970), p. 104.

40 *Letters, Conversations and Recollections of S. T. Coleridge*, ed. T. Allsop (London: Groombridge, 1858), pp. 106–7.

41 Samuel Beckett, *From an Abandoned Work* (London: Faber, 1958), pp. 9–10.

42 *Ibid.*, p. 10.

43 See, e.g., Andrews, *The Search for the Picturesque*, pp. 102, 128–30.

44 Beckett, *From an Abandoned Work*, pp. 10–11.

45 See Dickens, 'Mugby Junction. No. 1 Branch Line. The Signalman', in *Selected Short Fictions*, ed. D. A. Thomas (Harmondsworth: Penguin, 1976), pp. 78–90.

46 There are some connections to be made here with Freud, *The 'Uncanny'* (1919), in *Standard Edition*, vol. XVII, especially pp. 237, 240.

47 See Gilles Deleuze and Felix Guattari, *A Thousand Plateaus: Capitalism and Schizophrenia*, trans. Massumi (London: Athlone Press, 1988); Raimonda Modiano, 'The Legacy of the Picturesque: Landscape, Property and the Ruin', in the present volume.

48 Andrews, *The Search for the Picturesque*, p. 40.

49 This seems also to be the root of the extraordinary case of Frau Emmy von N., related in Josef Breuer and Freud, *Studies on Hysteria* (1893–5), in Freud, *Standard Edition*, vol. II, pp. 48–105.

50 J. G. Ballard, *The Unlimited Dream Company* (London: Cape, 1979), p. 222.

51 See Freud, *Psycho-Analytic Notes on an Autobiographical Account of a Case of Paranoia* (1911), in *Standard Edition*, vol. XII, especially pp. 17, 29–30.

52 See Jung, e.g. 'The Role of the Unconscious' (1918), in *Civilisation in Transition, Collected Works*, vol. X, pp. 3–28.

53 See Jung, e.g., 'Archetypes of the Collective Unconscious' (1954), in *The Archetypes and the Collective Unconscious, Collected Works*, vol. IX: 1, pp. 3–41.

54 See Jung, e.g., 'A Study in the Process of Individuation' (1950), in *The Archetypes and the Collective Unconscious, Collected Works*, vol. IX: 1, p. 328n.; 'Transformation Symbolism in the Mass' (1954), in *Psychology and Religion: West and East, Collected Works*, vol. XI, pp. 229–30.

55 I am thinking of, e.g., 'Sadak in Search of the Waters of Oblivion' (1812), 'The Destruction of Pompeii and Herculaneum' (1822) or 'Manfred on the Jungfrau' (1837).

56 In what follows, I have in mind analyses offered by James Hillman in, e.g., *The Dream and the Underworld* (New York: Harper and Row, 1979), pp. 50, 89, 182; *Re-Visioning Psychology* (New York: Harper and Row, 1975), pp. 109, 160, 163; and William G. Dory, 'Hermes' Heteronymous Appellations', in *Facing the Gods*, ed. Hillman (Dallas, Texas: Spring, 1980), pp. 115–33.

57 See Jung, *Symbols of Transformation* (1952), in *Collected Works*, vol. V, pp. 127–8, 258–9, 340; 'The Psychology of the Child Archetype' (1951), in *The Archetypes and the Collective Unconscious, Collected Works*, vol. IX: 1, pp. 158–60.

58 Knight, *The Landscape*, pp. 21–3.

59 Ernest Tuveson, *The Imagination as a Means of Grace* (Berkeley, Calif.: Gordon Press, 1960), p. 56.

60 Knight, *The Landscape*, p. 14.

61 Watson, *Picturesque Landscape*, p. 21.

62 Knight, *The Landscape*, p. 1.

63 See Klein, 'The Importance of Symbol-Formation in the Development of the Ego' (1930) and 'Love, Guilt and Reparation' (1937), in *Love, Guilt and Reparation, and Other Works 1921–1945*, ed. H. Segal (London: Virago, 1988), pp. 219–32, 306–43.

64 Gilpin, *Observations on the River Wye*, p. 47.

65 Gilpin, *Three Essays*, p. 7.

66 Thomas Newte, *A Tour in England and Scotland* (1791), quoted in James Holloway and Lindsay Errington, *The Discovery of Scotland* (Edinburgh: National Gallery of Scotland, 1978), p. 47.

67 Price, *Essays on the Picturesque*, vol. I, pp. 57–8.

CHAPTER 10

Agrarians against the Picturesque: ultra-radicalism and the revolutionary politics of land

David Worrall

Land is the basis of the Picturesque. It comprises the very features and structures of the Picturesque landscape: Picturesque buildings stand on it. The ownership of land in England was an issue vigorously contended by Spencean revolutionaries who were active in London and, in part, nationally from the early 1790s through to the translation of their ideas into the Chartist land programmes of the 1840s. According to the founder of the movement, Newcastle-born Thomas Spence, the land would be seized from landowners by the violence of a popular insurrection or *coup d'état* and then incorporated into national, parochially based, equally re-distributed ownership. Only in recent years have historians revealed the full extent of this political movement and its popularity among London and Irish ultra-radical activists.[1] This essay will show how a variety of texts represent the political contestation of land and will examine the role of the discourse of the Picturesque in this process. This matter is of some importance to the history of cultural reception and production. Jonathan Bate's *Romantic Ecology: Wordsworth and the Environmental Tradition*, a study of the role of Wordsworth's poetry in the assimilation of the concept of 'Nature', has sought to show that Wordsworth's championing of the idea of 'a sort of national property' led directly to Britain's two National Trusts and the National Parks schemes. Institutions such as these have had to act as a substitute for the natural right to land which was a right energetically pursued during the period assigned to literary Romanticism and the Picturesque movement. If 'all who walk in the National Parks are legatees of Wordsworth', it would be as well to realise that we have reached this position via a process which has dehistoricised the political debate over land ownership.[2] This debate is disclosed in the differences between the discourse of the Picturesque and the claims of contemporary ultra-radical politics.

The challenge to the Picturesque aesthetic is present in middle-class literary discourse. The political fragility of the aesthetic is evident in Jane Austen's *Northanger Abbey* (posthumously published in 1818). Near the top of Beechen Cliff, Henry Tilney gives 'a lecture on the picturesque' to such effect that Catherine Morland

> voluntarily rejected the whole of the city of Bath, as unworthy to make part of a landscape. Delighted with her progress, and fearful of wearying her with too much wisdom at once, Henry suffered the subject to decline, and by an easy transition from a piece of rocky fragment and the withered oak which he had placed near its summit, to oaks in general, to forests, the inclosure of them, waste lands, crown lands and government, he shortly found himself arrived at politics... (first edition, vol. I, pp. 263–4)

Henry Tilney's 'lecture on the picturesque' undergoes an entirely intelligible sequence of declension from 'the picturesque' to 'waste lands' and 'crown lands' until 'he shortly found himself arrived at politics'. The 'waste lands' signify the dilapidated redundancy of land-use which supplied the Picturesque with its aesthetic. 'Waste lands' and 'crown lands' were long-running unsolved problems, the signifiers of the under-cultivation of England to which William Cobbett referred in his 1816 *Letter to the Lord Mayor of London* saying that 'All is going to waste, and speedily converting itself to sterility. There is no species of wealth or power that does not spring from Agriculture: and if that decline, all must decline; if that perish all must perish.'[3] Waste lands, as Henry Tilney muses, might be fine for a 'lecture on the picturesque' but they were economically un-productive and consequently a contemporary political problem. 'Crown lands' were similarly out of production and similarly a focus of attention for those who contested the nature of the ownership of land. A Spencean revolutionary prospectus of September 1817, as reported by the spy John Shegog, stated that 'the Crown lands are to be considered as vested in the People', while a more genteel, post-Peterloo, correspondent to Home Secretary Lord Sidmouth asked 'whether there is any insurmountable obstacle to the cultivation of Crown Lands', arguing that such a move would 'encrease the Class of Husbandmen & yeomanry' and 'counterbalance' the effects of 'the Demagogue and Revolutionists' in 'crowded manufacturing districts'.[4] What Austen makes Henry Tilney consider is the political dimension of the Picturesque desire for unimproved, uncultivated, unproductive but highly fashionable landscape: food for the eye rather than for the body. It is no wonder that 'he shortly found himself arrived at politics' at the conclusion of his lecture on the Picturesque. Catherine Morland's subsequent premonition that '"something very shocking indeed, will soon come out of London"' characteristically figures contemporary fears of ultra-radical and agrarianist insurrections which made the full belly their objective.

Northanger Abbey – probably first written in 1803 – had been revised in the autumn of 1816, or very early in 1817, at almost exactly the time of the Spa Fields rising, which took place on Monday 2 December 1816.[5] Spa Fields was a concerted attempt by a Spencean revolutionary organisation to seize the metropolitan centres of power. Catherine's vision of 'a mob of three thousand men assembling in St George's Fields; the Bank attacked, the Tower threatened' had been mirrored in Spencean targets at the Spa Fields insurrection during which gunsmiths' shops were broken open (as advocated since October by Spencean handbills) and areas around the Tower were held for some hours. Nevertheless, Spa Fields was not a one-off event but part of the persistent presence of ultra-radical activity. Austen had completed most of *Northanger Abbey* in 1803, the year following the Spencean-sympathetic London *coup* plot of November 1802, led by Colonel E. M. Despard, which had similar targets and objectives.[6] In other words, 'Spence's Plan' and 'Spence's System', chalked up on walls for years in the locality, contained objectives as vividly political in 1816 as they had been in 1803.[7] Jane Austen's *Northanger Abbey* not only reveals a surprising awareness of ultra-radical agitation, but the novel remained as relevant and topical in 1816–17 as it had been in 1803 in its subtle commentary on the political implications of the Picturesque.

Henry Tilney's references to 'waste lands' and 'crown lands', as well as the Spa Fields rising itself, are reminders that the social and economic context of English literary Romanticism was starvation and famine. 1795–6, 1800 and the immediate post-war years were times of particularly bad harvests and/or food price rises: wartime England had its agricultural economy stretched to breaking point. The consumption of horse beans, horse flesh, turnips and nettles was an occasional feature of the emergency diet of wartime England. The less predictable effects of malnutrition in England varied from typhus in London to the delayed pick-up of a northern textile industry depressed by a second-hand market flooded with clothing and blankets as people pawned warmth for food.[8] The inefficient use of land and the consequent hoarding of scarce food for selling at high prices rankled with the lower classes. In *Northanger Abbey*, General Tilney's penchant for growing pineapples (vol. II, pp. 132–3) must be understood as the last word in socially insensitive husbandry for those deprived times. William Cobbett's comments in his *Letter to the Lord Mayor of London*, reflecting these concerns in the first post-war year of 1816, renewed protests about land 'waste' and agricultural 'sterility'. Much earnest advice about land efficiency had been offered by respectable writers following the bad harvest and food price exploitation of 1800. The millenarian economist George Edwards proposed 'a degree of compulsion', 'actually to press every where a sufficient quantity of the best arable lands' in the same manner, and with the same legality, as the press-gang, while the Whig–Foxite linen-draper Robert Waithman, also writing in 1800, advised 'the throwing...of the waste lands into cultivation'. According to Waithman's phrasing, 'waste' lands are the opposite of 'cultivated', but both descriptions of land types are significantly absent from the verbal and visual grammar of the Picturesque. The use of potentially productive land for Picturesque landscaped gardens or parks was particularly galling to the radicals, who advocated 'taxing parks and pleasure grounds' because 'for any advantage the public reap from them' they may 'be almost reckoned waste'.[9]

The Picturesque landscaped park came to be the target of a continued radical debate about land-use. In a speech made shortly after the disastrous harvest of 1795, London Corresponding Society member John Baxter condemned the same profligacy in land-use which caused Austen's Henry Tilney to falter: 'Do we not see splendid Houses rising in every part of the Town and Country, even elegant Dog-kennels[?]... Is not our Arable Land converted into Pasturage for...Horses for pleasure[?]'[10] A generation later, and several years after the end of the war, the complaint was essentially the same because the social and economic distress caused by the use of land for aesthetic rather than productive purposes continued to cause similar problems. In 1819, 'T.J.F.' the unidentifiable contributor to Thomas Davison's pro-Spencean journal *Medusa, or Penny Politician*, wrote of the rich who 'must have their fine parks and pleasure grounds while the poor, but for being deprived of that land, would be enabled to live in bodily comfort'. Under the unlikely guise of an article entitled 'The Necessity of Remodelling the Church', T.J.F. concluded: 'Let, then, every true-hearted reformer use his utmost endeavours for obtaining a radical, political and agrarian reform.'[11]

Northanger Abbey reflects anxieties about the irresponsible and inefficient use of land whose nationally incorporated ownership the Spenceans had made their objective. It is the persistence and textual ubiquity of the ultra-radical politics of land which I now wish to outline because it is against this political opposition that the Picturesque is defined in its historical moment. The appropriation of literary texts to bolster a radical case inimical to the concerns of the texts' authors had been a feature of Spencean radicalism since Thomas Spence's journal *Pigs' Meat* (1793–5). A striking example can be found in the Spencean appropriation of Robert Southey's *Wat Tyler. A Dramatic Poem.* The first speech at the Spa Fields meeting had reflected the concerns of the economically distressed when the speaker, James Watson Snr, declared to the crowd that 'we still have the Earth – which Nature designed for the support of mankind[.] The Earth is capable of affording us all the means of allaying our wants and of averting starvation.' It is this attitude to the abundancy of the 'Earth', to English soil, which formed an axiomatic objection to the privatisation, misuse or disuse of the land as far as the Spenceans were concerned. An inscription on a flag carried onto the fields told the story more cryptically: 'Nature To Feed the Hungry'. Watson's son, James Watson Jnr, followed him and made the speech which seems to have precipitated the rising:

for be it recollected that Watt Tyler rose for the purpose of putting down an oppressive Tax and would have succeeded had he not been basely murdered by William Walworth then Lord Walworth then Lord Mayor of London but if he was surrounded by thousands of his fellow Countrymen as I now am no Lord Mayor that ever existed would have stopped his Career (Huzzas)

It seems to be the determined Resolution of Ministers to carry every thing their own way … they mean to carry the business in defiance of the voices of the people (groans) Now I will ask, if they will not give us what we want shall we not take it (yes! yes!) Are you willing to take it? (yes, yes! from all quarters) Will you go and take it? (yes, yes) If I jump among you will you follow me? (cries of yes and loud acclamations)[12]

Two months later, Sherwood, Neely and Jones pirated Robert Southey's *Wat Tyler*, which had been written in 1794 in the Jacobin youth of the now Poet Laureate. Following an injunction from the author to stop publication, Sherwood, Neely and Jones thought it prudent (even though Southey had lost his case) to withdraw their edition: whereupon the radical publisher William Hone immediately reprinted it. Hone was deeply involved with the Spenceans in 1816/17: after the subsequent acquittal of Watson Snr on the charge of high treason at Spa Fields, at a meeting to discuss a Spence anniversary celebratory dinner he was 'heard to say "it was a Pity no bold fellow could be found to murder Lord Ellenborough"', the presiding judge at the treason trial.[13] Hone recognised that the 'radical pastoralism' of *Wat Tyler* both reflected and illuminated post-war Spencean attitudes.[14]

This example demonstrates the existence of a radically different concept of 'Nature' to the one which the canonical Romantic poets were helping to define and establish. 'Nature gives enough / For all', Southey had written in *Wat Tyler*:

> Abundant is the earth – the Sire of all
> Saw and pronounc'd that it was very good,
> Look round...
> There is enough for all...

Southey's revolutionary philosophy of class antagonism was articulated by his Wat Tyler in the simplest of terms, terms which make redundant the wasteful Picturesque ethic of land use: 'your hard toil / Manures their fertile fields.../ They riot on the produce!'[15] The social and economic meaning of the word 'Nature' as something 'To Feed the Hungry', was being lost to those empowering the word with a transcendentalist metaphysic. What the Spenceans found in *Wat Tyler* was an older 'Nature' of Southey's radical youth, one close to their own concept of nature as a prolific provider. 'Bears not the earth / Food in abundance?' asked Southey's John Bull. Twenty-five years later 'A Spencean Philanthropist' poet in the *Medusa* showed similar indignation 'While bounteous nature yields such store, / That man should know distress'.[16] Robert Southey's *Wat Tyler* could be made to speak the contemporary history of the Spa Fields rising and to concur implicitly with Spencean land objectives.

The radical press was quick to spot the affinities between young Southey and late Spenceanism. Quoting Southey's condemnation of those who 'riot on the produce' of the nation's 'fertile fields', T. J. Wooler's journal *The Black Dwarf* commented that these were 'Almost the very words of Watson in the Waggon [at Spa Fields]; and certainly the very idea better spoken.' 'Why is not Mr Southey

arrested, and sent to the tower [?]' *The Black Dwarf* remonstrated
sardonically, 'For ought we know the whole plot of the late riots, was
gathered from Mr Southey's poem.'[17] In another indication of the
ability of the radicals to bring about an embarrassing conjunction of
texts and authors, a few days earlier a spy had found a Spencean
gathering at the Mulberry Tree, Moorfields, reading aloud 'Part of
the Poem of Watt Tyler' alongside 'Tom Payne'.[18]

If the political fight for the productive meaning and semantic
control of 'Nature' was slowly slipping away from the radicals, the
strength of the artisan roots of the Spencean ideology was not in
doubt. Thomas Evans, a leading Spencean (though by then in the
process of renouncing physical force), was visited three weeks after
Spa Fields by the spy George Ruthven. Ruthven bought one of
Evans's own pro-Spencean books from him and asked about the
'riot' (as Ruthven termed it). Evans, he reported, 'expressed a
perfect Confidence that the Spencean System would sooner or later
prevail'.[19] Two months later, in February 1817, an informer
poignantly reported that at a well-attended meeting at the Nag's
Head, Carnaby Market, 'Evans stated &c that the Land was the
Peoples right &c [and] asked every Individual present if they agreed,
and each answered Yes upon their Honour.'[20] The ultra-radical
politics of land ownership had survived the débâcle of Spa Fields
intact, still with the capacity to function in ideological opposition to
the Picturesque.

In the long term, as in the short, the Spenceans proved to be
unsuccessful in their objectives. One of their most momentous defeats
was the loss of their fight for the ownership of the concept of 'Nature'.
For the Spenceans, 'Nature' was quite simply the provider of
'natural' abundance, an energy of the land which was free to be
tapped as a 'natural' right with no one having exclusive ownership
of either the land or the produce. With the loss of the Spencean
purchase on 'Nature's' meaning, 'Nature' could become an ideality,
a function of the aesthetic (as in the case of the Picturesque) which
could be tweaked, teased or neglected into shape. This loss coincided
with the marginalisation of the Spencean ideology in historical
narratives of English culture. Spencean politics in late 1816 and early
1817 were thoroughly mapped onto the English landscape and
political agenda: it is only now in the late twentieth century that
Western politics has, in its Green movements, sought to revive the
social and economic importance of 'Nature'. Wordsworth's reception

within the literary and cultural institution has played its own small part in the effacement of the Spencean alternative. It is significant that Wordsworth has become the national poet of uncultivated, pastoral, upland landscape, while other writers (like John Clare and the obscurer poets E. J. Blandford and Allen Davenport) who spoke for the English cultivated, tilled, lowland landscape have been neglected. Wordsworth's 'nature' was one manifestation of a steadily industrialising hegemonic 'culture' which had less and less to do with 'cultivation'. Bate's recent *Romantic Ecology* de-historicises Wordsworth's position. To argue that 'What is done to the land is as important as who owns it' is to neglect a visible and highly active political debate amongst Wordsworth's contemporaries.[21] The semi-literate black Spencean Robert Wedderburn, writing (or dictating) a contribution for Robert Shorter's journal the *Theological Comet, or Freethinking Englishman* in 1819 put the issue very simply: the 'wooden-headed gentry' needed to 'know that the produce of the land belongs to those who cultivate it'.[22] The gains made by transcendental concepts of 'Nature', to the loss of their materialist alternatives, are what I now want to outline in noticing how Wordsworth's ideas about land were developed with an awareness of the politics of the Spencean manifesto.

Wordsworth's cultural reception as the national poet of 'Nature' has ensured that Spencean ideas have long been neglected. Wordsworth (an exact contemporary of the Spencean debates) knew of their politics and developed his own land theory to avoid and counter them. In the same year (1801) that Thomas Spence was imprisoned for his seditious tract, *The Restorer of Society to its Natural State* (advocating enforced confiscation of land), Wordsworth had written to Charles James Fox about landowning Lake District small farmers, locally known as 'statesmen'. 'Their little tract of land', Wordsworth observed, 'serves as a kind of permanent rallying point for their domestic feelings, as a tablet upon which they are written.' In Wordsworth's formulation, land preserved as private property is the site of a personal domestic text which can be conveniently read and inspected by interested politicians. The land of the 'statesmen' can remain as private as their domestic and political affections and yet still be capable of interpretation by those who make it their business to read this 'tablet upon which [their interests] are written'. Private land can function, as it always has done, as a 'permanent rallying point' for those who have private interests vested in it. As a sure site of the self, in Wordsworth's politics the land escapes the promiscuous equalisation of the Spencean alternative, where land would be economically incorporated as the equal natural right of all.[23]

By the time of the 'alarmist' days of 1817, when Spencean organisation was mentioned in no less than three parliamentary *Committee of Secrecy* reports (*Report of the Committee of Secrecy, 19 February 1817*; *Second Report of the Committee of Secrecy, 20 June 1817*; *Report of the Secret Committee of the House of Lords, 23 June 1817*), Wordsworth's notion of land had become an extremely tortuous and illogical development of 'natural rights' theory, which attempted to make obsolete the right-to-land being promoted by the Spenceans. The Spencean ideology, as far as Wordsworth was concerned, contained a capital threat to the political and economic stability of property: 'Land[,] hitherto deemed the most stable species of property, will become the most insecure and treacherous', he wrote to Daniel Stuart, and his answer was to reform the Poor Rates. Wordsworth's ideas about Poor Rates make strange reading when compared to the ultra-radical Spencean plan. In the same letter to Daniel Stuart he did something which he does repeatedly in his poetry: he reified the experience of poverty by conferring on the landless poor the 'actual possession' of the '*real* estate of the Country'. According to Wordsworth, the poor really did own 'in actual possession' a significant percentage of the '*real* estate of the Country', because they were supported by that part of the population which owned land and paid the Poor Rates. Wordsworth claimed that 'this *absurd theory* [the Spencean system] does at present regulate the *practice* of the country' because the provisions of the Poor Rates acted as an equivalent for the 'actual possession' of the land. For Wordsworth, '*real* estate' was a metaphysical notion.[24] To put it more starkly, Wordsworth had a working knowledge of the Spencean alternatives and rejected them in favour of his notions about the metaphysics of land.

That Wordsworth should have thought it necessary to formulate and respond to the Spencean ideology is testimony to the purchase it had on contemporary political discourse. The anxieties of literary writers were, to be sure, well founded. The appropriation of *Wat Tyler* is a good example of the sort of illuminating embarrassment made possible by ultra-radicalism's efficient fugitive press, but within Picturesque discourse there were other resistive moves. A study of the landscape gardener Humphry Repton shows how the Picturesque relied upon aesthetic and political contradictions which Spenceanism contended.

For Humphry Repton, the appropriation of land by virtue of its ownership could function both as an improvement and as a denial of the Picturesque landscape. In the first part of his 'before' and 'after' *View from My Own Cottage* at Hare Street, near Romford, Essex, an elderly, one-eyed, one-armed, one-legged man stares unembarrassedly into Repton's estate (figure 10.1a).[25] This picture is of an amputee sailor, for Repton's *Fragments on the Theory and Practice of Landscape Gardening* was engraved in 1816, the first post-war year and the year of Spa Fields. The patch of common land behind him is 'covered with' droves of geese, indicating a useful function of land, but one essentially inimical to the Picturesque. To shut them (and the sailor) out from his view is the way to impose the Picturesque aesthetic onto the economy of the village. For his own backyard, so to speak, Repton uses the theory of the 'appropriation' of scenery that he had long been recommending to others interested in procuring Picturesque effects. How could Repton enjoy the view from his cottage when it 'looks as if it belonged to another'? When the view is not exclusive, it 'robs the mind of the pleasure derived from appropriation': 'A view into a square, or into the parks, may be cheerful and beautiful, but it wants appropriation; it wants that charm which only belongs to ownership, the exclusive right of enjoyment, with the power of refusing that others shall share our pleasure.' According to Repton, the 'unity and continuity' of 'unmixed property' is spoiled by the promiscuous gaze of the poor.[26] In other words, the private ownership of land was one of the prerequisites for the maintenance of the Picturesque. Repton, when it came to his own modest piece of property, did not shrink from taking over the common land (figure 10.1b). As he puts it, he 'Obtained leave to remove the paling twenty yards farther from the windows; and by the *Appropriation* of twenty-five yards of Garden, I have obtained a frame to my Landscape'.[27] To take a wider perspective, Repton was asserting the social and economic hegemony of the Picturesque aesthetic over Spencean ideology.

Repton's more serious problem was that he inhabited in his own historical moment the contradictions of the Picturesque. He could not see that the 'appropriation' of land was a political issue. The Picturesque demanded private ownership, or exclusive aesthetic appropriation, at a time when ownership was being contested: 'the

Fig. 10.1a   Humphry Repton, *View from my own Cottage, in Essex* [*Before*]. From *Fragments on the Theory and Practice of Landscape Gardening*.

most picturesque situation, and the most delightful assemblage of Nature's choicest materials, will not long engage our interest, without some appropriation; something we can call our own.'[28] Towards the end of his working life Repton's aesthetics of 'appropriation' experienced an economic contradiction which he was forced to negotiate.

Repton looked with growing personal discomfort at the new rich ('whose habits have been connected with trade') and their decreasingly paternalistic ways, but he was not in a position to be able to ignore their economic pre-eminence. *Fragments* exposes Repton in an unresolvable dilemma. On the one hand the exclusivity of his Picturesque aesthetic demands 'appropriation; something we can call our own', the 'exclusive right of enjoyment, with the power of refusing that others shall share our pleasure'. On the other hand, and in contradiction of his own private practice, Repton deplored the growing tendency of the new generation of landowners to shift

Fig. 10.1b   Humphry Repton, *View from my own Cottage, in Essex* [*After*]. From *Fragments on the Theory and Practice of Landscape Gardening*.

boundaries and encroach onto common land. A double plate in *Fragments* shows 'before' and 'after' views of a country road (figure 10.2). One illustration shows the Picturesque ideal of a simple road skirting an old and unfenced wood. The other shows the same scene but one now showing the economic effects those 'whose habits have been connected with trade' were having on Picturesque old England: 'the trees are gone, the pale is set at the very verge of the statute width of road, the common is enclosed'. Despite his own practices at his Hare Street home, described elsewhere in *Fragments*, Repton in this instance condemned the appropriation of the common land by *nouveaux riches* seeking to maximise and secure their estates. Repton claimed that he was appropriating common land in the interests of good taste while the typical new landed proprietor appropriated it for profit and boasted 'not that it produces corn for man, or grass for cattle, but that it produces him rent: thus money supersedes every other consideration'.[29] Although such contradictions between aes-

252 DAVID WORRALL

IMPROVEMENTS

Fig. 10.2   Humphry Repton, *Improvements*. From *Fragments on the Theory and Practice of Landscape Gardening*.

thetic and economic priorities are never allowed articulation in the *Fragments*, physical exclusion from the right to the land, whether by the tastefully Picturesque Repton or the new, grasping landowners, continued to irritate those of the Spencean persuasion.

In the revolutionary and aggressive post-war world, Repton deplored another aspect of the insistence of landowners on the privacy of their property. Now, the inviting 'ladder-stile was changed to a caution against man-traps and spring guns' to the exclusion of the seeker of the Picturesque.[30] While Repton regretted that the Picturesque wanderer or view-finder was dangerously hampered by these devices, the attempt to exclude access to the land continued to rankle with ultra-radical activists even when the revolutionary phase of their activism had developed into its Owenite, Co-operative and early Chartist manifestations. The shoemaker and author Allen Davenport, one of the most consistent promoters of Spencean and Co-operative ideas, appended to his 1845 autobiography a previously unpublished short story called 'The Spring Gun'. This tale is one of the subtlest indications of the persistence of an ultra-radical opposition to the physical curtailment of access to the land which the Spenceans claimed for the people. 'The Spring Gun' is interesting because, stylistically, it seeks to imitate and emulate the discourse of sensibility. Significantly, the tale is set soon after the Battle of Waterloo, during the economically distressed post-war years. In Davenport's short story, the heroine's lover has been 'accidentally killed by a spring gun' and she has been reduced by grief to a 'harmless maniac' frequenting a lonely shrubbery bower. It is to this spot, reached by a Picturesque 'sort of zigzag rout, discussing each point of improvement' and 'enchanted...by the beauties of the scenery', that the soon-to-be-enraptured 'Captain B.' is taken by his friend 'Mr Escourt'. If 'The Spring Gun's' sentimental writing makes any sense at all it is as a subtly grim condemnation of the new automatic weapons installed on estates to deter and injure trespassers, whether they were poachers or simply Picturesque-bibers taking some similar 'zigzag rout'. Although the story may have been written at any time up to 1845, Davenport's very violent speeches at Hopkins Street in 1819 make it likely that the point of his story is to give a salutary lesson in the consequences of the exclusive ownership of land: landowners would be included amongst those who must suffer.[31] Davenport's story is a politically quietistic piece, in contrast to the author's Regency activism, but 'The Spring Gun', if written in the 1830s or 40s, helps document the persistence of these agrarianist antagonisms.

If paling fences could be advanced across the land to both exclude and permit the Picturesque, according to whichever landowner's taste Repton was discussing, those same perimeter fences were also at that time becoming politicised and no longer merely the private 'frame to my Landscape' intended by Repton.[32] The Cato Street armourer, bill-sticker, hairdresser, musician and poet Edward James Blandford promoted the Spencean ideology in a series of poems published in the *Medusa* in 1819. In an April issue, Blandford published a poem called 'A REAL DREAM, Or, Another Hint for Mr Bull!' in which he described a visionary journey to 'richly verdant fields' where 'rustic swains and sylvan nymphs' live in 'sweet contentment' 'by the prospect cheer'd' and where 'Fruits and grain' grow 'abundant' in the 'fertile soil'. In short, in this Spencean state of 'Nature', land and 'equal toil' result in a plentiful 'produce shar'd', with no private ownership of land. The cultivation, seizure and equal division of land amounts to a Spencean counter-Picturesque, another ideology of land use which, in Blandford's 'A REAL DREAM', is visualised as being implemented by the revolutionary seizure of the great estates.

Returning from his visionary journey, Blandford comes back to the England of his own time where he finds 'an idle few are fed': 'insulted nature seemed amaz'd, / That proud profusion round these miscreants blaz'd.' Blandford's answer is another vision and one which requires us to make a historical leap back to the practicalities of arming an English revolution in 1819. In Blandford's poem the railings which surround the estates of the rich spring from their sockets and take their Spencean revenge:

> Could these dumb guards, while they these dens surround,
> Be moved to action, and to sense of sound,
> Could these dumb ranks of iron-railing speak,
> They'd from their stations start, – their yokes they'd break...
> The tongueless IRON then in accent steady,
> Replied "when wanted you shall find us ready!"[33]

Blandford's metaphor hides an instruction for arming: the use of iron-railings as pikes to bring down cavalry was known from the French Revolution. Pikes were the preferred weapon of contemporary revolutionaries: they were cheap, easily hidden (sometimes in privies) and had proved highly effective against the English army during the 1798 Irish rebellion.[34] Railings as pikes were also mentioned in the raucous Hopkins Street debating club, where the orator Robert Wedderburn told his audience one October night that 'if we can't all get Arms, theres them Iron Railing in front of these Big fellows Houses these will supply some with Arms'.[35] At the urging of Wedderburn and his like, a popular rising would ensure the breaching of the paling fence which demarcated the Picturesque 'frame' of the private domain.

In 1819 Picturesque and all private or Crown estates were under threat from the circulation of the Spencean ideology. Spencean ideas were well suited to simple didacticism. As a *Medusa* poem by an anonymous 'Spencean Philanthropist' put it:

> A country's land's the people's farm,
> And all that it affords;
> For why? divide it how you will,
> 'Tis all the people's still;
> The people's county, parish, town;
> They build, defend, and till.[36]

This easily understood philosophy was gaining some measure of nation-wide circulation and sympathy. An anxious clergyman in Paisley, Scotland, told the Home Office in October 1819 that:

An agrarian law is openly talked over among vast numbers of People... virulent hatred and contempt of all the higher ranks of Society, and even of the middling ranks, appear universally to prevail... Every pretence is laid hold of for large publick meetings...a marriage, a funeral; a fair...may be made equally a pretence to assemble; and then discuss the affairs of the Nation and revile the Government – Even women, forgetting the honourable station which the British constitution has placed them in, are forward in all these meetings.[37]

Throughout 1819 a core of Spencean activists in London, deeply infiltrated by spies, were plotting a *coup d'état* which was to result in the open trap of the Cato Street conspiracy.

The Cato Street group, which included Blandford (who had, to the alarm of his colleagues, been arrested in possession of a pike head in August 1819), operated in conjunction with an ultra-radical debating club at Hopkins Street, Carnaby Market in the present-day Soho. The club's premises in a ruinous loft were operated by Robert Wedderburn as a kind of ideological forum for disseminating and discussing revolutionary politics. Its surveillance by the Home Office was such that it is possible to have a good snap-shot of radical activity there. Blandford was not the only one to be thinking of taking over the great estates that year.

On 3 November 1819 at Hopkins Street a man called Perry, described by the spy as 'an Old Man of reduced Appearance', 'abused the Whigs without Mercy, and cautioned the Radicals against ever putting themselves under any Landed proprieter, they being all natural enemies of freedom and of "The People"'.[38] Perry's views are significant in another way because, in late 1819, there was enormous distrust in ultra-radical circles of landed people (like Hunt or Cartwright) who were seeking to nominate themselves as leaders of the artisan class. Eight days after Perry's speech, the Catholic priest and pamphleteer J. Chetwode Eustace (who seems to have organised his own surveillance of Hopkins Street) wrote to the Home Office with the information that there was a secret committee of ultra-radicals 'engaged in ascertaining the extent of the different Estates in every part of the United Kingdom'.[39] Eustace's covert soundings seem to corroborate the existence of this quickening desire to seize the land.

In October Robert Wedderburn 'spoke at great length, that there was no Constitution or Liberty in England since William the Conqueror – The day is now drawing near when the landholders must give up to us.'[40] In November an unidentified speaker at Hopkins Street claimed that 'the land ... had Got into too few peoples hands and that was the present complaint of the day'.[41] On Perry's night at Hopkins Street, Wedderburn finished his speech with the vigorous proclamation that 'Nothing can be done to interrupt the radicals, for the Land is the Strength of the Country and they will shortly possess themselves of that.'[42]

As it turned out, after the débâcle of Cato Street and the subsequent prosperity of the 1820s, the Spenceans never did possess the land. It remained a desire, an elusive projection of their needs, but their symbolic culture and discursive systems, their ways of thinking about an agrarian 'cultivated' society, lived on into the 1830s and 1840s in the Chartist Land Plan promoted by Feargus O'Connor and Bronterre O'Brien. Chartist agrarian propagandists could re-use *Spence's Songs* from the Napoleonic War period simply by substituting the word 'Chartist' for the word 'Spencean', but it was the earlier manifestation of radical agrarianism which was more directly revolutionary in its desire to implement a specific ideology through the popular overthrow of the state by physical force.[43] The Spencean ideology is a counter-culture firmly based upon the political and economic importance of land, the material which provided the basis of the symbolic practice of the Picturesque aesthetic. Riven by contradictions disclosed in its own texts and the subject of concerned social comment, the Picturesque faced its most direct and politicised threat from what may be called the Spencean counter-Picturesque: an ideology which contested the economic and political basis of the Picturesque claim to allow aesthetics to dictate the use of English land.

NOTES

1 See Iain McCalman, *Radical Underworld: Prophets, Revolutionaries and Pornographers in London, 1795–1840* (Cambridge University Press, 1988); Malcolm Chase, '*The People's Farm': English Radical Agrarianism, 1775–1840* (Oxford: Clarendon Press, 1988). The complexities of Chartism's ideological relationship with Picturesque and other land-scapes are discussed by Anne Janowitz in her essay in this volume, 'The Chartist Picturesque'.

2 Jonathan Bate, *Romantic Ecology: Wordsworth and the Environmental Tradition* (London: Routledge, 1991), pp. 47, 49.

3 William Cobbett, *William Cobbett's Letter to the Lord Mayor of London*, 7 December 1816. In 1816 Cobbett tried to assist copyhold tenants in his home parish to 'enclose small parcels of Waste-land' to support their families (see Ian Dyck, *William Cobbett and Rural Popular Culture* (Cambridge University Press, 1992), p. 110).

4 John Shegog, 26 September 1817, Home Office, Public Records Office, Kew (hereafter H.O.), 40/7 (1), 29; John Benton Higgon, 28 August 1819, H.O. 42/193, 62.

5 John Felperin, *The Life of Jane Austen* (Brighton: Harvester, 1984), p. 102, has briefly noted that Spa Fields may have been incorporated into the revisions of *Northanger Abbey*. By May 1817, Jane Austen was writing to Fanny Knight that 'Miss Catherine is put upon the Shelve for the present'; see R. W. Chapman (ed.), *Jane Austen's Letters To Her Sister Cassandra and Others* (1932), second edition (Oxford University Press, 1979), p. 141.

6 For an account of Spa Fields, but interpreted as a 'riot', see E. P. Thompson, *The Making of the English Working Class* (1963; Harmonds-worth: Penguin, 1980), pp. 691–6. See the enclosure, 'Britons to Arms!', 30 October 1816, H.O. 40/3 (3), 24. For the Tower as a target see *Trial of Watson* (London, 1817), vol. II, pp. 113–14; for the Bank as a target see T. Storer, 27 November 1816, H.O. 40/3 (4), 919. For Despard's

abortive *coup* and its Spencean associations, see David Worrall, *Radical Culture: Discourse, Resistance and Surveillance, 1790–1820* (Hemel Hempstead: Harvester–Wheatsheaf, 1992).

7 For Spencean wall-chalking see A. Kidder, *c.* December 1813, H.O. 42/136, 691.

8 See Roger Wells, *Wretched Faces: Famine in Wartime England, 1793–1801* (Gloucester: Alan Sutton, 1988), especially pp. 50–70.

9 George Edwards, *Effectual Means of Providing, According to the Exigencies of Evil Against the Distress Apprehended from the Scarcity and High Prices of Different Articles of Food* (London, 1800), pp. 22–3; Robert Waithman, *War Proved to be the Real Cause of the Present Scarcity ... with the Only Radical Remedies* (fourth edition (London, 1801)), pp. 58, 65. For Waithman's career see J. R. Dinwiddy, 'The "Patriotic Linen Draper"': Robert Waithman and the revival of radicalism in the City of London, 1795–1818', *Bulletin of the Institute of Historical Research*, 44 (1973), 72–94. Six years earlier, the activist translator of d'Holbach, William Hodgson (then in prison for sedition), had claimed that waste lands were 'a reproach to any government' when he asked that 'no land whatever shall be sufered to remain uncultivated, either for parks, pleasure grounds, common or otherwise' (*The Commonwealth of Reason* (London, 1795), pp. 81–2).

10 John Baxter, *Resistance to Oppression: The Constitutional Rights of Britons Asserted in a Lecture delivered Before Section Two of the Society of the Friends of Liberty* (London, 1795), p. 7.

11 T.J.F., 'The Necessity of Remodelling the Church', *Medusa*, 21 August 1819, pp. 211–14. David Cannadine has noted that Malthusian economics specifically encouraged 'conspicuous consumption' by the ruling classes ('In short, Malthus wanted the landowner to *spend*') in order to mop up, by the provision of luxury goods and services, the excess labour market produced by the procreativity of the lower classes. See 'Conspicuous Consumption by the Landed Classes, 1790–1830', in Michael Turner (ed.), *Malthus and His Time* (London: Macmillan, 1986), pp. 96–111, 103.

12 2 December 1816, H.O. 40/3(3), 895.

13 'B', i.e. Shegog, 30 June 1817, H.O. 40/7 (1), 2, 3. Hone knew Spence well enough for Francis Place, compiling notes for an unwritten biography of Spence, to correspond with him thirteen years later about Spence's life; see William Hone to Francis Place, 23 September 1830, British Museum Add. MS. 27808.

14 'Radical pastoralism' is a useful coinage I owe to Marilyn Butler.

15 Robert Southey, *Wat Tyler, A Dramatic Poem* (London, 1817), pp. 12, 19, 23.

16 *Ibid.*, p. 46; 'The Wrongs of Man, Or, Things as they Are', *Medusa*, 6 March 1819.

17 *The Black Dwarf*, 26 March 1817, pp. 140–1.

18 23 March 1817, H.O. 42/162, 280.

19 (G.R., 22 December 1816, H.O. 40/3 (4), 15.

20 Clarke, *c.* February 1817, H.O. 40/3 (4), 925.

21 Bate, *Romantic Ecology*, p. 46 and *passim*. Even E. P. Thompson's *The Making of the English Working Class* (London, 1963, revised 1980) now needs a new emphasis, one directed away from artisan industrial organisation and towards the rural labour and Spencean polemics which Thompson's book had been so remarkably prescient in recognising and introducing.

22 'R.W.', *Theological Comet, or Freethinking Englishman*, 6 November 1819, p. 124.

23 Ernest de Selincourt (ed.), *The Early Letters of William and Dorothy Wordsworth, 1787–1805* (Oxford, 1935), pp. 261–2. 'Wordsworth and the Real Estate' is the subject of a chapter of that title in Roger Sales, *English Literature in History: 1780–1830, Pastoral and Politics* (London: Hutchinson, 1983).

24 William Wordsworth to Daniel Stuart, 22 June 1817, in Ernest de Selincourt, *The Letters of William Wordsworth and Dorothy Wordsworth: The Middle Years, 1812–21* (Oxford: Clarendon Press, 1970), p. 379.

25 For Repton, see G. Carter, P. Goode, K. Laurie, *Humphry Repton: Landscape Gardener, 1752–1818* (Norwich: Sainsbury Centre for the Visual Arts, 1982).

26 Humphry Repton, *Fragments on the Theory and Practice of Landscape Gardening Including some Remarks on Grecian and Gothic Architecture* (London, 1816), pp. 233–5; and see *Sketches and Hints on Landscape Gardening*, reprinted in J. A. Loudon, *The Landscape Gardening and Landscape Architecture of the Late Humphry Repton Esq., Being his Entire Works on These Subjects* (London, 1840), p. 114.

27 Repton, *Fragments*, p. 235.

28 *Ibid.*, p. 235.

29 *Ibid.*, p. 192.

30 *Ibid.*, p. 193.

31 Allen Davenport, *The Life, and Literary Pursuits of Allen Davenport* (London, 1845), pp. 78–88. For Davenport's Hopkins Street speeches, see 18 October 1819, H.O. 42/ 197, 36; 27 October 1819, H.O. 42/197, 773, and see my discussion of Davenport's oratory and writing in Worrall, *Radical Culture*.

32 Repton, *Fragments*, p. 235.

33 *Medusa*, 17 April 1819.

34 For the use of pikes during the 1798 Irish rebellion, see Thomas Pakenham, *The Year of Liberty: The Story of the Great Irish Rebellion of 1798* (London: Hodder and Stoughton, 1969).

35 18 October 1819, H.O. 42/197, 36.

36 *Medusa*, 13 March 1819.

37 Rev. Monteath, 20 October 1819, H.O. 42/197, 216.

38 3 November 1819, H.O. 42/198, 428.

39 11 November 1819, H.O. 42/198, 202.

40 10 October 1819, H.O. 42/197, 394.

41 15 November 1819, H.O. 42/198, 77.

42 3 November 1819, H.O. 42/198, 428.

43 For Spencean symbolic culture see Worrall, *Radical Culture*. For Spencean aspects of Chartism, see Chase, ' *The People's Farm* ', chapters 6 and 7.

CHAPTER 11

The Chartist Picturesque

Anne Janowitz

This essay approaches an aesthetic topic from a practical perspective: that is, it addresses the relationship between the Picturesque and the political project of Chartism. Because the uprising at Newport in 1839 was one of the most important events within Chartist history, I draw here upon some Welsh materials to focus my larger argument. I locate in the Picturesque setting of Wales both the departure point and terminus of a discussion of the communitarian aesthetic associated with the poetry written between 1839 and 1850 by political activists and orators of the first self-organised working-class movement in Britain.

My aim has been to draw out some connections between the *latent* politics of the Picturesque and the *explicit* politics of Chartism and introduce some poems written in response to the failed Chartist insurrection at Newport in November 1839. At that time, Newport was a site at which aesthetically pleasing Picturesque ruins coexisted with the industrially productive port, receiving millions of tons of iron and coal from the industry of the South Wales coalfield each year. In marking the links between the Picturesque and the Chartist project, I address, as well, the relationship between Chartist poetry and Romanticism, a relation mediated through the poetic figuring of the *landscape*, itself often the representation of the concept of the *nation*. In the poems which address themselves to the actions and consequences of the Newport Uprising, the conflation of nation and landscape is particularly strong, as the alien shadow of the Australian landscape – where Chartists were transported to penal servitude – is cast along the contours of a more homely terrain.

This perhaps surprising category of the 'Chartist Picturesque' belongs as well to a larger argument I am at present developing about the role of poetry in British social and political movements. That larger argument traces the relations between Romanticism and

Socialism in poetry, from a common ground in Romanticism's commitment to both individualist and communitarian values. But though such an argument may appear rather far afield from issues of landscape, attention to the landscape aesthetic within the Chartist poetic may interest scholars of the Picturesque, since it engages the abundant work done over the last ten years on the politics of the Picturesque.

There has been an extensive critical discussion of the representational aims embedded within a hegemonic Picturesque ideology. In *Landscape and Ideology*, Ann Bermingham has taught us a vast amount about Picturesque painting with respect to the naturalisation of enclosure and in *The Dark Side of the Landscape*, John Barrell specified the politics within the georgic intentionality of landscape painting. In what is perhaps the most polemical presentation of the politics of the Picturesque, Marjorie Levinson demystified the poetic landscape of 'Tintern Abbey', opening up to analytical view Wordsworth's massive ideological evasion, in which, she argues, he erases the local culture of poverty for the sake of a culture of meditative poetry.[1]

All these discussions, however, even when they attend to the *representation* of the poor and the displaced, themselves focus on the building of a ruling-class aesthetic. It is useful then to see how a politically and culturally counter-hegemonic group, the Chartists, engaged with, and so put up for interrogation the seemingly fixed symbols and practices of the landscape aesthetic that had been so ideologically successful for hegemonic culture. Rather than generating a romanticised industrial landscape of works and pits, something industrial workers and political reformers would be quite unlikely to do, the Chartist Picturesque inhabits and then transforms a conventional poetic landscape, the specificity and *peculiarity* of the Chartist poetic being its yoking of explicitly political claims and aims to a landscape poetic that had, by the end of the 1830s, come to be habitually identified with concepts of aesthetic autonomy and a poetic of private meditation.

In her discussion of the fortunes of landscape painting in the Victorian period, Ann Bermingham points out that its ideological effectivity for the ruling class was diminished in proportion to the decline of country political power.[2] But as what Raymond Williams would call a *residual structure* available to a counter-hegemonic group, the Picturesque, generalised as a category of nativist landscape, was

quite pointedly appropriated as a tool of poetico-political intervention.[3]

My central contention in this essay, then, is that the Chartist poetic
landscape was created, after the *hegemonic* fashion for the Picturesque
had declined, as an invented nostalgia for a landscape which had
actually only been contradictorily available to those people identifying themselves as Chartists. The example of the poetry written by
and about exiled Welsh Chartists is a good place to make this point,
for their fabricated nostalgia was for a landscape to which, in fact,
they had a relationship of bondage, as colliers and hitchers and
hauliers. This relationship was a particularly complex one, moreover,
because of the juxtaposed and not always congruent claims of the
local Welsh component of Chartist self-definition and the larger
national movement for radical social and political change. From
exile in Tasmania, the Chartist figuring of exile picturesquely
metaphorises the defeat of the Uprising at Newport and, more
generally, defeat within a class struggle over cultural appropriation
of the meanings of the landscape. Success might have resolved the
problem of English domination within Britain by a Republicanism
with which not only Welsh, but Irish Chartists as well, could identify.

At the centre of the Picturesque landscape produced in poetry by
and about Welsh Chartists was an imaginary reconciliation of two
congruent, geographically juxtaposed but exclusive cultural systems
in Wales: the Picturesque tour, whose views presented to a distanced,
sensitive observer the benign integration of ruins and natural
formations, and the coal–iron industry, which produced the ma-
lignant assimilation of human forms into the tomb of the earth.

Malcolm Andrews's investigation of *The Search for the Picturesque* in
Britain between 1760 and 1800 demonstrates clearly how the
landscape aesthetic developed in the period just prior to Romanticism.[4] For the study of Romanticism, one thinks of Gilpin's trips
down the Wye and the Usk, trips which significantly pre-date the
rapid expansion of the coal–iron industry and the transformation of
the tiny villages of South Wales into the populous world of mining
culture, but whose stance *vis-à-vis* the landscape remains codified in
guide books throughout the nineteenth and twentieth centuries.
Gilpin describes 'hills, diversified with woods, and lawns... We could
distinguish little cottages, and farms, faintly traced along their
shadowy sides; which, at such a distance, rather varied, and enriched
the scene than impressed it with any regular and unpleasing shapes.'[5]

By the time of the 1841 *Commission Report on Employment in Mines* in the Western valleys, picturesque areas coexist with those filled with the misery of mining families, 'No regular water supply is obtainable. These supplies [are] always badly fouled with the drainage of the iron-works, collieries, and the use of drier banks as the only public lavatories.'[6]

Between the time of Gilpin's travels and of the Commission report, the massive transformation of the coalfield had been undertaken. In 1788, only 15 iron furnaces were working on the coalfield, while by 1839, there were 122. In fifty years, the production of iron increased by a factor of 36. In the counties most closely connected with both Gilpin and the Newport Uprising, Glamorgan and Monmouth, a primarily agricultural peasantry had turned over 61 per cent of its population to industrial jobs by 1841.[7]

Nonetheless, the landscape remained checkered with benign country vistas adjacent to areas of industrial devastation. And the relationship between the Wales of the Picturesque and that of the iron–coal industry was not only that of geographical juxtaposition; it was as well that of juxtaposition of the hierarchies of British class-society. The popularity of the Picturesque viewing of the landscape persists in Wales throughout the period of industrialisation, and South Wales remains a site of journeys and tours. A task of bourgeois Picturesque representation was to render fairly new political and industrial power as if it were permanent. That impulse, fragmented and diffused into a popular form, operates within texts like Thomas Roscoe's myopic 1839 *Wanderings and Excursions in South Wales*, which presents a Vale of Neath apparently untouched by industry, and 'possessing many subjects of great picturesque beauty'.[8] Not that the Picturesque tourist always refuses to concede the existence of the competing Welsh landscape. In 1830, Henry Gastineau traverses the Vale of Neath and notes that 'the country eastward, between Morris town and Neath, is miserably disfigured by the operation of the works'. But such a concession often belongs to the *appropriative* regard of the industrial Picturesque, within which, as Gastineau goes on, 'the coalery, at some distance on the river, is well worth visiting on account of [its] canal'.[9]

We can look, however, to a Chartist poet of the coal–iron industry to remind us that Picturesque Wales bore a more troubled relation to the coal–iron industry. Robert Lowery, a Chartist activist and orator, was originally associated with the Owenite movement, but then moved towards the physical force Chartists, and became a spokesperson for armed insurrection in 1839. His poem, 'The Collier Boy', published in *The Charter* in June 1839, turns on the contrast between 'yon child, with cheeks so pale', and 'the meads and woods and gurgling streams – /Soft cooling baths, in sunny hours/ Whose banks are blooming with gay flowers'. Lowery explicitly depicts the strata of earth hierarchically. The surface of the earth is bright and glorious, where 'each young heart hies/ To chase the gaudy butterflies...' while 'Entomb'd in earth, far, far away...Hard toil and danger doth employ/ For the dreary mine, the Collier Boy'. Two versions of the Welsh landscape, habitually exclusive because one belongs to the discourse of the aesthetic and the other to the discourse of social conditions (that is, the discourse of the Picturesque tour and the discourse of the Commission on Mines) are presented in Lowery's poem in a relationship of domination. One strain, then, within the Chartist landscape aesthetic is a demystificatory one, juxtaposing the aesthetic and the economic in a stark and highly contrastive manner, and might be recognised as a precursor in critical practice to *our* contemporary critical demystifying of the Picturesque.

Lowery's recourse to the landscape, moreover, is not an isolated instance within the relatively unstudied poetic practice and poetic theory of the orator–leaders and the anonymous labourer–poets of the Chartist movement, though if we were to rely on the literary evidence we have of the Chartist movement from the representation of Chartists painted by Carlyle, Mrs Gaskell or Disraeli, in the period after the defeat of the movement, we would think that Chartists were unkempt ignorant animals. One recalls Carlyle's description of Chartists as 'wild inarticulate souls' whose voices are in 'inarticulate uproar'. The persistent nineteenth-century literary depiction of Chartism as a movement of the sub-literate, almost sub-human, is, however, a good index of the anxiety provoked in the British middle class by the nation's first fully national and culturally autonomous working-class political and social movement for parliamentary reform and social transformation.

And this middle-class version of the Chartists as brutes is a particularly telling misrepresentation of the movement, since Chartism placed literature and literary practice near the heart of its political agenda. When we look at the actual literary culture that was produced within the Chartist movement as a whole, we are offered a surprising glimpse into a culture which asserted the importance of literature, and poetry in particular, to political intervention and to the making of a collective identity based on the universalising of the working class as the nation.

The poetry column in the central Chartist newspaper, Feargus O'Connor's *The Northern Star*, offers an immense array of poetic forms. Published from the late 1830s until 1850, the paper ran a weekly poetry column throughout its life. In 1839 the weekly circulation ran as high as 36,000 copies paid per week, and given an illiteracy rate of about one-third of the working class, the estimate is that each copy served between fifty and eighty readers/listeners in radical coffee houses, working-class taverns and reading rooms and working peoples' clubs.[10] In Wales in the 1830s over 400 working men's clubs and friendly societies were founded among the mining families, while beerhouses, according to one historian of the Newport Uprising, were visited by 'men, women and children ... at all hours of the day and night' for social events and meetings in addition to drink.[11]

Although many of the collier families were Welsh-speaking, the blend of artisans and miners within the Chartist movement suggests an increased growth of English as the language of the movement. Certainly, the poets who chose to commemorate the Newport Uprising did so with a view to the entire movement's use of the event and wrote their poems in English to be read by Chartists throughout Britain. Yet it was the peculiar cultural relation of Wales to England that made Chartism in Wales particularly revolutionary. As the Chartist leader Henry Vincent noted in his journal, 'Wales would make an excellent Republic'. And Ivor Wilks makes a strong case that because levels of alienation from state power were higher in Wales than in England, it was in Wales that an insurrection might best be launched.[12]

The sorts of poetic texts in the *Northern Star*'s columns that might have been read aloud range from lyrics based on popular ballad measure ('The Slave's Address to British Females', 'The Factory Girl's Last Hour') to great stretches of dramatic iambic pentameter ('Prologue to a new Drama, spoken by a Druid, on John Frost and the Insurrection at Newport'), as well as poems which belong to a more meditative mode ('A Fragment for the Labourer', 'Sonnets Devoted to Chartism' and many others).

Given how easily we accept the marginality of poetry to our

contemporary Anglo-American political world, what is striking and exciting about Chartist culture is not only the huge number of poems printed in Chartist publications, but also the importance assigned to poetry as an instrument of social change. Throughout Britain, Chartist political leaders used poems as political interventions, not just to represent political situations. Leaders incorporated poems into public addresses, rank-and-file Chartists used poems as a medium of correspondence in the columns of the *Northern Star* and some poets even produced texts with collective authors, such as a 'Song for the People' by 'Two Ultra-Radical Ladies'.[13]

Of interest to the study of Romanticism is the fact that activist Chartist poets and political theorists were particularly interested in, even preoccupied with, their inheritance from Romantic poetry. Romanticists working recently on poetic representation have engaged in the enunciation, description and critique of what we broadly call 'aesthetic ideology'. We have recently begun to understand more about the historical mechanisms of the ideology of aesthetic autonomy. Within the history of poetic structure, the lyric mode, and its shift into the central position in poetic hierarchy, has been variously linked to the explicit separating out of poetical and political intentions at the end of the eighteenth and the beginning of the nineteenth centuries. This separation has been characterised as the cultural vehicle of the Romantic ideology. Yet if this aesthetic ideology, the 'Tintern Abbey' ideology let us call it (to note its relationship with Picturesque ideology), marks a moment when politics and poetry appear to be separating out their explicit spheres of influence, Chartist poetry refuses such a separation and asserts itself *as* action. So, an anonymous poem tells us that 'The Voice of the People' 'rushes on, like the torrent's loud roar;/ And it bears on its surges the wrongs of the poor. / It's shock, like the earthquake shall fill with dismay, / The hearts of the tyrants and sweep them away.'[14]

Chartist poetics, then, makes an interventionist as well as a representational claim for the power of poetry. In the Glasgow *Chartist Circular*, a critic argues, 'Poetry is a lever of commanding influence... It penetrates to every nerve and fibre of society, stirring into irresistibility its innermost current, and spiriting into life and activity the obscurest dweller of the valley.'[15]

In refusing the separation between the aesthetic and the political, however, Chartist poetry does not abandon the Romantic poetry of meditation, even when it eschews the notion of a solitary consciousness. In fact, Chartist poetry exhibits a double commitment both to lyric forms and to political intervention, offering a utopian counter-statement to the notion of lyric as the terrain of landscaped solitude and secular transcendence through the extension of the unencumbered self, whose conventional representations are modelled on the Romantic poets.

The obviously Romantic cast to much Chartist poetry reminds us, however, that quite as much as an official Romanticism was incorporated into English nationalist and Imperialist culture, so did Chartist poets and poetry theorists theorise an *un*official Romanticism to ground a counter-culture that was not yet a marginal culture.[16] Against the example of Palgrave's 1861 anthology, *The Golden Treasury*, which was designed to export poetic superiority conveniently 'wherever the dominant language of the world is spoken' and which labels its most recent age, 'The Age of Wordsworth', we can set that of the Chartist John Watkins, author of two poems commemorating the Newport Uprising, who writes a sonnet exhorting, 'Chartists! What strive ye for? For liberty!/ 'Twas liberty inspir'd the British Bard/ Who surnam'd our Britannia – "The Free!"/ Byron, chiefest of poets! yes, 'Twas he.'[17]

The Romantic character of this quotation may begin to suggest the ways in which an attention to Chartist literature may in turn inflect a reading of more familiar Romantic texts and unsettle an Althusserian-based idea of a seamless Romantic ideology, for the subject of the relationship between Romanticism and Chartism intersects with the subject of middle-class and Chartist conceptions of literary culture right at the spot where British Romanticism is itself self-divided. That is, Romantic poetry offers at times a poetic of transcendence, lyric solitude and private meditation – performing the ideology of aesthetic autonomy; while, at other times, Romantic texts polemically invite political activism and poetic militancy.

Some Romantic poems stumble back into the Picturesque landscape from the urban and industrial fray, and from the increasingly hectic pressure of other consciousness. These poems, like 'Tintern Abbey', provide aesthetic spas, locations to cultivate an individual private poetic of transcendence. Others, however, (one need think only of 'The Mask of Anarchy' or *Jerusalem*) call on individuals to bind themselves into active communities and to take up collective, or communitarian, resistance, not only to 'mind-forged manacles', but also to the state and its military excrescences.

There is a double-intention then, within Romantic poetics, which can be discriminated as its individualist and its communitarian perspectives on identity formation. That is, one can conceptually link the poetry of solitude and meditation to individualism, that liberal conception of the individual as an 'unencumbered' self formed before, and voluntarily engaging in social groups. And one can link the poetry of intervention and political activism with communitarianism, which describes identity as built through and in relation to social goals and aims.[18] The shaping of twentieth-century literary criticism has, however, certainly declared the individualist emphasis within Romanticism to be the winner, which is why our classroom syllabi for nineteenth- and twentieth-century literature courses most often cherish meditative over interventionist poems.

What is of interest then within Chartist poetry (and in relation to the more familiar texts of Romantic poetry) is that kind of lyric which can be characterised by its presentation of a voice that is neither marginally solitary (as in Modernist avant-garde forms of oppositional art), nor representatively solitary (the Wordsworthian model). Rather, this voice is intended to embody a manifold rather than a singular poetic voice. As Samuel Laycock, a late Victorian Socialist poet analogised, perhaps sentimentally, in a poem part of and adverting to the collective work of a Northern poets' club, 'The pipes of an organ all vary in tone; / Their sound must be several, their music is one.'[19]

My own sense (after the sometimes numbing experience of reading hundreds of Chartist poems in *The Northern Star*), is that Chartist poetry at times foregrounds individualist and at times communitarian poetic ends, but that by the end of the 1840s, individualism came to dominate the Chartist aesthetic. That domination accompanied the demise of Chartism as a whole as a political force: individualist ideology finally transformed the collective and visionary notion of a revolutionary people's culture into the ameliorist models of reformism and labourism. At the same time, and this is one example of how Chartist literature carries residual cultural meanings from *before* the emergence of a homogeneous working class, visionary communitarianism, with its imagined community of working-class national identity, often drew upon anachronistic utopian models, those visions of community that had been central to radicalism in the seventeenth century and which persisted in circles of artisans. We hear this, of course, also in the peculiar lexicon of Blake's poetry. Chartism's own mix of artisans and industrial workers (and in Wales the shifting of farmworkers into coal–iron workers), who then engaged with textile outworkers and refugees from middle-class radicalism, together formed the uneven ground on which images of community were built which referred back to agrarian utopias (the Chartist land-scheme being one disastrous example) and forward to a revolutionary working-class movement. Part of this mix of residual cultural materials was the poetic elaboration of the landscape as the site of personal meditation, which became for Chartist poets the site of a potentially transformed collective identity.

The rhetorical vehicle for the Chartist poetic intervention was built through the notion of a repressed 'people's' national literary heritage, which Chartist poets and poetic theorists both *excavated* and *invented*. And with this concept of tradition we can return to the question of Chartist poetry as a poetic that interestingly engages with the Romantic Picturesque landscape.

For Chartist poetry is centrally a contestation of the received shape of literary tradition, within the larger context of the class struggle over the questions 'Whose nation? What people?', in which the issue of the nation was often congruent with, because figured as, the landscape itself. That class struggle over the proprietorship of the nation was clear to William Benbow, who first called for a general strike as soon as the betrayal of the 1832 Reform Bill had become apparent, and who speaks on behalf of the working class: the middle class and aristocracy are, he writes, 'the *jugglers* of society, the *pick-pockets* of society, the *plunderers*, the pitiless *Burkers*'. The working classes, on the other hand, 'do everything and enjoy nothing. The people are nothing for themselves and everything for the few. When they will fight for *themselves* then they will be the people.'[20] On the other hand, Henry Brougham, Whig Reformer and founder of the Society for the Diffusion of Useful Knowledge is equally confident: 'By the people, I mean the middle-classes, the wealth and intelligence of the country, the glory of the British name.'[21] In other words, in the period of the late 1830s and early 1840s, the definition and the geography of the nation were up for grabs, just as the two classes making their competitive claims for that 'imagined community' were in the process of defining themselves, of dialectically discovering and developing their class consciousness. In *Literature and Revolution* Trotsky argues that there can be no proletarian culture within bourgeois society.[22] But in an important sense, there was *not* in the late 1830s a confident national bourgeois culture in the manner that there would be by the middle of the century, and Chartist poetry quite interestingly exhibits the strains of a struggle to define itself literarily in a context in which the working class also was just coming into being as a coherent force. Chartist poetry and literary culture took on the task of wresting away the middle class's own *new* claim to universality and to nationality, by providing its own alternate, though equally mythic genealogy. And although some historians have argued that the Newport Uprising was an event of specifically Welsh nationalist provenance, the rhetorical claims of its myth-construction were more general ones, in the sense that it identified the cause as that belonging to all working people and their families across Britain. A newspaper commentator in the aftermath of the Uprising specifies the class competitive content of the idea of the nation when he writes in November 1839, 'the [untaught Welshmen of the Iron Works] began to think that they alone constituted the "Nation", and as such, conceived their recourse to arms as fully justified'.[23]

For the Chartist movement, then, the building of the working-class movement and the naming of a national culture were identified. Importantly, popular sovereignty would define the nation and the nation would be born, not from Painite and rationalist first principles, but out of and in relation to an inherited tradition, a tradition linked to the land. The nationalism of Chartism awkwardly but affectively intertwined the nationalism that we associate with the French revolutionary–democratic movement, which invented the nation-state in its modern form, and the earlier radical patriotism of community.[24] And this intertwining of older with contemporary ideas of the nation is itself linked both to the importance of the landscape as the site of community and to the jostling of human elements within Chartism itself: a movement made up of artisans, with their local traditions and customary practices, radical reformers, and new industrial workers, naming themselves as something new – the working class – but just as eager to give themselves a historical ground. So, Chartist poets and literary theorists tried to define working-class identity by yoking it to a national poetic tradition in which, they asserted, the history of the labouring poor had always been woven into poetic purpose. In aid of that intention, the *Chartist Circular* ran a year-long series of articles in 1839 on 'Politics of Poets'. Of course as Chartist poetry claims a past as well as a future, it finds that past only partially, fitfully, and with a necessary reliance upon the texts and poets from the culture from which it seeks to distinguish itself, insisting that Shakespeare, Milton and Burns were the ancestors of the contemporary Chartist poetic aesthetic. Claimed as closest forbears were the previous generation's apparent martyrs to liberty, Shelley and Byron. There is not space here to rehearse the complex sense of debt that Chartist poets felt to Byron and Shelley, but the following quotation from an article written on Wordsworth's death offers some sense of the stormy atmospherics surrounding the reputations of the Romantic poets as a group: 'In announcing his [Wordsworth's] death, we must acknowledge that we are not impressed with any heavy sense of sorrow, for we cannot include him in the list of those who, like Burns, Byron, and Shelley, have secured the lasting worship of the people by their immortal aspirations for, and soul-inspiring invocations to, Liberty. Unlike those Great Spirits, Wordsworth passes from amongst us unregretted by the great body of his country-men, who have no tears for a slave of Aristocracy and pensioned parasite of Monarchy.'[25] David Worrall's work on the importance of the Spenceans to the formulation of the Picturesque recovers another strand of inheritance within the genealogy of Chartist poets.[26]

Queen Mab and 'The Masque of Anarchy' were the Romantic poems most frequently reprinted and excerpted in Chartist poetry columns, where they appeared as well as Mary Shelley's note of 1819 that Shelley 'believed that a clash between the two classes of society was inevitable, and he eagerly ranked himself on the people's side'. But Shelley was also an important influence by way of his more meditative poetry. The point I want to stress here is that it was not simply the communitarian and interventionist side of Romanticism that influenced Chartist poetics. Most obviously much Chartist linking of intervention and poetry derives from and makes explicit Shelley's assertion in the Defence of Poetry that 'The most unfailing herald, companion and follower of the awakening of a great people to work a beneficial change in opinion or institution, is Poetry.' But Ernest Jones, Chartist poet and leader, wrote in an 1847 article that 'Shelley had the happy power of never swerving from a practical aim even in his most ideal productions.'[27]

Many Chartist poems do in practice attempt to link meditative idealism to the interventionist goals of the movement, but by transforming the individualist into a communitarian intention, within a poetic discourse that draws on the landscape poetic built in

the period of sensibility and Romanticism, rather than the more
public languages of antiquity, republicanism or satire. W. J. Linton,
for example, engages the sweep of the 'Ode to the West Wind' and
the atmospherics of 'Mont Blanc' to produce a sublime language of
the communitarian movement:

> Roll, roll, world-whelmingly!
> . . .
> It is accomplished!
> Melt us away!
> Gather ye silently!
> Even as the snow
> Buildeth the avalanche
> Gather ye, Now.[28]

Land, poetry and nationhood are continually identified in the
nineteenth-century arguments of class-consciousness. One might
recall once again here the imperialist mandate of Palgrave's *Golden
Treasury* and think also of Matthew Arnold's later assertion that the
glory of native nationhood was best measured by its poetry. Though
Arnold and Palgrave are in one sense collusive in the explicit
separation of politics and poetry, they are nonetheless eager to have
aesthetics serve politics. Chartist poetic theorists think quite differently: the glory of British poetry lies in the tradition of popular
sovereignty that, they argue, has always been its central purpose.
This assertion allows the Chartist poet to appropriate the landscape
of personal meditation for the uses of the class. Such a poetic
claim simultaneously reaches back before Romantic landscape
atemporality to the tradition of topographical poetry which used the
visible remains of history in the landscape as a set of general moral
markers, a tradition which had been virtually overgrown by the
detemporalising and individualising Picturesque sensibility of meditative poetry. This is a counter-hegemonic activity in that it rolls
back the bourgeois Picturesque dehistoricising of landscape, while
preserving the metaphorical power of such naturalisations. The
Chartist poetic landscape is revisioned from the perspective of the
working class imagined as 'the people': ''Tis the voice of the people
I hear it on high,/ It peals o'er the mountains – it soars to the
sky;/Through the wide fields of heather.'[29] The links amongst
pictured rurality, a people's tradition and a poetry associated with
that tradition, are articulated by a Chartist poet and orator, Gerald
Massey, in his 'Our Land', with its refrain, 'For our rare old land,

and our dear old land!/ With it's memories bright and brave!/
... Sing O! for the hour its sons shall band,/ – To free it of Despot and
Slave.' The forward movement of a democratic impulse is linked to
the antiquity of the soil, which is in turn linked to the poetry inspired
by that land, where 'Freedom's faith fierce splendours caught,/
From our grand old Milton's love'.[30] In the face of the economic
hardships accompanying industrialisation and the proletarianisation
of the peasantry, it was an easy poetic move to draw upon an
idealised picture of rurality to build up the utopian vision of a
possible future, and to modify that idealisation by repeopling the
landscape with a history of labour.

In some cases, Chartist poems invoke the landscape in order to
disengage it from the proprietorship of the ruling class: 'earth, its
mines, its thousand streams, the mountain-cleaning waterfall,/ –
God gave, not to a few, but all,/ As common property.' In others, the
land is figured more brutally as the battle-site of class struggle:
'There is blood on the earth, all wild and red/ It cries to our God
from the freeman's bed!/ It will not fade or be washed away.'[31]

There is, however, a self-defeating side to the retrospective
perspective. For in communitarianism lay a contradictory model:
the dream of a revolutionary working-class movement *and* the
obstruction built into its very antiquated character, since the
categories of the 'people's tradition' on the one hand, and the
working class under capitalism on the other, are not congruent. This
stubborn attachment to nativism acts as a political *encumbrance* in
what George Meredith captures ironically in 'The Old Chartist' in
the 1860s: 'Whate'er I be, Old England is my dam!... I'm for the
nation!/ That's why you see me by the wayside here,/Returning
home from transportation.'[32]

And certainly from the perspective of transportation the contours of
the landscape appeared mystifyingly attractive to the Chartist poetic.
I want to conclude by returning to the Newport Uprising, for John
Frost's exile to Tasmania, or as it was then called, Van Dieman's
Land, was a rich source for Chartist poetry after the collapse of the
insurrection of 4 November 1839.[33]

In the aftermath of the unsuccessful insurrectionary event, once
the Queen's Troops had occupied Newport and arrested the putative
leaders William Jones, Zephaniah Williams and John Frost, there
was a national campaign to save these men from being hanged and

quartered, the result of which was that they were shipped to the newly opened penal colony near Port Arthur, Tasmania.

A large number of John Frost transportation–exile poems appear in the British Chartist press, next to another popular topic of poems on the Uprising, the death of a child–martyr, George Shell. A series of meditative sonnets, 'Sonnets Devoted to Chartism', published throughout 1840 in the *Northern Star* by one of the Newport Chartists under the pseudonym of Iota, links the two heroes together in a sequence of landscape meditations, beginning, 'Once more I visit thee, sweet rural walk'.[34]

The anecdote of George Shell was widely disseminated. This young Chartist had written a poignant letter to his parents the night before the attack: 'Dear Parents, – I hope this will find you well, as I am myself at present. I shall this night be engaged in a struggle for freedom, and should it please God to spare my life, I shall see you soon; but if not, grieve not for me. I shall fall in a noble cause. My tools are at Mr Cecil's, and likewise my clothes. Yours truly, George Shell.'[35]

In Iota's sonnet beginning ''Tis long since last I came this pleasant way…' (Sonnet 1) Shell is given a elegiac context amidst a set of poems chiefly concerned with the landscape within which the Newport Uprising took place. Iota participates in the association of the continuity of land and poetic glory: 'Some future bard shall sing thy triumph, Shell… Thy patriot spirit hovering o'er the land/ That gave thee birth… shall have/ The joy, e'er long to see the glorious stand/ Which Walia – Scotia – England's slaves *can* make' (Sonnet 2). The sequence of eight poems as a whole belong to the landscape meditative mode, presenting that vague ahistorical antiquity that Picturesque landscape imparts to the rougher facts of historical ruin. The poet appears rather limited in utopian vision, however, for the future landscape which the sonnets imagine is not only derived primarily from memories of the past, but also maintains the past's inequities: 'Peace, and plenty and content in peasant's cot,/ And closely-huddled houses of the poor… Such and superior good the patriot contemplates' (Sonnet 8). Iota excuses the 'Patriot' Frost from insurrectionary intentions. The Patriot was searching for justice, in aid of that moment 'When men no more should be the slaves of gain,/ Nor infants die to fill the Moloch maw of despot lordlings…' No, Frost 'wandered o'er this pleasant way,/ With heart-felt ardor for his country's weal…' (Sonnet 3). 'His country' is the nation figured as a sweet rurality, and is meant to be sharply juxtaposed to the terrifying sublimity of the penal landscape in Australia where Frost serves his time even as Iota writes his sonnets.

John Watkins, a Chartist poet who wrote 'Lines on Shell', also wrote a play about Frost, extracts of which were published in 1841 in *The Northern Star*.[36] Watkins makes explicit the terror of transportation: 'Transport me! /I'd rather die – I'd far rather be hanged', Frost exclaims and then speaks a soliloquy filled with the agony of separation from that land which, however needful of change, remains the natural possibility for futurity. In this Chartist vision of Tasmania, art does not imitate a nature that itself benignly recalls a painting, but asserts instead the descent of the human into a terrifying and unfathomable nature, a sublime of terror: 'In such an irresponsive wilderness,' Watkins writes, 'Man is authoriz'd to torture man,/ And so exults in his most savage power...' Watkins implies that the British soil acts as a human brake upon cruelty because it is, in accordance with a Romantic conception of the dialectic of nature and mind, responsive, and hence, responsible.

To those in penal servitude in Australia and Tasmania, the picturing of British landscape was particularly sweet. In *The Fatal Shore*, Robert Hughes cites an early convict ballad of exile and rural loss: 'It's oft-time when I slumber I have a pleasant dream:/ With my pretty girl I've been roving down by a sparkling stream; / In England I've been roving, with her at my command,/ But I wake broken-hearted upon Van Dieman's land.'[37]

If the Chartist inheritance from Romanticism sometimes takes the form of the inspiration of Romantic communitarianism, for example, Blake's fantasy of the multiply personed Giant Man Albion, and at other times Chartist poetry takes the form of Romanticism's meditative individualism, it also at times interweaves the two. An anonymous poem on Frost's transportation very literally occupies one of Moore's *Irish Melodies*, changing only a few words of Moore's composition:

> He [Frost] recalls the scenes of his dear native land,
>   The hearts who to life had entwined him;
> And the tears fall uncheck'd by one friendly hand
>   For the joys he has left behind him.[38]

The revised version foregrounds the political content of the relationship between the exiled class leader and the beauties of his native land by linking Frost's individual sorrow to a collective potentiality of transformation: 'Nor soon shall the tears of his country be dried,/ Nor for long shall its efforts desist.' In Moore's version, we are given a solitary female mourner who will soon join her Irish patriot lover in death and her song will be lost in the grave.[39]

The history of the image of Britain as it was appropriated by convicts and settlers in Australia provides an interesting counterpoint to the domestic politics of the Picturesque, for the masking achieved via the ideology of the Picturesque was as effective in colonial as home terrain. The reality of Tasmania offered a landscape of agonising sublimity to the political convict which contrasted with a picturesque calmness of the dream of home; but for the military and the apparatus of the ruling class, the prison sublime was planted over with cuttings from the British Picturesque.

Bernard Smith's history of *European Vision and the South Pacific* provides a lot of primary material outlining the history of British responses to Australia and Tasmania. He traces an initial desire on the part of travellers to assimilate the exoticism of Australia to a native pattern which was then transformed into a shocking sense of the differences between Britain and Australia, and then later resolved into a more intentional strategy of using the Picturesque as a means of 'civilising' the culture and aesthetically shutting out the world of the penal colony.[40]

For example, a traveller in 1773 describes New South Wales as 'very pleasant and fertile... like plantations in a gentleman's park'.[41] As one historian suggests, it was the shaping categories of the Picturesque that in the first place rendered this new terrain *visible* to the British.[42] But a frightening sense of the cost of that visibility – its sham picturesqueness – is conveyed in the following letter home from a soldier at the end of the eighteenth century: 'The scene is beautifully heighten'd by a number of small islands on which may be seen charming seats, superb buildings, the grand ruins of stately artifices, etc., which at intervals are agreeably interrupted by the intervention of some proud eminence, or lost in the labyrinth of the inchanting glens that so abound in this fascinating scenery. 'Tis greatly to be wished these appearances were not so delusive as in reality they are.'[43]

A significant attempt was made in the first half of the nineteenth century to prune those delusive settings into more efficaciously Picturesque ones: George Thomas Blaney Boyes, a colonial auditor and artist in Tasmania, attempted to cultivate both local gardening and painting, hoping thereby to 'raise the standards of public taste' and stave off the encroaching barbarity from the influence of convicts on the children of settlers in Tasmania. One result of that attempt is captured in L. A. Meredith's memoir, *My Home in Tasmania*: 'The scenery around Newtown is the most beautiful I have seen on this side of the world – very much resembling that of the Cumberland Lakes: the broad and winding estuary of the Derwent flows between lofty and picturesque hills and mountains...But the most English, and therefore the most beautiful things I saw here, were the hawthorn hedges...It seemed like being on the right side of the earth again.'[44] For the military settler family, the Picturesque aesthetic was a mode of linkage back to Britain as well as a method of obscuring the presence of the penal world.

For the prisoners, on the other hand, the imagination of a Picturesque Britain was an appropriative reply to the terror of prison life. The sublime of servitude was foregrounded by John Frost himself when he returned to Britain in the 1850s. He lectured throughout the United States and Britain on the topic, 'The Horrors of Convict Life'. In the lectures he calls the Tasmanian experience 'the hardest kind of labour that any man could endure' in an alien environment, in mines which were the site of savage floggings and brutal male rapes.[45] What is striking in Frost's lectures is that he draws no parallel between servitude in Welsh mines and those of Tasmania. One senses that for the Chartist exile (and Frost remained a committed Chartist until his death), the affective power of a poetic Picturesque landscape had displaced the realities of the South Wales coalfield. And so too, had the autonomy of the Welsh experience been replaced by a more general, fabricated sense of a British homeland.

What I have been outlining here, from some varying points of view, is the contradictory appropriation of a rhetorical fashion by activist–poets within a counter-hegemonic group: the use of the landscape poetic was helpful to Chartist poets insofar as it, however marginally, linked the contemporary struggle to a communitarian past located in the countryside. It was helpful when it intersected with a vision of the future built on the premises of popular sovereignty, and when it was given poetic shape in images of the nation as belonging to a people defined as the universalising of the working-class. But the landscape poetic was a hindrance to the extent that it mystified the relationship between a rural past and a proletarianised present. And the irony of that rural myth becomes acutely palpable to us when we see it used to assuage homesickness amongst the transportees. The reality of the mines in Wales was not much less oppressive than that in Tasmania, though the nativist language offered a poetic terrain belonging not to the coalfield and the south, but a generalised British picturesqueness.

The repercussions of that nativist hindrance are historically marked, for Chartism as a movement was dead by the 1850s. From the ruling class came a thorough and successful campaign of ruining the autonomous institutions of working-class culture, and of extending the nation universalised as middle-class and imperialist. And from within the movement, the ideals of labourism came to replace those of Chartism. Labourism being, in the words of the historian John Saville, a 'theory and practice which recognized the possibilities of social change within existing society and which had no vision beyond existing society'.[46] Those possibilities, moreover, were firmly linked to the success of individualist ideology with its ethos of self-help, and its poetic of self-expression.

The vision within the communitarian impulse, however, and the idea of poetry as a social intervention imbued with a collective visionary purpose continues to inhabit less massive social movements and ought to have its history written. It finds its next significant chapters in the Socialist movement in the last decades of the nineteenth century and then in the 1930s in the British Communist movement. At present, in the United States, many multi-cultural and feminist and Marxist critics are being attacked by the Right, who accuse us of substituting a coercive criterion of 'political correctness' in the place of aesthetic value. I think that if we attend to and explore the counter-hegemonic life inscribed within the apparently coherent ideology of aesthetic autonomy, we may be able to recover those aesthetic categories so lately demystified, but then unfortunately abandoned as so much ideological detritus. We will be better able then to contribute to the making of a contemporary culture that is both interventionist and beautiful.

NOTES

1 See Ann Bermingham, *Landscape and Ideology: The English Rustic Tradition, 1740–1860* (Berkeley and Los Angeles: University of California Press, 1986); John Barrell, *The Dark Side of the Landscape: The Rural Poor*

in English Painting, 1730–1840 (Cambridge University Press, 1980); Marjorie Levinson, *Wordsworth's Great Period Poems* (Cambridge University Press, 1986).

2 Bermingham, *Landscape and Ideology*, p. 83.

3 Raymond Williams, *Marxism and Literature* (Oxford University Press, 1976), *passim*.

4 Malcolm Andrews, *The Search for the Picturesque: Landscape Aesthetics and Tourism in Britain, 1760–1800* (Aldershot: Scolar Press, 1989).

5 William Gilpin, *Observations on the River Wye* (1782; reprinted 1973, Richmond Publishing Company, Surrey), p. 50.

6 Cited in Ness Edwards, *John Frost and the Chartist Movement in Wales* (Abertillery, Mon.: Western Valleys Labour Classes, 1927), p. 5.

7 Ivor Wilks, *South Wales and the Rising of 1839* (London: Croom Helm, 1984), pp. 11–12.

8 Thomas Roscoe, *Wanderings and Excursions in South Wales; Including the Scenery of the River Wye* (London, 1836), p. 248.

9 Henry Gastineau, *South Wales Illustrated* (London, 1830), p. 28.

10 J. A. Epstein, 'Feargus O'Connor and *The Northern Star*', *International Review of Social History*, 21 (1976), 69–80, 97.

11 David J. V. Jones, *The Last Rising: The Newport Insurrection of 1839* (Oxford: Clarendon Press, 1985), pp. 30–1.

12 Wilks, *South Wales*, pp. 145, 236.

13 *The Northern Star*, 13 July 1839.

14 *The Northern Star*, 4 December 1841.

15 *The Chartist Circular*, 24 October 1840.

16 See 'Introduction', Y. V. Kovalev, *An Anthology of Chartist Writing* (Moscow: International Publishers, 1956).

17 John Watkins, *The Northern Star*, 29 April 1842.

18 My categories here derive from recent critiques of liberalism, in particular the argument developed by Alastair MacIntyre in *After Virtue* (London: Duckworth, 1981).

19 Samuel Laycock, *Collected Works* (Oldham, 1900), pp. 224–5.

20 William Benbow, *Grand National Holiday and Congress of the Productive Classes etc.* (London, 1832), p. 4.

21 See Eileen Yeo, 'Culture and Constraint in Working-Class Movements, 1830–1855', in *Popular Culture and Class Conflict 1590–1914*, ed. Eileen Yeo and Stephen Yeo (Sussex: Harvester Press, 1981), pp. 155–86.

22 Leon Trotsky, *Literature and Revolution* (Ann Arbor: University of Michigan Press, 1960), p. 186.

23 *The Silurian*, 16 November 1839. Quoted in Ivor Wilks, *South Wales and the Rising of 1839*, p. 231.

24 See E. J. Hobsbawm, *Nations and Nationalism Since 1790* (Cambridge University Press, 1990), for discussion of the meeting up of traditional and revolutionary democratic nationalisms; Ralphael Samuel (ed.), *Patriotism: The Making and Unmaking of British National Identity* (London:

Routledge, 1989), 3 vols., for the domestic tradition of patriotism; and especially Hugh Cunningham, 'The Language of Patriotism, 1750–1914', *History Workshop Journal*, 12 (1981), 8–33.

25 *The Democratic Review*, May 1850, p. 473.
26 See David Worrall's contribution to this volume.
27 Cited in Paul Foot, *Red Shelley* (London: Bookmarks, 1984), p. 241.
28 W. J. Linton, 'The Gathering of the People', *The English Republic*, 1851, pp. 136–7, cited in Brian Maidment, *The Poorhouse Fugitives: Self-taught Poets and Poetry in Victorian Britain* (Manchester: Carcanet Press, 1987), p. 40.
29 *The Northern Star*, 4 December 1841.
30 *The Friend of the People*, 21 December 1850.
31 'The Patriot's Grave', *The Northern Star*, 9 September 1843.
32 George Meredith, *The Poetical Works* (London: Constable, 1912), p. 117.
33 My main historical sources are: Ivor Wilks, *South Wales and the Rising of 1839*; David Williams, *John Frost: A Study in Chartism* (Cardiff: University of Wales, 1939); David J. V. Jones, *The Last Rising: The Newport Insurrection of 1839*.
34 Iota, 'Sonnets Devoted to Chartism', *The Northern Star*, 9 May, 27 June, 1 August, 15 August 1840.
35 *Welsh Labour History*, 1 (1970), p. 8.
36 *The Northern Star*, 30 November 1840; 2 January 1841.
37 Robert Hughes, *The Fatal Shore: A History of the Transportation of Convicts to Australia, 1787–1868* (London: Collins Harvill, 1987), p. 368.
38 J. H., 'Frost', *The Northern Star*, 2 May 1840.
39 Thomas Moore, *Irish Melodies* (London: Muse's Library, 1908), pp. 104–5.
40 Bernard Smith, *European Vision and the South Pacific, 1768–1850: A Study in the History of Art and Ideas* (Oxford: Clarendon Press, 1960), p. 135ff.
41 S. Parkinson, *Journal of a Voyage to the South Seas in His Majesty's Ship The Endeavour* (London, 1773), quoted in Smith, *European Vision and the South Pacific*, p. 133.
42 Paul Carter, *The Road to Botany Bay: An Essay in Spatial History* (London: Faber and Faber, 1987).
43 Quoted in Smith, *European Vision and the South Pacific*, p. 135.
44 L. A. Meredith, *My Home in Tasmania during a Residence of Nine Years* (London: 1852), quoted in Smith, *European Vision and the South Pacific*, p. 220.
45 John Frost, *The Horrors of Convict Life* (Hobart: Sullivan's Cove, 1857, reprinted 1973), p. 27.
46 John Saville, *The Labour Movement in Britain: A Commentary* (London: Faber and Faber, 1988), p. 14.

CHAPTER 12

The metropolitan Picturesque

Malcolm Andrews

I take it that it is part of the function of this volume to test the limits
of the conventional association of the Picturesque with landscape
aesthetics and the equally conventional view that the Picturesque is
a dead issue by the end of the Regency. That is what I aim to do in
this essay, by examining the idea of the Picturesque in a relatively
unfamiliar context, that of London in the nineteenth century. First, a
word or two about the tying of the term Picturesque to landscape
appreciation.

THE TERM 'PICTURESQUE'

William Gilpin had no particular wish to confine the term 'Picturesque' to a narrow range of rural subjects: 'I have always myself
used it merely to denote *such objects, as are proper subjects for painting*'.
According to his definition it followed that 'one of the cartoons [of
Raphael], and a flower piece are equally picturesque'.[1] In his usage
it was equivalent to the contemporary slang designation of paintable
subjects as 'pictorish', or 'pingible' (a term used by Richard Wilson).
But, as we know, the term was hijacked from its etymological
simplicity and broad applicability by, chiefly, the popularity of
Gilpin's scenic tours and the theoretical debates of the 1790s, and
became more exclusively reserved for discussions of landscape
aesthetics. It emerged in the nineteenth century as both a ridiculous
cliché and a concept of baffling complexity; and there it remains
today. 'Probably no word in the language (exclusive of theological
expressions) has been the subject of so frequent or so prolonged
dispute', wrote Ruskin in 1849. He continued:

yet none remain more vague in their acceptance, and it seems to me to be a
matter of no small interest to investigate the essence of that idea which all
feel, and ... with respect to different things, and yet which every attempt to
define has, as I believe, ended either in mere enumeration of the effects and

objects to which the term has been attached, or else in attempts at abstraction more palpably nugatory than any which have disgraced metaphysical investigation on other subjects.[2]

A salutary caution. I shall be returning a little later to Ruskin and his attempts to clarify or redefine the Picturesque. My point here is to signal an intention to retrieve it from its habitual application to the evaluation of landscape and rural life in the late eighteenth century and to work with it in the context of the Victorian city. There are three ways in which I propose to do this. The first is to consider the Picturesque as an architectural principle in the development of Victorian London. The second is to trace the rise of a kind of Picturesque tourism within the city itself and the translation into the metropolitan context of the aesthetics of poverty. The third is to indicate the way the Picturesque functions within a discourse of conservation as London develops. Finally the nature of the relationship between these three topics – the new architecture, urban tourism and the conservation movement – is suggested, but not developed in any extensive way.

THE ARCHITECTURE OF THE CITY

Eighteenth-century Picturesque was, in its formal manifestations, a reaction against both the transformation of the countryside during the agrarian and industrial revolutions, and the preference in architecture for symmetry, smoothness and regularity, the exercise of rational control in designing a domestic or urban environment. Dishevelled cottages, winding, rutted country lanes, the accidental, organic, heterogeneous structure of country villages are the vernacular antidotes to imported Palladianism in the Georgian villas and to the crescents, squares and terraces of Georgian towns, just as much as to the transformations of the countryside during the agrarian and industrial revolutions.

In the nineteenth century the Picturesque was invoked as a means of expressing similar anti-Georgian prejudices among those who were watching the rapid development of central London. Let me briefly trace this development, acknowledging a debt to Donald Olsen's excellent book *The Growth of Victorian London*. Near the beginning of Victoria's reign, the architect Sir John Soane deplored the 'disgusting insipidity and tiresome monotony' of Georgian estate planning in London. In 1868 the magazine *Builder* welcomed the transformation, by private wealth initiatives, of 'the dead walls and unmeaning windows of the Georgian style of street building, the poorest and least picturesque that was ever common in any civilised nation'.[3] Ten years later, the prolific travel-writer Augustus Hare, in his *Walks in London*, was pleased to note a change in the appearance of the streets:

Certainly street architecture appeared to be in a hopeless condition, featureless, colourless, almost formless, till a few years ago, but, since then, there has been an unexpected resurrection ... [the sooner architects recognise that] the greatest charm of a street is its irregularity the more beautiful and picturesque will our London become.[4]

Aggressive individualism, backed by private wealth, was giving a distinctive character to the redevelopment of nineteenth-century London. The city was celebrated for an idiosyncratic splendour wholly unlike contemporary Paris under Napoleon III's great rebuilding programme. The comparison between the two cities, often made in competitive terms, was taken up by the magazine *Building News* in 1889: 'the idea of Unity and State control permeated municipal architecture – a *régime* we find carried to an excess in Paris and many German cities. The assertion of the individual in the rebuilding of our streets is apparent to all who notice what has been done of late years.' As Donald Olsen has remarked, 'Economic individualism encouraged visual diversity.' In 1899, the president of the Society of Architects argued that, under this dispensation, the architect in London 'produces buildings which, from the broken appearance they give when grouped together, produce a pleasing and picturesque effect...far more...than a regular style could be'. A year earlier, the cultural anthropologist, Sir George Laurence Gomme had written: 'A ride on the top of an omnibus through any of the great routes...reveals, to those who have the feeling for the picturesque, beauties in London streets which are wholly local in character.'[5]

The Picturesque thus legitimates the architectural assertion of individualism – almost as a planning principle in central London. It is the opulent expression of *laissez-faire* policy, written into the public environment, and to be interpreted as a proclamation of the virtues of the British constitution. In this respect there is some politico-aesthetic continuity with Uvedale Price's ideological commitment to preserving in landscape design as much as in government, nature's untrammelled Picturesque inequalities:

A good landscape is that in which all the parts are free and unconstrained, but in which, though some are prominent and highly illuminated, and others in shade and retirement; some rough, and others more smooth and polished, yet they are all necessary to the beauty, energy, effect, and harmony of the whole. I do not see how a good government can be more exactly defined.[6]

The Picturesque love of the agency of accident, of letting nature take its course, translates comfortably into a political philosophy of *laissez-faire*. Victorian London, then, with all its brash, vivacious architectural idiosyncrasy, is the expression of the new age, emancipated from what it regarded as the drab uniformity and traditional hierarchical constraints of the previous age. In this respect, the Picturesque as presiding aesthetic is vigorously libertarian and progressivist. At the same time, this progressivist impulse is expressed in a bizarre range of pre-Georgian architectural styles. The new age had no architectural language of its own, except this revivalist eclecticism. As a commentator declared in 1885: 'Architecturally, London may be said to represent chaos itself...There is an incongruous diversity in the architectural fronts resulting from an anomalous collection of different styles.'[7] The new architecture was stylistically retrogressive in promoting its economically progressivist creed.

What most commentators seemed to mean when they invoked the Picturesque as an antidote to Georgianism was the breaking-up of uniform regular surfaces with lavish ornament and a more abruptly angular geometry of design. Sydney Smirke, the architect of the Carlton Club and the exhibition galleries at the Royal Academy, wrote in 1834:

We are, at present, a people deplorably devoid of a taste for the picturesque. Where except in this country, shall we find streets of interminable length, composed of houses without cornice, architrave, or any of the most simple features of architectural decoration?[8]

Variety of texture and colour was introduced along with a variety of building materials. Red brick, glazed brick, terracotta, carved stone, varied the facades of neo-Gothic, Flemish, neo-Italian Renaissance, neo-Elizabethan domestic, commercial and municipal buildings, side by side in the London streets.

Picturesque connotes, then, variety, idiosyncrasy and individuality, cornerstones of the new political and economic philosophy of the age – *laissez-faire*, self-help, entrepreneurial freedom.

THE AESTHETICS OF POVERTY

But the Picturesque sensibility was also traditionally attracted by scenes which were, on the face of it, quite antithetical to the flamboyant civic Picturesque of Victorian London. It was attracted by dilapidation and obsolescence in architecture and by the impoverished and marginalised in human beings. This notorious version of the Picturesque was referred to by Dickens after a visit to the Naples slums in 1845:

> The condition of the common people here is abject and shocking. I am afraid the conventional idea of the picturesque is associated with such misery and degradation that a new picturesque will have to be established as the world goes onward.[9]

As we have seen, there was indeed at this time a new Picturesque flourishing in the streets of central London: but it was not quite what Dickens had in mind. As if in answer to his call, a new, more ethically sensitive Picturesque was proposed eleven years later with the publication in 1856 of the fourth volume of Ruskin's *Modern Painters*; and I shall pick this up a little later. Just for now I wish to pursue the associations between Picturesque idiosyncrasy and poverty in the urban context. The civic Picturesque may be seen as a compensatory flourish, or 'displaced exhibitionism',[10] in the light not only of Georgian uniformity, but also of contemporary developments. The Victorian bourgeoisie was promoting architectural idiosyncrasy and individualism in a period when the powerful members of that class were themselves becoming more uniform, more submissive to the prevailing conventionalities of middle-class culture: sober, pious, industrious, earnest, as restrained in dress as in conduct. It was a culture concerned to define itself by the degree to which it could expel all traces of dandyism, just as, in its architecture, it repudiated the stucco facades of Nash's Regency terraces. Furthermore, the metropolis itself, according to some, was by now a formidable instrument for eroding or destroying the Picturesque in human beings. Tennyson in *In Memoriam* (Lyric 89) attributes such a view to Hallam:

> But if I praised the busy town,
>   He loved to rail against it still,
>   For 'ground in yonder social mill
> We rub each other's angles down,
>
> 'And merge' he said 'in form and gloss
>   The picturesque of man and man.'

Human idiosyncrasies, like nature's interesting deformities, can only mature when they have indulgent space and time. But the experience of the city is of constant social attrition. There is an interesting line of enquiry here, which unfortunately I do not have space to follow now. The main point I want to make is that natural Picturesque variety and individuality in the *social* rather than architectural context was thought to have survived only outside the culturally dominant middle classes, and particularly amongst the poorer classes, where there were apparently no such homogenising cultural constraints. A view of this kind was spelled out in an anonymous review of Dickens's *Hard Times* in 1854:

> In humble life, different occupations, different localities, produce marked and distinct hues of character: these differences are made more apparent by the absence of those equalizing influences which a long-continued and uniform education, and social intercourse subject to invariable rules of etiquette, produce upon the cultivated classes. Original and picturesque characters are therefore much more common among the poorer orders; their actions are simpler, proceeding from simpler motives, and they are principally to be studied from without.[11]

This associates the objects of Picturesque attention very clearly with the working classes. Indeed the colourful, vivacious, varied cockney street life of London constituted a tourist attraction itself. But the Picturesque attractions here were only for the short-sighted.

The metropolitan working classes were actually subject to other homogenising pressures: severe poverty being the most obvious. Furthermore, a destitute proletariat breeding rapidly in metropolitan slum areas presented an awesome social threat in a way wholly unlike the rural Picturesque prototypes, the idling peasant or small gypsy encampment. The latter figures were usually represented as isolated ornaments to a rural scene, perhaps adding to the Picturesque a slight frisson of the Sublime. But in the London Rookeries the street vagrants and communities of the poor become indistinguishable from the criminal underworld to which every citizen was immediately prey. These slums constituted a festering sore, the human casualties of Malthusian *laissez-faire* policies. In the open spaces of the countryside, the destitute and disaffected could be distanced in the spectator's view: they did not seriously disturb the security or the economy of the classes from which the Picturesque tourists generally came. Such detachment became harder to maintain in the metropolitan context. The Rookeries were the great incubators of moral, physical and political disease: crime, cholera and insurrection had their origins in such places, and in the crowded city no one, no matter what their social or economic level, could be sure of escaping contamination. This was a point repeatedly made by Dickens:

> That no one can estimate the amount of mischief which is grown in dirt; that no one can say, here it stops, or there it stops, either in its physical or its moral results, when both begin in the cradle and are not at rest in the obscene grave, is now as certain as it is that the air from Gin Lane will be carried, when the wind is Easterly, into May Fair, and that if you once have a vigorous pestilence raging furiously in Saint Giles's, no mortal list of Lady Patronesses can keep it out of Almack's.[12]

At the end of the eighteenth century, the Picturesque was founded largely on the aesthetics of poverty, neglect and decay. By the middle of the nineteenth century, in the great cities, such a taste was hard to indulge. Poverty now was on one's doorstep, not loitering at the boundary of one's country estate, or visible only on one's summer tour to the Highlands or North Wales. That is why Dickens argued for a new Picturesque, since the traditional Picturesque was associated with such misery and poverty:

> But, lovers and hunters of the picturesque, let us not keep too studiously out of view the miserable depravity, degradation, and wretchedness, with which this gay Neapolitan life is inseparably associated! It is not well to find Saint Giles's so repulsive, and the Porta Capuana so attractive... Painting and poetising for ever, if you will, the beauties of this most beautiful and lovely spot of earth, let us try to associate a new picturesque with some faint recognition of man's destiny and capabilities.[13]

In 1856 Ruskin offered the readers of *Modern Painters* a reconstructed Picturesque which incorporated an ethical response to scenes of poverty and decay, and which was to be distinguished from 'the low school of the surface-picturesque'. The lover of this lower Picturesque is the familiar, heartless, detached spectator:

> The shattered window, opening into black and ghastly rents of wall, the foul rag or straw wisp stopping them, the dangerous roof, decrepit floor and stair, ragged misery, or wasting age of the inhabitants, – all these conduce, each in due measure, to the fulness of his satisfaction. What is it to him that the old man has passed his seventy years in helpless darkness and untaught waste of soul? The old man has at last accomplished his destiny, and filled the corner of a sketch, where something of an unshapely nature was wanting.[14]

19 . The Picturesque of Windmills .

1 Pure Modern .   2.Turnerian .

Fig. 12.1   *The Picturesque of Windmills*. Illustration from Ruskin's *Modern Painters*, vol. IV (1856).

The lover and practitioner of Ruskin's higher Picturesque absorbs but transcends the surface Picturesque: s/he manifests a largeness of sympathy, a communion of heart with the subject in view. Ruskin offers the example of two windmill scenes in order to illustrate his distinctions between the two Picturesques (figure 12.1). Clarkson Stanfield's Mill (1, Pure Modern) is surface Picturesque. The artist has no interest in the functional value of the structure any more than he would in the human value of an old, decrepit labourer: his only interest is in its formal textural appearance. It is simply a rugged ornament in the landscape. Turner's Mill (2, Turnerian) is eloquent in all its details of long hardship endured. It is still a working mill and the artist has understood its functional mechanisms. It has a kind of heroic stoicism which the artist has absorbed and transmitted in his picture. I want to reserve for a later point the more specific application of Ruskin's higher Picturesque to the experience of London. Just for now I want to note Ruskin's response to what was by the mid-century an impatience, even revulsion, at the surface Picturesque's capacity to anaesthetise the social conscience at sights of poverty and decrepitude.

The metropolitan Picturesque had somehow to absorb, adapt or reconstruct the older relish for the antique, the ruined and the obsolescent, subjects which, in a rural context, seemed unaccountably glamourised by the depredations of time. And it had to do so in a way compatible with an awakened moral and social conscience, as one mid-century writer observed of a famous Rookery: 'The Minories may afford a study to the caricaturist, whilst the heart of the benevolent is smitten at the sight.'[15] Let me suggest two contexts in which some retuning of the Picturesque came about: the Picturesque tour of the metropolis and the conservation movement.

TOURISM AND CONSERVATION IN THE CITY

The Rookeries were in many respects the metropolitan counterpart to those rural casualties of the agrarian revolution: the impoverished migrant labourers, the old small-scale water-mills, clusters of ancient deserted cottages. Thomas Beames, the mid-century historian of the Rookeries, gives much the same account within the London context:

improvement has swept on with mighty strides; pity that there should remain the monuments of this olden time in the Rookeries of London, – that the close alley, the undrained court, the narrow window, the unpaved foot-path, the distant pump, the typhus or the Irish fever should still remind us of what London was once to all – what it still is to the poor.[16]

In a period of rapid change, as had been experienced over the architectural and industrial revolutions in the last decades of the eighteenth century, the remains of the obsolescent culture acquired an antique charm which grafted itself onto the new developing taste for the Picturesque. Thus Victorian London spawned dozens of books with titles such as *Picturesque Sketches of London, Pictorial Half-hours of London Topography, Scenes in Old London*. These constituted a particular genre of travel literature, somewhere between the reliable guide-book and the anecdotal exploration of the more obscure, old-fashioned street life of London. But in the 1850s several new circumstances compromised the pleasures of Picturesque tourism of London's older and shabbier corners. I will mention three. The Great Exhibition of 1851 promoted Britain as the world's most sophisticated and technologically advanced civilisation: a boast which was not easily compatible with publications drawing the attention of thousands of foreign tourists to the pockets of squalid poverty barely half a mile away from the Crystal Palace in Green Park. Secondly, in 1848 there had been an appalling epidemic of cholera, the worst of a number of outbreaks in the 1840s. It was public knowledge that this had originated in the slum areas of central London, and that public health was constantly at risk from the continued existence of such places. Thirdly, the Rookeries were potential breeding grounds for dissidence. With the examples of the 1848 European revolutions and the memory of the Chartist demonstrations in London fresh in the minds of the public, the threat posed by the Rookeries in the early 1850s was taken seriously:

Rookeries are among the seeds of revolutions;...taken in connection with other evils, they poison the minds of the working classes against the powers that be, and thus lead to convulsions, and seldom, we repeat it, are such evils found alone; the spirit of justice, which regarded the claims of labour in other respects, would scarce doom the working man to crowded dwellings and a forfeiture of the commonest blessings God has given to man: nor are recent events wanting in the same conclusions.[17]

One way in which the Picturesque tourism of London adapted itself to these changing attitudes, to a sharpening awareness of the need for reform, was for the guide-books to conduct the tourist into the Rookeries and offer lavish descriptions of their squalor accompanied with indignant gestures towards the system which allowed such conditions. This is the Picturesque masquerading as journalistic exposé, and thereby seeming to justify its inherent voyeurism.

There was, then, by the 1860s, pressure from several points on the old heartless surface Picturesque. It came from Ruskin's influential art criticism which was itself in the early 1850s becoming inseparable from his broader social critique, which made increasingly untenable that suspension of the moral sense so often involved in Picturesque appraisals. It came from caustic commentaries – such as those of Dickens – on the double standards of the English tourists. It came from the growing urgency of public debates about crime and sanitation in the metropolis, debates which issued in pressure-groups which in turn led to the constitution of various Boards and Associations to counter establishment *laissez-faire*. It came from the recognition, generally, that an unreconstructed Picturesque was incompatible with the prevailing cultural values of mid-Victorian England. As Thomas Hardy remarked in an essay later in the century, 'The Dorsetshire Labourer': 'It is only the old story that progress and picturesqueness do not harmonise.'[18]

I am not suggesting that the circumstances I have indicated put an end to the Picturesque tour of the metropolis, only that they complicated it. One of the richest examples of this tourist literature was Jerrold and Doré's *London: A Pilgrimage*, a text which still in 1872 addressed its task very much in the old surface-Picturesque idiom. As pilgrims 'in quest of the picturesque and the typical' they discovered a glut of material: 'The work-a-day life of the metropolis, that to the careless or inartistic eye is hard, angular, and ugly in its exterior aspects; offered us pictures at every street corner.'[19]

The Picturesque habit of mind was – and indeed still is – deeply ingrained as a response to the casualties of environmental and social change. By the 1870s it had become absorbed into a rather more socially sensitive discourse, that of the conservation movement. I want to examine one manifestation of this. In 1875 the Society for Photographing Relics of Old London was established. Between 1875 and 1886 the Society issued, annually, a series of photographic prints of pre-Georgian London buildings. What brought the Society into being was the wish to record, before its demolition, an old London coaching inn, the Oxford Arms. A later series was devoted to some of the old Southwark coaching inns. These were all rendered redundant by the railways, which, close to their own terminuses, built their own railway hotels. So the old cobbled courtyards, now sprouting tufts of undisturbed grass, and the tiers of galleries now undulating with age and decay, were picturesquely eloquent of an age gone by. The letterpress to the White Hart Inn prints (numbers 51 and 52) included the following: 'It is only fair to mine host of the "White Hart" to say that our views show nothing of what belongs to the existing tavern, which is very clean, very prosperous, and, to the lover of the picturesque, very uninteresting.'[20] Dirt and poverty were, of course, the constituents of the old heartless surface Picturesque. The Picturesque is mentioned in another, more suggestive context in this series. In 1877 the Society issued a group of photographs of St Bartholomew's Church and its immediate surrounds, with this letterpress:

The object of the present series is not to give a record of the church itself. The noble work of the interior, its massive Norman arches, grand proportions and magnificent tombs, could be far better rendered by the art of the etcher. Our aim...has rather been to show the picturesque manner in which the ecclesiastical and civil buildings are, as it were, dovetailed together in the quaintest nook of Old London.

Fig. 12.2   *The Poors' Churchyard* (1877).

This is illustrated in the views of the Poors' Churchyard, in particular that shown in figure 12.2. What exactly is Picturesque about this? The surface Picturesque is certainly there in the closely packed variety of building materials – plaster, brick, slate, tile and old-fashioned weatherboarding. But the letterpress is suggesting the attractions of another kind of variety – the functional diversity of buildings which nonetheless seem to be organically connected. This had always stimulated a specific kind of Picturesque pleasure: and is no doubt related to a favourite subject of some of the earlier watercolourists, such as Michael Angelo Rooker.

I suspect that the appeal of the Poors' Churchyard is stimulated by, if not partly originates in, certain cultural anxieties in the later Victorian period. In the last part of this essay I want to test this suspicion by reintroducing the two topics raised earlier: the architectural development of Victorian London; and Ruskin's reconstruction of the Picturesque in *Modern Painters*.

Development in central London was marked by an extraordinary architectural diversity, as we have seen. Underpinning that diversity was a highly self-assertive individualism. There was also something else at work. In 1899 the author of a book on the growth of nineteenth-century cities wrote:

The city is the spectroscope of society: it analyzes and sifts the population, separating and classifying the diverse elements. The entire progress of civilization is a process of differentiation, and the city is the greatest differentiator.

London's redevelopment in the nineteenth century was marked by social and professional differentiation. 'Subdivision, classification, and elaboration, are certainly distinguishing characteristics of the present aera of civilisation,'[21] observed G. A. Sala in 1859. Individual buildings had individual, specialised functions: purpose-built offices, banks, restaurants, hotels, department stores. Separate, purpose-built work places necessitated purpose-built residential areas; these in turn segregated in social status. In the architecture and topography of later Victorian London one could read something like the atomisation of a society in its domestic and professional functions. The dark side of the spirit of individualism and segregation was observed earlier in the century, when Frederick Engels saw new and sinister phenomena in the concentration of people in the streets of great cities:

Hundreds of thousands of men and women drawn from all classes and ranks of society pack the streets of London. Are they not all human beings with the same innate characteristics and potentialities? Are they not all equally interested in the pursuit of happiness?...We know well enough that the isolation of the individual – this narrow-minded egotism – is everywhere the fundamental principle of modern society. But nowhere is this selfish egotism so blatantly evident as in the frantic bustle of the great city. The disintegration of society into individuals, each guided by his private principles and each pursuing his own aims has been pushed to its furthest limits in London.[22]

The growing anxiety over this fragmentation of community, so evident in the physical and social experience of Victorian London, was of course a driving force behind the work of some of the great

Victorian writers: Carlyle, Ruskin, Dickens. It found expression in a variety of broader movements, from Romantic medievalism to pioneer Socialism. The anxiety also finds expression in these photographs. In drawing attention to the dovetailing of ecclesiastical and civil buildings in a nearly forgotten nook of old London, the photographer, like a social anthropologist, finds a melancholy trace of a lost culture, one which baffled those differentiations of function and social rank which marked the new London. The small scale, the intimacy of this complex of ecclesiastical, academic, commercial and domestic buildings is underlined in the Society's letterpress to the collection of photographs of the area around St Bartholomew's:

Cloth Fair... still preserves, far beyond any other portion of London, mediaeval characteristics. Here are narrow walled lanes, where two persons can pass one another with difficulty. In another the occupants of one house could literally, and without danger or difficulty, shake hands from windows on opposite sides of the way. The explorer may thread covered passages from which he can note details of domestic life passing within easy ken.

The appeal of this image – its 'mediaeval characteristics' – has a related source, I think, which arises out of Ruskin's distinctions between lower and higher Picturesque. In trying to exemplify the nature of his 'higher picturesque' response to particular objects, he chooses the old tower of Calais church. It certainly qualifies as Picturesque in the 'lower sense': it is partly ruined – 'eaten away by the Channel winds, and overgrown with bitter sea grasses'. But the observer of great moral sensitivity will discern other qualities:

The large neglect, the noble unsightliness of it; the record of its years written so visibly, and yet without a sign of weakness... its carelessness of what anyone thinks or feels about it,... above all it completely expresses that agedness in the midst of active life which binds the old and the new into harmony... the links are unbroken between the past and present.[23]

He compares this with current English attitudes towards their past:

We, in England, have our new street, our new inn, our green shaven lawn, and our piece of ruin emergent from it, – a mere *specimen* of the Middle Ages put on a bit of velvet carpet to be shown, which, but for its size, might as well be on a museum shelf at once, under cover... Abroad, a building of the eighth or tenth century stands ruinous in the open street; the children play around it, the peasants heap their corn in it, the buildings of yesterday nestle about it, and fit their new stones into its rents, and tremble in sympathy as it trembles. No one wonders at it, or thinks of it as separate, and of another time; we feel the ancient world to be a real thing, and one with the new.[24]

Victorian London, in asserting itself as the great modern metropolis, the capital city of progressive individualism, was obliterating evidence of that sense of continuity and community which Ruskin found essential to the health of a culture. Victorian London, in its topography and architecture, was not only segregating and classifying socially, economically and professionally: it was also differentiating *historically* – it was alienating its present from its past – in spite of its revivalist new architecture, in spite of its unbridled enthusiasm for the restoration of old buildings. It was producing a deracinated culture. I say 'in spite of' enthusiastic restoration projects: for Ruskin, the rupture was largely *because* of restoration:

Nominal restoration has...hopelessly destroyed what time, and storm, and anarchy, and impiety had spared. The picturesque material of a lower kind is fast departing – and for ever. There is not, so far as we know, one city scene in central Europe which has not suffered from some jarring point of modernisation... A few lustres more, and the modernisation will be complete: the archaeologist may still find work among the wrecks of beauty, and here and there a solitary fragment of the old cities may exist by toleration, or rise strangely before the workmen who dig the new foundations... [or, one may say, be sought out by the antiquarian photographer]. But the life of the Middle Ages is dying from their embers, and the warm mingling of the past and present will soon be for ever dissolved.[25]

The experience of the metropolis has shown that revivalism and restoration, ostensibly acts of homage to the past, are actually obliterating that inheritance by supplanting it with the present age's versions of the past. It was, of course, happening everywhere in Britain, but nowhere so swiftly as in London. Reconstructed antiquity, however reverently executed, could never satisfy the sentimental purists of the conservation lobby, who were, in many respects, the descendants of the Picturesque tourists and connoisseurs of a century earlier. This comes from the speech of the chairman to the first meeting of the Society for the Protection of Ancient Buildings held in June 1878, the year after the issue of the Poors' Churchyard prints, and about a century on from the first rush of enthusiasm for Picturesque tourism:

Now with regard to picturesqueness. The touch of time gives what nothing else can do, and beautifies in a way that nothing else can. Why, even a plain simple barn or brick wall of 300 years old is a beautiful and interesting object which cannot be formed now... To see this sort of thing [wholesale restoration] going on is nearly enough to bring tears into the eyes (Hear, hear).[26]

The Picturesque is thus embedding itself in the discourse of conservation. It is there in the letterpress to the photographs of old London. It is there in the speeches of the Society for the Protection of Ancient Buildings (secretary, William Morris). It is there in the literature of the National Trust, which was established in 1895. And it remains indispensable to the promotional language of the Heritage industry today. The experience of the metropolis in the nineteenth century helped to refashion the Picturesque and equip it for a new role on the stage of cultural politics.

NOTES

1 William Gilpin, *Three Essays*, second edition (London, 1794), pp. 36–7.
2 John Ruskin, *The Seven Lamps of Architecture* (1849), chapter 6, para. 11: E. T. Cook and A. Wedderburn (eds), The Library Edition *The Works of John Ruskin*, 39 vols. (London, 1903–12), vol. VIII, p. 235. This edition is hereafter cited as *Works*.
3 Donald J. Olsen, *The Growth of Victorian London* (London: Batsford, 1976), pp. 33, 49.
4 Augustus Hare, *Walks in London*, 2 vols. (London, 1878), vol. I, pp. xxix–xxx.
5 Olsen, *Victorian London*, pp. 61, 63–4.
6 Uvedale Price, *Essay on the Picturesque*, new edition, 2 vols. (London, 1796–8), vol. I, p. 39.
7 Olsen, *Victorian London*, p. 64.
8 Sidney Smirke, *Suggestions for the Architectural Improvement of the Western Part of London* (London, 1834), p. 19.
9 Dickens, in a letter to John Forster, 11 February 1845: M. House and G. Storey (eds.), *The Letters of Charles Dickens* (Oxford: Clarendon Press, 1965–), vol. IV, p. 266.
10 These terms are employed in Ann Bermingham's discussion in this volume of fashion and the Picturesque: see pp. 91–2.
11 Anon., (reviewing *Hard Times*) *Westminster Review*, NS vol. VI (October 1854), pp. 604–8.
12 Dickens, in a speech to the Metropolitan Sanitary Association, 10 May 1851: K. J. Fielding (ed.), *The Speeches of Charles Dickens: A Complete Edition* (Brighton: Harvester–Wheatsheaf, 1988), p. 128.
13 Dickens, *Pictures from Italy* (London, 1846), p. 240.
14 John Ruskin, 'Of the Turnerian Picturesque', *Modern Painters*, vol. IV (1856), chapter I, para. 12: *Works*, VI, 19–20.
15 Thomas Beames, *The Rookeries of London* (London, 1850), p. 102.

16 *Ibid.*, p. 17.

17 *Ibid.*, p. 198.

18 Thomas Hardy, 'The Dorsetshire Labourer' (1883): reprinted in Harold Orel (ed.), *Thomas Hardy's Personal Writings* (London: Macmillan, 1962), p. 181.

19 Gustave Doré and Blanchard Jerrold, *London: A Pilgrimage* (London: 1872: Dover Publications, 1970), pp. 2, xxxi.

20 There is no pagination in the publications of the Society for Photographing Relics of Old London.

21 Olsen, *Victorian London*, pp. 19, 21.

22 F. Engels, *The Condition of the Working Class in England in 1844*, trans. and ed. W. O. Henderson and W. H. Chalmer (Oxford: Basil Blackwell, 1958), pp. 30–1.

23 John Ruskin, 'Of the Turnerian Picturesque': *Works*, vol. VI, pp. 11–12. Ruskin's contrasting of the English and Continental attitudes to ruined architecture is also discussed in Raimonda Modiano's essay in this volume, 'The Legacy of the Picturesque'.

24 *Ibid.*, pp. 11–13.

25 John Ruskin, 'Samuel Prout', *Art Journal*, vol. CXXXIX (March 1849), pp. 76–7: *Works* XII, 314–15.

26 Report of the First Annual Meeting of the Society for the Protection of Ancient Buildings, 21 June 1878.

Index